On Writing Short Stories

On Writing Short Stories

Francine Prose
Joyce Carol Oates
Tom Bailey
Frank Conroy
Andre Dubus
Robert Coles
C. Michael Curtis

edited by
TOM BAILEY

New York ❦ Oxford
OXFORD UNIVERSITY PRESS
2000

Oxford University Press

Oxford New York
Athens   Auckland   Bangkok   Bogotá   Buenos Aires   Calcutta
Cape Town   Chennai   Dar es Salaam   Delhi   Florence   Hong Kong   Istanbul
Karachi   Kuala Lumpur   Madrid   Melbourne   Mexico City   Mumbai
Nairobi   Paris   São Paulo   Singapore   Taipei   Tokyo   Toronto   Warsaw

and associated companies in

Berlin   Ibadan

Published by Oxford University Press, Inc.,
198 Madison Avenue, New York, New York, 10016
http://www.oup-usa.org

Library of Congress Cataloging-in-Publication Data

On writing short stories / edited by Tom Bailey.
    p.   cm.
Includes bibliographical references.
ISBN 0-19-512272-0 (pbk.)
1. Short story—Authorship.   2. Short story—Technique.
I. Bailey, Tom, 1961– .
PN3373.P77 1999   99-35471
808.3'1—dc21   CIP

Printing (last digit): 9 8 7 6 5 4 3 2 1

Printed in the United States of America
on acid-free paper

for my teachers

Jane Wells
Richard Spilman
John Vernon
Barry Targan

Contents

PART THREE
Magazines, Journals, and Quarterlies Publishing Short Stories

Tobias Wolff

Foreword

*T*hough I read them attentively and write them myself, I can't say what a short story is. Every time I come up with a definition I remember some indisputable classic that makes nonsense of my terms. When is a short story not a short story but an anecdote, a tale, a novella? Does it have to be written down with literary intention, or can it be part of an oral tradition? Must a true short story illuminate the world beyond itself? Must it engage us morally? Is there some essence that we can recognize as *short story* without being able to put it into words?

These are hard questions, and I'm content to watch others in this book wrestle with them. I will ask another question—not what is the short story, or how is it made, but why? Why short stories—why do they matter to us? And they do, they do. Look at the passion, even reverence, with which the writers in this book speak of Chekhov and Joyce and Anderson and Hemingway and Babel and Flannery O'Connor and Katherine Ann Porter and Raymond Carver, of all those who've drawn life from the form, and breathed life back into it.

But beyond passion, beyond reverence, there is a certain tone we use in discussing short stories that we do not use about novels. You can hear it in these pages. It is a tone close to that of shared confidence, even, occasionally, confession, as if the moments we recall from certain stories arise from our own experience—as if we were not readers but accomplices to the desperate reunion of Chekhov's adulterous lovers Gurov and Anna in that seedy opera house with its pathetic snobs and teenage loiterers and sour violins and haze of smoke above the chandelier. We speak of such scenes as we would of our own memories. And that may be the particular power of the short story—the way it imitates memory.

General statements about literary forms, about almost anything, are fated to die of exception if inanity doesn't get them first. But I'm curious, and willing to hazard a guess, as to why certain stories, once read, have this singular ability to reappear to us with the texture and force of personal recollection. This is not an argument about the superiority of the story form to, say, the novel. Neither is inherently more true or sincere than the other. At their best, both are the result of conscious artistry, even when that artistry effaces itself to give an impression of naturalness, simplicity, spontaneity. But it is the case that most of us remember the past in terms of stories. Certainly that's how we recall it to each other. And the stories we tell are generally limited in duration and cast of characters, otherwise we couldn't remember them or bring them to a close. Though our experience is continuous, our perception of it as having shape and meaning presents itself in slices or bursts. The story form excites the immediate, intimate feeling of memory by mimicking its narrative habits and accepting its limits. The novel behaves differently. The novel by its very length relies on the continuity of a particular world and set of circumstances, and a patiently unfolding narrative design dramatic enough to sustain our interest and our willingness to defer understanding to a distant conclusion—qualities remote from our usual ways of recalling the past.

Whatever the reason, stories matter. Robert Coles, in his essay "Taking on the World," quotes the Southern writer and early civil rights activist Lillian Smith as saying that "even theoretical physicists have a story that makes sense of the world." (I like that *even*.) And of course she's right, except that we don't have just one story, we have many stories that make sense of the world—that's how we do it. When children come home from school they pass on their grievances and victories in stories, stories of stout friends and traitors and interventions by powers of darkness (mean teachers) and light (nice teachers). Their parents do the same after a day of work. When our friends die we gather and recall them in stories, and that is a true recalling, for in telling their stories we call them back to speak and move among us again. Spiritual teachers as distant and different as Chuang Tzu and Jesus habitually spoke in parable and allegory. We sense in them an impatience with the discourse of argument, precept, logic-chopping abstraction, high thought nobly phrased. They spoke to their followers in story not as a concession to their naivete but because only story can express the most difficult, paradoxical, unparaphraseable truths of life as it is actually lived.

Of course the literary short story—the subject of this book—is not the same thing as the tribal myth or the religious parable or those instinctive narratives by which we describe our quarrels and love affairs. But the family resemblance is strong, and disarming. We always have a welcome ready for the old stories, and the new story slips in under that welcome, and draws on all its privileges and powers. "When Miss Emily Grierson died," Faulkner writes, "our whole town went to her funeral. . . ." We bend forward, like children overhearing an interesting visitor start a story in the next room. *The whole town,* we think. What kind of town was this, and what kind of woman was she, that such a thing could happen? So we attend. And we remember. And in our remembering we make this strange world more and more our own, until we come in time to feel like those old men in their brushed Confederate uniforms who'd never known Miss Emily but still speak of her "as if she had been a contemporary of theirs, believing that they had danced with her and courted her perhaps, confusing time with its mathematical progression, as the old do, to whom all the past is not a diminishing road but, instead, a huge meadow which no winter ever quite touches. . . ."

Tobias Wolff

Preface

*O*n *Writing Short Stories* is a collection of original essays by writers, teachers, and editors who give voice—*voices*—to the ongoing dialogue about the art and craft of writing short stories. The book also offers a touchstone selection of eighteen short stories. A list of the addresses and the editors of magazines, journals, and quarterlies that publish short fiction is included at the end for the writer who feels ready to begin submitting his or her own work for consideration. Writing exercises help writers put the practices of craft to work for themselves.

Writers are fiercely independent, and *On Writing Short Stories* respects their autonomy by not presuming to offer itself as a too-systematic apparatus for learning to write short stories. The opening essay asks, "What Makes a Short Story?" and the possibilities for an answer are explored by giving consideration to demonstrable aspects of craft in the essay "Character, Plot, Setting and Time, Metaphor, and Voice." The importance of reading as part of the process of teaching ourselves how to write short stories is emphasized in the essay "Reading as a Writer: The Artist as Craftsman," and the significance of the give and take of concrete peer critique in workshops, where most fiction writing is taught, is brought to light in "The Writer's Workshop." Beyond workshops, the essays turn our attention to process and revision in "The Habit of Writing," and pause to wonder why we bother to write short stories at all in "Why Write? Taking on the World." In the essay "Publishers and Publishing," an editor offers advice on how to publish what we have written once we have come to terms with what we have discovered about writing short stories for ourselves. The eighteen short stories offered here are good stories, interesting stories, heartfelt stories, foundational stories, and stories that push the envelope of narrative fiction. Reading them will create a working forum for the short story form.

And the dialogue goes on. But now it is a dialogue in which we find ourselves wholly involved.

ACKNOWLEDGMENTS

Influences in putting together a book such as *On Writing Short Stories* are many and varied. I first wish to acknowledge the teachers under whom I studied and whose voices can be heard in both the ideas for the essay topics here as well as in the selection of short stories in the anthology. They are Jane Wells, Richard Spilman, John Vernon, and Barry Targan. I would also like to thank my former colleagues in The Expository Writing Program at Harvard University, especially Pat Kain, Tom Perrotta, Maxine Rodburg, and The Sosland Director, Nancy Sommers, for offering their time and advice. This book grew out of my desire for a text that could *stand on the shoulders* of the good books I have used for years in my own workshops: Janet Burroway's *Writing Fiction,* Ann Charters's *The Story and Its Writer,* Richard Marius's *The Writer's Companion,* and John Gardner's *The Art of Fiction.* I am pleased to be able to recognize my indebtedness. My appreciation goes out to the writers, teachers, and editor who valued the idea for the book enough to become a part of it—Francine Prose, Joyce Carol Oates, Frank Conroy, the late Andre Dubus, Robert Coles, and C. Michael Curtis. I would also like to thank Loren I. Noveck, Project Editor at Oxford University Press, for her patience, and D. Anthony English, Senior Editor at Oxford University Press, for his unflappable support during our work together on this book. Without his sponsorship, *On Writing Short Stories* would not have been possible. Thanks also to my mother and father, Elizabeth and Carl, who were there in a pinch when the time came to proof for press.

And, finally, thanks to my wife, Sarah LeWine, my most demanding—and my most forgiving—editor.

Tom Bailey

Contributors

FRANCINE PROSE is the author of nine novels, including *Hunters and Gatherers, Bigfoot Dreams,* and *Primitive People,* two short story collections, and most recently a collection of novellas, *Guided Tours of Hell.* Her essays and stories have appeared in *The Atlantic Monthly, Harper's, Best American Short Stories, The New Yorker, The New York Times, The New York Observer,* and numerous other publications. She writes regularly on art for *The Wall Street Journal* and is a fellow of the New York Institute for the Humanities. The winner of Guggenheim and Fulbright Fellowships, two National Endowment of the Arts grants, and a PEN translation prize, she has taught at the Iowa Writers' Workshop, the University of Arizona, the University of Utah, and the Bread Loaf and Sewannee Writers' conferences. A film based on her novel *Household Saints* was released in 1993.

JOYCE CAROL OATES is the author of a number of works of fiction, poetry, drama, and criticism. Her most recent novels are *We Were the Mulvaneys, Man Crazy, My Heart Laid Bare* and *Broke Heart Blues.* Her most recent short story collection is *The Collector of Hearts.* She is Professor of Humanities at Princeton University and has been a member since 1978 of the American Academy of Arts and Letters.

TOM BAILEY currently holds the Winifred and Gustave Weber Professorship in the Humanities at Susquehanna University where he is an Assistant Professor. A graduate of the Iowa Writer's Workshop, he earned his Ph.D. in English Literature from the State University of New York at Binghamton. Before coming to Susquehanna University, he taught in the Expository Writing Program at Harvard University. His short stories have appeared in *DoubleTake, The Greensboro Review, Black Warrior Review, The High Plains Literary Review, The Crescent Review,* among other journals and magazines, and have been anthologized in *New Stories from the South, Streetsongs: New Voices in Fiction,* and *The Pushcart Prize 2000.* He is a recipient of a National Endowment of the Arts Fellowship.

FRANK CONROY is the director of the Iowa Writer's Workshop at the University of Iowa. He is the author of *Stop-Time, Mid-Air,* and *Body & Soul.*

The late ANDRE DUBUS is the author of one novel, seven collections of stories, including *Separate Flight, The Last Worthless Evening,* and *Dancing After Hours,* one collection of novellas, and two collections of essays, the most recent of which was *Meditations from a Moveable Chair.* He received numerous awards for his writing, including two Guggenheim Grants, two National Endowment of the Arts Fellowships, and a MacArthur Foundation Fellowship, as well as the Jean Stein Award from the American Academy of Arts and Letters and the Rhea Award for the Short Story. He taught writing and literature at Bradford College in Massachusetts for over twenty years.

ROBERT COLES is the James Agee Professor of Social Ethics at Harvard University and the founding editor of *DoubleTake* Magazine. His aim is to take on moral matters through the study of literature. He is the author of more than 1300 articles, reviews, and essays in newspapers, magazines, journals, and anthologies. His 60 books include: *Walker Percy: An American Search, The Old Ones of New Mexico, Flannery O'Connor's South, The Moral Life of Children,* and *The Call of Stories: Teaching and the Moral Imagination.* He is a winner of the Pulitzer Prize and a MacArthur Foundation Fellowship. Most recently he was awarded the Presidential Medal of Freedom.

As Senior Editor of *The Atlantic Monthly,* where he has worked since 1963, C. MICHAEL CURTIS edits virtually all *The Atlantic Monthly*'s fiction. He is the editor of five anthologies of short fiction—*American Stories: Fiction from the Atlantic Monthly, Volumes I and II, Contemporary New England Stories, Contemporary West Coast Stories,* and *God: Stories*—and has published poetry, essays, reporting, and reviews in *The Atlantic Monthly, The New Republic, The National Review,* and many other periodicals. He has taught creative writing and composition at Cornell, MIT, Tufts, Boston University, Simmons College, Bennington College, Northeastern University, and elsewhere. Since 1994 he has served as director of the New England Writers Workshop, held each June at Simmons College.

PART 1

On Writing Short Stories

What Makes a Short Story?

*T*here must be more difficult questions than "What makes a short story?"

What is man, that Thou art mindful of him? What does a woman want? What is love? What walks on four legs at dawn, two legs at noon, three legs in the evening? What can you say about a twenty-five-year-old girl who died? Tell me where is fancy bred, in the heart or in the head?

Yet all of these seemingly impossible questions are, in fact, far easier to address than the deceptively straightforward matter of what constitutes the short story. For all of these classic puzzlers—except for the sphinx's riddle—suggest variant solutions and multiple possibilities, invite expansion and rumination, whereas any attempt to establish the identifying characteristics of the short story seems to require a narrowing, a winnowing, a definition by exclusion. A short story is probably this—but definitely not that.

The real problem is that the most obvious answer is the most correct. We *know* what a short story is: a work of fiction of a certain length, a length with apparently no minimum. An increasing number of anthologies feature stories of no more than a humble page, or a single flashy paragraph, and one of the most powerful stories in all of literature, Isaac Babel's "Crossing Into Poland," less than three pages long, is capacious enough to include a massive and chaotic military campaign, a soldier's night of troubled dreams, and the report of a brutal murder. Similarly, Cynthia Ozick's "The Shawl" is only four pages long.

But, nearing the opposite end of the spectrum, Robert Boswell's "The Darkness of Love" is over forty pages. After a certain point (to be on the safe side, let's say seventy or eighty pages, though one short-story theoretician has argued that Conrad's "Heart of Darkness"—not one word more or less—defines the outer limits of the form) the extended short story begins to impinge on novella territory.

Lacking anything clearer or more definitive than these vague mumblings about size, we imagine that we can begin to define the short story by distinguishing it from other forms of fiction, by explaining why it is not a sketch, a fairy tale, or a myth.

And yet some of our favorite stories seem a lot like the sort of casual anecdote we might hear a friend tell at a dinner party. Somerset Maugham, in what must have been a demented moment, claimed that many of Chekhov's great stories *were* anecdotes and not proper stories at all. ("If you try to tell one of his stories you will find that there is nothing to tell. The anecdote, stripped of its trimmings, is insignificant and often inane. It was grand for people who wanted to write a story and couldn't think of a plot to discover that you could very well manage without one.") And just to confuse things further, many fairy tales—the best of Hans Christian Andersen and the Brothers Grimm—are as carefully constructed, as densely layered, as elaborately crafted as the stories (or are they tales?) of, for example, Hawthorne and Poe.

Why do we feel so certain that a masterpiece such as Tolstoy's "The Three Hermits" is a short story, though it so clearly bears—and takes so little trouble to hide—the stamp of its origins in "an old legend current in the Volga district" and though its structure has more in common with the shaggy-dog story than with the artful, nuanced studies of Henry James, who, in fact, was quite insistent that a short story "must be an idea—it can't be a 'story' in the vulgar sense of the word. It must be a picture; it must illustrate something . . . something of the real essence of the subject."

Just to take on James, always something of a challenge, let's look at "The Three Hermits," which could hardly be more of a "story," in the most fabulously, unashamedly "vulgar sense of the word." The protagonist, if we can call him that—we know nothing about his background or the subtler depths of his character, absolutely nothing, in short, except that he is a Bishop of the Orthodox Church—is traveling on a ship that passes near an island on which, he hears, live three monks who spend their lives in prayer. The Bishop insists on being ferried to the island, where he meets the hermits—again described with a minimum of the sort of physical and psychological description that, we have been taught, is essential for fiction in general and for the short story in particular. One of the monks is tall "with a piece of matting tied round his waist"; the second is shorter, in a "tattered peasant coat"; and the third is "very old, bent with age and wearing an old cassock." To his horror, the Bishop discovers that the hermits have their own way of praying ("Three are ye, three are we, have mercy on us") and have never heard of the Lord's Prayer.

The bulk of the story, the shaggy-dog part, concerns the Bishop's efforts to teach these comically slow learners how to pray correctly—a Herculean task that consumes the entire day and that is completed, more or less, to the visitor's satisfaction. That night, as the Bishop is sailing away from the island, he sees a light skimming toward him across the water. "Was it a seagull, or the little gleaming of some small boat?" No, in fact, the radiance is an aura surrounding the hermits, flying hand in hand over the water, desperately chasing the Bishop's boat because they have forgotten what they learned from the church official, who—educated at last—tells them, "It is not for me to teach you. Pray for us sinners."

Even in summary, this story retains some of its power to astonish and move us, and yet the full effect of reading the work in its entirety is all but lost. Which brings us to one of the few things that *can* be said about the short story: Like all great works of art, it cannot be summarized or reduced without sacrificing the very qualities that do in fact distinguish an amusing dinner-party anecdote from a great work of art—depth, resonance, harmony, plus all the less quantifiable marks of artistic creation. This is especially true of stories in which the plot line is not so clear, so succinct, so distilled to its folkloric essentials, and of writers who achieve their effects almost entirely by the use of tone, by the accretion of minute detail, and by the precise use of language.

What can we possibly—accurately—conclude about Turgenev's "Bezhin Meadow" when we hear that it concerns a few hours that the narrator spends among a group of peasant boys who scare themselves and each other by telling ghost stories? At the end of the story, we learn—in a sort of brief epilogue— that one of the boys was killed a short time after that evening on the meadow. When we hear it summarized, the plot seems sketchy and indistinct— why is this not a vignette or a "mood piece"? But when we read the story itself— a work of art that feels utterly complete and in which every sentence and phrase contributes to the whole—we are certain, beyond any doubt, that it is indeed a story. We cannot imagine anything that needs to be added or omitted.

What remains of the humor and breathtaking originality of Katherine Mansfield's "Daughters of the Late Colonel" when we describe it as a story about two childlike (but ostensibly adult) sisters attempting to get through the days following the death of their father? What survives of the many small gestures and lines of deceptively whimsical dialogue that lead us to understand that the distribution of power between the more "grown-up" sensible Josephine and the fanciful, impulsive, skittish Constantia is the same as it must have been in early childhood? What remains of Josephine's certainty that their dead father is hiding in his chest of drawers, or of his former nurse's—Nurse Andrew's—upsetting, "simply fearful" greed for butter, or of the "white, terrified" blancmange that the cook sets on the table, or of that final, elliptical moment of forgetting in which we intuit the impossible and tragic cost of remembering?

It is hard to *recognize* Chekhov's "The Lady with the Pet Dog" from the following description: A jaded womanizer falls deeply in love despite himself and for the first time, and in the course of that love affair discovers that his whole world—that he himself—has changed. How sentimental and obvious it sounds, how romantic and unconvincing. Yet when we actually read the story, we feel that it is of enormous, immeasurable consequence and resonance, and that it tells us all we need to know about Gurov and Anna's whole lives. We feel that the story's details—the slice of watermelon in the hotel room, the description of Gurov's wife's eyebrows—are as important as its "action," and that if we left out these details, the perfect but somehow fragile architecture of the story would begin to crumble.

Not much remains of the short story, retold in summary—but not *nothing*. For this also can be said, of the short story: If we find a way to describe what the story is *really* about, not its plot but its essence, what small or large part of life it has managed to translate onto the page, there is always *something* there— enough to engage us, and pique our interest.

But isn't the same true of novels? What do we lose when we try to explain what *Mrs. Dalloway* is *about?* Or when we become hopelessly enmired in the tangles—lovers, generations, narrators, stories within stories, frames within

frames—of *Wuthering Heights?* Or when we say that we just read the most har-
rowing novel about a provincial French housewife whose life is ruined by her
silly and impractical fantasies of love and romance? The answer's the same:
Nearly everything, though some "germ" (to quote James again) stays ineradi-
cably present.

A similarly illusory distinction that is often made between the short story
and the novel claims that the short story—unlike its more expansive or discur-
sive older sibling—works more often by implication, by indirection, that it more
frequently achieves its results by what has *not* been said or what has been left
out. But although it is undeniably true that certain stories function this way—
the situation that has caused all the trouble between the lovers in Ernest Hemingway's "Hills Like White Elephants" is never directly mentioned in the course
of the lovers' painful conversation—it is also true that in the greatest works of
fiction, regardless of their length, every line tells us pages *more* than it appears
to communicate on the surface. So even in Proust's *In Search of Lost Time*—
hardly the most concise and economical of novels—each seemingly insignificant phrase and incident assumes additional meaning and resonance as the
book progresses; every incident, every minor exchange takes on levels of significance that we cannot hope to apprehend until we go back and reread the
whole. In fact the most important way to read—the way that teaches us most
about what a great writer does, and what *we* should be doing—is to take a story
apart (line by line, word by word) the way a mechanic takes apart an automobile engine, and to ask ourselves how each word, each phrase, and each sentence contributes to the entirety.

In their efforts to define the formal qualities of the short story form, critics
are often driven back to invoke basic Aristotelian principles (short stories, we
hear, have a beginning, a middle, and an end) and to quote the early masters
of the genre, writers who must have had, one supposes, a more sharply focused
view of the new frontier toward which they were heading. So introductions to
anthologies, textbook chapters, and surveys of the latest developments in the
academic field of "short story theory" are all fond of invoking Edgar Allan Poe's
notion of the "single effect."

> A skillful literary artist has constructed a tale. If wise, he has not fashioned his
> thoughts to accommodate his incidents; but having conceived, with deliberate
> care, a certain unique or single *effect* to be wrought out, he then invents such inci-
> dents—he then combines such events as may best aid him in establishing this
> preconceived effect . . . in the whole composition, there should be no word writ-
> ten, of which the tendency, direct or indirect, is not to the one pre-established
> design. And by such means, with such care and skill, a picture is at length painted
> which leaves in the mind of he who contemplates it with a kindred art, a sense of
> the fullest satisfaction. The idea of the tale has been presented unblemished,
> because undisturbed, and this is an end unattainable to the novel.

More recent—and also frequently quoted—is V.S. Pritchett's characteristi-
cally elegant and incisive formulation:

The novel tends to tell us everything whereas the short story tells us only one thing, and that, intensely. . . . It is, as some have said, a "glimpse through," resembling a painting or even a song which we can take in at once, yet bring the recesses and contours of larger experience to the mind.

And Chekhov—whom some readers (this one, for example) consider the greatest writer of the modern short story—had himself some very definite ideas on the necessity of keeping things simple:

In planning a story one is bound to think first about its framework; from a crowd of leading characters one selects one person only—wife or husband; one puts him on the canvas and paints him alone, making him prominent, while the others one scatters over the canvas like small coins, and the result is something like the vault of heaven: one big moon and a number of very small stars around it. . . . It is not necessary to portray many characters. . . . The center of gravity should be in two persons: him and her. [to A.P. Chekhov, 1886] . . . One must write about simple things: how Peter Semionovich married Maria Ivanovna. That is all.

Certainly this is true of his own "The Lady with the Pet Dog," in which the center of gravity seems to turn—slowly at first, and then more and more intensely—around those all-important "two persons."

No sensible reader could argue with Pritchett or Poe. But then again, few readers could explain exactly what "a single effect" is, or what precisely is the "one thing" that our favorite short story is telling us so intensely. And Chekhov should have known—and *did* know—better, since many of his most successful and beautifully realized stories encompass a good deal more than "him and her" or the nuptial arrangements of Peter Semionovich and Maria Ivanovna.

Indeed, the minute one tries to make any sweeping declarations about the proper limitations or boundaries of the short story, one thinks (as with any "rule" for the writing of fiction) of an example—a masterpiece!—that embodies the very opposite of the law that one has just proposed. So let's take just a few of the many assumptions that the casual reader—or the student hungry for some definitive parameters—might make about the short story.

Perhaps we should begin by addressing Chekhov's statement about that big moon and those very small stars, about that "him and her" whose interaction should form the core of the story. One might assume that for reasons of economy or artistic harmony, the short story should limit itself to depicting the situation of a main protagonist or at least a somewhat restricted—a *manageable*—cast of characters. And many stories do. There are only three major characters—the narrator, his wife, and the blind man—in Raymond Carver's "Cathedral." And only one character, really, in Poe's "The Pit and the Pendulum." In Flannery O'Connor's "Everything That Rises Must Converge" the "him and her" are the overbearing, heartbreaking mother and her snobbish and long-suffering son Julian. And in James Baldwin's "Sonny's Blues," the narrator and Sonny are the big moon around whom the others—Isabel, the mother and father, the other musicians—revolve.

But who, one might ask, is the "big moon" in Tim O'Brien's "The Things They Carried," or in Chekhov's own "In the Ravine," a story that focuses not on any central character, but on the life of an entire community, Ukleevo, a village that "was never free from fever, and there was boggy mud there even in summer, especially under the fences over which hung old willow-trees that gave deep shade. Here there was always a smell from the factory refuse and the acetic acid which was used in the finishing of the cotton print." In this polluted and horrifically corrupt little hamlet, the most powerful family—a clan of shopkeepers—devotes itself to lying and cheating their neighbors; their dishonesty and general depravity are repaid, eventually, by heartbreak and ruin.

The story does have a villain, the vicious Aksinya (who, as the very worst person in her family, naturally is spared the destruction that befalls the somewhat less culpable others), and a heroine, of sorts, the innocent peasant girl Lipa, who does not appear until quite a few pages into the story. Nonetheless, we feel throughout that Chekhov is less interested in depicting particular destinies than in painting a broader picture; the story is the literary equivalent of a monumental canvas, crowded with figures—Rembrandt's "Night Watch," for one. We never know exactly, we can never answer that question that writing teachers so often ask: Whose story is it?

But even the story that lacks a central character should, presumably, limit itself to a single point of view, a controlling intelligence that guides us through the narrative. Or should it? Once more the answer seems to be: not necessarily. "Sonny's Blues," "Cathedral," and John Updike's "A & P" are examples of short fictions that stay fixedly within the consciousness of their narrators. Kafka's "The Judgment" adheres more or less faithfully to the close-third-person viewpoint through which we observe the tormented last hours of Georg Bendermann.

Yet another of Kafka's stories—"The Metamorphosis"—also begins in the close third person, with the understandable astonishment of Gregor Samsa, who (when we meet him) has just woken in his bed to find that he has been transformed, overnight, into a giant insect. And there the story remains until the narrative must leave the room in which Gregor is imprisoned in order to follow the action in the other parts of the apartment and chart the effects that Gregor's peculiar transformation has had on the members of his family. Finally, after Gregor's death, the story can—for obvious reasons—no longer be told from his point of view, and a more detached omniscience describes the process by which his parents and his sister repair themselves and go on with their lives after the regrettable but unavoidable demise of the unfortunate Gregor.

Still other stories pay even less heed to the somewhat schoolmarmish admonition that they color neatly within the lines of a single perspective. In "The Lady with the Pet Dog," we feel that Chekhov is constantly shifting his—and our—distance from Gurov. Sometimes (for example, in the scene in which he watches the sunset) we feel that we are looking through his eyes, and down into his soul; at other moments (when he first sees Anna and toys with the idea of seducing her) we feel that we are watching him with a somewhat greater and more ironic remove.

Alice Munro's "Friend of My Youth" begins with a dream that the first person narrator has about her mother, and then narrates the rest of the story from the point of view of "my mother" with occasional, stabilizing swings back to that initial "I." Katherine Mansfield's "Prelude" moves seamlessly from one family member to another, exposing the innermost—tormented or fortuitously ignorant—thoughts of an extended family: a mother and father, their children, and the mother's unmarried sister. Tatiana Tolstaya's "Heavenly Flame" behaves as if it has never heard of the whole issue of point of view, and skips around from character to character, alighting from time to time on a sort of group perspective, a "we" representing the minisociety vacationing at a country house near a convalescent home. And though John Cheever's "Goodbye, My Brother" begins in the first person plural—not the royal *we* or the editorial *we* but the family *we*—we readers soon understand that this plural ("We are a family that is very close in spirit") is by its very nature ironic, and functions as a key to the fortress and the prison in which the narrator chooses and is forced to reside. Much of the story, in fact, is about the efforts to break away from that "we" (the Pommeroy family) so that point of view becomes, in an intriguing way, part of the plot—and the problem—of the story.

But even if the short story refuses to fall in line with any of our notions about the number and range of its characters, and the importance of a single perspective, shouldn't it observe the most (one would think) easy to follow of the Aristotelian conventions, the prescriptions concerning the length of time that the action may comfortably span? It's true that "Hills Like White Elephants" nearly restricts itself to the real time of a single conversation, and that Tillie Olsen's "I Stand Here Ironing" takes place entirely during a session at the ironing board.

On the other hand, "Sonny's Blues" moves back and forth through decades of the two main characters' histories, covering the most significant parts of the lifetimes of two men; at the same time, it fits a huge wedge of social history into the confines of a short story. And Lars Gustafsson's "Greatness Strikes Where It Pleases" takes, as its subject, the existence—and especially the inner life—of an unnamed retarded man, who grows up in the country and spends his later years in a home. In the space breaks, the black space between sections, months, days, or years elapse—blank spots that, we soon realize, matter far less than we might have supposed, since our hero has been liberated by consciousness from the narrow strictures of time:

> At the end of the '50s, his parents died. Nobody tried to explain it to him, and he didn't know in what order they died or when, but when he hadn't seen them for a few years—his mother would visit him regularly twice a year and always brought him candy and apples, an anxious lot of apples, as if the lack of apples were his problem—he started to miss them, in some vague fashion, about the way you might all of a sudden long for mustard or honey or a certain kind of floury gravy with just a taste of burned pork.

As much as we might like the short story to keep its borders modest, crisp, and neat, the form keeps defying our best efforts to wrap it up and present it in a tidy package. Pick up those helpful, instructional books—Anyone Can Write a Short Story—and you're bound to find one of those diagrams, those EKGs of the "typical plot line," its slow ascent, its peak and valley (or peaks and valleys) meant to indicate the tensing or slackening of dramatic interest.

But any attempt to draw such a chart for a story such as Bruno Schulz's "Sanitarium Under the Sign of the Hour Glass"—with its labyrinthine plot turns and disorienting switchbacks—will look less like that comprehensible medical or seismographic chart than one of those webs spun by those poor spiders whom scientists used to torment with doses of mind-altering drugs. How does one draw up a chart for "The Things They Carried," which is structured like an obsessive, repetitive list of *stuff*—the materials that a group of Vietnam soldiers are humping through the jungle—and contains, hidden inside, a story of life and death.

Some stories have huge amounts of plot—it has been said that Heinrich von Kleist's "The Marquise of O." was used, unedited, as a shooting script for Eric Rohmer's full-length film (of the same name) based on the novella. And some stories—John Updike's "A & P," Raymond Carver's "Cathedral"—have, by comparison, almost no plot at all.

The understandable longing to keep things tidy and nice and neat also leads many critics and teachers to put the "epiphany"—the burst of under-standing, self-knowledge, or knowledge about the world that may occur to a character at some crucial point in the story—at the highest peak of that EKG graph, like the cherry on a sundae. Some even insist that this sort of mini-enlightenment is necessary for the short story—is, in fact, a hallmark and sine qua non of the form.

It's my understanding that the word epiphany first came into common cur-rency—in the literary rather than the religious sense—in connection with the fiction of James Joyce, many of whose characters do seem to "get something" by the end of many of his brilliant stories. Sometimes, characters in stories do learn something. By the end of "Sonny's Blues," the narrator has had a vision (however unwelcome and unwilled) of what music means to his brother, and of what sort of musician his brother is. The recognition that her precious new hat is the very same one worn by the black woman on the bus has over-whelming—and tragic—consequences for the mother in "Everything That Rises Must Converge." Gurov learns one startling lesson after another in "The Lady with the Pet Dog," and the story ends with the realization that "the hardest part was still before" the two lovers. But just because Joyce's or Baldwin's or Chekhov's or O'Connor's characters wise up, even for a moment, doesn't mean that anyone else's characters do, or should be expected to.

One could spend pages listing short fictions in which characters come out the other end of the story every bit as benighted as they were in the first sen-tence. By the end of "Everything That Rises Must Converge," Julian could hardly *not* know that something has happened to change his life. But the story con-cludes before he—or the reader—has had a chance to intuit what that change is, or what it will mean. It's hard to say what the unnamed narrator learns in Samuel Beckett's thrilling and upsetting story "First Love." To claim that every short story should include a moment of epiphany is like insisting that every talented, marvelous dog jump through the same narrow hoop.

It is simply not true that a character always learns something in the course of a short story. Heaven forbid that someone should *have* to see life or the world in a brighter or darker light, that someone *has* to be changed—or, even worse, improved. How deadly dull it would be if that were the case for all those stories in all those anthologies—all those epistemological light bulbs going on, one right after another.

A story creates its own world, often—though not always—with clear or mysterious correspondences to our own, a world in which we are too involved to keep track of what anyone is learning. While reading the story, we enter that world. We feel that everything in it belongs there, and has not been forced on it by its reckless or capricious creator. In fact, we tend to forget the creator, who has wound the watch of the story and vanished from creation. We may feel this world is something like life and at the same time better than life, since this short-story world—unlike life—has reached some miraculous ecological balance, so that everything in that world has been put there for a reason.

Unlike most novels, great short stories make us marvel at their integrity, their economy. If we went at them with our blue pencils, we might find we had nothing to do. We would discover there was nothing that the story could afford to lose without the whole delicate structure collapsing like a souffle or meringue. And yet we are left with a feeling of completeness, a conviction that we know exactly as much as we need to know, that all of our questions have been answered—even if we are unable to formulate what exactly those questions and answers *are*.

This sense of the artistic whole, this assurance that nothing has been left out and that nothing extraneous has been included, is part of what distinguishes the short story from other pieces of writing with which it shares certain outward characteristics—what separates it, for example, from the newspaper account, which, like the short story, most often features characters and at least some vestige of a plot. But the newspaper version of "The Lady with the Pet Dog"—MAN'S AFFAIR TURNS SERIOUS—manages to leave out every single thing that makes the story so beautiful, significant, and moving.

Everything in the story resonates at its own unique, coherent, and recognizable pitch, along with everything else in the story, creating an effect that Joyce described—quoting Aquinas, and in another context—as "wholeness, harmony, and radiance." As readers, we may feel that after finishing the story we understand something new, something solid. And we recognize the short story (what *is* a short story *is*) in a visceral, quasi-physiological way; we feel—to paraphrase what Emily Dickinson said about poetry—as if the top of our head had come off. Maybe that is something like what Poe meant by his unity of effect—the short work of fiction, so beautifully made that it cannot be broken down into components or spare parts. Reading a masterpiece like Chekhov's "The Lady with the Pet Dog," we cannot think of anything we would add, anything else we need to know; nor is there anything extra or superfluous.

To understand what a short story is requires reading dozens and dozens of them, far more than the examples collected in this anthology, more than the additional stories mentioned in this essay. By reading many and varied examples, we develop an almost instinctive sense of what a short story is, so that when we read one we recognize it, just as we recognize our own instincts and emotions. We know what a short story is, just as we know what it is to be afraid, or to fall in love.

To really communicate the entirety of what a short story has given us, of what it has done for us, of what it has helped us understand or see in a new way, would involve repeating the whole story, every one of our favorite stories, the stories in this anthology, and also the stories I have mentioned above—stories that lovers of the short story should know practically by heart. It would mean quoting all those stories sentence by sentence, line by line, word by word—the only real answer to that most difficult of questions: What makes a short story?

Reading as a Writer

THE ARTIST AS CRAFTSMAN

AND YET THE ONLY EXCITING LIFE IS THE IMAGINARY ONE.
—Virginia Woolf, *Diary*, 21 April 1928

O f course, writing is an art. And art springs from the depths of the human imagination and is likely to be, in the final analysis as at first glance, idiosyncratic, mysterious, and beyond easy interpretation. We think of that supreme artist of solitude, Emily Dickinson, in the ecstatic grip of inspiration—"Did you ever see a soul at the *white heat?*"—and we think of the youthful Franz Kafka in the throes of writing his first story, "A Judgment," working through the night to convert the "tremendous world I have in my head" into prose to release its pressure, he hopes, without "tearing me apart." We think, with less unqualified admiration, perhaps, of the youthful Jack Kerouac, who didn't so much compose his memoirist novels as plunge head-on into them, typing compulsively through the night fueled by alcohol, Benzedrine, and mania to create what he called "spontaneous prose": *On the Road,* which made him both famous and notorious overnight, was written on a single taped-together sheet of Chinese art paper forming a prodigious 150-foot roll through Kerouac's manual typewriter. We think of Herman Melville's similarly ecstatic bouts of inspiration in the composition of his masterwork *Moby Dick,* and we think of D. H. Lawrence's fluid, seemingly artless storytelling in such classics as "The Blind Man," "The Horse Dealer's Daughter," "The Rocking-Horse Winner," and *The Escaped Cock*. Without such rushes of feeling, private and untrammeled, there can't be creativity. And yet, inspiration and energy and even genius are rarely enough to make "art": for prose fiction is also a craft, and craft must be learned, whether by accident or design.

And here we arrive at a very different truth: that the writer, even the writer who will seem to readers and reviewers strikingly original, has probably based his or her prose style and "prose vision" upon significant predecessors. Consider the no-longer-young unpublished poet Robert Frost studying with excruciating care the poems of Thomas Hardy, to the point at which the cadences of Hardy's language, if not the noble bleakness of Hardy's vision, would be so absorbed into Frost's soul as to become indistinguishable from it; with the astonishing result, which no one including Frost might have foretold, that Frost would one day become as great a poet as his predecessor, and far more widely read in the United States than Hardy has ever been. Consider the young Flannery O'Connor, drafting her first novella, to be titled *Wise Blood,* and discovering Sophocles's *Oedipus Rex* and Nathanael West's *Miss Lonelyhearts,* both of which made a profound, lasting impression upon her: Sophocles for the tragic dignity of Oedipus's self-blinding, which O'Connor replicates in *Wise Blood;* West for his acerbic style, his cruel genius for caricature, and his young male Miss Lonelyhearts as a Christ-fanatic in denial of his faith, very like O'Connor's young Christ-fanatic Hazel Motes. O'Connor's indebtedness to Nathanael West is pervasive through her fiction, and even a mature work like "Everything That Rises Must Converge" retains the Westian turn of phrase, sharp, revealing yet funny, a comic tone abruptly turned savage in the story's concluding paragraphs. Consider one young, exuberant Herman Melville, so struck by his contemporary Nathaniel Hawthorne's collection of allegorical tales *Mosses from an Old Manse* that he revised his plans for *Moby Dick,* shifting its comic-picaresque tone to a far graver, more elevated, and tragic tone and creating in the process what is arguably the most powerful American novel of the nineteenth century, if not of the twentieth as well. Consider William Faulkner, a young writer in his mid-twenties casting about for a voice, a point of view, a vision, taking up and discarding such disparate models as Algernon Swinburne, Aldous Huxley, and even his contemporary Ernest Hemingway before discovering the more temperamentally kindred James Joyce, as well as Gustave Flaubert's *Madame Bovary* and Joseph Conrad's *The Nigger of the Narcissus,* masterpieces of consciously wrought prose that would have an incalculable influence upon Faulkner; as, in turn, Faulkner's idiosyncratic poetic prose would have an incalculable influence upon writers as diverse as Gabriel García Márquez and Cormac McCarthy. And there is Ernest Hemingway, generally credited with having transformed American prose by way of his minimalist, rigorously unsentimental vision, and yet immensely influenced by such distinguished predecessors as Mark Twain and Sherwood Anderson, without whose refinement of American vernacular, particularly in such masterpieces as *The Adventures of Huckleberry Finn* and *Winesburg, Ohio,* the famous Hemingway style might not have developed.

Sometimes, a writer of stylistic brilliance denies or is unaware of having been influenced by another writer, for as Virginia Woolf notes in her diary for 20 April 1935:

> Do I instinctively keep my mind from analysing, which would impair its creativeness? I think there's something in that. The reception of living work is too coarse and partial if you're doing the same thing yourself.

Here is Virginia Woolf mulling over the phenomenon of James Joyce's *Ulysses,* which she could not have failed to recognize not only as a work of astonishing genius but one that would alter the very concept of prose fiction irrevocably:

I should be reading *Ulysses,* and fabricating my case for and against. I have read 200 pages so far—not a third; and have been amused, stimulated, charmed, interested, by the first 2 or 3 chapters . . . ; and then puzzled, bored, irritated and disillusioned as by a queasy undergraduate scratching his pimples. And Tom [T. S. Eliot] thinks this on a par with *War and Peace!* An illiterate, underbred book it seems to me; the book of a self taught working man, and we all know how distressing they are, how egotistic, insistent, raw, striking, and ultimately nauseating. (*Diary,* 16 August 1922)

Woolf's protestation, which descends even to class snobbery, surely arises from simple jealousy, if not envy, for the energy and inventiveness of *Ulysses.* Here Woolf senses herself confronted by literary genius beyond her own; however grand her ambition for transforming English fiction, she could not have failed to register how anemic and "impressionistic" her own style is compared to Joyce's. Yet, in *To the Lighthouse, The Waves,* and most of all *Between the Acts,* Woolf will be clearly influenced by the revolutionary Joycean language so like music to the inner ear and elliptical in its communication of ephemeral states of mind, in contrast to the nineteenth-century notion of "character."

Often, "influence" is not immediately discernible but may be said to suffuse a younger writer's sensibility, rather more in the way of character than in writerly terms. Anton Chekhov and Leo Tolstoy could not be more different as artists, and as visionaries, yet Chekhov revered Tolstoy as he did no other writer:

His illness frightened me and kept me in a state of tension. I dread Tolstoy's death. If he died, a large vacuum would be formed in my life. In the first place, I never loved any human being as much as I do him. I am an unbeliever, but of all faiths I regard his as the nearest to me and the one that suits me best. Second, when Tolstoy is part of literature, it is easy and agreeable to be a writer; even the knowledge that you have not accomplished and never will accomplish anything is not so terrible, for Tolstoy makes up for all of us. His activity justifies all the hopes and expectations that are pinned to letters . . . (letter to M. O. Menshikov, 28 January 1900)

Yet Chekhov continues in this letter to shrewdly criticize Tolstoy for the "too theological" *Resurrection,* only just published.

In the same way, though there is hardly a glimmering of the ever-subtle Jamesian sensibility in her prose fiction, Flannery O'Connor spoke of reading Henry James with enormous respect and attention. Ralph Ellison closely studied Ernest Hemingway and Gertrude Stein yet would seem to have learned far more, as a craftsman of sentences, from William Faulkner. The lyric fabulist Eudora Welty admired Anton Chekhov, the supreme realist; Henry David Thoreau, with the eye of a visual artist for the rich details of the natural world, and a precise prose style to communicate that vision, loved the mythopoetic Homer and such religious-mystic works as the Vedic *Upanishad,* the most non-specific, philosophical, and non-naturalistic of texts. Richard Wright may have believed himself influenced by Dostoyevsky's *Crime and Punishment* while writing *Native Son,* but apart from the surface similarity of plot, there would seem to be little of the Russian's deeper, profoundly religious consciousness in this startling novel of black American ghetto life and racism. We can understand to a degree why Henry James was fascinated by Honoré Balzac, not least by Balzac's great celebrity in the nineteenth century; yet Balzac as a stylist would seem to have had no effect upon James at all, and the melodrama of his characteristic plots is totally missing in James, where human relations of a subtle kind, and often merely interior revelations, constitute drama. (As when, in the quintessential James story, "The Beast in the Jungle," the middle-aged bachelor-protagonist finally realizes what most readers would have quickly discerned, that his is a life in which "nothing" has happened.) Yet, surprisingly, here is Henry James musing to himself in his notebook after having read a story by Sarah Orne Jewett, a minor contemporary of his whose best-known work is *Tales of New England:*

> February 19, 1899
> Struck an hour ago by pretty little germ of small thing given out in 4 or 5 lines of charming volume of Miss Jewett . . . A girl on a visit to new-found old-fashioned (spinster-gentleman) relation, 'idealized her old cousin, I've no doubt; and her repression and rare words of approval, had a great fascination for a girl who had just been used to people who chattered and were upon most intimate terms with you directly and could forget you with equal ease.' That is all—but they brushed me, as I read, with a sense of a little—a very tiny—subject. Something like *this.* I think I see it—*must* see it—as a young *man*—a young man who goes to see, for the first time, a new-found old-fashioned (spinster-gentleman) cousin . . .

Here follows a dense, and intense, paragraph in which James rapidly limns an outline for a story (to be titled "Flickerbridge," reprinted in *The Better Sort*) that clearly would not have been imagined, still less composed, without the inspiration of Sarah Orne Jewett's "The Tone of Time." Henry James's great notebooks, available in a single volume edited by his biographer Leon Edel and Lyall H. Powers, are highly recommended for young writers. This remarkable gathering of notes to himself by a writer of genius is filled with gems, revelations, and surprises, more obsessively detailed even than Virginia Woolf's diary.

> I have my head, thank God, full of visions. One has never too many—one has never enough. Ah, just to let one's self go—at last: to surrender one's self to what through all the long years one has (quite heroically, I think) hoped for and waited for—the mere potential, and relative, increase of *quantity* in the material act—act of application and production. One has prayed and hoped and waited, in a word, to be able to work *more.* And now, toward the end, it seems, within its limits, to have come. That is all I ask. Nothing else in the world. I bow down to Fate, equally in submission and in gratitude. (14 February 1895)

The inspiration a writer takes from a predecessor is usually accidental, like the inspirations of our lives; those individuals met by chance who become integral to our destinies. We meet—we "fall in love"—we are transformed. (If not always permanently, memorably.) Obviously, a writer is most permeable to influence when he or she is young; adolescence is the fertile turbulent period, a time of luminous dreams and dream-visions when the examples of our elders loom large before us and would appear to be showing us pathways we, too, might take. As a young, already ambitious poet, Sylvia Plath, the perfectionist, typed out poems by such then-popular poets as Sara Teasdale, lamenting in her diary (1946), "What I wouldn't give to be able to write like this!" In her twenties, Plath was so determined to be a writer of salable short stories that she coolly dissected the stories of the Irish Frank O'Connor: "I will imitate until I can feel I'm using what he can teach." (Quoted in Ted Hughes, introduction to *Johnny Panic and the Bible of Dreams,* by Sylvia Plath, 1979.) Plath learned from writers as different as Wallace Stevens and James Thurber; she analyzed stories published in *Seventeen, The New Yorker,* and *The Ladies' Home Journal;* her diary is breathless with self-admonitions and pep talks:

> First, pick your market: *Ladies' Home Journal* or *Discovery? Seventeen* or *Mlle?* Then pick a topic. Then think.

> Send it off to *The Sat Eve Post:* start at the top. Try *McCall's, Ladies' Home Journal, Good Housekeeping* . . . before getting blue.

> I want to hit *The New Yorker* in poetry and the *Ladies' Home Journal* in stories, so I must study the magazines the way I did *Seventeen.*

> I will slave and slave until I break into those slicks. (quoted in Jacqueline Rose, *The Haunting of Sylvia Plath,* p. 170)

In the similarly frank, though not nearly so obsessive, memoir *Self-Consciousness,* John Updike speaks of his country-bred childhood in which he was "in love with not writing but with print, the straight lines and serifs of it, the industrial polish and transcendence of it"; and of his early admiration for works as various as Eliot's "The Waste Land," Faulkner's *Requiem for a Nun,* the prose of James Joyce, Marcel Proust, and Henry Green. (Joyce, Proust, and Green glimmer yet in Updike's tessellated style, along with Vladimir Nabokov, a later discovery.) Yet in the much-anthologized, irresistible "A & P," Updike's most popular story, the voice of American vernacular—Mark Twain, Sherwood Anderson ("I Want to Know Why"), J. D. Salinger (*The Catcher in the Rye*) as predecessors—is fitted to distinctly Updikean themes of class and sexual attraction.

John Gardner, another ambitious young writer even in adolescence, spoke of typing out works of exemplary fiction in order to "feel" the prose rhythms of another's language; Gardner was a particular admirer of Tolstoy, whose moralizing, didactic tone is echoed in Gardner's fiction. In D. H. Lawrence's *Studies in Classic American Literature,* Lawrence reproduces much of the prose of works he admires (Poe's "Ligeia" and "The Fall of the House of Usher," Hawthorne's *The Scarlet Letter,* Melville's *Moby Dick*) commenting so minutely on the passages as to seem a kind of coauthor. This is an extraordinarily sympathetic, uncannily intimate criticism, in which Lawrence hotly discusses ficti-

tious characters like Hawthorne's Hester Prynne as if they were not mere constructs of language, but somehow *real:*

> Unless a man believes in himself and his gods, *genuinely;* unless he fiercely
> obeys his own Holy Ghost; his woman will destroy him. Woman is the nemesis
> of doubting man. She can't help it.
> And with Hester, after Ligeia, woman becomes a nemesis to man. She bolsters him
> up from the outside, she destroys him from the inside. And he dies hating her, as
> Dimmesdale did . . .
> Woman is a strange and rather terrible phenomenon, to man. When the subcon-
> scious soul of woman recoils from its creative union with man, it becomes a
> destructive force. It exerts . . . an invisible destructive influence. The woman [like
> Ligeia] is sending out waves of silent destruction of the faltering spirit in men . . .
> She doesn't know it. She can't even help it. But she does it. The devil is in her . . .
> A woman can use her sex in sheer malevolence and poison, while she is *behav-*
> *ing* as meek and good as gold. ("Nathaniel Hawthorne and *The Scarlet Letter*")

Readers of Lawrence's similarly passionate fiction will recognize his narrative
voice in such passages, in which textual "analysis" is taken to an extreme of
identification and empathy. For Lawrence the moralist didn't believe that art is
merely aesthetic or self-expressive, still less entertaining, but the primary ves-
sel of truth:

> Art-speech is the only truth. An artist is usually a damned liar, but his art, if it be
> art, will tell the truth of his day. And that is all that matters. Away with eternal
> truth. Truth lives from day to day . . .
> The artist usually sets out—or used to—to point a moral and adorn a tale. The
> tale, however, points the other way, as a rule. Two blankly opposing morals, the
> artist's and the tale's. Never trust the artist. Trust the tale. The proper function of
> a critic is to save the tale from the artist who created it. (Introduction, "The Spirit
> of Place")

D. H. Lawrence is as intransigent, and controversial, a figure in our own time
as he was in 1917–1918, the time of *Studies in Classic American Literature,*
when he was involved in the composition of his most complex and ambitious
novel, *Women in Love.*

   An eager, eclectic reader in his youth, F. Scott Fitzgerald, who would
become famous, and notorious, at an even younger age than Jack Kerouac,
with the publication of *This Side of Paradise* (1920) when he was only twenty-
four, was influenced to varying degrees by Joseph Conrad, Theodore Dreiser,
T. S. Eliot, James Joyce, Andre Malraux, Ernest Hemingway, Booth Tarkington,
Thomas Wolfe—and Gilbert and Sullivan; in his letters to his daughter Scottie,
at the time a freshman at Vassar, he urges her particularly to read Daniel Defoe's
Moll Flanders, Dickens's *Bleak House,* Dostoyevsky's *The Brothers Karamazov,*
Henry James's *Daisy Miller,* Joseph Conrad's *Lord Jim,* and Dreiser's *Sister Car-
rie*—works of literary and cultural distinction Fitzgerald wished to emulate.

   One of the most imitated short story writers of the past several decades,

Raymond Carver, acknowledged his indebtedness to such precursors in the form as Chekhov, Isaac Babel, Frank O'Connor, V. S. Pritchett, and Ernest Hemingway; in *Fires: Essays, Poems and Stories* he notes in the introduction that he has affixed to the wall beside his desk a fragment of a sentence from a Chekhov story: "... and suddenly everything became clear to him." Carver speaks of Lawrence Durrell and Henry Miller as writers he admired who had no obvious influence on his prose style, nor is there any immediately discernible Chekhovian influence in his writing, as there would seem to be, clearly, an echo of Hemingway in Carver's pared-back, minimalist prose with its emphasis on dramatic dialogue; but the spiritual influence of Chekhov suffuses his later work, like the tenderly comic, anecdotal "Cathedral" with its subtle epiphany arising from a sighted man's identification with a blind man: "It was like nothing else in my life up to now." (The affinity with D. H. Lawrence's similarly tender, passionate story "The Blind Man" is evident here, too.) And Carver's last published story, "Errand," the most unusual work of fiction in Carver's career, is actually about Chekhov's final days and death, and an incident following his death, virtually transcribed from a biography of Chekhov but narrated in an urgent, poetically distilled style unlike Carver's characteristic conversational style; as if, approaching his own death (from lung cancer) at the young age of fifty, Raymond Carver had fashioned a new voice for this story of the premature death, at the age of forty-four (from tuberculosis) of his hero Chekhov. Carver's artistry in the short story comes to a culmination in such powerful stories as "Cathedral," "A Small Good Thing," "Feathers," and "Errand," as he had defined it in his preface to the Franklin Library limited edition of *Where I'm Calling From:* the attempt to be "as subtle as a river current when very little else in my life was subtle."

In his homage to Nelson Algren, the novelist and filmmaker John Sayles remarks that "the people who influence you aren't necessarily who you're going to write like, but the fact of their existence, of the existence of their characters, the spirit in them, opens up a possibility in your mind." So too Nelson Algren greatly influenced Russell Banks by the strength of his personality. Cynthia Ozick succumbed to an early, near-fatal fascination for Henry James; a quirkily original stylist, Ozick has acknowledged what might be called moral or spiritual influences in predecessors as varied as Anthony Trollope and Isaac Babel, Edith Wharton and Virginia Woolf, Isaac Bashevis Singer and Saul Bellow, Bruno Schulz and Primo Levi, and her now nearly forgotten contemporary Alfred Chester. In adolescence Maxine Kumin was enthralled by W. H. Auden, and Nicholas Christopher by Dostoyevsky and John Donne. Unlikely, or perhaps elliptical, models are the norm: Maureen Howard pays tribute to Willa Cather, whose fiction differs radically from her own; the experimental novelist Bradford Morrow pays tribute to Ralph Waldo Emerson, who wrote no fiction; the experimental/minimalist Black Mountain poet Robert Creely pays tribute to the New England poet Edwin Arlington Robinson, author of the popular "Miniver Cheevy," "Richard Cory," and "Mr. Flood's Party."

More logically, it would seem to us, Stephen King, one of the best-selling writers in American, if not world, history, acknowledges a direct debt to his predecessor in Gothic horror/"weird" fiction, H. P. Lovecraft, who died nearly penniless after a desperate career publishing in pulp magazines without having seen a single hardcover collection of his stories. The postmodernist Gothic writer Joanna Scott acknowledges Poe as a significant predecessor. Another postmodernist, Paul West, acknowledges "the sound and fury" of Faulkner's seductively extravagant prose style; Rick Moody, the suburban milieu and "indirection" of John Cheever; Mona Simpson, the solitary heroism of Henry James; Quincy Troupe, the originality and "astonishing, American language" of Ralph Ellison. Peter Straub, one of a small number of literary writers who are also writers of genre, acknowledges an admiring kinship with Raymond Chandler, though Chandler was a pioneer of the genre called "hardboiled mystery/detective" and Straub is an experimentalist in "Gothic horror." (For a number of these acknowledgments, and others, see *Tributes: American Writers on American Writers: Conjunctions 29.*) Virtually all of these tributes derive from the young writer's impressionistic reading in adolescence.

Is there any moral to be drawn from this compendium, any general proposition? If so, it's a simple one: *Read widely, read enthusiastically, be guided by instinct and not design. For if you read, you need not become a writer; but if you hope to become a writer, you must read.*

❧ ❧ ❧

THAT IS THE MISSION OF TRUE ART—TO MAKE US PAUSE AND LOOK AT A THING A SECOND TIME.
                                                              —Oscar Wilde

To the writer of fiction, reading fiction is a dramatic experience. It's often tense, provocative, disturbing, unpredictable. *Why this title? Why this opening scene, this opening paragraph, this opening sentence? Why this particular language? And why this pacing? And why this detail, or lack of detail? And this length, and this ending—why?* Because as fellow writers we realize we're not reading mere words, a "product"; we understand that we're reading the end result of another writer's effort, the sum total of his or her imaginative and editorial decisions, which may have been complex. We know, as perhaps ordinary readers, nonwriters, wouldn't care to know, that despite romantic notions of divine inspiration, no story writes itself; whatever the original inspiration, the story before us, whether a classic like Chekhov's "The Lady with the Pet Dog" or Ernest Hemingway's "Hills Like White Elephants," or a story by an American contemporary like Cynthia Ozick's "The Shawl" or Andre Dubus's "A Father's Story" has been consciously, in some cases painstakingly, *written*. It has been extricated, excavated, out of the privacy of the individual imagination and positioned in a communal space, on the printed page. Its interior, secret emotions and associations for the writer mean nothing now. It has become an autonomous creation, in a sense a small vehicle of words that moves us through time, or in some cases fails to move us. *Why was this story written? Is this story significant enough to have warranted the effort first of its own composition, and secondly of the reader's participation? Is it original? Is it convincing? Is its language appropriate? Am I a slightly different person for having read it than I'd been previously? Will I urge others to read this story, and will I want to reread it myself and to read other work by the author? Above all, what have I learned from this story—as a writer?*

Henry James spoke of the artist as, ideally, one upon whom nothing is lost. This is particularly true for the writer of prose fiction who must populate his or her imaginary worlds with "real" figures; and the worlds containing them must give the illusion of being "real" as well. What a writer *is* intellectually, morally, spiritually, emotionally will radiate through the work, like light on an overcast day on which there's no visible sun, so that all things appear illuminated equally. Yet we can change our characters, we can deepen our souls, certainly we can become more mature, more sensitive and observant through the discipline of writing, as photographers "see" more sharply through a camera lens, and one of the ways we can effect such change is by approaching the art of writing as a craft. In Annie Dillard's *The Writing Life* there's an illuminating exchange:

> A well-known writer got collared by a university student who asked, "Do you think I could be a writer?"
>
> "Well," the writer said, "I don't know . . . Do you like sentences?"
>
> The writer could see the student's amazement. Sentences? Do I like sentences? I am twenty years old and do I like sentences? If he had liked sentences, of course, he could begin, like a joyful painter I knew. I asked him how he came to be a painter. He said, "I liked the smell of the paint."

"THE LADY WITH THE DOG": A MASTERPIECE OF CHEKHOVIAN ART

. . . EVERY MAN HAD HIS REAL, MOST INTERESTING LIFE UNDER THE COVER OF SECRECY AND UNDER THE COVER OF NIGHT.
—Anton Chekhov, "The Lady with the Dog"

Composed in 1899, when Chekhov was thirty-nine years old, at the height of his literary powers yet in a meditative, melancholy phase of his life, this most famous story of Chekhov's may well have been fueled by the author's own memories of "secrecy" and the "cover of night." And its subtly elegiac tone, so powerfully evolving out of the passion of adulterous love, is surely a consequence of Chekhov's brooding upon his own steadily failing health. (He was dying by degrees of tuberculosis and had only four more years to live.) The sophisticated, cynical Gurov is a deft, elliptical portrait of Anton Chekhov in his dissatisfactions with himself as a man who felt estranged—"cold and uncommunicative"—in the company of men yet came alive in the company of women. As the prematurely aging Gurov comes passionately alive in the company of Anna Sergeyevna, who is half his age, provincial and limited in education and experience:

> Why did she love him so much? He always seemed to women different from what he was, and they loved in him not himself, but the man created by their imagination, whom they had been eagerly seeking all their lives; and afterwards, when they noticed their mistake, they loved him all the same. And not one of them had been happy with him. . . . And only now when his head was gray he had fallen properly, really in love—for the first time in his life. (translation by Constance Garnett, 1917)

To know certain biographical facts of Chekhov's life isn't at all essential to an understanding of this story, but it's instructive to know that Chekhov was in fact borrowing heavily from his own life in composing it. For what we can make of our own experiences, including even our ambivalent feelings about ourselves, is as legitimate a subject as any for fiction.

First of all, the title: Chekhov's titles are direct and unpretentious, rarely "poetic" or didactic, yet significant nonetheless in symbolic or mythic terms. (So *The Three Sisters* and *The Cherry Orchard,* his greatest plays, have titles with both literal and mythic meaning: the "three sisters" suggests the three fates, and the cherry orchard suggests the Garden of Eden.) "The Lady with the Dog"—frequently translated, "The Lady with the Pet Dog"—is obviously descriptive, and literal; yet it suggests an ironic juxtaposing of lady/woman/female with "male": in this case the girlish, extremely feminine and religious Anna Sergeyevna who loves Gurov deeply and without restraint, though she perceives herself as an adulteress and a "low, bad woman," and the more experienced and jaded Gurov, a "dog" by contrast. Yet, Chekhov suggests, the lady is fated to love the dog, and the dog, the lady. This is their highly Chekhovian, which is to say bittersweet and irresolute, fate.

A young writer, confronted with "The Lady with the Dog," is apt to miss its extraordinary ease of craft, for Chekhov isn't a self-regarding stylist in the mode of James Joyce, Marcel Proust, Vladimir Nabokov; his prose is luminous and translucent, never ornamental. In 1900, having just read "The Lady with the Dog," Chekhov's friend and fellow writer Maxim Gorky wrote to him excitedly, saying that Chekhov was "killing" Realism, for after Chekhov "no one can go further than you along its path, no one can write so simply about such simple things as you. After . . . your stories, everything else seems coarse." (Quoted in *Chekhov,* by Henri Troyat, p. 239.) Yet it isn't quite the case that Chekhov is "simple"—unless classic elegance is simple. The most accomplished art may be to disguise "art" altogether. Chekhov's language is direct and even conversational, never self-conscious or "poetic"; his use of metaphor is rare, and always precisely chosen. For instance, when Gurov is first beginning to fall in love with

Anna, he compares her to other women with whom he has had affairs, including

> very beautiful, cold women, on whose faces he had caught a glimpse of a rapacious expression—an obstinate desire to snatch from life more than it could give . . . and when Gurov grew cold to them their beauty excited his hatred, and the lace on their linen seemed to him like scales.

"Like scales"—for these cold, rapacious women are like snakes. By contrast, the inexperienced Anna is imaged as "'the woman who was a sinner' in an old-fashioned picture." Gurov is as much in love with his vision of Anna as with Anna herself; he's in love with his own fading youth, and with a nostalgia for a more moral, more profound, "old-fashioned" past.

One of the distinctive features of a Chekhov story or play is its seemingly conversational tone. This "voice" is always intelligent and sometimes whimsical, playful, ironic; occasionally, as in "The Lady with the Dog," it becomes explicitly philosophical and analytical. Gurov's consciousness pervades the story even before we come to know him. There's an apparently impersonal, omniscient opening line:

> It was said that a new person had appeared on the sea-front: a lady with a little dog.

It was said is a modern analogue of *Once upon a time.* Immediately we're introduced to what is in fact Gurov's introduction to "a fair-haired young lady of medium height, wearing a beret; a white Pomeranian dog was running behind her." It's a graceful cinematic opening that brings us into the astute consciousness of Gurov, a man whom even "bitter" experience hasn't discouraged as a lover of women. Following a few necessary paragraphs of exposition focusing upon Gurov's bourgeois background and character, we move into the first dramatized scene between Gurov and the young lady whom he's deliberately befriended. Part I is only three masterfully condensed pages; Part II, a little more than seven pages, brings us swiftly to the consummation of the love affair, its central dramatized scene in which Gurov confronts the remorse of Anna, which is unsettling to him, and the parting of the lovers which they believe to be final: "It's time for me to go north," thinks Gurov. "High time!"

Yet the adulterous love story that the principals believe to be over is not over. As in other Chekhovian works, seemingly casual actions have serious, protracted consequences. Gurov realizes that he has fallen in love with Anna; contrary to his sophisticated character, he makes a desperate trip to Anna's provincial hometown and with no warning confronts her at the opening night of an opera. This powerful scene is also cinematic: Chekhov notes the glamor and bustle of the opera house, establishing an ironic counterpoint to the intensely private and emotional experience the lovers are undergoing. Following this climactic scene, Part IV is a four-and-a-half page coda spanning years in the lives of the lovers as they continue to meet surreptitiously. (What of their domestic lives? What of Anna's children? Only their love affair is highlighted, as in a play involving just two characters.) Few serious writers even attempt to write love stories of this sort, which are achingly realistic and yet skirt senti- mentality and bathos, but Chekhov's art raises "The Lady with the Dog" to a kind of tragedy, as the irresolution at the conclusion of *The Three Sisters* sug- gests tragedy in the very banality of thwarted ideals. Gurov and Anna love each other, we're told, like "tender friends"; yet their anguish is such that they yearn to be "free from this intolerable bondage." Yet happiness for them lies precisely in that there's no evident solution to their predicament:

> And it seemed as though in a little while the solution would be found, and then a new and splendid life would begin; and it was clear to both of them that they had still a long, long road before them, and that the most complicated and diffi- cult part of of it was only just beginning.

"The Lady with the Dog" has the depth and breadth of a novella, like so many of Chekhov's stories. Where most short fiction focuses upon a brief time period, or may contain a single dramatized scene, this story takes its lovers through years of their lives and projects them into a speculative future. Throughout, Chekhov maintains a precisely orchestrated *background* to his dramatic *foreground:* first, we're in the idle summer resort of Yalta; then we're in Moscow, in winter, where Gurov's lyricism is confounded by a companion's banal comment on food ("You were right this evening: the sturgeon was a bit too strong!")—which may well be an ironic comment on erotic love; then we're at the opera house, and at last in a room in the Slaviansky Bazaar Hotel in Moscow, an impersonal setting for the lovers' passion. The story's secret core, so to speak, is this phenomenon of the intensely private, secret life lived in the very midst of a public, extroverted life; as Gurov thinks, in the epigraph above, most men live their true lives under "the cover of secrecy and of night":

> All personal life rested upon secrecy, and possibly it was on that account that civ- ilized man was so nervously anxious that personal privacy should be respected.

The story's theme is like a bobbin upon which the thread of the narrative, or plot, is skillfully wound. Without the bobbin, the thread would fly loose. Lack- ing this thematic center of gravity, the story of "fated" lovers would be merely sentimental and unoriginal.

   In general, fiction of a high quality possesses depth because it involves absorbing narratives and meritorious characters and is at the same time a kind of commentary upon itself. In Chekhov, as in a number of other writers included in this anthology, "fiction" is counterpointed by "commentary" in a delicate equilibrium. The commentary can be extricated from the fiction, as Raymond Carver chose a succinct epiphany from Chekhov to affix to his wall: ". . . and suddenly everything became clear to him." But the fiction can't be extricated from the commentary, except at the risk of reducing it to a mere con- catenation of events lacking a spiritual core.

"Hills Like White Elephants":
Writerly Grace Under Pressure

I met a girl in Prunier . . . I knew she'd had an abortion. I
went over and we talked, not about that but on the way
home I thought of the story, skipped lunch, and spent that
afternoon writing ["Hills Like White Elephants"].
                    —Ernest Hemingway, *Paris Review* interview

What felicitous use to have made of a single afternoon: skipping lunch, and composing a four-page masterpiece.

(In fact, according to biographer Kenneth S. Lynn, Hemingway spent several days on his honeymoon in 1927 revising an earlier draft of a story set in the Ebro Valley in northern Spain, which would evolve into "Hills Like White Elephants." But Hemingway's version makes a superior anecdote.)

Ernest Hemingway often spoke with admiration of "grace under pressure" as an ideal of character in literature and in life. His was a masculinized vision of strength fortified by will, and it's as readily applicable to the art of fiction itself: Grace is what we might call fluidity, smoothness, "inevitability" of narration, and pressure is the need to keep the story as tightly crafted, as pared to its essentials, as possible. "Hills Like White Elephants" is a single-scene story, a very brief one-act play. In dramatic literature, the tauter the scene, the more emotionally effective; if the scene is protracted or repetitive and the audience gets ahead of the play, there's a slackening of attention; but if the scene is too short and underdeveloped, the dramatic experience will be thin, slight, sketchy, forgettable. The goal for the writer is to *fully realize* his or her material: to discover the ideal balance between fluidity of narration and background exposition, description and amplification.

In a brilliant miniature like "Hills Like White Elephants," as in the kindred "A Very Short Story," Hemingway's goal is to move us swiftly and unerringly from Point A to Point B. There are only two characters, "the American and the girl with him" (whom contemporary writers would probably call a "woman" since she would seem to be over eighteen). We don't know the names of these characters because they are evoked purely for this fragment of a scene, a "he" and a "she" whose attitude toward the unnamed "thing" (presumably an abortion) is antithetical; we are not intended to imagine lives for these characters beyond the scene in the train station bar. Short as it is, "Hills Like White Elephants" achieves a startling and dramatic closure, as perfect a match of content and form as the dazzling sonnets of William Butler Yeats.

The young writer can instructively contrast "Hills Like White Elephants" with the more complex, more leisurely "The Lady with the Dog" and with other more developed Hemingway stories like the classics "The Snows of Kilimanjaro" and "The Short Happy Life of Francis Macomber," which are structured like compact novellas. It's possible to imagine alternative, fuller versions of this

story, written by the author in a later and more meditative phase of his life
(Hemingway was only twenty-eight when he wrote "Hills . . .") in which the
past relations of the young woman and her callow companion have been
explored with thematic reference to the present situation; these characters
would have names, histories, personalities, and their experience might merge
with our own. For longer fiction has the distinct advantage of involving the
reader emotionally, while minimalist fiction has the advantage of short, sharp,
declarative art: surprise and revelation.

Note how the scene is set in the first, precisely written paragraph: as in
"The Lady with the Dog," we open with what might be called a quick cinematic
"establishing" shot.

> The hills across the valley of the Ebro were long and white. On this side there was
> no shade and no trees and the station was between two lines of rails in the sun.

How subtly it's suggested subliminally that romance of a kind is in the distance,
across a valley; while "on this side" there's no shade and it's "very hot" and the
primary concern of travelers is "What should we drink?"

Rare in Hemingway, yet altogether convincing here, a woman—a "girl"—
is the bearer of a visionary truth, as she is the potential bearer of a child whose
father would like it aborted. She is the one of the two who has an eye for poetic
metaphor: She observes that the distant hills resemble white elephants while
her companion says flatly, "I've never seen one," and drinks his beer. The girl,
who surely hasn't seen a white elephant either, responds with a taunt, "No, you
wouldn't have." In this brief exchange, their personalities are effectively contrasted and a sense of their discord is established. The story reaches a pitch of
understated emotion as the two discuss the possibility of an abortion without
ever quite naming what the "awfully simple operation" is; the girl, gazing out
across the river valley, responds in a rush of inspiration which her companion,
concerned with his own welfare, tries to block:

> "And we could have all this," she said. "And we could have everything and
> every day we make it more impossible."
> "What did you say?"
> "I said we could have everything."
> "We can have everything."
> "No, we can't."
> "We can have the whole world."
> "No, we can't."
> "We can go everywhere."
> "No, we can't. It isn't ours any more."
> "It's ours."
> "No, it isn't. And once they take it away, you never get it back."

(Who is this mysterious "they" who can take the world from us? So Hemingway
has elsewhere evoked a kind of impersonal, godless fate that lies in wait for
individuals who violate an unstated moral code.)

Judging from this exchange, the reader can assume that the man and the girl have been debating this issue for some time, without resolution; that the girl will probably give in ("Then I'll do it. Because I don't care about me"); that their relationship, which they call love, won't endure the strain of the abortion and its emotional aftermath. Hemingway seems to be suggesting, oddly for one with his well-known antagonism for traditional religion and morals, that we provoke punishment when we "violate" nature and the natural laws of sexual reproduction, when we live purely for ourselves, like these deracinated American travelers of the 1920s in a post-World War I malaise of the spirit. What is notable about the story, apart from its powerful theme, is of course Hemingway's highly stylized, wonderfully honed language. In this time, now decades past, such blunt, direct speech and the recording, in prose, of "the way people really talk" (even if they don't in fact really talk this way but with far less art) had the force of a revolution in consciousness. And Hemingway's idealism shone through the flawed, often wounded actors of his imagination as challenge and guidance for us all:

> From things that have happened and from all things that you know and all those you cannot know, you make something through your invention that is not a representation but a whole new thing truer than anything true and alive, and you make it alive, and if you make it well enough, you give it immortality. That is why you write and for no other reason . . .

(See *Writers at Work,* The Paris Review *Interviews,* edited by George Plimpton, 1963.)

The short stories gathered in this anthology have been selected because they represent, in most cases, works of prose fiction that have transcended their immediate times and the occasion of their first publications. They represent, to the individual and very diverse writers, solutions in prose to problems of aesthetic form. *I have to tell* is the writer's first thought; the second thought is *How do I tell it?* From our reading, we discover how various the solutions to these questions are, how stamped with an individual's personality. For it's at the juncture of private vision and the wish to create a communal, public vision that art and craft merge.

T O M   B A I L E Y

Character, Plot, Setting and Time, Metaphor, and Voice

*I*n "The Craft of Stories," a writing course which I began teaching at Harvard and now teach at Susquehanna University, we study how writers make short stories—how they build the essential shaping elements of character, plot, setting and time, metaphor, and voice. To help us begin to see fiction from this point of view, I like to ask my students to imagine themselves as carpenters. I have them run their fingers over the edge of the conference table we're sitting around to get a feel for what I mean. I wonder aloud what we'd find (other than graying gobs of gum) if we flipped the table upside down and took a look at it from that perspective. How was it made? Did the builder bother to bevel the edges? What wood did he or she choose—maple, oak, or cherry? Does the cut go with or against the grain? The legs seem sturdy. Were they glued? Bolted? Was the careful time taken to countersink the screws? Were they counterbored? Perhaps dowels were used.

To talk about the piece that is our conference table—to voice the work we see—or as craftsmen and craftswomen to say how a story is working (or not working!) on the page—we first need a language to respond. We need words, specific words, working words. Surely no one is more aware of this need than we writers, and for writers and readers of short stories terms such as character, plot, setting and time, metaphor, and voice help us to begin to define what it is we do when we make fiction. Such terms let us know what we mean when we talk about a story, whether it is a published story we have read, a story we are writing, or a draft of someone else's story that is up for workshop.

The Voice of Desire: Character

In this section we will consider the importance of character in literature, "round versus flat" characters, primary and secondary characters, points of view, direct and indirect methods of characterization, and dialogue.

From some good authority somewhere I once heard it said that there are only a dozen plots available to the author: basic Cain and Abel conflicts of brother against brother, or King Lear-like tragedies of betrayal, tales of revenge such as Hamlet's righting his father's "foul and most unnatural murther," seminally sharp, bittersweet bites of the apple—the loss of innocence Adam and Eve suffer in the Garden of Eden—Ahab's maniacal hunt for the great white whale. But when we walk into a bookstore or local library and scan the shelves of fiction, we find ourselves faced not with twelve titles, but perhaps as many as 12,000. Where did all these plots come from, we say. Didn't I hear from some good authority somewhere that there are only a dozen plots available to the writer? Then how can there be so many books? So many different stories?

Then we recall the many characters we've met in our reading. No two seem just the same. No matter how similar the story line of *King Lear*—where an aged patriarch puts his daughters' love to the test—and Jane Smiley's novel *A Thousand Acres,* the characters remain distinctly different. They may find themselves in similar situations—they may even meet similarly tragic fates—but the characters who people both stories remain separate for us because they're full-up with their own desires—sharply drawn by the defining lines of their own motives, wishes, wants, needs, likes and dislikes, prejudices, the sum of where they grew up and how they were raised, the histories of their parents and grandparents and great-grandparents, their cultures, their talent for playing Chopin or lowering their head and blindly busting a football up the two hole, their failings at their job or second marriage, IQ or other kinds of "smartness" such as the ability to feel, *intuit*—their very *whoness*. As we read, we get to know such things about our characters, these myriad concerns that shape and power them, and so simply knowing the story before we begin doesn't give *them* away.

Character in literature is the always shifting and changing element that makes each story different no matter how similar the "plot" (a word we'll discuss on its own terms later). Character, in writing fiction, acts as the x variable in what would otherwise be a too-obvious and easily enumerated, fixed equation.

Character pumps as the heart of fiction. It is character—and the "love and honor and pity and pride and compassion and sacrifice" characters live, to quote the "verities" William Faulkner gave us in his Nobel Prize acceptance speech—that, as Raymond Carver says in "On Writing," "carr[ies] news from their world to ours."

ROUND VERSUS FLAT CHARACTERS

But what is character? Or, rather, *who?* And, as writers, how do we make people stand up and take shape on the bright white flatness of the page?

In his book *Aspects of the Novel,* E. M. Forster speaks of "round" and "flat" characters. Flat characters are flat because they exist in one dimension. Flat characters are stand-ins for ideas, merely good or too simply evil; they are caricatures of people, cartoons: Snideley Whiplash types or even Snow Whites. They do not exhibit a human being's possibilities for emotion, for action and reaction, given the *x* variables of *whoness* mentioned before.

These possibilities shape round characters. Round character act in a particular way because of some specific *desire.* Janet Burroway in her book *Writing Fiction* notes that "Aristotle rather startlingly claimed that man *is* his desire." This desire, the need that makes him or her, can be termed the character's **motivation,** and this motivation is formed by the complexities inherent in any character's often contradictory aspects of self. Aristotle called these contradictory properties of self a character's "consistent inconsistencies."

Before offering an example of a round character, Anders in Tobias Wolff's "Bullet in the Brain," we should pause to make a preliminary distinction between **primary** and **secondary** characters. To help us get started let's say that **primary characters** are usually made to carry the brunt of meaning in a story and so must necessarily be complex enough to have any **realization** the story might offer. They are built to experience **epiphanies.** (Two more terms that we will give their due a bit later.) If we can, for our purposes here, briefly define an epiphany as a change in perception, and the primary character as the narrator of the story—or focus of the narration—whose perception changes, then the primary character must be round enough, complete enough, and reveal enough "consistent inconsistencies" to hold the possibility for change. A **secondary character** might necessarily be less developed—"one of these cash-register-watchers, a witch about fifty with rouge on her cheekbones and no eyebrows," who's been waiting "fifty years" for somebody like Sammy, the checkout boy in John Updike's "A & P," to make a mistake ringing up her purchase.

These witches, or the "houseslaves in pin curlers . . . pushing their carts" up and down the aisles of Sammy's A & P world act in the story like extras in a movie. They are necessary, but their perceptions do not change; they are not invested with the possibility for change as is Sammy, our narrator, whom we spend the entire story getting to know. "A & P" is Sammy's story; at the end, it is Sammy who walks past "the electric eye" of the automatic door to find "the sunshine . . . skating around on the asphalt," Sammy who has the "realization": "and my stomach kind of fell as I felt how hard the world was going to be to me hereafter." Sammy is the primary character; the "witches" and "houseslaves" are secondary characters. Even the girls who walk into the A & P in "nothing but bathing suits," Queenie, and Plaid, the "chunky one," and "Big Tall Goony-Goony (not that as raw material she was so bad)," who play such a vital role in Sammy's transformation, are secondary characters. Each has a part to play in

Sammy's drama, but each leaves the A & P (so far as we know) unchanged by Lengel's scolding. They exist in the story as Sammy sees them. In a sense, they are Sammy's creations: how he describes them is more a reflection of Sammy and how he views the world than who they "really" are.

Tobias Wolff's short story "Bullet in the Brain" is *primarily* about Anders, a world-weary critic whose withering cynicism gets him shot in the head when he "burst[s] out laughing" in the face of a third-rate secondary character, a clichéd pistol-toting bank robber, who pokes his weapon under Anders's chin as he stands in line and says, "Fuck with me again, you're history. *Capiche?*"

The story, which is only six pages long, fleshes out what appears at first to be the lopsided, one-dimensional cynicism that Anders's character exhibits from the moment he enters the bank: "Anders couldn't get to the bank until just before it closed, so of course the line was endless and he got stuck behind two women whose loud, stupid conversation put him in a murderous temper." Then the bank robbers burst in and tell the teller to "get [her] ugly ass in gear and fill that bag." As a "book critic known for the weary, elegant savagery with which he dispatched almost everything he reviewed," Anders has become bored to death by everything he sees and hears, everything he has read or is tiredly reading now. We don't know exactly when "he began to regard the heap of books on his desk with boredom and dread, or when he grew angry at writers for writing them . . . when everything began to remind him of something else," we only see him as he is here, in this moment before he is shot as he stands in line critiquing the robbers: "Oh, bravo. *Dead meat.* Great script, eh? The stern, brass-knuckled poetry of the dangerous classes."

But it is in this here and now of Anders's moment of reckoning that we are given the hint of who he was before, or, under different circumstances, who he might have been. It is the *possibility* of another side to Anders's character, our understanding that there was a time when he wasn't bored to death, a time when "his eyes had burned" at hearing a professor of his recite *Aeschylus* in Greek, or the "respect he had felt" after reading a novel by a college classmate, a time when Anders actually experienced "the pleasure of giving respect," that makes him *round*.

The story slows the moment for us, shifting the remaining microsecond of Anders's life into "brain time" as the bullet, "scattering shards of bone into the cerebral cortex, the corpus callosum, back toward the basal ganglia, and down into the thalamus," sets off "a crackling chain of ion transports and neuro-transmissions"—in short, sparking a single flashbulb pop of memory in stark relief against all that Anders does *not* recall about his life, a single remembrance that makes Anders whole. "This is what he remembered. Heat. A baseball field. Yellow grass, the whir of insects, himself leaning against a tree as the boys of the neighborhood gather for a pickup game . . . Coyle and a cousin of his from Mississippi" who, when asked what position he'd like to play, says, "Shortstop. Short's the best position they is." It is this "They is" that Anders hears, words at which he remembers being "strangely roused, elated, by . . . their pure unexpectedness and their music."

Of course, Anders will soon be dead, "[t]hat can't be helped," but as the bullet "leave[s] the troubled skull behind, dragging its comet's tail of memory and hope and talent and love into the marble hall of commerce" we find Anders wholly defined. *"They is, they is, they is" is* the "soft chant" we're left with, the call for us to completely understand the tragic life story of who Anders really, *roundly,* is, how he became who he was, the acerbic critic standing in line late at the bank. This moment is *our* realization of Anders as more than critic. In his appreciation for and awe at this simple phrase, we can view him in 3D, so to speak. And though we may be surprised at our discovery, we are not shocked. The fact is Anders had it in him all along, whether we knew we knew it or not.

Considering this example of a round character, it would seem the writer's job is to offer us such seemingly contradictory possibilities. But how do we actually go about doing this? After all, the page *is* flat even if our primary characters can't be.

POINT OF VIEW

In any discussion of how writers create round characters, **point of view** (or POV) is an important concern. At its most basic, POV can simply be thought of as the character who holds, or is held in the eye of the camera, our **narrator** or the focus of the **narration.** Through the eyes, perceptions, or directions of a narrator or narration, we *view* (i.e., *experience*) the story.

Any story is told with three possible points of view: **first person** (I, We), **second person** (You), or **third person** (He, She, It). Each choice of POV has its advantages and disadvantages, its freedoms and limitations. First person may offer the freedom of slinging around a strong voice, to invoke the narrator of Louise Erdrich's "Saint Marie": "So when I went there, I knew the dark fish must rise. Plumes of radiance had soldered on me. No reservation girl had ever prayed so hard. There was no use in trying to ignore me any longer. I was going up there on the hill with the black robe women. They were not any lighter than me." Such a voice is strong—mesmerizing—but it can be limiting, confining vocabulary to that particular character's level of diction. In "A & P," Sammy shows himself to be awfully perceptive, terribly sharp, but he would never use the word *lascivious* in describing McMahon's "sizing up the girl's joints." Such a word denotes another character, demanding another POV.

In choosing POV we not only consider the *person* in which the story is told—*first person, second person,* or *third person*—but whether it will be **subjective** or **objective**. In "Bullet in the Brain," the first half of the story is told in *third person subjective,* "*Anders* had conceived *his* own towering hatred for the teller, but *he* immediately turned it on the presumptuous crybaby in front of *him*" (italics mine). The second half, beginning at the point at which Anders is shot and so no longer has the ability to narrate, is told from the distanced perspective of *third person objective,* "The bullet smashed Anders' skull and ploughed through his brain and exited behind his right ear. . . ."

All this can seem confusing at first, but it's really as simple as who tells the story and the distance employed by the writer between the teller and the tale that is told.

First Person (Subjective)

The anthology in Part Two of this book offers examples of stories told in **first person subjective POV,** including Tillie Olsen's "I Stand Here Ironing," Raymond Carver's "Cathedral," John Updike's "A & P," Susan Minot's "Lust," James Baldwin's "Sonny's Blues," Louise Erdrich's "Saint Marie," Joyce Carol Oates's "Heat," and Andre Dubus's "A Father's Story." Read through any two of these stories. You will quickly see that each of them has several things in common.

Right away you may notice that first person is by its very nature *subjective*. The speaker is the subject, even if the story seems to be about someone or something else. In Tillie Olsen's "I Stand Here Ironing," the narrator is concerned about the call she's received from the guidance counselor from school who has phoned to talk about the narrator's daughter, Emily: "I wish you would manage the time to come in and talk with me about your daughter. I'm sure you can help me understand her. She's a youngster who needs help and whom I'm deeply interested in helping." And though the story is *about* her daughter's troubles, it is the narrator's own guilt, shame, understanding, and, finally, "wisdom" that the counselor's call causes to "move . . . tormented back and forth with the iron": "Even if I came, what good would it do? You think because I am her mother I have a key, or that in some way you could use me as a key?"

Another common denominator of stories told in first person is the unique **voice** of the narrator. Listen to "Bub," of Raymond Carver's story "Cathedral," as he describes the blind man, his wife's friend, who has come to visit them for the weekend:

> I've never met, or personally known, anyone who was blind. This blind man was late forties, a heavy-set, balding man with stooped shoulders, as if he carried a great weight there. He wore brown slacks, brown shoes, a light-brown shirt, a tie, a sports coat. Spiffy. He also had this full beard. But he didn't use a cane and he didn't wear dark glasses. I'd always thought dark glasses were a must for the blind. Fact was, I wished he had a pair. At first glance, his eyes looked like anyone else's eyes. But if you look close, there was something different about them. Too much white in the iris, for one thing, and the pupils seemed to move around in the sockets without his knowing it or being able to stop it. Creepy. As I stared at his face, I saw the left pupil turn in toward his nose while the other made an effort to keep in one place. But it was only an effort, for that eye was on the roam without his knowing it or wanting it to be.

Or Luke Ripley in Andre Dubus's "A Father's Story":

> My name is Luke Ripley and here is what I call my life: I own a stable of thirty horses, and I have young people who teach riding, and we board some horses

too. This is in northeastern Massachusetts. I have a barn with an indoor ring, and outside I've got two fenced-in rings and a pasture that ends at a woods with trails. I call it my life because it looks like it is, and people I know call it that, but it's a life I can get away from when I hunt and fish, and some nights after dinner when I sit in the dark in the front room and listen to opera. The room faces the lawn and the road, a two-lane country road. When cars come around the curve northwest of the house, they light up the lawn for an instant, the leaves of the maple out by the road and the hemlock closer to the window. Then I'm alone again, or I'd appear to be if someone crept up to the house and looked through a window: a big-gutted grey-haired guy, drinking tea and smoking cigarettes, staring out at the dark woods across the road, listening to a grieving soprano.

My real life is the one nobody talks about anymore . . .

Or, again, Marie from Louise Erdrich's "Saint Marie":

So when I went there, I knew the dark fish must rise. Plumes of radiance had soldered on me. No reservation girl had ever prayed so hard. There was no use in trying to ignore me any longer. I was going up there on the hill with the black robe women. They were not any lighter than me. I was going up there to pray as good as they could. Because I don't have that much Indian blood. And they never thought they'd have a girl from this reservation as a saint they'd have to kneel to. But they'd have me. And I'd be carved in pure gold. With ruby lips. And my toenails would be little pink ocean shells, which they would have to stoop down off their high horse to kiss.

All of these characters have particular manners of speaking, distinctively voicing their understanding of the world. What they say—and how they say it—is who they are. They are drawn for us not so much from physical descriptions but from what they choose to tell us and the words they use to describe what they see. (Sammy: "She was a *chunky kid,* with a *good* tan and a *sweet broad soft-looking can* with those *two crescents* of white just under it, where the sun never seems to hit, at the top of the backs of her legs." [Italics mine.]) The cragginess of language, the words they choose (Bub: "Creepy."), even the syntax— the way the words are grouped, *at the top of the backs of her legs.*"—tell us much about them—a hint of their sensibilities, social class, age, education, taste, dislikes, intelligence, and the view they have of the world.

We can guess a lot from the way people talk and when we choose to tell a story from the first person point of view, it is our job as writers to be as true to the person speaking as is possible. It isn't about *us.* And no matter how much we might be interested in what Carver, as a writer, may have to say about "Cathedral," he can't simply interject his own commentary—not if he wants to remain true to the narrator of the story. This is the narrator's story. When the narrator wonders aloud to his wife if he might take the blind man who is coming to visit them bowling, we are getting a big hint of who this character is, complete with all his limitations and contradictions.

At a reading Andre Dubus once gave, a man from the audience asked him how he created his characters. Dubus had been drinking water from a plastic

Dixie cup. It was empty, and he picked it up and set it down, picked it up and set it down again. He pointed at the cup and, in reference to a female character he was then trying to write about in the first person POV, said, "I try to *be* that cup." Some days, in three or four hours at his desk, he said, he could only manage four sentences that were *hers*.

Another aspect of *first person subjective* is the possibility of a "we" narrator. A good example of this is William Faulkner's "A Rose for Emily." The narrator remains undisclosed. We are never told whether it is a woman or a man, but much is revealed by the fact that this narrator can speak for the town:

> So the next day we all said, "She will kill herself"; and we said it would be the best thing. When she had first begun to be seen with Homer Barron, we had said, "She will marry him." Then we said, "She will persuade him yet," because Homer himself had remarked—he liked men, and it was known that he drank with the younger men in the Elks' Club—that he was not a marrying man. Later we said, "Poor Emily" behind the jalousies as they passed on Sunday afternoon in the glittering buggy, Miss Emily with her head high and Homer Barron with his hat cocked and a cigar in his teeth, reins and whip in a yellow glove.

The voice is aged, gray-haired itself, a bit stagy-grand, certainly gossipy; complicity is understood. This is *our* town, *our* story. Miss Emily is *our* concern and what happens to her is about *us*.

Second Person (Subjective/Objective)

Second person as a narrative technique has the strange effect of both distancing the narrator and going so far as to include us in a more general, objective universal narrative.

In Susan Minot's "Lust," the narrator begins her story in the first person, but as the list of boys she's "fucked"—Leo, Roger, Bruce, Tim, Philip, Johnny, Eben, Simon, Mack, Paul, Oliver—grows out of control she distances herself from the act in which she has become merely "a body waiting on the rug." She "disappears" from her own narration, replaced by a more objective, less personal (perhaps less painful) way of viewing what she knows full well she's doing to herself:

> After sex, you curl up like a shrimp, something deep inside you ruined, slammed in a place that sickens at slamming, and slowly you fill up with an overwhelming sadness, an elusive gaping worry. You don't try to explain it, filled with the knowledge that it's nothing after all, everything filling up finally and absolutely with death. After the briskness of loving, loving stops. And you roll over with death stretched out alongside you like a feather boa, or a snake, light as air, and you . . . you don't even ask for anything or try to say something to him because it's obviously your own damn fault. You haven't been able to—to what? To open your heart. You open your legs but can't, or don't dare anymore, to open your heart.

Second person can be a powerful POV. But it does have the disadvantage of calling attention to itself as a *technique*. We are somehow more aware that we're in second person than first and third, which have the curious ability to "disappear" themselves, leaving us more completely—more believingly—inside the "dream" of the narrative. Second person is also filled with presumption. "You would go to the store and buy a six pack of Red, White and Blue beer for $1.98," I might write. But you might already be shaking your head. *You* would, you say, not *me*.

Third Person

After a reading introducing his collection of stories *Bear and His Daughter,* Robert Stone was asked why he never wrote in the first person POV. The woman asking the question, an older woman wearing a big, drooping hat with a blue plastic flower attached, wondered if, perhaps, first person wasn't, well, a little "tacky," which got a laugh. Stone laughed, too, but then he rubbed his chin, considering it. He wagged his head; with his full beard and glasses he looked like a kind of Walt Whitman up there. No, he said, it wasn't that first person was "tacky," but, as a writer, he did feel its "limits." In third person he felt *stronger*. He could still gain the effect of first person—still get that close subjective POV—but he wasn't as confined. I took him to mean that he felt that he could simply *do more* in third.

Third person POV puts distance between the writer and his or her subject. It can offer the writer a way to see beyond what the character can see. Third person also allows the writer more freedom in the use of language. Vocabulary is not determined solely—though of course it must be a consideration—by the word choice of the character.

For the purpose of discussion, third person POV can be separated into three dominant perspectives, **subjective, objective,** and **omniscient.** These points of view do not necessarily have to exist separately. Rather, they are like primary colors that the writer, like the painter, may use boldly as blue or mix with yellow to gain green. Part of the beauty of third person—the strength of which Stone spoke—is the seemingly unlimited effects, chances and choices, shadings of color, such a perspective affords the writer to explore his or her subject.

THIRD PERSON SUBJECTIVE

Anton Chekhov's "The Lady with the Pet Dog" is a perfect example of the full use of a third person subjective. The perspective is set from the beginning:

> A new person, it was said, had appeared on the esplanade: a lady with a pet dog. Dmitry Dmitrich Gurov, who had spent a fortnight at Yalta and had got used to the place, had also begun to take an interest in new arrivals. As he sat in Vernet's confectionery shop, he saw, walking on the esplanade, a fair-haired young woman of medium height, wearing a beret; a white Pomeranian was trotting behind her. . . .
>
> "If she is here alone without husband or friends," Gurov reflected, "it wouldn't be a bad thing to make her acquaintance."

One of the beautiful things about this opening is the fluidity with which Chekhov, utilizing every nuance of the third person subjective POV, moves us from the interest at the "appearance" of the "lady with the pet dog" to the understanding that we have of Gurov's apparently offhand interest in "making her acquaintance." It is understood that if she is "alone" then he would like to manage an affair with her.

It is worth our while to take note of the artistry being displayed. From the first line of the story, Gurov's sensibilities and his desire have been quietly invoked. By the fourth paragraph, Chekhov has already managed to set the wheels of the story into motion and has found a moment to still the forward momentum and begin to build the foundation of Gurov's motive, the history of reason behind his desire to go to bed with the lady with the pet dog, whom he will soon come to know as Anna Sergeyevna.

In third person subjective POV we are intimately tied to Gurov's perceptions throughout the story; the narrative seems subjective in much the same way a first person POV would be subjective. We "hear" what Gurov hears "was said," and we see what he sees, that she's "alone" in the "public garden and in the square," we "reflect" with him as he thinks to himself "it wouldn't be a bad thing to make her acquaintance." And yet the third person subjective POV distances the perspective just enough to allow us to take a step back in the fourth paragraph to note *about* him, that Gurov was

> under forty, but he already had a daughter twelve years old, and two sons at school. They had found a wife for him when he was very young, a student in his second year, and by now she seemed half as old again as he. She was a tall, erect woman with dark eyebrows, stately and dignified and, as she said of herself, intellectual. She read a great deal, used simplified spelling in her letters, called her husband, not Dmitry, but Dimitry, while he privately considered her of limited intelligence, narrow-minded, dowdy, was afraid of her, and did not like to be at home. He had begun being unfaithful to her long ago—had been unfaithful to her often and, probably for that reason, almost always spoke ill of women, and when they were talked of in his presence used to call them "the inferior race."

And we haven't blinked! Chekhov has used third person subjective to move without a hitch from what Gurov sees, to his reflections, to a long outside view of his life. The POV has allowed the writer to intrude without being intrusive.

I love to read Chekhov; it's as if he isn't there! But it is Chekhov's apparent absence, of course, when we stop to consider the seamless effects this flawless third person has wrought, that makes us note how powerfully present he really is.

During a trip to Oreanda, as Gurov and Anna sit silently together on a bench "look[ing] down at the sea," we are introduced to a furthering of the third person POV perspective. Thus far we have "seen" with Gurov, "reflected" with him, stepped outside to take a long view of his history, but in this scene we are taken into his consciousness. We are nearly as close as we can get; we enter a reverie with him:

Yalta was barely visible through the morning mist; white clouds rested motionlessly on the mountaintops. The leaves did not stir on the trees, cicadas twanged, and the monotonous muffled sound of the sea that rose from below spoke of the peace, the eternal sleep awaiting us. So it rumbled below when there was no Yalta, no Oreanda here; so it rumbles now, and it will rumble as indifferently and as hollowly when we are no more. And in this constancy, in this complete indifference to the life and death of each of us, there lies, perhaps, a pledge of our eternal salvation, of the unceasing advance of life upon earth, of unceasing movement towards perfection. Sitting beside a young woman who in the dawn seemed so lovely, Gurov, soothed and spellbound by these magical surroundings—the sea, the mountains, the clouds, the wide sky—thought how everything is really beautiful in this world when one reflects: everything except what we think or do ourselves when we forget the higher aims of life and our own human dignity.

The thought is beautiful; it is profound; but it may also seem to us a little sappy, sentimental. Gurov seems poised on the verge of epiphany—a realization about life that will change him forever—and indeed he is! But it is not the realization he expects. He is in love, but doesn't know it yet. He's never been in love. At this moment, he is simply a man sitting next to a "young woman who in the dawn seemed so lovely," but she is not yet *Anna*. The reverie brings us closer than ever to Gurov. But he can see only so far, we see, even when examining life as closely—as intimately—as he may well ever have up to this point in his life.

Third person subjective POV has allowed Chekhov a cut diamond's planes of perspective. The complexities of his character are prismed before him for us, not yet clearly understood, but invaluable in marching toward our discovery of Gurov's love. Here, at the end of the story, Chekhov manages to squeeze one last bit of art out of the seemingly simple third person subjective perspective, making a move to loom large over the fate of both characters without ever necessarily leaving Gurov's POV and yet managing to echo out beyond it:

And it seemed as though in a little while the solution would be found, and then a new and glorious life would begin; and it was clear to both of them that the end was still far off, and that what was to be most complicated and difficult for them was only just beginning.

This story is so well crafted that the subtleties of third person POV can be easily missed. For me, that is Chekhov's mastery in this story: *not* showing his genius. My advice? Read it again! And again and again and again!

THIRD PERSON OBJECTIVE

A contrast to the *third person subjective POV* Chekhov uses to tell the story of Gurov in "The Lady with the Pet Dog" is a story such as Hemingway's "Hills Like White Elephants," which is told primarily in a distanced **third person objective POV.**

The camera pans into the story showing us a view of "[t]he hills across the valley of the Ebro [which are] long and white" before settling "[o]n this side" where "there [is] no shade and no trees and the station [is] between two lines of rails in the sun." We focus on the American and the girl, Jig, sitting "at a table in the shade, outside the building." They're trying drinks while they wait for the "express from Barcelona" which "would come in forty minutes . . . stop . . . at this junction for two minutes and [go] on to Madrid."

On a first reading, my students often finish the story unaware that the situation centers around Jig's decision of whether or not to have an abortion. The word "abortion" is never used, and the camera in this extraordinarily brief story has remained detached, *objective*, throughout except for a few vital moments when the focus shifts in close, giving us a quick subjective perspective: "The girl stood up and walked to the end of the station. Across, on the other side, were fields of grain and trees along the banks of the Ebro. Far away, beyond the river, were mountains. The shadow of a cloud moved across the field of grain and *she saw* the river through the trees" (italics mine).

"And we could have all this," she says. "And we could have everything and every day we make it more impossible."

Jig, as we get to see in this quick glimpse of what she sees, "just knows things." Her knowing is shown to us in the fertility of the valley, a hope "far away," the life of the river that she sees "through the trees," the "shadow of a cloud" that passes over everything.

But if we get to see this bit of what Jig sees, are allowed to feel for an instant what she feels, then why the objective POV?

Why isn't the word "abortion" used? It is spoken of as "an awfully simple operation." Why not just say it? (Why not have Jig think about *it?*) Is "it" a trick? At the end, are we supposed to guess? Is the answer to the story, "Oh, they're talking about an abortion!" Obviously not. The story isn't a who-done-it, the point is not the mystery. So, we ask, what is the effect of not simply spelling out what the "operation" is? Perhaps it's because the third person objective POV forces us to focus our attention on the actions and dialogue of the characters, giving us a seat at the station, as it were, to let us observe what they do and say for ourselves:

> "It's really an awfully simple operation, Jig," the man said. "It's not really an operation at all."
> The girl looked at the ground the table legs rested on.

The fact is we have no choice but to focus on what *they* choose to focus on, to see what *they* see. The abortion is the combustible inner engine for the story, the central concern, the drive that puts their love through this test. But it is the tension of this "operation" charging the air between them that works to *show* their lives. We are enabled to objectively experience their "love" for ourselves. We needn't be told.

Jig begins,

> "And you really want to?"
> "I think it's the best thing to do. But I don't want you to do it if you don't really want to."

"And if I do it you'll be happy and things will be like they were and you'll love me?"

"I love you now. You know I love you."

"I know. But if I do it, then it will be nice again if I say things are like white elephants, and you'll like it?"

"I'll love it. I love it now but I just can't think about it. You know how I get when I worry."

"If I do it you won't ever worry?"

"I won't worry about that because it's perfectly simple."

"Then I'll do it. Because I don't care about me."

"What do you mean?"

"I don't care about me."

"Well, I care about you."

"Oh, yes. But I don't care about me. And I'll do it and then everything will be fine."

It is the very objectification of the abortion that throws the dialogue about love in which the American and the girl are engaged into stark relief. We might, at first, believe the man's protestations. But he protests too much! The man is slowly exposed for what he is, selfish and self-centered. He loves himself. But Hemingway doesn't need to tell us this, nor do we need Jig to explain that he's a heel or to say how desperately she wants to stop traveling and trying drinks and settle down into a more complete love—to fulfill the possibilities of love that she has glimpsed in the hills across the Ebro. There's no need. We have *seen* them for ourselves. We *feel* it! Actions, we find, *do* speak louder than words—they scream even while "sitting at the table . . . smil[ing]."

"Do you feel better?" the American asks, coming back from carrying their bags around to the other side of the station, stopping to "dr[i]nk an Anis at the bar" where all the other people are "waiting reasonably for the train."

"I feel fine," Jig replies. "There's nothing wrong with me. I feel fine."

Third Person Omniscient

Strictly speaking, **third person omniscient POV** means all-seeing, all-knowing. When I think of an omniscient POV, I can't help but think of a God-like scope. In third person omniscient, we may levitate above a scene or shift at will from one character's consciousness to another's—the author seems to know all. The writer may make pronouncements, predict futures. The author is an intimate part of the goings-on: a storyteller to be reckoned with, even when the reader momentarily forgets his or her presence.

In our anthology, "The Things They Carried" by Tim O'Brien comes closest to an omniscient POV. "The Things They Carried" alternates POV between Lt. Jimmy Cross's third person subjective and an all-seeing third person omniscient told by an unseen narrator who has knowledge of the soldiers who play a part in the story and the war in Vietnam:

The things they carried were largely determined by necessity. Among the necessities or near necessities were P-38 can openers, pocket knives, heat tabs, wrist watches, dog tags, mosquito repellent, chewing gum, candy, cigarettes, salt tablets, packets of Kool-Aid, lighters, matches, sewing kits, Military Payment Certificates, C rations, and two or three canteens of water. Together, these items weighed between fifteen and twenty pounds, depending upon a man's habits or rate of metabolism.

After cataloging each of these "necessities," the narrator goes on to list the items each man carried: "Henry Dobbins . . . carried extra rations; . . . Dave Jensen . . . carried a toothbrush, dental floss, and several hotel-size bars of soap he'd stolen on R&R . . . Ted Lavender, who was scared, carried tranquilizers until he was shot in the head outside of the village of Than Khe in mid-April." The men are now referred to as "they." It isn't Jimmy Cross speaking. We're not quite sure who it is, but this *who* knows everything about the men, he knows the bulk of the burden they really "hump" is the "unweighed fear."

This broader POV allows us to view the war, if not objectively, then at least from a "higher" plateau than Lt. Jimmy Cross, who is stuck "humping" in the sweat of the jungle, focused on the letters he carries "from a girl named Martha, a junior at Mount Sebastian College in New Jersey. They were not love letters, but Lieutenant Cross was hoping, so he kept them folded in plastic at the bottom of his rucksack." And it is this perspective that at the end, after Ted Lavender is shot, when Lt. Jimmy Cross burns the letters and "dispense[s] with love" and "form[s his men] into a column to move out toward the village of Than Khe," allows us a separate realization of which Lt. Jimmy Cross, as narrator trapped by third person subjective POV, is not capable.

CHARACTERIZATION

When I was working toward my Ph.D., I lived on an old farm in upstate New York that doubled as a day camp during the summer. I used to earn extra money—indeed about all the money I did earn in those days of trying to survive on a state school stipend—working the grounds. The Bronsons owned the place, and when I was driving his old 1950s Chevy tractor, Mr. Bronson, then in his seventies, used to come hustling after me across the football field waving his hands wildly over his head like some kind of air traffic controller. He would point at the way the field lay downsloped or caution me about the rocks around the edges of the tennis court. He hated, he said, to be a Master of the Obvious, but shouldn't I mow so that I was always crossing uncut grass?

I, too, hate to be a Master of the Obvious, but having considered the importance of *character* and possible *points of view,* it seems we should touch back briefly to cover two methods of *characterization,* **indirect** and **direct.**

As we have seen, the best possible characterizations simply *show* who characters are, exampling their desires through scenes, by having them *act* as themselves. Remember Anders's acerbic reply to the women standing before him in the bank or the guffaw in the face of the robber that gets him shot in the head, or the way Sammy has made the shoppers in the A & P into actors and actresses in his own little drama ("what do these bums *do* with all that pineapple juice?"), or the way the narrator in "Cathedral" talks about the blind man, his wife's friend, who is coming to visit them: "Maybe I could take him bowling." What these characters have said about others has drawn a perfect portrait of who they are for us. *How* they are is part and parcel of *who* they are. This is *indirect characterization* at work.

Undoubtedly, though, there are times when the writer needs to employ *direct characterization*. Sammy's description of the girls who enter the A & P is a good example of *direct characterization:*

> They didn't even have shoes on. There was this chunky one, with the two-piece—it was bright green and the seams on the bra were still sharp and her belly was still pretty pale so I guessed she just got it (the suit)—there was this one, with one of those chubby berry-faces, the lips all bunched together under her nose, this one, and a tall one, with black hair that hadn't quite frizzed right, and one of these sunburns right across under the eyes, and a chin that was too long—you know, the kind of girl other girls think is very "striking" and "attractive" but never quite makes it, as they very well know, which is why they like her so much—and then the third one, that wasn't quite so tall. She was the queen. She kind of led them, the other two peeking around and making their shoulders round. She didn't look around, not this queen, she just walked straight on slowly, on these long white prima-donna legs. She came down a little hard on her heels, as if she didn't walk in her bare feet that much, putting down her heels and then letting the weight move along to her toes as if she was testing the floor with every step, putting a little deliberate extra action into it.

Sammy has perfectly drawn the girls for us; he has animated them and even offered insight into their relationships to each other, all from the picture he presents of them walking near-naked through the A & P. But now that we're aware of POV and *characterization,* we can't help but be clued to the fact that Sammy's noticing them, the words he uses to describe them, and the inferences he draws about them, say as much—if not more—about him as about the girls. His directly characterizing them, indirectly characterizes him.

I've always gotten a kick out of this paragraph of *direct characterization* from Ron Hansen's novel *Desperadoes:*

> Eugenia Moore was her alias; she was baptized Florence Quick. She was five-feet-nine inches tall and twenty-five years old and wore her blond hair in a bun. She was brown-eyed and pretty, if somewhat boyish, with teeth so white it looked like she'd never drunk tea. She had a sultry voice and a sturdy, broad-shouldered body and breasts that were not large; her hands were strong and branch-scratched and calloused; she chewed her fingernails down so close to the quick they looked like cuticle. When she wasn't in boots she was barefoot, but that evening she was wearing a white calico dress with ties on the sleeves and looked more like a lady than she was. She'd been to Holden College and she taught school for two years and there was a lot of that in her speech; when she didn't hear what was said completely, she'd say, "I beg your pardon?" She had

blond bangs that she kept brushing with a finger as she talked. She said meeting us was a pleasure and glided away to sit at a smaller table by the burlap-curtained front windows. Her face was brown from the sun.

From this fun description, we come to know Eugenia Moore completely, far beyond the fact that's she's "pretty" (though even the choice of that word tells us a lot).

Another aspect of *direct characterization* is when **exposition** is used to tell us about a character. The first two-thirds of Andre Dubus's "A Father's Story" are a veritable expository accounting—Luke Ripley explaining who he is: "My name is Luke Ripley and here is what I call my life . . ." This telling—or *re*telling—of who he is is important to the story so that when the action begins, when his daughter knocks on his door late one night with the news that she's hit someone with the car, we don't have to hesitate in the recounting of what happens from that moment on to find out why Luke Ripley does what he does. His *motive* has been solidly established. What Luke Ripley does may surprise us, but it doesn't shock us. We've spent the entire story learning who he is through both direct and indirect characterization, and given who he is, Luke Ripley—"the father of a girl"—could do nothing else.

DIALOGUE

Of course one of the best ways of having characters describe themselves or others—gaining the benefits of both direct and indirect characterization—is through their own words. Go back and listen again to the American and Jig as they sit at the little table at the train station in Hemingway's "Hills Like White Elephants." What they say and how they say it shows us so much more about them than reams of exposition could. **Dialogue,** which in fiction is simply the written version of the way characters speak, is another form of dramatization, of letting the characters show themselves for who they are.

But dialogue can be tough to write. The writer has to be a good mimic. You have to develop an ear for the ways people speak, the Boston "ca*r*," which makes a name like Arlene sound like *Ah*-lene. Lately I've noticed a lot of writers seem to be returning to the use of phonetic spellings, "Ah-lene, pahk de cah!" to capture the way characters sound when they talk. Obviously, when well done such soundings can be fun and effective, a good way for the reader to hear an approximation of the voices and nuances of dialects, the accents of speech, but they can be terribly distracting. Substituting "goin'" for "going" is not the only way to capture the way a character speaks, or who that character is.

To think about ways in which to capture believable sounding dialogue on the page, look back at any of the stories we've read thus far. Besides phonetic spellings, note the way writers work to capture the syntax of characters' speech—the ordering of their words in a sentence—and strive to choose the exact words they would use.

Hemingway, a writer often touted for the "naturalistic" dialogue he wrote, doesn't really write naturalistically at all. Where in the pauses of the difficult conversation between the American and Jig in "Hills Like White Elephants" are all the "wells . . ." and "ohs" and "you knows" that litter daily speech, even, I'm sure, the speech of the 1920s? These naturalistic touches are cut, edited out by the writer in favor of lines of speech that directly advance the character's concerns and the tensions of the story.

In Toni Cade Bambara's "The Lesson," Sylvia, the narrator, speaks up for herself:

> Back in the days when everyone was old and stupid or young and foolish and me and Sugar were the only ones just right, this lady moved on our block with nappy hair and proper speech and no makeup. And quite naturally we laughed at her, laughed the way we did at the junk man who went about his business like he was some big-time president and his sorry-ass horse his secretary. And we kinda hated her too, hated the way we did the winos who cluttered up our parks and pissed on our handball walls and stank up our hallways and stairs so you couldn't halfway play hide-and-seek without a goddamn gas mask. Miss Moore was her name. The only woman on the block with no first name. And she was black as hell, cept for her feet, which were fish-white and spooky. And she was always planning these boring-ass things for us to do, us being my cousin, mostly, who lived on the block cause we all moved North the same time and to the same apartment then spread out gradual to breathe.

Sylvia's narrative voice is naturalistic in the way we've noted above. She seems to be rambling on. Bambara uses phonetic spellings such as "cept" for *except* and "kinda" for *kind of*. The misspellings work well here; they don't get in the way. Bambara uses them to capture Sylvia's speech without distracting us unnecessarily. But look carefully at how else, besides phonetic spellings, she has managed to do this. Note the repetition of the words "hated" and "laughed" in rolling the rhythms of Sylvia's speech, and the curious way Bambara has Sylvia drop the expected "hated her" for "hated the . . ." Listen to the words, the language, Sylvia chooses: "laughed the way we did at the junk man who *went about his business* like he was some *big-time* president and his *sorry-ass* horse his secretary." (italics mine)

In capturing the actual conversation—the dialogue—between the children who go with Miss Moore to be taught the lesson of the disparity of wealth between Harlem and one thousand dollar toy sailboats at FAO Schwarz, Bambara uses the same techniques:

> "This is the place," Miss Moore say, presenting it to us in the voice she uses at the museum. "Let's look in the windows before we go in."
> "Can we steal?" Sugar asks very serious like she's getting the ground rules squared away before she plays. "I beg your pardon," say Miss Moore, and we fall out. So she leads us around the windows of the toy store and me and Sugar

screamin, "This is mine, that's mine, I gotta have that, that was made for me, I was born for that," till Big Butt drowns us out.

"Hey, I'm going to buy that there."

"That there? You don't even know what it is, stupid."

"I do so," he say punchin on Rosie Giraffe. "It's a microscope."

"Whatcha gonna do with a microscope, fool?"

"Look at things."

"Like what, Ronald?" ask Miss Moore.

The first thing we notice is how well the dialogue here shows the characters. We clearly imagine slow, pudgy Big Butt and the upright Miss Moore. They seem to naturally give voice to themselves and their predicament of place: "Can we steal?"

As writers we also observe the way Bambara keeps using tags such as "Miss Moore say" and "Sugar asks" to keep us abreast of who is speaking, but note how she quickly drops such lines when who's speaking is obvious. Beginning a new paragraph every time the speaker changes is another useful technical way we keep who's saying what straight.

A pet peeve I have is when writers overload lines of attribution with unnecessary adverbs: "Whahoo!" I shouted boisterously. Most times (not all, not all) such tags are better left off. If the dialogue is doing its job, there's no need to explain. "He said" or "she asked"—though they may seem boring or uninspired—become nearly invisible in our prose.

What else can we learn from the above passage? Bambara uses actions or gestures from her characters— " 'I do so,' he say punchin on Rosie Giraffe"—to punctuate and emphasize the way something was said. And she does not waste a line. Everything said—everything the characters say and the way they say it—advances the story.

We like hearing and seeing people speak. So, dialogue is a good and useful way of characterization. But what if you have a tin ear? What if you have trouble imitating the way people speak?

I read everything I write onto tape. This allows me to listen to the words I've written, and I find I can sometimes *hear* a gap in tension in a story more readily than I can see it on the page. These gaps, for me, are often overly long passages of exposition, of telling that interrupts the action. But listening to what I've written on tape helps me hear my characters' voices, too. And it forces me to say what they would say—"Morning, Jack!" "Morning, Bob!" "Cripes, this trick knee! It'll snow by morning, mark my words. Say, did you get that tire on the truck fixed yet?"—and to put the tension of what they're saying to the test, asking myself how it cogs the concerns of the story as a whole. Go so far as to read your written dialogue in their voice—"*Ahh*-leene!"—though you might want to try it when no one else is in the room. Also, try keeping a journal in which you record actual conversations you've overheard on the bus while standing in the aisle swaying over a mother and daughter on their way back from shopping for discount wedding dresses at Filene's Basement. Or you might rehearse conversations by your characters, keeping at heart some central concern, such as the issue of whether or not to have an abortion (or which dress to buy, when the crux of the discussion is really the husband the bride-to-be has chosen) in each word a character speaks. Writing dialogue is just like the other aspects of crafting our prose. It means writing it, and then writing it again and again until it sounds right.

A Last Word on Character

Character is the *who* that stories are all about and **point of view** is the distance that controls both our seeing and our feeling through characters. The possibilities for character and for our seeing through character, though they may seem limited by the mere fact that we've enumerated them here, are virtually limitless—I want to stress that! The designations here act as guidelines to consider—something like how ice or snow affects road conditions and the driver's consideration of curves on any road when deciding how fast to drive—not laws—like a 55 mile per hour speed limit enforced by the highway patrol—by which you must abide or suffer the penalty of a ticket. The writer's own inventiveness, judgment, talent, and style are the only real controls.

Writing Exercises

Below I've offered several writing exercises that emphasize the different aspects of character on which this section has focused. Work on each as you see fit and try not to put too much pressure on yourself. These are, after all, exercises. *Trying* is what they're all about.

1. Getting started. If character is the single most important aspect of fiction, then why not begin by imagining a character? I've found this exercise works best if you bring to mind people you know or have seen—or a kind of Mr. or Mrs. Potato Head mix of people. Say, your cousin, Jimbo, or your Great-aunt Smyrna. List everything you can about a character, from his or her name, to shoe size (9 1/2 EEE), to first grade teacher Mrs. Lawson (with her scrub of red hair), to the kind of ice cream he or she likes to eat, Ben and Jerry's Double Fudge Chunk!
2. Once you've made a list, try putting your characters into motion. Have them do something as simple as walk into Angelo's, a dark, delicious little pizza joint on Broadway, or give them engine trouble when they are alone on a windy little mountain road at night. In a page or so, try to show us as much of the above list as possible and probable, given their particular situation.
3. If you've written the above page in first person point of view, try switching it to second person, then to third person subjective, then

third person objective, then third person omniscient. You'll find it isn't as easy as simply exchanging "I" for "he" or "she." Consider the allowances you've had to make for the changes in point of view. Consider the opportunities such a change opens up.

4. To practice characterization, build on the first person point of view experimented with above by having your narrator characterize him or herself by describing someone or something else, a cousin from Mississippi who's come to visit for the summer or a sunrise at a resort by the sea. Using a third person subjective POV, have your characters move into a direct scene in which they use the continuing action to offer us exposition about themselves. In third person omniscient POV, use direct characterization to describe the appearance and peculiarities of your narrator.

5. Write down a conversation that you've heard recently. What, at heart, is the central concern of what was said? Try interspersing the dialogue with gestures and actions. You might also try writing the dialogue without using "he said" or "she said," while working to keep who's speaking clear. If you have a tape recorder, listen to what you've written. Having listened, what changes would you make? Make them, read it, and listen again.

❦ ❦ ❦

The "Why?" Behind the Power of Plot: Shaping the Short Story

In this section we will build on our understanding of writing about character to include a further discussion of motivation in determining structure, discussing conflict, climax, and resolution, tension and action, the difference between a story and a plot, as well as a consideration of the role of epiphany in shaping the short story.

"Fiction is a lie," Eudora Welty writes in her essay "Place in Fiction," and we're forced to admit it's true. Even if we attempt to tell a "true" story about our Great-aunt Smyrna, we soon find ourselves having to make decisions about what aspects of the "truth" to include (Smyrnie, as we all called her, *was,* in fact, married twice, but the first marriage isn't important to the vacation she took at Ruby Falls. So. . . .) As Maupassant wrote in "The Writer's Goal," "To make things seem real on the page consists in giving the complete *illusion* of reality, following the logical order of facts, and not servilely transcribing a pell-mell succession of chronological events in life." He puts forth "that writers who call themselves realists should more accurately call themselves illusionists."

Indeed, it comes as no surprise that stories are illusions. They are created; they are *made* of words on a page.

The word "made," though, seems to imply that stories are somehow prefabricated. I have the same problem with talking about the **structure** of a short story. Talking this way makes me feel as if all we have to do as writers is conveniently fit our characters into a sort of jig that holds all the structural elements of the short story in place, nail them quickly up—a real bang-up job— and be done with it. To return to my opening analogy of our being carpenters— craftsmen and craftswomen—this would be an enterprise more fitting to the manufacture of picnic tables for a public works operation than to the *crafting* of one finely wrought oak conference table. "Shaped" allows for a discovery of form that will manifest itself from the necessities forced on it by the nature of its own telling—by the job it sets out to perform. Our fine oak conference table may turn out to be recognizable to, say, a picnic table—the table, like the short story, is, after all, a *form*—but it is shaped by and for its own particular use. In a sense, although it is made, it has molded itself. The short story is shaped in much this same way. And so even though the short story as a form will be recognizable, each particular story must stand structurally on its own, shaped to its own demands, as singly separate as "A Father's Story" is from "The Shawl," as "Bullet in the Brain" is from "Saint Marie," as "A & P" is from "I Stand Here Ironing."

The point is that there is no set structure for writing a short story. To paraphrase Sherwood Anderson, it is the shaping of a particular story that wakes the writer screaming and kicking his or her covers off in the middle of the night. But to help guide us, we can consider the particulars that shape short stories.

MOTIVATION

"We are our desires." Aristotle's statement *feels* true, doesn't it? And it is this truth—our desires, any character's motivation—that powers the shaping of the short story.

None of us does anything without a motive—a *reason*. We don't get up off the couch and go to the store unless we are driven there because we have run out of trash bags and shampoo. Nor can we continue to think of ourselves as honest if we cheat the cashier out of the extra $5.00 he or she handed us in change unless we can somehow justify it as "luck," or perhaps our own little way of getting back at "the system." If we stop in the parking lot counting our change, and then turn on our heels and walk the money back inside, it may be precisely because we, too, worked as cashiers at some point in our lives and we know at the end of the night when the register comes up short, it won't be the system that "catches it," but Bob or Yolanda, Hamish, or our hero from "A & P," old Sammy himself. When Aristotle says that *we are our desires,* it is these sorts of driving motivations he has in mind. What we want and how we go about satisfying that want show who we are. We live by such desires; we are destined to *be* by such needs.

In fiction as in life, **motivation** is the heart and soul of any character's action or inaction. Aristotle's maxim holds true in determining the career our character pursues—book critic, cashier, owner of horses—or something as seemingly inconsequential as the candy she may choose in line at the Stop and Shop, say Jolly Ranchers fortified with vitamin C over a Mounds bar, because she's just come from the doctor's office where she's learned, much to her joy, that she's pregnant. She eats two; she suspects it's twins!

Without motivation, a character has no need to move, to act or react—enjoin, coerce, ridicule, praise, lie—and so if our characters lack strong motivations, chances are we won't have much of a story. No one will want to do anything; their need won't be strong enough to get them up off the couch and out the door. There will be no impetus for a story to be told.

Characters want, they *need,* often desperately so, and this *desire* or *motive,* rising in direct *conflict* with an opposing desire or obstacle toward a moment of crux, a *climax,* which has some *resolution, The End,* a "complete story," in Flannery O'Connor's words, in which "nothing more relating to the mystery of that character's personality could be shown through that particular dramatization," has classically defined the basic architecture of the short story.

CONFLICT, CLIMAX, AND RESOLUTION

In class I like to draw on the blackboard a paradigm for the classic composition of the short story:

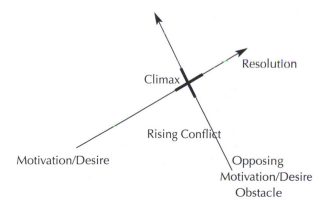

In "Creative Writing 101," Raymond Carver says: "Try as I might, I couldn't muster a great deal of interest or really understand this side of things, the stuff he [his teacher, John Gardner] put on the blackboard." And I have to admit such tell-tale mappings do make the spontaneity we feel when we read a great short story appear mechanical. Revealing the "illusion" can make the course that we took for fun seem like drudgery, but in learning to shape a short story such models do help us to see how a short story may come to be.

In thinking of these basic components of the short story—*motive, conflict, climax,* and *resolution*—I'm again reminded of painting, in which a good composition is defined by a clearly marked contrast in values, that is, seemingly simple gradations of light and dark. Winslow Homer said his entire career as a painter could be characterized by his struggle to define such values. In shaping his or her own short story, the writer is faced with a similar struggle—to set down clearly defined values, in our case, motives, in juxtaposition to one another. It is this juxtaposition of "values" that creates the *conflict* that escalates a short story.

Conflict in a story is the ratcheting roller-coaster-car-like climb of motive set against motive, obstacle against desire—it is the friction, the energy generated by conflict, a character's struggle and need, that hastens a short story forward. *Conflict* is not merely *action,* which, to borrow from one of my favorite television shows when I was a kid, *The Dukes of Hazzard,* I always think of as a corner-squealing car chase, Bo and Luke Duke being pursued by Boss Hog and his boys. Action will sweep a story along for a while, but action must be the effect of motive. Bo and Luke are being chased because they've vowed to put an end to Boss Hog's plan to rig all the pool tables in town.

Climax in the story occurs when rising desires collide. In "A & P" the climax occurs when Sammy says, "I quit." In John Steinbeck's "The Chrysanthemums" the climax occurs when Elisa sees her flowers, which the tinker has dumped on the side of the road. In "The Lady with the Pet Dog" the climax occurs when Gurov, with Anna in his arms, catches sight of himself in the mirror and realizes he's in love. **Resolution** is the next step, how the climax is resolved (or goes unresolved!). Sammy walks out the door to "feel how hard the world is going to be to [him] hereafter"; Elisa ends up slumped against the seat crying "weakly—like an old woman"; Gurov and Anna huddle together believing how "the solution" to their being forced to live apart "would be found." A resolution is an end for a story, but it is not necessarily *The End.* To return to Flannery O'Connor, the resolution makes a "complete story in which nothing more relating to the mystery of that [character's] personality could be shown through that particular dramatization."

And so, looking back to our diagram on the blackboard even if we find we can't "muster a great deal of interest [for] this side of things," perhaps the diagram can help us better understand how conflicting motives help to create a narrative in which we read to find out not only *what* happens, but *how* it happens, *to whom* it happens, and, most importantly, *why* it happens.

STORY VERSUS PLOT

In *Aspects of the Novel,* E. M. Forster writes that "'The king died and the queen died'" is a story, whereas "'the king died and then the queen died of grief' [is] a plot." The difference, as he describes it, is that "in a STORY we say 'and then?' [and that] in a PLOT we ask 'why?'"

This "why?" is the character's motivation, which gives reason to events. Without reason, without this "why?," events remain stuck in "their time sequence," and become powered simply by action, merely satisfying what Forster calls the "cave-man's insistent and then? and then?" to find out what happens next. This makes for a **story,** which is propelled from event to event. The queen in the above **plot** longs for her dead husband. She is in deep mourning. And no matter what other concerns she may have—a state funeral to attend, a prince or princess to look after, the responsibilities of state, being queen in a kingdom cast into a fit of chaos—the loss of her love compels her every thought and action, determining the reason behind her every move, ghosting her thinner and thinner because she cannot eat, the ache of emptiness hollowing her cheeks, until she too passes away—leaves her life behind to join her husband in the only way she now can, wedded once again by death. The queen is dead; that's the "and then" end of the matter, but discovering the *why* behind her death allows us to dispel the merely sequential. The exploration of the story is of her grief, freeing us from abutted actions, beginning with the day of the king's death, perhaps, before taking us back to their first meeting when she was a girl of three and then forward to the time the king, a young prince of fifteen, gave her her first kiss, in the garden, as they sat on the marble steps overlooking the fountain.

Maupassant's "The String" is a near-perfect example of the way the "why?" works to determine events—the *cause and effect*—relying on the motivation of character to create tension, taking a short story beyond action, past the "and then? and then?" of what happens next to discover the "why?" of its happening, which lies at heart of its *plot.*

Maître Hauchecorne is extraordinarily "economical like a true Norman, [who] thought that everything useful ought to be picked up." He's so frugal in fact that when he sees a bit of string on his way to the square of the little town of Goderville with the rest of the peasants on market day he bends down and picks it up, "painfully, for he suffered from rheumatism." But Maître Malandain, the harness maker, who's standing, arms crossed, in his doorway, has seen him do it. Maître Hauchecorne is embarrassed; he and Maître Malandain have "had a quarrel on the subject of a halter" and they remain in long-standing dispute, "being," as we're told, "both good haters." Embarrassed to be seen picking up a "bit" of string, Maître Hauchecorne "hid his find quickly under his smock" and "pretended to be still looking on the ground for something which he [did] not find." He then continues on, without acknowledging his enemy, "his head thrust forward, bent double by his pain."

When it turns out that Maître Fortuné Houlbrèque of Manneville has lost his "pocketbook containing five hundred francs and some business papers," Maître Hauchecorne finds himself summoned to the Mayor's office. Maître Malandain, who saw him pick up the pocketbook, has turned him in! Immediately Maître Hauchecorne understands. He's *innocent;* he can explain! It wasn't a pocketbook he picked up but a piece of string. And here it is! he says, *voilà!,* and produces the unusable snippet from his pocket. The mayor, as we may imagine, looks dubiously at him.

Even when the pocketbook is found, and Maître Hauchecorne's innocence is proven (he thinks), no one believes him. They wink and laugh, laugh and wink, yuk it up more and more each time he tells his tale. And he tells his tale of "innocence" again and again.

At the end of the story, Maître Hauchecorne dies because no one will believe that he's innocent.

> He died early in January, and in the delirium of his death struggles he continued to protest his innocence, and to repeat his story:
> "A piece of string, a piece of string—look—here it is."

In "The String" Forster's point about the *why?* is put to the test. Maître Hauchecorne is innocent of stealing the pocketbook—we know he's innocent—the sequence of events has borne that out, but there's a catch, a kick. As Maître Hauchecorne tells us:

> with his Norman cunning [he] was capable of doing what they had accused him of, and even of boasting of it as a good trick. His innocence seemed to him, in a confused way, impossible to prove, for his sharpness was well known. And he was stricken to the heart by the injustice of the suspicion.

Maître Hauchecorne's desire is to prove his innocence. But the irresolvable conflict is his own "inner" guilt. The climax of his conflict is his realization that he is fully "capable of doing what they had accused him of, and even of boasting of it as a good trick." His innocence is impossible to prove—and indeed it is impossible to prove because, at heart, Maître Hauchecorne *is* guilty of the crime. He dies suffering the dilemma of his own "why."

The *story* of "The String," according to Forster's definition, might be the fact that Maître Fortuné Houlbrèque of Manneville's pocketbook was "stolen." We ask "and then? and then?" to find out what happened to it, but the *plot* routes us back to the "why?" of our primary character, Maître Hauchecorne, who was "wrongly" accused. His death, we discover, is inextricably rooted in his heart's desire to be a "cunning and thrifty Norman."

EPIPHANY

We have noted the components that seem to shape short stories—*motive, conflict, climax, resolution*—and we have begun to take into consideration the difference between a *story* and a *plot* as a way to get at the *why?* behind how to put a story together for ourselves. But it seems to me there still remains a question about what happens at the *end* of a short story. Consider yet again what Flannery O'Connor said about the end of a short story. A story for her is "complete . . . when nothing more relating to the mystery of that [character's] personality can be shown through that particular dramatization."

Resolution is the term we are currently using to signal the completion of a short story. By resolution we mean that there has been some answer—not necessarily the right answer or the final answer, no guaranteed solution—but *an* answer to the conflict. Maître Hauchecorne dies; Sammy leaves the A & P. But, if we pay close attention to O'Connor, the term resolution seems to lack something. It doesn't take full account of either the change in perception of the primary character or the newly gained understanding of the reader—"relating to the mystery of that [character's] personality"—that we feel has occurred when we've finished most short stories.

There are three terms bandied about to explain this "mystery": **realization, denouement,** and **epiphany.** An argument could be made here that, close as they are, each has a slightly different shading or take on the moment of recognition in a story. Realization, for instance, seems (somehow) less life altering than the term epiphany, and denouement feels quieter, more gentle, closer to the word *insight* perhaps, than the shock O'Connor often uses to rock her characters into completeness. Allowing for these subtle differences, let's use the word *epiphany* to further explore O'Connor's idea of "completeness."

James Joyce took the word epiphany from Christian doctrine—the epiphany was the moment when Christ was revealed to the three magi—and coined it for literary purposes to mark the moment in a story at which something is shown that had not been known before. But epiphany is not simply a showing. Even for literary purposes, the term retains part of its mysticism. It is a magical moment, a felt moment, and the change it signals, no matter how seemingly subtle, is irrevocable.

To begin a class discussion of the way *epiphany* works I often use an exercise given to me by Maxine Rodburg, Director of the Writing Center at Harvard; students are asked to consider the following two statements, the first from Flannery O'Connor and the second from Eudora Welty:

Flannery O'Connor: I often ask myself what makes a story work . . . and I have decided that it is probably some action, some gesture of a character that is unlike any other in the story, one which indicates where the real heart of the story lies. This would have to be an action or a gesture which was both totally right and totally unexpected; it would have to be one that was both in character and beyond character; it would have to suggest both the world and eternity.

Eudora Welty: In going in the direction of meaning, time has to move through a mind. What it will bring about is an awakening there. Through whatever motions it goes through, it will call forth, in a mind or heart, some crucial recognition.

The exercise then asks, "What are these two writers talking about?"

In the heated discussion that inevitably ensues I'm less concerned that we come up with a single "correct" definition of an epiphany than that we give our thoughts a good stirring.

If the *beginning* of a story sets into motion a character's desire in a given situation—say Maître Hauchecorne's picking up the string—and the *body* of the story is the *dramatization* of events that lead to a *climax*, the *resolution* of which is *The End* of the short story, then it stands to reason that the end of the *plot* (for it to be a plot and not merely a story, to answer the "why?" and not simply the "and then?") needs to take us beyond *resolution*—the end of what happened (Hauchecorne dies)—to *meaning*.

In "Writing Short Stories," Flannery O'Connor says she prefers the term "meaning" to "theme" when talking about a short story, and I agree. "People talk about the theme of a story," O'Connor writes, "as if the theme were like the string that a sack of chicken feed is tied with. They think that if you can pick out the theme, the way you pick the right thread in the chicken-feed sack, you can rip the story open and feed the chickens. But this is not the way meaning works in fiction." *Meaning* lets us talk about what the story has to say; what the *story* says, what the characters, and we as readers, have *experienced*. As O'Connor says, there's only one way to say what the meaning of a story is and that's to read the story.

To quote her in entirety:

> . . . Perhaps the central question to be considered in any discussion of the short story is what do we mean by short. Being short does not mean being slight. A short story should be long in depth and should give us an experience of meaning. I have an aunt who thinks that nothing happens in a story unless somebody gets married or shot at the end of it. I wrote a story about a tramp who marries an old woman's idiot daughter in order to acquire the old woman's automobile. After the marriage, he takes the daughter off on a wedding trip in the automobile and abandons her in an eating place and drives on by himself. Now that is a complete story. There is nothing more relating to the mystery of that man's personality that could be shown through that particular dramatization. But I've never been able to convince my aunt that it's a complete story. She wants to know what happened to the idiot daughter after that.
>
> Not long ago that story was adapted for a television play, and the adapter, knowing his business, had the tramp have a change of heart and go back and pick up the idiot daughter and the two of them ride away, grinning madly. My aunt believes that the story is complete at last, but I have other sentiments about it—which are not suitable for public utterance.

For O'Connor, when the man deserts the idiot daughter and drives off "nothing more relating to the mystery of [his] personality could be shown through that particular dramatization." The end is the moment of realization of who he is, at heart, in essence. Forster's "why?" which drives the story has been fully "revealed" and what happens to either of them after that isn't the point.

I would call this moment the story's *epiphany.*

Welty calls fiction a "lie"; Maupassant calls it an "illusion." Real life is full of vagaries, but not fiction. Nothing in a short story is random. Short stories exist for their moment of effect. They are directed, *made.* Writing is an *art.* And although the idea that any piece of art should have a job to do seems unpopular these days, as writers this moment—which we can point to and call an *epiphany*—offers us a target at which to aim the meaning of the story we've written. In other words: *In considering how to shape the short story, it is this moment of insight at the end that helps us determine where the conflict of the story begins and how the dramatic action might progress.* In working to discover the shape of our stories, we can have our own "epiphanies." Suddenly we see the why of what we've done (or are going to do).

In his essay "Against Epiphanies," which is included in his book *Burning Down the House,* Charles Baxter makes a good case against a certain kind of epiphanic ending. The words "I've had a major revelation," he writes, "typically fill me with dread." Baxter, it seems to me, is arguing against *unearned* epiphany. "Suddenly, it seems, everyone is having insights. Everyone is proclaiming and selling them. . . . Everywhere there is a glut of epiphanies. Radiance rules." Baxter's point is that epiphanies have become *de rigeur;* we have come to expect them and feel cheated in a story if we don't get one.

It is the idea that a story must have an epiphany that Baxter rejects—not the work earned epiphanies perform, though he admits to a "prejudice" against epiphanic stories. Baxter "[doesn't] believe that a character's experiences in a story have to be validated by a conclusive insight or a brilliant visionary stop-time moment." He lobbies for the anti-epiphanic story, which, he writes, "is perfectly capable of sneaking its own visionary eloquence through the back door," though he concedes "it has been and probably will always be a kind of minority writing: quarrelsome, hilarious, and mulish. . . . Instead of a conclusive arrival somewhere, we end, or rest, at a garden of forking paths, or an apartment complex where no one knows how to start the car, but everyone has an opinion, possibly worthless, about the matter."

Baxter's objection should be kept in mind; for one thing, it keeps us honest! The curtain has been yanked back, and Charles Baxter is staring straight back at us. Epiphany must reveal the "mystery" of character in conflict. Pat endings or simplistic moralizations, summaries of emotion, and quick fixes may be termed epiphanies, but they will not punctuate good stories. Stories that are guilty of such things will read like the contrivances they are; they will not convince us with the earned effects of a *true* "illusion." They will not feel complete. Such endings are more in keeping with the taste of O'Connor's aunt.

A LAST WORD ON SHAPING THE SHORT STORY

Much of the discussion in this section on shaping the short story concerns process. How can we write the beginning of a story if we have to know the end first? Well, we can't. Not a *finished* story. We must listen to our characters (see

Andre Dubus's essay in this book, "The Habit of Writing," p. 90), carefully consider their desires in crux. The moment in a story that we call an epiphany is often as much a discovery for the writer as it is for the characters involved. At a reading I heard Tobias Wolff give, he said that if his characters didn't discover something from the story how could he? Beyond the advice of listening to our characters to help us discover how to shape our short stories, there are concrete ways of saying what we mean when we go to work building any story. *Motive, conflict, climax, resolution,* and *epiphany* are the signposts that can help map our way to discovering how to "complete" a story for ourselves.

Writing Exercises

1. Compare the shapes of the short stories you've read from the anthology. Choose three and draw a paradigm of how each is shaped. Do the three stories you've chosen follow the diagram we've drawn? Consider the differences and similarities of each.
2. Now try the above exercise with one of your own stories. Map out a story you've written. Then answer these questions: Is the motive in your story clearly defined? Is there a clearly defined conflict? Where does the climax in the story occur? How is the climax resolved? Is there an epiphany? Has the epiphany been "earned?" In your own estimation, is your story "complete?" If not, where does the map you've drawn reveal a weakness?
3. "'The king died and the queen died'" is a story; "'The king died and then the queen died of grief' [is] a plot." The difference, as Forster describes it, is that "in a STORY we say 'and then?' [and that] in a PLOT we ask 'why?'" Considering the above definition, is the story you have outlined a "story" or a "plot?" In a page or two engage your reasons by keeping strictly to the terms of Forster's definition and using specific examples from your own story to prove your points.
4. Try your hand at the epiphany exercise. What *are* O'Connor and Welty talking about anyway? In a page or two take what they have said into account, and using what they've written as a springboard, offer your own understanding of epiphany. Use specific instances from the stories you've read in the anthology to help explain your points.

❦ ❦ ❦

The Lesser Angels of Fiction: Setting and Time

In this section we will examine the ways in which setting acts as a backdrop, creates atmosphere, helps to establish believability, enhances tension through situation, powers motive, or serves as metaphor, and we will consider fictional time, exploring scene, summary, flashback, and slow motion.

"Place," Eudora Welty writes in her essay "Place in Fiction,"

is one of the lesser angels that watch over the racing hand of fiction, perhaps the one that gazes benignly enough from off to one side, while others, like character, plot, symbolic meaning, and so on, are doing a good deal of wing-beating about her chair, and feeling, who in my eyes carries the crown, soars highest of them all and rightly relegates place into the shade.

And yet place, or setting as we'll call it, and time must be given their due— lesser angels though they may be. Without them we wouldn't have a story! Let's consider each separately.

SETTING

"Where we are is who we are, Miss Moore always pointing out," says Sylvia, the irrepressible narrator of Toni Cade Bambara's "The Lesson," a short story about a bunch of children from "the slums" who take a field trip to Fifth Avenue to enter FAO Schwarz's grand toy store only to find they've touched down in a world where a "toy sailboat" costs "one thousand one hundred and ninety-five dollars." They are shocked, and are ripe for an awakening about their own place on the planet—whether Sylvia wants to learn Miss Moore's *pointed* lesson or not: "Not that I'm scared [of going inside], what's there to be afraid of, just a toy store."

Even for a lesser angel, the setting in "The Lesson" seems to be doing *a lot* of wing-beating, a veritable flurry of fluttering. And here we can quickly see a few of the jobs setting may be responsible for in a short story. Setting can work as a **backdrop** for the character's actions, a stage like the showroom floor of FAO Schwarz; it can help create a certain **atmosphere,** happy and seemingly carefree as Sylvia and her friends harass the cab driver all the way downtown and then, suddenly, somber, as they come face to face with the price tags in the windows of the toy store; setting enhances **believability**—we recognize FAO Schwarz, whether we've ever been to the toy store before or not. A "real" place (even if it were made up!), a store on Fifth Avenue in Manhattan that is stocked with thousand dollar toy sailboats and three hundred dollar microscopes, a paperweight for four hundred and eighty dollars, makes us believe in the characters and their reactions. They've come to FAO Schwarz from a place where "thirty-five dollars could buy new bunk beds for Junior and Gretchen's boy . . . and the whole household could go visit Grand-daddy Nelson in the country . . . pay for the rent and the piano bill too." Setting, as we see plainly in "The Lesson," can power a story as **motive.** As Miss Moore says, *Where we are is who we are.* And as an integral part of the story's **situation,** setting may also help create the conflict of a story. It may also act as a **metaphor,** significantly enhancing the meaning that takes place on its "stage."

Setting as Backdrop

Setting as backdrop is the most basic way in which place works in a short story. Setting in this case *sets* the stage where the conflict of the story takes place. When the curtain rises on a story such as Hemingway's "Hills Like White Elephants," we see before us "The hills across the valley of the Ebro . . . long and white . . . the station . . . between two lines of rails in the sun . . . the warm shadow of the building and a curtain, made of strings of bamboo beads . . . The American and the girl . . . at a table in the shade, outside the building. . . ." Setting here seems a lesser angel in that its job is relatively straightforward. The story has to take place somewhere. So now the stage is set, and now the girl can ask, "What should we drink?"

Setting and Atmosphere

Beyond its job as backdrop, place can set the mood of a piece and help us feel a character's emotional state. John Gardner used a writing exercise that we can try ourselves to show the significance of setting on the **atmosphere** of a story.

Imagine your character is poised on the rise of a ridge, overlooking a wide valley. In the valley sits a barn, an old Ford pick-up, a John Deere tractor and implements, a cultivator, maybe a planter, a disk. Day is breaking.

Your job as writer is to describe this scene from the point of view of the farmer whose barn this is. The catch? The farmer's son or daughter has died that night. Use the setting to describe the scene in a way that helps us feel what he's feeling. Do *not* mention the child's death.

Many students want a rainy day, a weepy, cloudy afternoon, say, to make their job (they think) easier. They want the sky to cry. The point is the valley, the sunrise, old farm implements, the lean of a barn, the dark maw of its double-door—wheat standing straight up, glistening with dew—can all *work* for you in creating a mood. As Raymond Carver says in "On Writing," each of these

"commonplace things and objects" can be "endow[ed] with immense, even startling power."

The danger, Carver goes on to warn us, is that

> If the words are heavy with the writer's own unbridled emotions, or if they are
> imprecise and inaccurate for some other reason—if the words are in any way
> blurred—the reader's eye will slide right over them and nothing will be achieved.
> The reader's own artistic sense will simply not be engaged. Henry James called
> this sort of hapless writing 'weak specification.'

Consider again our section on character. In a particular point of view, we
feel everything that character feels, see everything that character sees, tastes,
smells, senses, and hears. The setting can be shown to reveal these things and
these "things" will reveal the character and what he or she is feeling.

This use of setting as mood works in the objective point of view as well.
In "Hills Like White Elephants" the descriptions appear fairly flat; Hemingway
does not overwork the "hills across the valley of the Ebro" or overemphasize
the fertility on the "other" side of the Ebro. "On this side," we know, "there [is]
no shade and no trees . . ." But we certainly feel these things—we are left sitting with the American and the girl in "the warm shadow of the building"—we
are placed firmly "between two lines of rails in the sun." The atmosphere of the
story has lent an air of expectancy to the conversation to come.

Setting is the obvious backdrop of the short story; it may also help create
the atmosphere of the piece, the *mood*—as the Gardner exercise reveals. What
is less obvious is when setting is at work on our readers without their knowing
it. Setting goes to work to quietly convince them to believe in a story by creating the illusion of a "real" place on the page.

Setting and Believability

"Fiction," Flannery O'Connor writes in "Writing Short Stories," "is an art that
calls for the strictest attention to the real—whether the writer is writing a naturalistic story or fantasy." In fact, O'Connor

> would go so far as to say that the person writing a fantasy has to be even more
> strictly attentive to the concrete detail than someone writing in a naturalistic
> vein—because the greater the story's strain on credulity, the more convincing the
> properties in it have to be.

Setting aids the writer in this way by creating a world to which we can
relate, where we can live, even if it is the world Z377^XXXXIII in the Tetrame-
ter Climatic Zone. It is this "strictest attention to the real" that makes us *believe*.
It is the "thousand dollar sailboats" in Bambara's "The Lesson" or the "two lines
of rail in the sun" in "Hills Like White Elephants," or a simple "curtain made
of strings of bamboo beads hung . . . to keep out flies" that helps the story

come alive for us. Such concrete details help make the made-up mirage shimmer of our stories as possible as the skyscrapers that we "know" rise above FAO Schwarz.

Setting as Situation

Less obvious still might be the way the setting of a short story stresses the tensions inherent in a situation. In "Hills Like White Elephants" the scene set for us is one of waiting and transience. It's "very hot and the express from Barcelona would come in forty minutes. It stopped at this junction for two minutes and went on to Madrid." There is the contrast of "hills across the valley of the Ebro" and the bareness on their side of the river where "there was no shade and no trees and the station was between two lines of rails in the sun." At first, the description seems merely a way to satisfy the first job of our lesser angel, that of setting the stage. But though we may not yet *know* it, we have already begun to *feel* the waiting, the discrepancy of scenery, the either/or *choice* to be made—and there's a time limit—forty minutes. Back to O'Connor's "Writing Short Stories":

> The peculiar problem of the short-story writer is how to make the action he describes reveal as much of the mystery of existence as possible. He has only a short space to do it in and he can't do it by statement. He has to do it by showing, not by saying, and by showing the concrete—so that his problem is really how to make the concrete work double time for him.

The place in which these two characters find themselves—waiting at a crossroads station for the train that will take them to Barcelona—creates the *moment* of the story. Something is at issue. Our couple is at a crossroads in their relationship as well. They have forty minutes before the "express from Barcelona" arrives to whisk them off into their lives. The setting, in all its detail, makes us feel the impending arrival of the train—and the pressure of the lifelong decision to be made.

Setting as Motive

When we advance to setting as motive, our lesser angel sheds her hummingbird flutters for the wings of an eagle, soaring higher and higher. Setting swiftly becomes more than the stage for a short story. Because a short story is, above all, short, and because it must show, using every technique at its disposal to enhance the intended *meaning,* the importance, the vitalness of setting in the short story begins to loom large.

Where we are is who we are. For Sylvia there is no escaping that fact: she lives in "the slums." Setting can act as motive; it can drive a character's actions.

John Steinbeck's "The Chrysanthemums" begins with a long cinematic shot of the Salinas Valley and, once again, at first setting might seem little more than a staging:

> The high grey-flannel fog of winter closed off the Salinas Valley from the sky and from all the rest of the world. On every side it sat like a lid on the mountains and made of the great valley a closed pot. On the broad, level land floor the gang plows bit deep and left the black earth shining like metal where the shares had cut. On the foothill ranches across the Salinas River, the yellow stubble fields seemed to be bathed in pale cold sunshine, but there was no sunshine in the valley now in December. The thick willow scrub along the river flamed with sharp and positive yellow leaves.

This description appears to be exactly what we expect of our lesser angel. She has her part to perform, relegated to the "shade" as she may be, and when called on she performs it beautifully. Certainly the setting here does justice to itself as a backdrop for the characters and events to come. We can perfectly picture the Salinas Valley, its "black earth shining like metal where the shares had cut" and the "flam[ing] . . . sharp and positive yellow leaves" of the "willow scrub along the river." We have acknowledged its boundaries, a great valley surrounded by mountains, covered by a "high grey-flannel fog of winter" that isolates it "from the sky and from all the rest of the world."

The stage is dutifully set before the camera pans past "Henry Allen's foothill ranch" with its plowed orchards and cattle to focus on Elisa Allen, our primary character, at work in her flower garden. Now the story can begin, though, in fact, the setting has already put it into motion.

A second reading of "The Chrysanthemums" helps us see a possible reason for waiting to introduce Elisa until the fourth paragraph of the story. Subsequent readings reveal the Salinas Valley—and Steinbeck's taking such careful time to describe it—as vital to understanding Elisa's motive in the story.

Elisa is as rooted in the valley as the chrysanthemums that she grows in her little garden behind the confines of her fence. She, too, is a product of that small square of soil—that particular patch of earth.

Elisa *appears* strong: "Her face was lean and strong and her eyes were as clear as water. Her figure looked blocked and heavy in her gardening costume, a man's black hat pulled low down over her eyes." Her "terrier fingers destroy . . . pests before they could get started" And when her husband Henry comes back from making a deal over thirty head of cattle and marvels at her gift for growing flowers, saying, "I wish you'd work out in the orchard and raise some apples that big," Elisa's "eyes sharpen." "Maybe I could do it, too," she replies, "I've a gift with things, all right." Elisa seems ready to take on the world.

And yet the world is a big place, scary. The garden is safe; it is known territory.

The truth we are to discover is that Elisa *is* as strong as she wishes to appear, but she has also been shaped by her place in the "closed pot" of the

Salinas Valley. She is a product of a world in which her job is to take care of the house (even the mud mat is "clean") and grow flowers (Elisa, it seems, is childless). When an emissary from beyond the mountains rattles up in his "old spring-wagon, with a round canvas top on it like the corner of a prairie schooner," we feel as sure of Elisa as she seems to be of herself.

But, after a brief conversation in which the tinker shows an interest in her flowers, she ends up fawning before the tinker, on her knees in the dirt:

> Elisa's voice grew husky. She broke in on him, "I've never lived as you do, but I know what you mean. When the night is dark—why, the stars are sharp-pointed, and there's quiet. Why, you rise up and up! Every pointed star gets driven into your body. It's like that. Hot and sharp and—lovely."

From such an emotional display, we might not be surprised if Elisa, acting like the woman she appears to be, pulled the tinker to earth with her and satisfied her fantasies. At best, we imagine her climbing up on the seat of his wagon to see the world with him. But Elisa does neither. Instead, she sends one of her *chrysanthemums* with the tinker to give to "a lady down the road a piece," when he's told her the lady would like a "few seeds." As he drives away,

> Elisa stood in front of her wire fence watching the slow progress of the caravan. Her shoulders were straight, her head thrown back, her eyes half-closed, so that the scene came vaguely into them. Her lips moved silently, forming the words, "Good-bye—good-bye." Then she whispered, "That's a bright direction. There's a glowing there." The sound of her whisper startled her. She shook herself free and looked about to see whether anyone had been listening.

Of course, we know the tinker was just trying to make a sale. He needed a few pots to mend and he made up the story of the woman "down the road" to gain Elisa's favor. He wasn't interested in Elisa or her "smelly" flowers. But Elisa has taken her "act" of sending a chrysanthemum out into the wider world as a symbol of her strength. "I'm strong," she boasts to Henry when he returns from rounding up the cattle for the sale, "I never knew before how strong." It isn't until she is on her way to dinner in town with Henry that she sees the speck on the road. She knows immediately what it is, her flowers, which the tinker has dumped "to keep the pot." "He had to keep the pot," she says. "That's why he couldn't get them off the road."

Elisa is more than merely disappointed. As the "roadster turned a bend . . . she saw the caravan ahead. She [swung] full around toward her husband so she could not see the little covered wagon and the mismatched team as the car passed them." She does not look back.

Elisa is reduced to asking Henry if they can "have wine at dinner." To which Henry replies, "Sure we could. Say! That will be fine." Elisa then appears to rally, to gain back a bit of the grit she showed earlier; she asks about the prize fights to which Henry jokingly offered to take her at the beginning of the story: "[D]o the men hurt each other very much? . . . I've read they break noses, and blood runs down their chests. I've read how the fighting gloves get heavy and soggy with blood." Henry is shocked. He looks at her. "What's the matter, Elisa?" he asks. He's already noted that she's changed again. He offers to take her to the fights if she wants to go.

But Elisa doesn't want to go. She "relaxed limply in her seat. 'Oh, no. No. I don't want to go,'" she says. "'I'm sure I don't.' Her face was turned away from him. 'It will be enough if we can have wine. It will be plenty.' She turned up her coat collar so he could not see that she was crying weakly—like an old woman."

Elisa is devasted. She can no longer blame her place on anyone but herself. The Salinas Valley is a man's world; indeed, we're told at the beginning of the story that it is "Henry Allen's foothill ranch." A man in the world of this story can wander around at will "following the nice weather." And even Elisa in her garden looks man-like in her man's hat and man's gloves. But she has taken pride in showing her strength as a woman. In sending her chrysanthemums out into the world, she has seen the "brightening" of possibility for herself. Proud of showing her strength, seemingly confident, she is here all but destroyed. Her resolve, her idea of herself, her dream of escape, her belief in her strength, have all been dashed. And by what? A vagabond tinker tossing out her flowers? No, Elisa has been laid bare as "the black earth [left] shining like metal where the shares had cut." Elisa can no longer kid herself. She has seen herself clearly for who she is, a woman shaped by her place. She has the desire to escape *herself,* the motive, but not the will. It simply isn't *in* her. She will remain behind the safety of her fence on her husband's farm.

Setting as Metaphor

Back at the station in "Hills Like White Elephants," the girl

> stood up and walked to the end of the station. Across, on the other side, were fields of grain and trees along the bank of the Ebro. Far away, beyond the river, were mountains. The shadow of a cloud moved across the field of grain and she saw the river through the trees.
>
> "And we could have all this," she said, "And we could have everything and every day we make it more impossible."
>
> "What did you say?"
>
> "I said we could have everything."
>
> "We can have everything."
>
> "No, we can't."
>
> "We can have the whole world."
>
> "No, we can't."
>
> "We can go anywhere."

"No, we can't. It isn't ours any more."

"It's ours."

"No, it isn't. And once they take it away, you never get it back."

"But they haven't taken it away."

"We'll wait and see."

This dialogue reveals the metaphorical nature of setting. By **metaphor** (the complexities of the term will be discussed in the next section) I mean the figurative meaning behind the literal. The hills are, in fact, just hills. We saw them for ourselves in the opening paragraph. Jig, however, sees them as something else, something more. In them, she recognizes fertility, a fullness, their lushness and possibility; she sees in the view an Elysian vision of completeness, all the possibilities for their life together, a paradise of love: "And we could have all this . . . And we could have everything and every day we make it more impossible."

Literally, of course, they cannot have the valley. They can't buy it; they can't take it with them. The conversation that ensues between the couple clearly draws this contrast between the figurative and literal. Jig sees the mountains as "white elephants" to which the man says "I've never seen one." She replies: "They don't really look like white elephants. I just meant the coloring of *their skin* through the trees" (italics mine). Jig realizes the possibilities in the view across the Ebro stretched out before her, but the man remains rooted to his chair, sipping his beer, focused on Jig's pregnancy: "But I don't want anybody but you," he says. As the story proceeds, the setting takes on mass, weight; what is at stake between the characters stands revealed to us in their separate interpretations of the place in which they find themselves. The girl sees fertility, possibilities for growing their love; the man has "never seen" a white elephant, and he refuses to imagine one. He refuses to see anything in his surroundings other than tracks that will take him to a place where he can solve his "worry."

Hemingway often spoke of the "iceberg principle," in which the bulk of the story lay under the water with only the top ten percent *showing* on top. The ten percent of the setting shown in "Hills" takes on the weight of the metaphorical bulk of the story we begin to feel for ourselves.

TIME

To begin our talk about fictional **time,** I'd like to return to the quotation from Eudora Welty that we used to begin our discussion on epiphany:

> In going in the direction of meaning, time has to move through a mind. What it will bring about is an awakening there. Through whatever motions it goes through, it will call forth, in a mind or heart, some crucial recognition.

Fictional time is not real time. Fictional time, like character in fiction or setting, is "illusory." Fictional time gives us the felt-meaning of time, but the fact of time—however long it takes us to sit down and read a short story, perhaps thirty minutes to an hour—has little to do with the months that pass in a fifteen-page story like "The Lady with the Pet Dog."

How, then, does time work in fiction?

Scene

To begin, let's look at Welty's line again. "In going in the direction of meaning, time has to move through a mind. . . ." It occurs to me that Welty is talking about *scenes* when she says "time has to move through a mind." Fictional time can be *felt* through the dramatization of events that make up a short story.

In Flannery O'Connor's "Everything That Rises Must Converge," we "stand . . . before the hall mirror" with Julian and his mother as she prepares to go to her "reducing class." She is trying on her new hat—"a hideous hat" with "a purple velvet flap [which] came down on one side of it and stood up on the other; the rest of it was green and looked like a cushion with the stuffing out"—while Julian stands beside her, with "his hands behind him, appear[ing] pinned to the door frame, waiting like Saint Sebastian for the arrows to begin piercing him."

"Maybe I shouldn't have paid that for it," his mother says, "No, I shouldn't have. I'll take it off and return it tomorrow. I shouldn't have bought it."

Julian "raise[s] his eyes to heaven. 'Yes, you should have bought it,' he sa[ys]. 'Put it on and let's go.'"

And so, O'Connor puts the story into motion by creating a **scene.** The scene puts the story into present time, allowing us to see and hear what the characters are seeing and hearing as they prepare to leave. Scene, because it gives direct experience, is the foundation of fictional time.

Summary

The above scene starts "Everything That Rises Must Converge" into motion, but O'Connor has chosen to begin the story itself with **summary:**

> Her doctor had told Julian's mother that she must lose twenty pounds on account of her blood pressure, so on Wednesday nights Julian had to take her downtown on the bus for a reducing class at the Y. The reducing class was designed for working girls over fifty, who weighed from 165 to 200 pounds. His mother was one of the slimmer ones, but she said ladies did not tell their age or weight. She would not ride the buses by herself at night since they had been integrated, and because the reducing class was one of her few pleasures, necessary for her health, and *free,* she said Julian could at least put himself out to take her, considering all she did for him. Julian did not like to consider all she did for him, but every Wednesday night he braced himself and took her.

Summary affords us the fictional time to be brought up to speed. It gives us a block of necessary information that influences the scene we are about to see,

but that, in other respects, exists outside of their present trip to the Y. Summary
can take on blocks of time, years, weeks, an hour, or a day, or as O'Connor
uses it here, give a broad (though pertinent) overview of the history of the
characters.

Flashback

O'Connor also employs **flashback,** another manipulation of fictional time, in
which we move from a direct scene into another scene, usually from the past.
As Julian and his mother walk through their dilapidated neighborhood toward
the bus stop, she says,

> "I remember going to Grandpa's when I was a little girl. Then the house had dou-
> ble stairways that went up to what was really the second floor—all the cooking
> was done on the first. I used to like to stay down in the kitchen on account of
> the way the walls smelled. I would sit with my nose pressed against the plaster
> and take deep breaths. Actually the place belonged to the Godhighs but your
> grandfather Chestny paid the mortgage and saved it for them. They were in
> reduced circumstances," she said, "but reduced or not, they never forgot who they
> were."
> "Doubtless that decayed mansion reminded them," Julian muttered.

And then he flashes back, using the transition, "He never spoke of it without
contempt or thought of it without longing":

> He had seen it once when he was a child before it had been sold. The double
> stairways had rotted and had been torn down. Negroes were living in it. But it
> remained in his mind as his mother had known it. It appeared in his dreams reg-
> ularly. He would stand on the wide porch, listening to the rustle of oak leaves,
> then wander through the high-ceilinged hall into the parlor that opened onto it
> and gaze at the worn rugs and faded draperies.

The flashback differs from the summary in that an actual scene is created.
A flashback is, most simply, a scene within a scene.

The trouble with flashbacks is that, first, they interrupt the forward movement of a scene—in this scene the dialogue between Julian and his mother—
and risk stalling the tension created by direct interaction of the characters. And,
second, flashbacks invariably call attention to themselves. A smooth transition
that leads naturally into the flashback is a must, such as the one O'Connor uses
above. A good transition will help pave the way from the present moment of
the story, the direct scene, into the past—this telescoping into another scene
that informs the moment at hand.

The danger of the flashback, I'm always aware, is that it can become a kind
of crutch. Scenes are the most powerful way to convey feeling because they are
the most direct, the most immediately felt. Summary is a telling and flashback

is an interruption, even if it leads into a scene. But they are both useful tools for the fiction writer who needs to exercise all levels of time—past, present, and future—to fill out the motivations in the world of the characters who have been created.

Slow Motion

Slow motion also interrupts the march of the scene in a story—and so the use of it comes with that yellow flag of caution—but it does allow us to practically freeze-frame an important moment and give the reader time to absorb the significance of what is happening. In "Everything That Rises Must Converge," we slow for the moment of impact after Julian's mother has handed the little black boy a penny. The boy's mother, who has been on the bus growling and smoking, smoldering like an active volcano, finally explodes:

> The huge woman turned and for a moment stood, her shoulders lifted and her face frozen with frustrated rage, and stared at Julian's mother. Then all at once she seemed to explode like a piece of machinery that had been given one ounce of pressure too much. Julian saw the black fist swing out with the red pocketbook. He shut his eyes and cringed as he heard the woman shout, "He don't take nobody's pennies!" When he opened his eyes, the woman was disappearing down the street with the little boy staring wide-eyed over her shoulder. Julian's mother was sitting on the sidewalk.

Now, we know this must have happened quickly, in the blink of an eye—a purse swung by a big woman moves *fast*. But it is a critical moment in the story, a vital action, and O'Connor uses slow motion to closely focus our attention on the event. The truth of how well it has been done is that we hardly realize time has slowed at all; rather, we feel we have expanded into the moment.

A LAST WORD ON SETTING AND TIME

Though setting and time may well be "lesser angels," they play important roles in any short story. The setting can act as a backdrop or help to create the mood for a piece, lend it atmosphere; setting can be the foundation on which the believability of a story is built; it can serve as the motive for a character's action or work to enhance the story as a metaphor of events. Time in fiction is the clock that puts the work into motion. Through created scenes, we show, as Welty said, "time moving through a mind," working to give the reader O'Connor's "experience of meaning." Time may cog forward as direct showing or cover entire decades expansively in summary. Flashbacks may be used to move from present time to give the moment the illumination of past events, and slow motion can shift the gears of any moment to let us dwell on its significance.

Setting and time may be lesser angels, but without their flurried "wing-beating," a story will never make it off the ground, much less soar.

Writing Exercises

1. Try John Gardner's setting exercise. Remember: Do not tell us the father's child is dead. Work to show!
2. To help better see the layered workings of fictional time, write a short piece that, like the example from O'Connor's "Everything That Rises Must Converge," begins with summary and then moves into a direct scene, work a transition from that scene into a flashback, and end in slow motion. This exercise is a great way to see how the uses of fictional time make the story tick.

❦ ❦ ❦

"The Connectedness of All Living Things": Metaphor

In this section we will explore the uses of figurative language, including simile, metaphor, and symbol.

I have always thought of metaphor as the writer's muscle: the bulk of strength the writer gains by making, as O'Connor says, "the concrete work double time." Whether we're speaking about the hills across the Ebro which, Jig says, "don't really look like white elephants. I just meant the coloring of their skin through the trees" or the fence that serves to mark the boundaries of Elisa's world in "The Chrysanthemums" or the wind that whispers like the voice of God around Luke Ripley as he feels for the pulse of the boy his daughter has hit with the car in "A Father's Story," it is metaphor—or to consider it more fully—the entire scope of figurative language, including simile and symbol—that gives a story its mass.

FIGURATIVE LANGUAGE

I have used the term **metaphor** to head this section but, strictly speaking, there are three variations on figurative language: **simile, metaphor,** and **symbol.**

Simile

A simile is announced by *like* or *as*. In William Faulkner's "A Rose for Emily," Emily is described as

> a small, fat woman in black, with a thin gold chain descending to her waist and vanishing into her belt, leaning on an ebony cane with a tarnished gold head. Her skeleton was small and spare; perhaps that was why what would have been merely plumpness in another was obesity in her.

This is straight description. So far, the narrator has simply given us the picture of her condition, but in the next two lines simile is used to further emphasize this "obesity":

> She looked bloated, *like* a body long submerged in motionless water, and of that pallid hue. Her eyes, lost in the fatty ridges of her face, looked *like* two small pieces of coal pressed into a lump of dough as they moved from one face to another while the visitors stated their errand. (Italics mine.)

Wow! we say. "Gross!" The simile—this likeness the narrator has drawn—goes beyond mere description. The comparison enlarges our understanding. Miss Emily isn't fat; she's "bloated," and the image of a body, waterlogged and drained of all color, flashes to mind.

When simile is done well, it feels *true*—the comparison drawn by *like* or *as* adds, enlightens, resonates, a believable connection. But when similes are off, ugh! False similes make us smile or laugh out loud. And we're not laughing with the writer!

"Winners of the 'worst analogies ever written in a high school essay' contest" was posted in the copy room of the Expository Writing Program at Harvard. Below are a few doozies:

> Her hair glistened in the rain like nose hair after a sneeze. (Chuck Smith, Woodbridge)

> John and Mary had never met. They were like two hummingbirds who had also never met. (Russell Beland, Springfield)

> McBride fell 12 stories, hitting the pavement like a Hefty Bag filled with vegetable soup. (Paul Sabourin, Silver Spring)

Similes, by the very nature of the risk they take in going beyond concrete description to comparing something actual in the story to something else, draw attention to themselves, and so they must be true. A true simile has the power to awaken us to a deeper connection and to round out a flat description. But a false simile obscures and unnecessarily complicates the very description it is trying to enhance.

Metaphor

Robert Boswell's long short story "The Darkness of Love" is about Handle, a black New York City policeman, who fears that he has become a racist. In an attempt to try to come to terms with the turmoil he feels, Handle takes time off from his job, and retreats to the home of his wife's parents in Tennessee.

In the beginning of the story, Handle recounts a tale told by his wife's family that, he says, "before he'd met his in-laws [Marvin and Annalee]. . . shaped his opinion" of them:

> Their old dog, Hoot, had gone blind. Marvin speculated it stemmed from eating inky cap mushrooms, but Annalee insisted age had blinded the yellow dog. Too old to adjust, Hoot would become confused in the big yard, howling until someone came after him. He began shitting in the living room and lifting his leg on the furniture. Marvin couldn't bear the thought of putting Hoot to sleep. He'd found the dog as a pup, cradled in the boughs of the purple magnolia that marked the northeast corner of their property. Who put the dog there and why, they never discovered, but Marvin attached significance to finding a puppy in a tree. Annalee finally solved the problem. She made a trail with bacon grease from the front porch to the old barn where he liked to pee, to the thick grass near the purple magnolia where he liked to shit, and back to the porch. The old dog ran this circle the last two months of his life. When he finally died, Marvin insisted they bury him under the purple magnolia. Annalee dug the hole and buried the dog. The tree promptly died, leaving Marvin to speculate on the connectedness of all living things. Annalee argued that she may have severed the taproot while digging the grave, but Marvin ignored her.

On a literal level, the tale that Handle recounts characterizes Marvin and Annalee for us as well as it did for Handle. We get to see for ourselves their love and kindness for Hoot as Annalee devised a trail of bacon grease "from the front porch to the old barn where he liked to pee, to the thick grass near the purple magnolia where he liked to shit, and back to the porch"—and we grin at the oddness of Marvin's "finding a dog in a tree." The "significance" Marvin attaches to that aspect of this family tale, the very fact that they make so much of it, telling and retelling it every time they get together, is crucial for us in how we come to understand them as people as well as their relationship, their dependence and reliance on each other, as a family. But Marvin recognizes the figurative importance of the story as well, which leads him after the dog dies to "speculate on the connectedness of all living things" and to wave away Annalee's literal explanation that she must have severed the taproot when she was digging Hoot's grave.

The tale serves as a *metaphor*. The story of Hoot is a real event in their lives, and their recounting it works as a dramatic scene in the story, but our figurative understanding of what it means transcends these happenings. "The connectedness of all living things" that Marvin gives serious consideration is a story that represents the interdependence of all life, not just the dog and the tree, but each of us to each other and to other living things as well. Members of a family depend on each other in this way; it is their very "connectedness" that *makes* them a family, and when a family member is lost, the family withers. We recognize the likeness, the metaphor echoes out a larger truth.

The basic difference between a metaphor and a simile is that the metaphor *is* the thing it is being compared to rather than simply being *like* it.

Symbol

Symbol differs from simile and metaphor in that a symbol is an object or sign that carries its own weight of meaning. A cross is a well-known symbol and bears the weight of its own meaning—its religious significance—despite the dramatic action of the story. Symbols can also be created inside a story. Consider the white doll that Marilyn's grandmother gave her in "The Darkness of Love." The characters in the story are all Black, and Marilyn has had a dream in which white dolls with blue eyes are raining from the sky. Handle thinks it a "beautiful nightmare." But Louise sees the symbol: "We all have white dolls in us, whether we like it or not." The characters have been influenced by whites. The doll is the symbol of that influence. The white, blue-eyed doll assumes a meaning of its own.

A LAST WORD ON METAPHOR

In his essay "The Writer's Workshop," included in this book, Frank Conroy says that the greatest "failure" he finds in the young writers he teaches at Iowa is that they try to "write over their heads." "Most writers," he says,

> began writing as an extension of their love of reading. They were excited by books even as children, perceiving a kind of magic going on in narrative which they were eventually drawn to emulate. As they grew older they simply plunged into literature and became used to reading over their heads. They *eagerly* read over their heads. When, as adults, they try to write they are often as much preoccupied with magic—effect, simile, metaphors, mood, etc.—the fancy stuff—as with meaning. They are intoxicated with the seemingly endless power of language, an intoxication that can be dangerous. For while it is true that reading over one's head is good, writing over one's head is very bad indeed. An almost certain guarantee of failure, in fact.

Of course, it is this "magic," the "fancy stuff," that attracts many of us to writing in the first place. We get a charge out of "finding" symbols or discovering the hidden agenda of some metaphor in a story or novel—this is the *real* stuff, we think, *literature*—and we, too, want to pack our stories with the charge of such discoveries.

Metaphors (similes and symbols) are the most natural things in the world!

We don't need a literature professor to help us feel them, nor as writers do we need to overburden a scene with symbolism for the sake of symbolism. The best metaphors are born naturally out of the story. When Hemingway's Jig looks off across the Ebro, given who she is, given where she finds herself with the American in their relationship together, both physically and spiritually, because of their *situation,* she can't help but yearn for the lushness and possibilities she sees before her. She is that close, and that far away from realizing her "dream": "And we could have all this. . . ." The metaphor of fertility is captured in her state of mind, the growing of their love, and by seeing the "coloring" of their "skin" through the trees, we feel the conflict between what she views there, the very real possibilities in the fleshing out of the hills, and what the man, in his practiced practicality, *sees* for "real."

A bit of practical advice about metaphors: Do the hard work of capturing character first. Invest that character with a desire and place your character in a setting that reflects or informs the situation. Then, as the story takes shape, look to sound its depths by capitalizing on every aspect of craft at your command that we have spoken of thus far, including highfalutin metaphor.

Writing Exercises

1. Part of the job of a simile is to make comparisons fresh—to give your reader a new experience of the thing you are describing. To begin this exercise think of the most worn cliché you can imagine—Old Billy was sharp as a tack!—and as Pound said, "Make it new again." Create a true simile preserving the meaning of the cliché.
2. In a paragraph or so, attempt an extended metaphor. Begin with a simple concept, such as a family tree.
3. Locate a symbol or metaphor that you have discovered in one of the stories you have read from the anthology. Beyond noting that it is a symbol or metaphor, show all the ways you see it working to inform the story as a whole.

The Writer's Signature: Voice

In this final section we will sound the basics of style—language, sentences, and paragraphs—to help us to better hear the writer's voice.

IT IS AKIN TO STYLE, WHAT I'M TALKING ABOUT, BUT IT ISN'T STYLE ALONE. IT IS THE WRITER'S PARTICULAR AND UNMISTAKABLE SIGNATURE ON EVERYTHING HE WRITES. IT IS HIS WORLD AND NO OTHER. THIS IS ONE OF THE THINGS THAT DISTINGUISHES ONE WRITER FROM ANOTHER. NOT TALENT. THERE'S PLENTY OF THAT AROUND. BUT A WRITER WHO HAS SOME SPECIAL WAY OF LOOKING AT THINGS AND WHO GIVES ARTISTIC EXPRESSION TO THAT WAY OF LOOKING: THAT WRITER MAY BE AROUND FOR A TIME.
—Raymond Carver, "On Writing"

To begin our discussion on a writer's **voice** in "The Craft of Stories," I have my students write a *pastiche,* a time-honored literary tradition, a high compliment—one writer writing in living imitation of another. I ask them to choose two writers from the syllabus. Then I have them rewrite one important scene from a story by Writer A using the voice of Writer B. Next they write the reverse: a scene by Writer B using the voice of Writer A.

This is a whole lot tougher than it may seem at first—as well as a whole lot more fun. To make the assignment work, we not only have to think carefully about a writer's **style,** which we see at work on the page—the "particular and unmistakable" way he or she uses **language** to create **sentences** to build the blocks of **paragraphs** that they use to shape short stories—we must also consider the writer's **vision,** his or her view of the world that he or she has brought to us through their work. "It is his [or her] world," as Carver says, "and no other." Voice, we discover in working through the exercise, is "akin to style . . . , but it isn't style alone," it is more than style, beyond style: it is the writer's "special way of looking at things" and the way he or she has found to "give artistic expression to that way of looking." Voice is the *sum* of who the writer is on the page, the totaling of everything he or she brings to the art and craft of the short story.

Reading the pastiches out loud in class is often hilarious. We might get a dose of Flannery O'Connor's violent retribution on Lengel in the world of Sammy's "A & P." At Sammy's "Fiddle-de-doo," he may well end up stroked-out dead on the green and white tiles of the store. Or, in the scene in Chekhov's "The Lady with the Pet Dog" where Gurov is stretched out with his slice of watermelon and Anna is in tears after they have made love for the first time, we may hear the American from Hemingway's "Hills" make the laconic reply "Well, I love you." The results are always insightful. We find ourselves amazed at how difficult even seemingly simple voices such as Hemingway's or Chekhov's are to capture. It proves as tough as Hemingway always said it was to write "one true sentence." We quickly realize that the violence O'Connor ends her stories with cannot strike lightning-like out of the blue. To pull it off we find we need her vision—that *something more* Carver spoke of that we discover for ourselves in trying to imitate her style, the voice that breathes into the prose of O'Connor or Chekhov, Hemingway or Carver, into the prose of any writer, its life.

Style

Each of us as a writer has his or her own **style**—whether we recognize it or not. Our prose style is as original and unique to us as our thumbprint. Much of the struggle of the beginning writer is working toward rendering our *particular and unmistakable way of looking* into words. This may seem something of a paradox: how can you have a style and not recognize it? Coming into your own style is a lot like growing up. It takes time—years sometimes—for us to "find out who we are" in our prose. The discovery of our style works in much the same way. I believe it is part personality, part experience, part taste, and part sensibility.

Our individual style is undoubtedly influenced by the authors we like to read. As writers, we do not exist in a vacuum—read Joyce Carol Oates's essay "Reading as a Writer: The Artist as Craftsman" (p. 13). As Frank Conroy says, "Much has been done for us." We don't have to invent language or the fact of paragraphs. But we can sound out our own unique way of putting words and sentences together—our style—we can think of new ways to shape our stories.

Richard Marius, a novelist and former director of the Expository Writing Program at Harvard, once told me how Gordon Lish saw Marius as he passed by his editor's office door at Knopf and called out to him with a grin, "It's all in the sentences, Richard!" It is a bedrock truth we discover again and again as writers. Sentences and the words they're born of are everything to the writer.

In an effort to think through the making of our own style—in an attempt to come to terms with our own voice—let's turn back to the basics of language, the sentences and paragraphs, of which any writer's signature is composed.

Language

In "On Writing," Raymond Carver tells of the three-by-five cards that he kept "tape[d] . . . to the wall beside [his] desk." One of the cards read: "Fundamental accuracy of statement is the ONE sole morality of writing. Ezra Pound." "It is not everything by ANY means," Carver cautions, "but if a writer has 'fundamental accuracy of statement' going for him, he's at least on the right track."

The words we use in our writing must be the right words—the *exact* words. There is a *huge* difference between the verbs "walked" and "skipped" or "jumped" and "lunged." One does not work interchangeably with the others. Only one can be correct given the mood and specific objective of the particular action that needs to be conveyed. It is the writer's job to make sure the word fits.

I often turn to poetry to make the point of our choosing the right word for the work of any particular sentence, bringing a few poems to class that we pass around and then read out loud. Short stories are no less attentive to language than poems—*nothing in a short story is random*—but because the language of a poem is even further distilled it is easier to see any word's individual responsibility. Below is a poem of Marianne Moore's:

THE FISH

wade
through black jade.
    Of the crow-blue mussel shells, one keeps
adjusting the ash heaps;
        opening and shutting itself like

an
injured fan.
    The barnacles which encrust the side
of the wave, cannot hide
        there for the submerged shafts of the

sun,
split like spun
    glass, move themselves with spotlight swiftness
    into the crevices—
        in and out, illuminating

the
turquoise sea
    of bodies. The water drives a wedge
    of iron through the iron edge
        of the cliff; whereupon the stars,

pink
rice-grains, ink-
    bespattered jellyfish, crabs like green
    lilies, and submarine
        toadstools, slide each on the other.

All
external
    marks of abuse are present on this
    defiant edifice—
        all the physical features of

ac-
cident—lack
   of cornice, dynamite grooves, burns, and
    hatchet strokes, these things stand
      out on it; the chasm side is
dead.

Repeated
   evidence has proved that it can live
   on what can not revive
      its youth. The sea grows old in it.

What becomes obvious here is the reliance of each word on the next, their musicality, and the powerful, building effect of the poem as a whole. Take out any word and the rhythm fails, a beat drops, an image becomes vague, meaning is missed. Because each word is so carefully chosen, the words together sound as if they had *always* been there as a poem, natural to the page. This "naturalness" is the mark that the writer has done his or her job.

We can see the same care of words at work in *any* paragraph of *any* short story in our anthology. This care has been won through hard work. In my classes, I like to say, "Nothing is written, everything is rewritten." We work and rework draft after draft until every word holds fast. In your own writing, ask yourself what would happen if you removed one word, any word. If the meaning of the sentence would tumble and crash without it—that's the word you want.

Sentences

"It's all in the sentences, Richard!"

Sentences are the basic building blocks of communication between writer and reader. Words in and of themselves lack direction; sentences give our language a place to go, work to do.

When I teach sentences (and paragraphs, too), I use Richard Marius's book on writing the essay, *The Writer's Companion*. In his chapter "Writing Sentences," he says, of the "fundamental principles of sentences":

Sentences make statements or ask questions. We learn to make sentences naturally when we learn to talk because we have to make statements if we are to be understood by members of the community where we live. Although some people imagine that they do not speak in complete sentences, we in fact nearly always do unless we are answering a question or adding information to a sentence we have already made. To say that a sentence is complete is only to say that it makes a comprehensible statement.

Most sentences make their comprehensible statements by naming a subject and by making a statement about that subject. Clauses, phrases, and other kinds of modifiers may amplify the basic statement just as harmonies may amplify the theme of a melody. Everything in the sentence should serve the basic, central statement. When you write a sentence, you should know exactly what that basic statement is. Are you telling how somebody acts? Are you explaining that something exists in a certain way? Are you saying that something happens? If you do get confused with one of your sentences, stop and ask yourself what is the most important statement you are trying to make in that sentence. Name the subject, and as simply as you can, tell what you want to say about it. Once you have arrived at that thought, revise the sentence so that it clearly conveys what you want to say.

The basic tenets of sentences that Marius sets forth pertain to fiction writers as well as to writers of the essay. Sentences are shaped to the need of the statement or question the writer wishes to convey. Sentences come into being through revision, endless revision. Sentences are tightened, honed—until, finally, like finding the right word, they stand, hard-polished, though the reader may not even notice (we hope!) the painstaking work we've put into them.

Marius, in his chapter on "Writing Sentences," goes on to state twenty or so "principles" of "writing good sentences." You may have heard some of these principles paraphrased before: "Be direct!" "Use the active voice." "Combine thoughts to eliminate choppy sentences. "Begin most sentences with the subject." "Be economical with adjectives!"

Beyond memorizing such principles and working to put them into practice, the best way I know to improve sentences is to read other writers. Specifically, read to see how they have managed their sentences. Read writers with a variety of styles. John Gardner once told Carver to read all the Faulkner he could get his hands on and then to read all of Hemingway to flush the Faulkner out of his system. Reading such writers and then attempting a variety of sentences on your own, with attention to the principles stated above and an eye on the intent of the statement or question you're trying to make, is about as good advice as anyone can offer.

Paragraphs

It *is* all in the sentences, certainly, but those sentences—each statement or question—must be strung together with other sentences to make **paragraphs.** These paragraphs are the blocks we use to build our short stories.

Paragraphs are constructed in one of two ways. As Marius points out in his chapter on paragraphs, in one type of paragraph, removing any single sentence—like pulling a word from a sentence—confuses or disrupts the meaning of the paragraph as a whole. The second type of paragraph is controlled by a general statement. The sentences that follow refer back to the first. Reordering these sentences has little to do with the overall idea of the paragraph.

The wide use of cutting and pasting by writers who use personal computers reveals much of how paragraphs work in a short story. In shaping a story, I've often found I can move paragraphs (or even entire scenes) to gain or heighten effect and to clarify meaning. Moving paragraphs often shows me whether or not the sentences they contain are necessary. Moving paragraphs in this way helps me test the tension or direction of a piece. In the draft stage, I find I write a lot, usually in long blocks. In homing in on the meaning I begin to see emerging from a story, I find myself cutting and then consolidating sentences until each paragraph and thus, the story, stands firm.

How long should a paragraph be?

A paragraph could be a single word, Yes!, or it could run on for several pages. (Read Cormac McCarthy!) Keep in mind that it's easier for your reader—and for you as the writer—to keep track of the development of a short story if each step is set out clearly. These steps are your paragraphs. We can almost always find a good place to separate long blocks of text. Often when we divide long blocks of text the transitions are natural, the *flow* is there. All it takes to make such a simple break and gain clarity is to punch the return key. If only all aspects of writing could be so easy!

A LAST WORD ON VOICE

And what does all this have to do with style—with finding your own voice as a writer? Language, sentences, and paragraphs are the tools all writers have at their disposal. Each of us has a voice. Reading how other writers have used language, sentences, and paragraphs and then striving to put down our own "particular and unmistakable" view of the world, utilizing what we've learned, help us to begin to realize ourselves on the page—to sign our signature as the writers we were meant to be.

Writing Exercises

1. Write a pastiche. Choose two writers. Then rewrite one important scene from a story by Writer A using the voice of Writer B. Next write the reverse: a scene by Writer B using the voice of Writer A. Remember, you may have to change a scene to allow for a writer's vision. Voice is "akin to style . . . but it isn't style alone." The best part is reading these aloud.
2. As we did in the section on "Shaping the Short Story," draw a paradigm of the structure of one of your paragraphs. In a page or so write about how you see each sentence working. Now consider the job of the paragraph in the story as a whole.
3. During the course of a week, search for one word that you read or hear misused. Look for one word that is perfectly used. Make yourself aware of one wordy or inaccurate sentence. Collect one "true" sentence.
4. Pick a paragraph from a short story you have read and annotate the piece to show how each word is pulling its weight. Then, in a page or two, make every possible connection of every word's significance to the story as a whole.

A LAST WORD ON CHARACTER, PLOT, SETTING AND TIME, METAPHOR, AND VOICE

Sitting around the conference table waiting for class to begin, I'm often asked if I *really* believe anyone can be taught to write fiction. My response is a heartfelt and immediate, unequivocal *Yes!* Craft can be taught. We can learn to bevel the edge of a table; we can be instructed in the truths of wood grains. Cherry works beautifully for a dining room table; locust is better for making nearly indestructible fence posts. But can we really teach someone to be a great writer or even a very good writer? This isn't a question the would-be writer needs to ask. To paraphrase Faulkner, the beginning writer is too busy learning to wait to be taught. But a good teacher can offer guidance, give direction—there are terms to consider that help us talk about what it is we do when we shape short stories, "rules" worth our consideration, even if there are no laws we must obey. But as I've stressed again and again, at The End, it is only the judgment of the individual writer in application of the craft of stories, striving to *make it new* again in his or her own way, that will leave the signature that others may still be reading in such a class, around just such a conference table, a hundred years from today.

FRANK CONROY

The Writer's Workshop

As far as I know, the term, "writer's workshop" first came into usage some sixty years ago when Iowa University, with the blessing of the Board of Regents, decided to accept "creative" theses in partial fulfillment of the requirements toward earning certain advanced degrees. Quite a radical idea at the time. Write a string quartet toward a Ph.D. in music. Paint paintings for a Master of Fine Arts. Mount a ballet for dance, or write a play for theater. Despite the initial scandalization of the academy, the idea spread rapidly and is now commonplace. The words "writer's workshop" to describe what all those prose writers or poets were doing in all those university classrooms may have been chosen more for their reassuring overtones of craft guilds, handmade artifacts, etc. than for any descriptive precision.

Certainly writer's workshops around the country reflect wildly different assumptions about what the work should be, what the goals are, and how progress might be measured. Some are simply therapy sessions, attempting to create a warm, nurturing environment in which writers are encouraged to express themselves, release their putative creative energies without fear, and see what happens. Some have a political agenda—feminist art, black art, social protest art. Some have an aesthetic agenda—minimalism, realism, metafiction, etc. There are writer's workshops specializing in horror fiction, detective fiction, children's fiction, science fiction, and so on. There are workshops that have almost nothing to do with writing, where the texts are little more than an excuse for primal scream catharsis on one hand or new age channeling on the other. So it follows that in talking about a writer's workshop it must be made clear just whose workshop is under discussion. I will attempt to describe my own at the University of Iowa.

Every Tuesday at 4:30 in the afternoon I meet with about a dozen students. We have all picked up copies of the material we're going to talk about—texts generated by the two student writers who are "up" that week—and have read them several times over the weekend, made editorial comments in the margins, and written letters to the authors attempting to describe our reactions to the texts. These letters are quite important—first because they are written before any public discussion and hence are not corrupted by what may be said in class, and second because they tend to be more supportive, more personal, and sometimes more trenchant than what the writer of the letter might say in class. Thus if a story is torn apart during workshop, the letters, which are read one week later (since I keep them and read them myself during that time), can work to cheer a student up and encourage more work.

We talk for two and a half hours. The author of the text being examined generally remains silent, which some observers find surprising, but which I encourage. If there is a tension between the writer's intentions for the text and what the text, standing alone, appears to actually be doing to the readers, that is a tension the writer should face, and think about. As well, the writer's temptation to defend his or her work can lead to wasted time.

But let me back up now, to the first meeting, when we have no texts before us and I try to give a general sense of what I think our work should be. I announce right away that I reserve the right to be wrong, because not to do so would severely restrict my ability to talk at all. Narrative fiction is complex, judgments can be subjective, tastes differ, and rules seldom hold.

I further state that the focus of our attention will be the texts, and our goal will be to expand our awareness of how language functions on the page. We will stop with the text, and resist the temptation to go through it and talk about the author. Remarks, thoughts, and reactions to a given piece of writing should be addressed to the room as a whole and not to the author, whose presence, for the rest of us, is superfluous. We are studying the text, what the text actually is rather than what the author might have wanted it to be or thought that it was.

The people in my workshop are usually in their late twenties, very bright, exceptionally well read by modern standards, ambitious, and in thrall to books and literature. As sophisticated as they are about other people's writing, they are often quite naive about their own, half assuming, for instance, that when they write their souls are on their pages and that an attack on the page is an attack on the soul. I try to make the point that when the soul is truly on the page the work has risen past the level at which it makes much sense for us to talk about it. Victory has been achieved and the work passes over to the attention of students of literature, culture, and aesthetics. We, on the other hand (and I include myself), have more immediate goals. We're trying to write better prose, and to struggle through whatever we have to struggle through in order to do it. In a not entirely ancillary way, we want to get published, as a confirmation of the value of the work, and a partial authentication of the worker in the chosen role of writer. These latter passions are tacitly understood as part of the general background of the workshop, but it fairly soon becomes clear that in only the most minimal sense are they a function of the quality of the work. Better to separate, even if somewhat artificially, the text from the author, and keep our attention on the language.

Chalk in hand, I go to the blackboard and suggest that it might be helpful to think about the relationship between the writer and the reader. A common error is to use the following model of a transportation exchange.

Writer ⎯⎯⎯⎯⎯▶ Text ◀⎯⎯⎯⎯⎯ Reader

The writer creates a story and puts it into a code (language) that is the text. The reader decodes the text and receives the story. Simple transportation from the writer/creator to the reader/witness.

But what really goes on is more complicated. The language statement "yellow pencil" can carry no actual color. The reader must add the color with the mind's eye for the full image to emerge. Likewise, the reader's energy is needed to hear tones of voice in dialogue, to infer information that the text only implies, to make full pictures from the text's suggestive sketches of the physical world, to respond to metaphor, and on up to higher and higher levels. The reader is not a passive witness to, for instance, Hemingway's "Hills Like White Elephants." He or she is pouring energy into the text, which, as a result of severe discipline, has been designed to elicit, welcome, and *use* that energy. Indeed, without work from the reader the story doesn't make much sense. (What are they going on about? Where is the train taking her and what is she going to do there?) So the above model is wiped from the board and another put in its place.

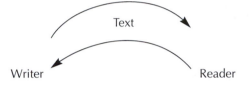

This model purports energy from the writer (the act of writing) aimed at the reader, and energy from the reader (the act of reading) aimed at the text. The text here is thought of not as a single plane or page in space, but as the zone where the two arcs of energy overlap.

This model suggests that the reader is to some extent the cocreator of the narrative. The author, then, must write in such a way as to allow the reader's energy into the work. If the text is unintelligible it falls short of the zone and the reader is blocked. If the text is preemptive and bullying it goes past the zone, smothers the incoming energy, and the reader is blocked. In either case the dance of two minds necessary to bring a living narrative into existence is precluded. Note that no judgment is made about how to handle the reader's energy once it has been allowed in. Great demands can be made of the reader, or lesser, depending on what's afoot. The point is, without the active participation of the reader's mind and imagination, absolutely nothing will happen. As well, the model says nothing about the degree or intensity of the energy from the two sides in relation to one another. Obviously it takes *very* much more energy (and time) to write good prose than it does to read it.

All right, the students say, assuming we buy the idea of the zone for the moment, what can you tell us about getting into it, or writing toward it? I respond that that is what we will be doing all semester, and that in preparation I will put forward some unproven but possibly useful ideas.

Most writers began writing as an extension of their love of reading. They were excited by books even as children, perceiving a kind of magic going on in narrative which they were eventually drawn to emulate. As they grew older they simply plunged into literature and became used to reading over their heads. They *eagerly* read over their heads. When, as adults, they try to write they are often as much preoccupied with magic—effect, simile, metaphors, mood, etc.—the fancy stuff—as with meaning. They are intoxicated with the seemingly endless power of language, an intoxication that can be dangerous. For while it is true that reading over one's head is good, writing over one's head is very bad indeed. An almost certain guarantee of failure, in fact.

When we write we are not alone, starting everything from scratch, however much it might feel that way. Literature is a continuum—moving and changing to be sure—but much has already been done for us. Conventions have been established. When we make paragraphs, use punctuation, follow (flexibly) the rules of grammar, and so forth we are borne by the flow of that continuum. We can employ an omniscient third-person narrator without having to explain who is narrating because Flaubert and others cleared that particular problem away. A tremendous amount has been done for us. Literature is a river, full of currents and cross-currents, and when we write we are in it, like it or not. If we grow too forgetful, we can drown.

At the blackboard again I draw the following box.

Meaning   Sense   Clarity

This is the first order of business in trying to write toward the zone, the first signal to the reader that his or her energy is welcome, the first announcement of a common ground.

1. Meaning. At the literal level, the writer's words must mean what they say. The author, having chosen them, must stand fully and firmly behind them. *Obese, fat, chubby, heavy,* and *stout,* for instance, have different meanings. They are not interchangeable. *He sat down with a sigh* means that the sitting and the sighing are happening at the same time, which precludes a construction such as *"I'm too tired to think," he said as he sat down with a sigh.* The reader will undoubtedly get the drift and will separate the sighing from the saying, but the writing is sloppy from the point of view of meaning. It doesn't, at the literal level, mean what it says. Errors of meaning are quite common in lax prose, and there are more ways of making them than I can list here.

2. Sense. The text must make sense, lest the reader be excluded. *The boy ate the watermelon* makes sense. *The watermelon ate the boy* does not, unless the author has created a special world in which it does. Unmotivated behavior in characters doesn't make sense to the reader, who is also confused by randomness, arbitrariness, or aimlessness in the text. The writer must recognize the continuous unrelenting pressure from the reader that the text make sense. It can be strange sense, to be sure, but the reader has to be able to understand the text to enter it.

3. Clarity. Strunk and White tell us not to use ten words where five will do. This is because the most compact language statement is almost always clearer than an expansive one. The goal is not brevity for its own sake but *clarity*. The reader expects the writer to have removed all excess language, to have distilled things to their essences, whether the style is simple or complex. If the writer has not done this work the reader is less enthusiastic about putting energy into the text, less sure about being on common ground. As well, clarity has aesthetic value all by itself. To read Orwell is to get real pleasure from the clarity of the prose, and this is true whether or not one agrees with the politics that are so often embedded in his work.

In my opinion the struggle to maintain meaning, sense, and clarity is the primary activity of any writer. It turns out to be quite hard to do, demanding constant concentration at high levels, constant self-editing, and a continuous preconscious awareness of the ghostly presence of a mind on the other side of the zone. Many enthusiastic inexperienced writers (even some experienced ones) would like to skip this struggle, or evade it while maintaining that of course it has some importance, but the real action occurs at higher levels, up where the fancy stuff is, the stuff that so moves them as readers. I maintain that any attempt to write from the top down will likely fail. I put forward the idea of a sort of pyramid

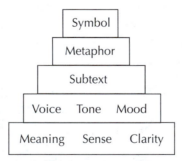

in which the higher levels have a chance to become operative only as the levels below become operative. The most common error one sees in talented young writers is the attempt to work from the top down rather than the bottom up. A good workshop can save people a tremendous amount of time if it can correct this error. The pyramid is reductive, no more than a thought experiment, really, but it strengthens writers. A great deal of what makes good writing is mysterious and beyond our power to control directly, but we need not be entirely helpless in our attempts to approach that state in which we might, possibly, increase our chances of doing good writing. You cannot really teach a baseball player how to become a great hitter, says Kurt Vonnegut, with regard to teaching writing, but you can teach him where to stand in the box, how to shift his weight during the swing, how to follow through, and a dozen other things he'll need to know before he can become even a good hitter.

Against this general background, then, we begin to look at student texts. Everyone is warned that my remarks are likely to be negative, that experience has shown me that my positive remarks aren't likely to have the same impact, which is too bad, but seems to be the case. I will search out every weakness in the prose that I can, explaining as carefully as I can precisely why I consider each particular discovered weakness to be an actual weakness, rather than some idiosyncratic response to the text of my own. I will tear the prose apart until I get prose sufficiently strong that it does not tear. This approach creates a good deal of nervousness in the students at first, but as the semester progresses that problem eases. They begin to see that the texts are being looked at, not the authors, and that the process is oddly impersonal (especially if it's someone else's work under discussion) and generally rational. We put to the test my assertion that if there is some large, abstract problem with a story, or a series of problems—"It's thin." "It lacks energy." "It lacks narrative drive." "It's frustrating to read." etc., etc.—the seeds of the problem can *always* be found at the microlevel of language, the words and sentences on the page. That is at least a place for the author to start actual work to strengthen the story rather than simply throwing up one's hands in despair. Another draft, and then again another draft, until one has gone as far as one senses one can reasonably go.

Much of this work has to do with meaning, sense, clarity, and working from the bottom up vis-à-vis the pyramid. We spend time and effort trying to find out what's wrong, leaving it to the author to fix it. (Again, some observers find this surprising. My own feeling is that, in prose, any given problem is most likely susceptible to many different solutions, and that the author's solution is the one that counts. As well, writing even a simple sentence should be done slowly and carefully within the context of the whole narrative, and never off the top of one's head in a classroom.) I often use the class as a sort of panel to verify the existence of a problem. "How many of you thought they were still in the kitchen when it turns out they were in the living room?" (We don't vote—it's a question of nodding heads.) If there is a consensus we go to the language to find out why we thought they were still in the kitchen. If this sounds trivial we should remember Virginia Woolf's comment after being asked how her three hours of writing had gone one afternoon. (I paraphrase.) "Very well. I got them through the French doors and out onto the patio." She was quite serious.

As we read closely and compare our readings many different kinds of problems can be seen to crop up in the texts. We learn the danger of giving the reader insufficient information—how the reader will simply make something up to fill the vacuum. "You mean they were brothers? I thought they were gay lovers and that's why the macho bartender got on their case." We talk about the Loose Reader, who is able to create the most fantastic cathedrals in the air out of the smallest slips of the author.

We discuss matters of technique and of craft. "This is a first person story told by Lucy, and since she never went to the trial how can she know all this stuff about the quality of the light coming through the courtroom windows?" We ruminate on the seductiveness of the first person, how it seems easy initially but subsequently becomes very hard. We look at texts in which the author seems trapped in the first person, unable to find a way to look around the narrator, or rise above the narrator. We discuss strategies to avoid such pitfalls.

Inevitably we will come upon a text that is hiding in abject naturalism, where the author creates chronological lists of events rather than selecting some events over others. "I don't know what is important in this story. I don't know what I'm supposed to be paying attention to because everything is treated the same. I mean all this stuff could happen, but what's the point? What am I supposed to make of it?" The question is rhetorical, of course, because if the text doesn't answer it, it doesn't get answered. The text stands alone, without an explicator, as it does in life.

Because writing is an extension of reading, and because the students have been reading all their lives, it is understandable that the two activities might blur somewhat in their minds. Although it is certainly a good thing that their writing is informed by their reading—indeed, at the most basic level they wouldn't be able to write anything at all if it weren't—it has its dangers. The creation of metaphors and similes, for instance. "The boy hopped up and down," writes a particularly bright student whose intuition, sense of rhythm, and experience as a reader tell her a metaphor or simile is needed to complete the sentence, "like beads of water on a hot frying pan." In the rush to meet the demands of intuition and rhythm she has written a weak metaphor. She has forgotten the basic function of the device, which is to make something crystal clear, to reduce to essence. She has tried to *amplify, to add on,* rather than reduce.

Consider John Banville's description of a sound from a very young, practically newborn infant. "In his cot the child made a sound in his sleep like a rusty hinge being opened." He could have stopped with "sleep," but he particularized the sound, reduced it, as it were, by bringing in the rusty hinge. (Creating a frisson of recognition for anyone who's had a child.) Updike's comparison of the Colosseum to a "ruined wedding cake" is a visual reduction of great power. The point is these experienced writers understand the function of metaphor and simile. The bright student did not. She allowed the reader in her, the mimetic reader, too much power over the writer in her at that particular moment in composition. Once again, it is up to the student to come up with a solution to the hopping child sentence. Workshops cannot teach the magic of making thrilling metaphors, but they can at least discuss their function, what it is they're supposed to be doing. Precision.

A problem that sometimes comes up is a narrative that looks like a story—controlled language, dialogue, description, some kind of plot or shape—but is in fact only a mimetic stringing together of various devices that the writer has absorbed as a reader. I do not mean copying, I mean empty writing. Techniques learned while reading narratives that are actually about something are applied in the creation of texts whose raison d'être is nothing more than the recreation of the techniques for their own sakes. Lacking any emotional or intellectual engine, pressure, or emerging reason why the reader should continue to read, such texts are stillborn. Happily, this is most often a short phase for young writers, but it can require a good deal of energy to get past it. In truth, writing is a mixture of knowing what you're doing and not knowing what you're doing. The late John Cheever told me he never once knew the ending to any of his short stories, and had to discover the ending and how to get there while in the act of writing each one of them. So even to a master it is not an entirely unknown experience to look down at what you've written, decide it looks like a story, and go forward on faith. The author creates the text and the text whispers to the author, but for this to happen there must be pressure, the text must be in the service of something even if the author is not yet quite sure what that something is, there must be forward momentum. Mimetic texts are invariably static. Neither do they whisper what they want to become.

The workshop cannot tell or teach a student what his or her text should be in the service of. Such presumption would be outrageous. It wouldn't work in any case. If the text is to have pressure it must be the author's pressure, which can only come from the inside.

Many elements of good narrative fiction cannot be directly learned in a workshop. Narrative drive, metaphor, depth of characterization, wit, dynamics of pitch, humor, narrative authority, and a dozen other things are simply too complex to be broken down intellectually. We should certainly talk about them—talk around them—when they come up in a text, but I suspect that in the end it is the intuitive preconscious forces at work in the writer that matter the most, a certain tense alertness to language being perhaps the most basic. Workshops can help students to dare to trust intuition, or at least lessen their fear of it. Experienced writers know Hemingway was correct when he said the larger part of the iceberg is hidden under water, and they know that when they are doing their best work more is going on than they can consciously describe. So be it. The art lifts the artist.

Art cannot be made by committee. Any such use of a workshop will be counterproductive. Thus the student who is "up" should not be looking for solutions from the other students or from the teacher. The student should be looking for problems in the text that he or she had not been aware of. In a good workshop this becomes clear in a matter of hours. (Failure to understand this had led to many a canard from uninformed commentators about what they imagine to be going on at Iowa—the existence of an "Iowa short story," for example, or the assumption that a prevailing aesthetic or style exists that is drummed into the students. Not so. The Iowa Workshop attempts to respond to what each student brings, and each student is unique. The briefest look at the variety in the work of the students—to say nothing of the famous graduates—is the proof.)

Neither can art be made by learning a set of rules and applying them, as is the case, say, with solid geometry. The young writer may well be guided by hints or suggestions that might look like rules, but are in fact only observations not meant to be applied universally. I am reminded of working on a tune with the late jazz musician Paul Desmond—myself on piano and the master on saxophone. At one point, improvising the voicings as I moved from one chord to another, Paul stopped the music, leaned over the keyboard, and showed me a better way to do it. "Usually," he said, "but not always, we try to retain all notes common to both chords." Exactly so in a writing workshop. Suggestions are made in that spirit—"usually, but not always."

The workshop concentrates on matters of craft, as it should, but hints, suggestions, and thought experiments flow continuously through the semester, offerings whose usefulness is privately determined by each student. Here is a list, for instance—notes jotted down by one of my students over a period of three weeks—suggestive of the sorts of things that come up: "Characterization is built not through repetition but through layering. . . . The text should imply, so the reader can infer. . . . Dramatization is crucial. Too much telling infantilizes the reader. . . . The text informs the alert writer as to its manifest destiny. . . . [Cheever!] Written dialogue is very different from spoken, or 'real' dialogue . . . degraded language can degrade a character . . . a text must not have amnesia, each sentence should be linked to all that came before . . . rhythms should vary" and so forth and so on. These are observations of my own springing from the discussion of various student texts. Part of the workshop experience is older writers working with younger writers, a sort of atelier where the older writers, who have presumably produced significant work, imply that they have "been there" about some issue, and put forward thoughts for what they are worth. Students seem eager for such information, and I've sometimes wondered if they are not in fact training me to give it, so quickly do they reach for their pens when I get into that mode. I do believe they understand that the value, if any, of such observations is their ability to expand the way one thinks about certain problems rather than their efficacy in immediately solving them.

Many good things happen outside the classroom. At Iowa, the students are in residence for two years in what is for almost all of them a mildly exotic environment: a calm college town in the midwest where they tend to eat in the same restaurants, go to the same bars, theaters, concerts, and grocery stores. They get to know each other very well, and many of them find two or three contemporaries who prove to be particularly sensitive, particularly smart and sympathetic readers. A good deal of discussion about one or another text goes on in coffee houses or even over the telephone as a student tries out a couple of paragraphs at one o'clock in the morning. (Allan Gurganus, for instance, found some special readers when he was a student here years ago whom he still consults.) The value of this dynamic cannot be overstated, and may well be a critical factor in the integration of whatever may have been learned in class.

At Iowa young writers get to work with at least four different teachers during the course of their stay. Each teacher has his or her own approach, using methods only indirectly connected to the others, so that the students become aware that the process is more circular than linear. But a common theme is that the students should be focused on process rather than project. Typically students tend to cling to the texts that got them into the workshop in the first place, deeply and understandably worried that the magic might not strike again, that the magic is unpredictable. They mistakenly think that only their strong work is significant and that their weak work is a total waste of time. They fear being exposed as impostors.

The workshop asserts that it is process that counts. All the work is necessary to move process forward, hence it is all valuable. Every writer creates weak, middling, and strong work. No one ever knows when lightning will strike, and we are all, much of the time, waiting for it. But we are not passive. We write, we struggle, we take risks. We work to be ready for the lightning when it comes, to be worthy of it, to be able to handle it rather than be destroyed by it. (Success has ruined more writers than failure.) Writing, sayeth the workshop, is a way of life. You either sign on or you don't.

The Habit of Writing

I gestate: for months, often for years. An idea comes to me from wherever they come, and I write it in a notebook. Sometimes I forget it's there. I don't think about it. By *think* I mean *plan*. I try never to think about where a story will go. This is as hard as writing, maybe harder; I spend most of my waking time doing it; it is hard work, because I want to know what the story will do and how it will end and whether or not I can write it; but I must not know, or I will kill the story by controlling it; I work to surrender. I know a political scientist who writes books. Once I told him that I try simply to go to the desk and receive what will come. He said he did the same. I said: "I thought you guys used outlines. Don't you already know what you want to say?"

"No," he said. "It all happens at the typewriter. I never get any work done by thinking."

The Zen archer does not release the arrow; he concentrates, breathes; the arrow releases itself, and the target draws it to itself.

I gestate, and when I am blessed, I am working on one story while another is growing in me. I begin to see characters' souls, sometimes their faces. I give them bodies and names. That is all I need, for most of my ideas are situations, and many of them are questions: *What if?* What would happen if a man's daughter accidentally killed a man by hitting him with her car, and did not stop but drove home and told her father? When I see the first two scenes, I begin writing. This truly means that the first two scenes show themselves to me. I may be watching a movie or driving my car or talking with a friend, and here come the scenes. It means it is time. The story is ready for me to receive it. Then I must write, with the most intense concentration I can muster.

In 1979 I was at someone's house, at a party, and I met a lawyer. By then I had been writing for a quarter of a century, since I was seventeen years old. He asked me what was the hardest part of writing. I said: "I just learned what it is. Concentration. I don't mean ridding the mind of bills and heartbreak and other things. I mean absolute concentration on one word. Becoming the word."

"I'm a Zen archer," he said, "and lately my concentration has been bad."

We talked about pitchers, how sometimes they lose concentration during a game, and can't get it back. And he said: "In this country, they'll forgive you for losing concentration while writing a story, or trying a case, or pitching a baseball, or shooting an arrow. But there's one place they won't: in bed. They'll always say 'You don't love me.'"

I repeat this because it's funny and profound. If we can lose concentration—and we do, we do—performing a natural act that animals can perform as easily as some of them kill, and if we lose concentration performing this with one we truly love, two lovers in harmony in body and spirit, how can we expect anything while writing but a very difficult and intense struggle simply to concentrate on discovering one word after another, and putting them on a blank page till the page is no longer blank? And filling a page with words means nothing of itself. We have to make those words into human beings, while writing the story; and if we do it well enough, that reader will remember these fictional people, as if they actually walked the earth, and entered, however briefly, the reader's life. Anyone who wants to write should read Joseph Conrad's Preface to *The Nigger of the Narcissus;* I have read nothing better about writing prose, giving life to imagined characters.

I told the lawyer *concentration* because of a story I was working on then. It's called "Anna." A few years earlier, I'd read in the *Boston Globe* about a man who robbed a bank in Boston, then went to a phone booth and called his girlfriend in Florida to tell her about it; she asked him where the phone booth was, then whispered to her boyfriend to go next door and call the Boston Police; then she kept the cuckolded bank robber on the phone till the police came. I wrote this in my notebook, and wrote: "story of betrayal." In those days I was still planning stories. I only wrote one of them, in 1968 or 1969, exactly as I had planned it, and it was dead long before I put the final period on the page; I had not given free will to the young woman in the story I dropped into the wastebasket. So I knew stories would never become what I planned them to be and that, with draft after draft, they would tell me what they were. I usually wrote five or six drafts; generally the first draft was terrible and several only showed me what the story was not, and generally what it was not was precisely what I had thought it would be. A novella, *Adultery,* took seven drafts, four hundred typed pages (I write in longhand, then type) to get the final sixty pages. This was foolish, or seems foolish now, but perhaps I needed it for those twenty-five years before I confronted "Anna," which threw me on my back, then raised me up to a new way of working.

Of course I have to plan some things. With "Anna" I had to plan a robbery. I went to see my pharmacist, told him what I was doing, and asked him how much money someone could steal from a drugstore. He said very little from his, because he had regular customers who charged everything; but he said that from a drugstore on a highway, especially one that sold money orders, a robber could get two thousand dollars. So I made up a drugstore in a shopping center on Route 1, north of Boston, not far from Haverhill, where I live, and where Anna and Wayne lived, a young, unmarried couple, he a maker of hamburgers at Wendy's, she a clerk at a convenience store. But I planned too much, still, after a quarter of a century, believing these things would happen. Even though, in my late twenties, I had written a novel, *The Lieutenant,* and my protagonist had broken my heart when he failed to climb one more rung on the moral ladder; even though character after character in stories had broken my heart, doing things I wished they would not. The young man in "Anna," because he had no money, had only a hunting knife as a tool for their first robbery of the drugstore. I planned how later he would get a gun. They lived upstairs in an apartment building and on the ground floor was a widow. She would kill herself with gas from the stove. He would smell the gas and go into her apartment, open the windows, and find, in her bedside table, a pistol she had chosen not to use. He would escalate, robbing now with a gun, robbing several places, and Anna, in fear and maybe good conscience, would betray him to the police. I actually wrote all of this nonsense in my notebook; writing it down makes it feel like it must happen. That is why I call it nonsense.

The story is in Anna's point of view. I began it slowly, writing about her, then moved to the robbery. But it was very difficult for me to become her. I kept telling friends: "As far as I know, I don't know anyone who's committed armed robbery." I kept writing, trying for those five pages a day, but each day I felt as though I were watching Anna from a distance, and I could not get inside of her, become her. Then one day or night I decided to try a different approach. I told myself that next day at the desk I would not leave a sentence until I knew precisely what Anna was feeling. I told myself that even if I wrote only fifty words, I would stay with this. By now Anna and Wayne had robbed the drugstore and had driven to a liquor store in their own town, but the store was closed, so they went to the neighborhood bar where they were regulars.

At my desk next morning I held my pen and hunched my shoulders and leaned my head down, physically trying to look more deeply into the page of the notebook. I did this for only a moment before writing, as a batter takes practice swings while he waits in the on-deck circle. In that moment I began what I call vertical writing, rather than horizontal. I had never before thought in these terms. But for years I had been writing horizontally, trying to move forward (those five pages); now I would try to move down, as deeply as I could.

I always stop writing for the day in mid-sentence, a trick I learned from Ernest Hemingway when I wrote a paper about him while I was a college freshman. That was his method, and his advice to writers: stop in mid-sentence, while it is going well (I stop in mid-scene too), then exercise your body and forget the story and let the subconscious do the work. On that first morning of vertical writing, I read the half-sentence, with Anna and Wayne in the bar, hunched my shoulders and leaned toward the page one more time, then slowly dove. Very slowly. I worked on feeling all of her physical sensations. There are probably too many tactile details in that story, there are probably too many in every story I've written since "Anna," but that is the only way I can work. And something happened, in that bar with Anna.

I did become her, through her senses. *You must know what a glass of beer feels like in her hand,* I told myself; *you must know everything.* While they stood at the bar, I learned this: she truly loved Wayne. Now, I was excited. I had not written many words, and suddenly I knew that this was a story about two people who loved each other. It was not a story of betrayal. Walls fell down and everything was open: I knew nothing of what would happen next, and that was frightening—though simple to solve—but it was wonderful, it was elating, I was both lost and free. There were no more plans. The widow remained in the story, but there would be no suicide, no gun, no more robberies. Now what?

They were still in the bar. *Just follow them home,* I told myself, and since then I have believed that you can write a story simply by becoming a character and following that character home. Or through a day or a night. Who among us is not a story, or several of them, every day? So I went home with Anna and Wayne. Next day I woke with her, felt her bad hangover, went to work with her. Then what? I followed her home. Now, when working on a story, I keep telling myself: *Just follow the dots; become the character and follow; there will be a story.* So that night after work, Anna and Wayne went to the mall. Her hangover was still bad. They bought things. They went home and carried the things upstairs: a record player, a television set, a vacuum cleaner. They left the things and walked to the bar. They had not bought food or beer; I *noticed* that; I did not plan it. They had forgotten their nearly bare refrigerator. On the way to the bar they walked past a car dealership. I almost wrote that, through the large windows, the new cars showed them what they would never be able to buy, showed them the economic futility of their lives. But I decided not to point this out; maybe a reader would notice. I was still following the dots: they went to the bar because of their hangovers, and the spiritual fatigue caused by the mall's stimulation, and by their spending money on dead yet good things that would give them comfort but not hope. In the bar they drank, then went home, where in bed they sadly talked, knowing now that they could never get everything. And then I knew it was a story about America too, about the things we are expected to buy and love, and the things that are supposed to give us equality with other Americans, and fulfill our souls. Next day Anna took their clothes to the laundromat and washed them. The story was done. I had written slowly every day, and in one draft it was done.

Because I wrote it vertically; if I had written it horizontally, I would have discovered in the first or at least an early draft that it was not a story of betrayal, or even a story about robbers. In the fifth or sixth draft I would have written the story as it wanted me to. When I have finished a story in longhand, I read it into a tape recorder. Doing this makes me see things I had not seen before, probably because reading aloud is a physical act that heightens my concentration. Remember: before each day's work I read the manuscript from the beginning; so, by the time I have finished a story, I have read sentences as many as a hundred times or more. While reading aloud I change things: often I cut or compress. The day after I record the story, I listen to it, and usually have a few changes to make, but not as many as when I read it aloud. Then it is ready to type. When I wrote horizontally, I wrote an average of three stories a year, in a good year. Writing vertically, I still write three stories a year, in a good year.

My stories often stop; I think this happens less since I began writing vertically. While I was writing horizontally about sixty-five percent of my stories stopped, and would not move. I do not believe in forcing a story. If it stops, it is telling me that I am not seeing it or hearing it. I could force it, impose action on it, but it would be false. So I lay it aside, and start another story, and wait for the motionless story to put itself into motion and to tell me it is moving now, and I should turn to it. A story called "The Fat Girl" stopped after the young woman's roommate put her on a diet and she lost weight. Simply stopped. I put it in a drawer. A year or more later I was walking on a small town sidewalk when those words came into my mind, from the air, the sky, from God knows where: *Get her married.* That night I wrote, and the next day, and the story was done.

I gestate. In 1985 I wrote a story, "A Father's Story," which came in one longhand draft, one tape recording, then a typed draft. I don't remember how many weeks or months I spent writing the story, but the work truly began years before I wrote the first sentence. I used to walk, fast and happily, for five miles, for conditioning and peace of soul and clearing of clutter from my mind. On one of these walks, an idea came: *Write about a man of faith. Make him a good-field no-hit infielder who plays triple A ball and knows he will never play in the major leagues.* When I got home, I wrote that in my notebook. Much later, months, maybe a year, while I was on my conditioning walk, another idea came: *What is the morality of a hit-and-run accident? I know the civil law; but what is the moral obligation, if you have accidentally killed someone? Can you flee?* I wrote that in my notebook. At least a year later—oh, I miss those conditioning walks, now that I am in a wheelchair; they gave me transcendence and opened me to the voices—another idea came: *Why not make the man of faith not a ballplayer but the father of a hit-and-run driver?* I wrote that in my notebook and it felt right.

Now I did have to think. Unlike my government, or American voters, or both, I believe I have to give jobs to my characters. I also had to decide whether the driver would be a son or a daughter. An instinct told me to make her a daughter, because the father may treat her differently than he would a son. I did not know how, or even if he would treat her differently. It was an instinct, and I have faith in those. Nearly absolute faith, when the instincts are about writing. So: a father and a daughter, and a false start. I gave the father a convenience store with a coffee and lunch counter; probably he had a wife and other children; I don't remember. Nor do I remember why he did not work as a character. I was interested in his owning this store where police officers from his small town would come to drink coffee; they would be his friends—casual ones, but still friends—and he would be concealing his daughter's crime from them. But the story stopped, and I laid it aside. I do not understand these things; I think part of my work is not to understand. Not long ago I wrote a story called "All the Time in the World." Again and again, it stopped about midway through, when the woman in the story met a man whom she would love and marry. All I wanted to do was write a story about how and why a man and woman met each other. But when the man—Ted Briggs—entered the story, it stopped. He was a slender, angular man; I gave him the body of a man I know. One day, while I was not writing the story, I saw him differently: he was a broad and strong man with a cane and a limp from a knee wounded in Vietnam, and an alcoholic who no longer drank. This new body gave Ted Briggs something richer: he was a man, wounded in body and spirit, and from this I got another story I wrote later, "Falling in Love," about Ted when he was drinking and taking erotic love too easily. With Ted's new body and soul, "All the Time in the World" moved dot after dot after dot.

I imagined a new man for "A Father's Story": I used the body of a man who owned a riding stable where I used to bring one of my daughters for Sunday afternoon lessons, in the 1970s, when she was in high school. I gave this man the riding stable. Now he had a body and a job. And I took away his wife, made him a divorced Catholic, so that his faith would be action: he will not remarry and he tries to be celibate, and almost perfectly is. His children are grown, and he lives alone, and I gave him a priest as his best friend.

But I was not ready to begin. He had a name, Luke Ripley, and work, and he went to daily mass and cared for his horses. It was time for me to immerse. I read William James's *Varieties of Religious Experience.* Then I reread Kierkegaard's *Fear and Trembling;* this was in the winter of 1983 while I was teaching at Bradford College in Haverhill. I asked a woman friend, a philosophy teacher, if she would like to team-teach *Fear and Trembling* in an open seminar, without grades or credit, and she said she would. We somehow announced this seminar, saying we would meet one night a week, for as long as all of us wished. Then we started, and students came to the classroom; I don't remember how many times we met, only that, for the last night, the woman and I met with one female student in the neighborhood bar. Now I was ready, and the story did not take a long time to write; I finished it in April. A blizzard came one school day that April, canceling classes. At my desk, while snow blew outside, I knew my story was ending. I stopped, in mid-sentence, mid-scene. Next day the sky was clear, but I called the registrar and told her I wasn't feeling well and could not teach, and I went to my desk. I had to know how this story would end. And that day it did end, and in its closing lines, I knew.

Nearly everything in that story surprised me. I had planned how the accident would happen. That was all. The story is in the first person, and I knew that its beginning would have to establish, for a reader, that Luke was a man of faith. All I had to work with was his going to daily mass, and his nearly perfect refusal to make love out of wedlock, therefore his refusal to date women, and to consider marriage forbidden by the Catholic church. I had nothing more.

But on the first page Luke took my pen and moved: he talked about his solitary life, about his rituals of loneliness, about God, and his priest friend, and his marriage and children. I kept telling my wife: "He won't stop talking. *Nothing* is happening, and I can't make him shut up." That was at times when I was away from the desk, and worrying about those words in the notebook on the desk, but I should not have been worrying, or thinking about Luke Ripley. This is hard work: trying to free yourself from thinking about what you have written that day and will write tomorrow.

I taught two classes every weekday afternoon, and that freed me. At night I had homework, reading novels and stories for the literature classes; and my wife and I always, on weeknights, went to a movie or watched one on video.

Then there was sleep. Of course the day after the April blizzard, I could no longer wait, and I went to my desk. I should not have worried about Luke talking on and on; for at the desk, I did not worry. I *was* him, I spoke; I also listened to him. But not from a distance, the kind I had had from Anna till I began to write vertically. No, I listened to him as he listened to himself. I will paraphrase E. M. Forster because I don't remember where I read this: How can I know what I think about something till I hear what I have to say about it? This is profound, I believe, and universal; when we speak from the heart, with no plan, no point to make, we discover truths we did not know that we knew. So at the desk Luke's talking filled me, surprised me, and I was one with it and with him.

I believe "A Father's Story" was twenty-six typed pages, and for the first thirteen of those—in longhand, slowly, vertically—Luke Ripley talked. Finally he stopped and told the story of the accident, and his daughter coming home to him. Then I could tell my wife: "He's finally stopped talking; something is finally *happening*." There is a strong wind blowing that night, in the story, only because one night I woke up to go to the bathroom and outside a strong wind was blowing and I thought: *I should put wind in a story*. Near the end of the story's action, I began, while writing, to see images: Luke and his daughter riding horses together, and I thought that would be the final scene. Only because I was seeing it. It did not become the final scene. And, as Luke was helping his daughter conceal the crime, I discovered something: in his first thirteen pages of talking he had said, that, in love, feeling should be subordinate to action. Yet here he was, acting only because of his feelings—love for his daughter—and paying no heed to his belief in good action, no matter what one feels.

The story's action ends; Luke's daughter drives home to Florida. He talks again. On my last day of longhand work, the sunlit day after the blizzard, I left my desk to make another cup of tea and said to my wife, "He's talking again. Now he's talking to *God*." I took the tea to my desk, picked up the pen Luke was holding anyway, and held on, while he talked to God. God talked too; Luke gave Him his lines. Then he stopped and, with gratitude and joy, I placed at the end of the story its final period.

ROBERT COLES

Why Write? Taking on the World

*I*n 1965 my wife Jane and I had just returned from the American South, where we had both become involved full-time in the civil rights movement. She had become a high school teacher of English and history, I had been trained in child psychiatry and pediatrics—and both of us had spent five years with the children of Louisiana and Georgia who had initiated school desegregation under most unfavorable circumstances: riots, constant threats, even boycotts by families opposed to "race mixing," a constantly used phrase at that time. Indeed, even as we were talking with African-American boys and girls, and their parents, we were also getting to know white youngsters who had their own reasons to be perplexed, troubled by a sudden shift in what was held to be lawful, proper.

For many months I brought to that "field work" the thinking and language of medicine and the social sciences. I was a reader of *The New England Journal of Medicine, The American Journal of Psychiatry, The International Journal of Psychoanalysis, The Psychoanalytic Study of the Child*. Before I went South I had done hospital research in Boston—an effort to learn how children afflicted with polio, with leukemia, managed psychologically under such circumstances. The writing I did to describe that work tells not only of the thinking I encountered in various youngsters, but of my own way of seeing things—formulations, paradigms, theoretical constructs.

Not that such a way of expressing myself (and of course, regarding others) met with the approval of everyone I knew. My wife, Jane, kept asking me this: "Where are the children themselves—their voices?" Then, there was the older man whose poetry (the first two books of *Paterson*) had been the subject of my undergraduate thesis, whose example had inspired me to go to medical school, and whose friendship had sustained me during the demanding years there (for which I was ill-prepared): Dr. William Carlos Williams, himself no stranger to sick or worried children. I would send him drafts of the articles I was writing, or I would go see him in Rutherford, New Jersey, and tell him what I was doing, what was on my mind, and he would listen attentively, quietly only so long. I can still hear the response, the refrain actually: "The voices, the voices—where are they?"

I wanted to please this then ailing physician, this wonderfully original, brilliantly knowing poet, novelist, essayist, this huge, shaping presence in my own life (and that of so many others), but I also had acquired a way of listening to others and a manner of putting forward what I'd heard—really, a sense of who I was: a researcher whose job it was to analyze "respondents," "subjects," "informants"—such distancing words an aspect of an investigator's necessary, important "objectivity." The result was a certain sense of achievement (the publication of my work in several journals), but also a strong sense of disappointment, chagrin in two individuals whom I both respected and loved.

In the South I began to hear other voices of concern, even alarm—voices of those who also lamented the absence of voices in the early reports I was submitting of the studies I was doing. In particular, I was receiving some strongly worded advice, if not remonstrance, from two novelists whom Jane and I had been lucky, indeed, to meet: Lillian Smith and Margaret Long. Both of those writers, born Southerners, had dared state their determined opposition to segregation when (the 1930s, the 1940s) that state of affairs seemed beyond any effective challenge. Now, as a consequence of the Supreme Court's 1954 decision (*Brown v. Board of Education of Topeka*) a major struggle was taking place in cities such as New Orleans and Atlanta (where Jane and I were doing our work), and both of those women, like others of their persuasion, were anxious to do all they could to help change not only the laws of, say, Georgia (where they lived) but influence their fellow white citizens, so long unblinking in their acceptance of what was commonly called a "way of life," meaning the strictly enforced educational and social and cultural and political separation of the races.

Mostly I was using my tape recorder in the homes of the African-American and white children who were daily experiencing the breakdown of that long institutionalized apartness, but every once in a while I asked certain adults to help me understand what was happening in those early years of the civil rights movement, and one such person was Lillian Smith, whose novel, *Strange Fruit,* with its story of miscegenation, had shocked even my native Boston when it appeared in 1944—indeed, the book was banned in the city. Here is what I heard Ms. Smith say in 1962 in her Clayton, Georgia, home as we talked of her life as a novelist unafraid of the unconventional, the illegal, and as we talked of the work I was then doing, and trying to put to words:

People need bread and water for their bodies to stay alive. But they also need to figure out this life. Even theoretical physicists have a story that makes sense of the world—that's what unites us all, the rich and the poor, the educated and the ignorant, the white folks and the Negroes, the ones who live on Park Avenue in Manhattan and my neighbors here in this rural part of Georgia. For years I ran a camp, while writing the rest of the year, and before that I taught school; and I realized how needy, how *hungry* the young are for those stories: we're the story-telling creature! Our stories change, of course, as events happen in our personal lives and in the neighborhood where we live, or in our nation—and so there is a new story, developing now, and we have to hear it, know it, share it with others.

Some years ago the Klan decided they'd had enough of me. They'd built me and my books and my camp into a big story, their story: Lillian Smith the race-mixer, and Lillian Smith the communist. They figured that the way to really do me in, without getting themselves into big trouble—charged with murder—was to burn my house down. They kept telling people that the house was where I wrote all that "filthy race-mixing stuff," and it was all based on "truth"—that I had "lots of niggers, *men*" who came and stayed here. Once, when we had a group of white and Negro people from across the South stay here, for a conference on education, the Klan and their supporters spread the word that I had "a hundred nigger men" up here—that was the kind of person I was, they kept saying, and you know, the townspeople in Clayton, they didn't agree with me on "race," and yet, they had to respond to that story, and they did [so] not by arguing with it (they basically were on the Klan's side, against any and all integration), but by calling upon their day-to-day common sense. After all, they knew me well. I came to the post office everyday, and I shopped in the same stores they did, so, when they heard this story, of "Miss Lil" (as they called me) "sleeping with a hundred nigger men," they mused a bit, and came up with their own story: "I guess she's a better woman than we thought"—that went around, from person to person and the laughter undid the Klan allegation, the rumors.

Eventually, the Klan did burn my place down, and you know, plenty of folks, who you and me would call "segregationists," or "Klan-sympathizers," came up to me and told me they were sorry, and they were mad. I'll never forget what a woman told me in the post office: "They tried to silence you, scare you to silence, because they're afraid that you have a way with words, and that gets people to stop and think. Now, they've given you a new chapter to write—they've made it worse for themselves, not better!" This was no Yankee liberal! She was against "race-mixing" too; she was the wife of a man who worked in a sawmill, and she hated going to "Northern-bought" Atlanta, but she'd picked up on something important, something real big—that when people disagree and fight it's the same as when they come together in friendship and love: they describe in their minds, to one another, what is happening; they use words, make sentences, develop a story. You know, after that fire, people began to turn on the Klan (not on a lot of their views, I regret to say); they pictured me an odd, defenseless *lady* who "deserves respect," even if I have "these crazy ideas." The way people rallied around me was through narrative, not polemics—and frankly, even a polemic has to have a storyline if it's to sustain itself in the minds of people.

I recall and summon those tape-recorded words, that statement, that story, because it was part of an unforgettable afternoon for Jane and me: Lillian Smith had listened to some of the interviews we had done with children, their parents and teachers, had looked at the drawings and paintings of those boys and girls, had read two psychiatric articles I'd written and a draft of a psychoanalytic one—and pronounced herself more than a little dissatisfied. She urged quite a different tack; she urged that I write what I'd then and there been telling her, the accounts of what happened in one situation, in another, to this particular child, that one. Nor was she being "practical," or "political." She deeply believed that I was, in a sense, "failing" these children through the manner of my presentation of their situation, their experiences, *them,* to others, and she told me so vigorously, vividly—by implication, through her personal remarks (as with those above), and more pointedly through a sustained aria of sorts with respect to the virtues of fiction, the limitations of psychological and social theory.

Meanwhile, Margaret (Maggie) Long, who was the editor of *New South,* a periodical published by the Southern Regional Council (a group of white and African-American laymen who wanted to see an end to segregationist laws and practices) was constantly trying to get me "to tell a story or two to our readers." She once amplified in this way: "If you've got to go talk child psychiatry or psychoanalysis, go do so—but please don't stop there! Give us the kids—give us their words and what they do, the details of their lives, the things that happen to them." That, in a letter, and a brief note from Dr. W. C. Williams bluntly, as always, urging a similar approach (he of "no ideas but in things") made me, at last, begin to try to describe particular moments in particular lives—the incidents I'd observed or heard recounted, the kind of language used, the clothes worn, the toys picked, the pictures drawn, the facial expressions witnessed, the gestures used. For *New South,* rather than *The Journal of Child and Adolescent Psychiatry,* I wrote a piece titled "Separate but Equal Lives," which was, really, a story of two young lives, one that of an African-American youth, the other that of a white one—brought together by high school desegregation in Atlanta. A friend of mine showed the essay to Oscar Lewis, whose anthropological work had then become available to a wide audience because he chose to present his observations through biographical narratives—tape-recorded interviews edited, of course, but more than that: shaped into arresting, accessible stories. Indeed, in the middle 1960s, as I was struggling hard with what to do with a growing number of tape-recorded interviews and notes and children's drawings and paintings, I met Professor Lewis at a *Daedalus* conference (many social scientists assembled for a discussion of America's racial problems) and soon enough I heard his voice saying what others had said: "Find your own way of pulling it all together—bring the life you see and hear to others in a way that they remember." Not yet wholly convinced, I remember wondering, as I heard that advice, what the editors of various scientific journals would make of that line of reasoning.

By 1966, after eight years of working in the South, I was back in Boston. I had been asked by Erik H. Erikson to join the ranks of his assistants in an undergraduate course he offered at Harvard. We were teaching psychoanalytic psychology—of a kind Erikson had formulated in books such as *Childhood and Society* and *Young Man Luther:* the life of the mind evoked in its relationship to social and cultural forces, not to mention historical events. Erikson was trained in child psychoanalysis, but he had learned to write for a general audience—he was, originally, an artist, and he became, it can be said, a deep-thinking portraitist, who knew how to convey the many sides of those he attended as a biographer: Gorki in *Childhood and Society,* the Luther who relatively early in his life dared stand up to a corrupt ecclesiastical authority, and ultimately, Gandhi. We all loved using his books, exploring his ideas in the company of the bright, eager students who flocked to the course. Concepts such as "identity" and "identity crisis" (now absorbed into the American vernacular) were the meat and potatoes of Erikson's theoretical writing, and we worked hard to do justice to their complexity, their allowance for, even respect for ambiguity and irony and contradiction and inconsistency—such a contrast with the reductionist inclination of so much social science.

When Erikson lectured on his own ideas he invariably moved from the abstract to the concrete. He drew on his work as a clinician; he told us stories about this patient or that one—about the melancholy, sometimes the hilarity, that goes with, as Freud put it, "the psychopathology of everyday life." Once, in the midst of an account of a youth's experiences Erikson stopped to tell us how the patient's troubles had reminded him of his own adolescence—and then, this: "In psychoanalysis, we learn to understand others through self-understanding, and we learn *that* [the latter] through the stories we tell to our analysts, and their interpretation of the stories." He paused, added an afterthought, with a smile: "I suppose the analyst is the literary critic who examines these personal statements, one after the other, and interprets them."

A statement of the obvious—yet, a remark intended in its implications to connect, most broadly, the humanities to the social sciences, and specifically, the fictional narrative to the clinical "write-up," a phrase those of us who went to medical school keep using when we talk about what we have to put into our patients' hospital records. Some of us who taught with Erikson, encouraged by his way of seeing things (and way of putting things), suggested that we read novels or short stories—a means of showing the students that contemporary ideas, offered in a course listed in a university's catalog under the rubric of "social sciences," could be explored by men and women who wrote books titled *David Copperfield* or *The Brothers Karamazov* or *Sons and Lovers*. But Erikson demurred; he felt those novels were quite demanding in their own right, would sidetrack us from the pointed psychological explication which for him was the mainstay of his lecturing. Moreover, he was frank to tell us that there were only so many days in his life, that he had enormous "reading obligations," as he called them, and so no time to take on himself some of the novels we wanted put on the syllabus, used in his teaching.

Once, as he talked about "identity" in the meetings he had with we who taught the various "sections" of his course, several of us mentioned Ralph Ellison's *Invisible Man*—which, we earnestly felt, addressed precisely and suggestively the same matters we'd heard our professor discuss in a lecture the previous day. Under some hard-to-ignore insistence from us, Erikson relented, agreed to take on that novel. A few weeks later we realized that a busy, hence somewhat reluctant, reader had become an outspoken fan. We were given permission (those of us who wanted it) to use *Invisible Man* in our sectional teaching—and even encouraged to use a short story or two, if we so desired. (The work of Richard Wright, of James Baldwin, of Flannery O'Connor, of Eudora Welty had been brought up as we discussed with Erikson the South and its racial struggles, then very much in the daily news, and so on the students' minds as well as ours. A good number of our students had become involved in the civil rights movement, had ventured South in a volunteer effort.)

I will never forget those classroom days in the late 1960s and early 1970s. As with children and parents, our students are constantly teaching us how to do our work. Their questions stir us to thought, elicit ideas from us that we never knew we possessed. I had been trained to keep an eye on the faces of my patients, their gestures, the signs and signals their bodies silently sent my way. All too often in school we overlook those indications of interest or decided disinterest; and only gradually did I begin to realize, at times, no matter the energy I was putting into a particular class, that the students were not engaged, were apathetic—as their impassive faces, their collectively slumped look more than conveyed. Yet, when we came to fiction, be it Ellison's novel, or Flannery O'Connor's stories, or those of Chekhov, I kept noticing a change: talk flowed, but also, the young men and women before me stirred, used their hands, looked wide-eyed, nodded in agreement with what was said or shook their heads in dissent. Those stories not only contained their respective kinds of magic, but prompted in this or that class a responsive magic—concentrated attention, a commitment of heart as well as mind, and not least, a noticeable autobiographical strain in the discussions, the written assignments.

We were lucky to have occasional visits by Professor Erikson in our various sections, and we were lucky, too, that he wanted active, honest conversation rather than the reflexive compliance that all too readily can inform learning at any stage of its activity. To this day I remember an exchange between Erikson and a student who was majoring in psychology and sociology, who had taken few literature courses, and who, nevertheless, had found in the fiction we were reading a kind of breakthrough intellectual experience. She wanted to know how and why—what it was about "Ward Six," for instance, that caused her to think about psychology and psychoanalysis in ways not prompted by the textbooks she'd read in such abundance in so many courses. Erikson had not read that particular Chekhov story, but he was quite willing to address the larger matter of literature as a means of understanding human affairs. He told the students of Freud's essay "Dostoyevsky and Parricide"—the renunciation, albeit reluctant, in it of the explanatory zeal otherwise so prominent in psychoanalytic writing: "Before the problem of the creative artist analysis must, alas, lay down its arms." We also heard a tactful renunciation, if not refutation, on Erikson's part. He thought it a mistake for Freud to use the word "problem" in connection with an effort to understand a writer's work. Moreover, he thought that the crux of the matter wasn't personal—a particular novelist's special gifts of insight—but rather, "methodological." He paused long enough for all of us to realize that we needed clarification—and we got it: "Even at our best we are not going to be able to offer you the kind of psychological wisdom you'll find in Dostoyevsky or Chekhov—or many other novelists."

Wordlessly, we wondered why—and again he waited for a few seconds (a long time in a classroom) until he became forthcoming. In science, he pointed out, and its stepchild social science, the urge is to generalize, formulate, hence the considerable danger of an unwitting or unapologetic reductionism. In a short story or a novel or a play, however, the opposite holds: The writer is intent (in accordance with the work that he or she is doing) on rendering the

individual, the idiosyncratic, even—on supplying us not with general statements but the details of this human scene, that set of circumstances. As a consequence, we are brought close, in fiction, to a dense complexity, whereas in
the social sciences we are encouraged to seek (and enjoy) abstractions, formulations, and so we know about "minds in general," as he put it, but we don't
get into "a character's mind as it connects with all the nearby life happening."
Afterward, I had only my scattered notes, with a few of his remarks noted,
taken as he talked in that Adams House seminar room in the fall of 1968, but I
wrote out my appreciative sense that our class had been encouraged to go
beyond the set limits of a college course in "human development" (Erikson's
"field" as described in the university catalogue)—in favor of an attempt to learn
what is, well, just plain human: how fate, chance, luck, and circumstance bear
down on us, and to what possible effect.

Several years later Erikson had retired from teaching—a big disappointment for many students, and for those of us who taught them. I had gone to
live in New Mexico with my family—there to talk with Native American children (Pueblo, and in Arizona, Hopi) who lived on reservations, and also with
boys and girls whose parents spoke mainly Spanish, or whose parents were
descended from families of Spanish origin. So doing, I was hearing many stories, indeed—especially from the elderly members of the families whose children I was getting to know. These grandparents and great-grandparents were
held in high esteem by their kin, by their neighbors, and were closely attended
as they talked of the past, told of moments in time. So often, too, those "old
ones of New Mexico," as I kept describing them in my notebooks, were repos-
itories of moral reflection. They had lived long and hard lives, had struggled
mightily with the land high up in the hill country (near towns such as Truchas,
Madrid, El Valle), and had thereby earned not only survival but a stoic wisdom,
a wry sense of humor, a calm irony with respect to life's ups and downs, so
inevitable and unpredictable.

In home after home I heard those men and women, near the end of their
lives, talk about the various events that had befallen them and others—modest
accounts of ordinary, hard-pressed, yet strong-willed lives as they had unfolded. Later, as I transcribed what had been spoken, and thought about what
I'd heard, I realized that in essence I'd been given stories, stories of great power
and beauty—tales of ambition and disappointment, of yearning and loss, of
great hope and unyielding sadness or regret, and not least, of unassailable pride
(even acknowledged vanity) and an unselfconscious humility that, to this day,
I find unforgettable—it was as if, I sometimes have thought, that master storyteller Tolstoy was prompting certain comments and ways of self-expression
behind the scenes, out of a desire, yet again, to construct one of those moral
fables that so obsessed him after his twin triumphs of *War and Peace* and *Anna
Karenina*. Indeed, an eighty-two-year-old woman who knew that the end was
near asked word for word what Tolstoy asked in one of his moral fables: "How
much land does a man need?" She posed the question, actually, for the same
reasons that he had: a sense of dismay that a cousin had been so greedy for so
long; a disapproval of his way of doing things, and, really, of his way of being;

and by implication, a desire on her part to put various matters on the table, make clear her disapproval of what had taken place.

At one point, as she was in the middle of a chronicle—an account of lust for land that in the end spelled ruin for a family whose various members fought each other as if they were the children of King Lear—she paused to spell out her rationale for telling a tale; and no wonder as I struggle here to do justice to story-telling as a means of personal contemplation and instruction, not to mention pleasure, I recall her words of twenty-six years ago:

> I'm trying to leave my memories to others—they're all I have now. I close my eyes, and I see people and I hear their words and I recall what they did, what happened, and then I try to gather all that together, so that my children and my grandchildren and my great-grandchildren will know what to think about life—they'll not be so surprised when something good or bad comes around the corner. My grandmother sometimes told me to describe my day for her. In the evening, that's what she liked, for us to tell her what we'd "done with the day"—or she'd add, "what the day has done to you." So, we'd tell her, and then she'd tell us back what she thought was important. She'd take our hundred or thousand words and give us ten back, and they said it all. Now, I myself go on with too many of those words—but I hope I've learned to tell my stories so that a little of what I say sticks with people, the way my grandmother's talk stuck with me.

She was trying hard, in her own way, to sort through the memorable moments in her life, pull some of them together in spoken narratives that would, in turn, become poignantly or starkly remembered occasions in the lives of her offspring, their offspring. "My last job here," she once let me know, "is to pass along to others what I've seen, and to remind them that they'll be doing the same. You make things happen when you're young, and then, when you're old, you tell what you did, and what you saw others do." But she knew that the manner of telling also matters—more so than she herself once realized:

> I used to hear my grandmother talk, and I thought she was just saying whatever came into her head at that time. Now I know better. Now I know that you have to be careful; you have to figure out what's important and what's not important. You have to win over your own family, so they'll keep paying attention. I try to get smiles from my grandchildren [when she tells her stories], and if someone cries when I speak of trouble, and sickness, and hard times, then I know I'm doing all right; but if people are struggling to keep their eyes open, and they don't succeed [in doing so], and then they do for a while, but I can see that they're not interested—then I know it's my fault: I'm not pulling them into the memories I'm giving them. You've got to put your heart into what you say, or sleep will take away your own family from you.

She knew in her bones about plot, character portrayal, compelling dialogue; about rising dramatic tension and the inevitable and desirable denouement in a narrative; about the importance of "background"—the evocation of a mood through careful observations of life's particulars, nature's passing parade. One minute she could be quietly informative, descriptive, offer desert or mountain landscapes put to word; at other times she became moodily introspective or excitedly determined to convey comedy or tragedy or mere farce. "She has her favorites," members of her family would tell me—by which they meant that she knew who to summon, for what reason, in connection with her constant effort to put various matters on record, to make a record of all that once took place. She knew, in that regard, how to stir others to laughter and tears, to perplexity and doubt that only her own further words could clarify, resolve, or sometimes, heighten in hopes of any performer's great wish: sustained attentiveness, the voluntary thralldom of someone who at all costs wants to know what will happen. "Even when she repeats herself, I tip my hat to her by forgetting what I once heard her say"—a loyal son, true, but also an appreciative theatergoer whose kitchen serves as a stage for his mother's reveries most vividly conveyed.

In 1977, I was back in Cambridge trying to make sense of what I'd learned in the American Southwest and in Alaska, where Eskimo grandparents also felt strongly the responsibility of handing along orally the stories they'd been told, and the stories that told of their experiences in the villages they'd inhabited (most of my time was spent in Noorvik, on the Kobuk river). By then, Erik H. Erikson had retired, and I had begun a stint of volunteer teaching in a much troubled urban high school located in Roxbury, a part of Boston where mostly African-Americans live. I taught stories by James Baldwin and Richard Wright, and poems by Langston Hughes. I also used some stories by Zora Neale Hurston. I had a hard time there—the students were not much interested in going to school, and often were not reluctant to tell me so. I fear I wasn't "strong" enough with them—I didn't know how to answer their truculent indifference or their casual rowdiness (or worse) with a show of determination, conviction, ingenuity, and not least, moral purpose. I tried (and failed) to please those students, to earn from them a commitment to learn that they had no intention of offering with any ease or for any sustained length of time. Finally, I decided to quit—and on my last day, I told them why. I also told them how I'd gotten "there," to the classroom in which we all sat. I described my work in the South during the school desegregation struggles of the early 1960s, and specifically, I told them certain stories—portraits of particular children, a recounting by me of what others had let me know in conversation or through the drawings or paintings they did.

The class was now, for the first time, silent—eerily so. I assumed I was being given a polite goodbye—until, at the end, several students asked whether they could one day see some of the pictures I'd mentioned. I said yes, immediately—and only later realized that I had just bid them all an unqualified farewell. I returned, though, with some slides of the artwork I'd mentioned—and told the class more stories about the children who'd used the crayons and paints years earlier. I read some Langston Hughes poems I'd used in class earlier, and some excerpts from Baldwin's fiction and essays, which I'd also called upon weeks before. Now they were paying heed—and I was wondering what had prompted this turn of events. After that second class discussion of those civil rights days, I realized I could stay at my job, and I also realized, weeks later, what had happened: my own life had somehow become engaged with theirs through the stories told them under the dramatic auspices of a proclaimed departure, itself a story of sorts. When I overheard one of the tougher students in the class, a self-described "cynic," telling one of his friends "that dude has been around," I knew that I'd managed to grab the attention of these young people, hold it for a while (long enough to establish a bit of mutual trust) through the drama of my announced leavetaking and the compelling authority of relayed, experienced narratives as they connected with the personal lives of those who heard them. Eventually, I would be able to encourage these young men and women to write their own stories, and to comment seriously, effectively on the fictional stories they'd hitherto been so loath to accept as worthwhile.

In the midst of such teaching (1978) I was asked to teach at Harvard University. I had no great interest in lecturing on the subject matter of my profession—if anything I felt that psychiatric and psychoanalytic jargon were all too much a part of the thinking, the talk of secular, late-twentieth-century America: psychology as a religion of sorts for many essentially materialist folks, who believe, finally, in themselves, their bodies and their emotions. I wanted to teach short stories, and was allowed to do so, and have done so, now, for two decades in a variety of settings in a large university: with college students, medical students, mainly and consistently, but also with law and business students, and in the graduate school of education, and even with young would-be architects or physicians in the midst of their residencies (psychiatry, pediatrics, internal medicine). Again and again I call upon the same short fiction in my undergraduate lecture course—William Carlos Williams's "Doctor Stories," Tillie Olsen's four stories that make up *Tell Me a Riddle,* Raymond Carver's last collection, *Where I'm Calling From,* Flannery O'Connor's *Collected Stories,* Tolstoy's "The Death of Ivan Ilych" and "Master and Man," any number of the pieces that are to be found in John Cheever's *Collected Stories,* most especially "The Housebreaker of Shady Hill," "The Sorrows of Gin," "The Enormous Radio," and "The Country Husband" (one more searing and affecting than the other!). I also use short stories by Tobias Wolff, by Richard Ford, by Charles Baxter, by Richard Yates, and by the great master of the genre, Chekhov. I ask the students to read novels, as well (*Invisible Man,* of course, and *Their Eyes Were Watching God,* and *Middlemarch,* and *Great Expectations,* and *Jude the Obscure,* and *The Moviegoer,* and *The Diary of a Country Priest*)—but the students especially take to pieces of shorter fiction, and not out of a lazy reluctance to spend the required time and energy to go through, say, George Eliot's demanding prose, many hundreds of pages long. Rather, they find certain short stories hard to forget—insinuating, it can be said: The reader takes the story to heart, and lives with it for a good long while.

During my office hours, it is usually the stories that I hear mentioned—their great effect on the students, who speak with huge excitement or with aching sadness or with a kind of anxiety that tells of a true home run with respect to an author's impact on a reader. "The Use of Force," "I Stand Here Ironing," "The

Artificial Nigger," "In the Garden of the North American Martyrs," "Ward Six," "Cathedral," "A Small, Good Thing," and again those four aforementioned Cheever stories keep being acknowledged by these young people as bearing down hard on their consciousness, their reflective life, and yes, as "undermining" as well. That last word was used again and again by one of my college students—he claimed that Cheever and O'Connor and Carver and Olsen, whom he playfully called the "four horsemen of the apocalypse," were "subversive," did "sabotage" to his accepted notions of what matters in life, and how it ought to be lived. He insisted on pursuing that line of thought, even though I found it somewhat exaggerated, and indicated as much through a surprised look, a series of questions meant to give him second thoughts. He was, however, tenaciously set in his opinion, unyielding in his conviction that Johnny Hake, for instance, in his perceptions as a temporary (secret) outlaw, quietly and decisively challenged the kind of materialism most of us simply take for granted, and protect ourselves from seeing with any analytical or, needless to say, moral clarity. "He's a subversive," I kept on hearing. His thoughts, as he goes to work and walks the streets frequented by his fellow stockbrokers, lawyers, and businessmen on the rise or already at the top, are "a threat to the status quo, mine." The student spelled out the reasons for that claim this way:

> I'm headed for Wall Street; or I *was* going in that direction. But I've been haunted by Hake—and by the other Cheever stories. Those people are successful in the sense that they live well, in fancy city apartments, or nice suburban homes, but they are so *miserable,* so wrapped up in themselves, so pitiable—and now I keep wondering whether that's what I want. No critique of that world—not sociology, not philosophy, not economics, not Weber or Santayana or Marx, and not even my Catholic religion [the Papal encyclicals of the nineteenth century deploring capitalist greed and standing up for the rights of the worker] could get to me the way Cheever does!

A brilliant student, erudite and inclined toward the abstract (as in George Eliot's remark about one of her characters as possessing a mind that was "theoretic"), this senior was tempted sorely to turn his back on what seemed like an express elevator waiting to take him to the very top of American commercial life: he had been admitted to a combined "law and business" graduate program at Harvard University. Instead, he spoke of an enlistment in the Peace Corps, and beyond that, a career as a school teacher. In that last regard, he kept going back to Carver's "Cathedral," which he pronounced "awesome," and not in a frivolous way meant to dismiss rather than encourage further, intense scrutiny. He found in that story a moral metaphor—a statement about what ought to matter: individuals breaking out of their self-preoccupations, finding in one another a kind of searching companionship that gets to the origins of that word, as in Jesus taking bread with His disciples, or as in (another Biblical image) the blind leading the blind, handing one another along, for all their obvious frailties, vulnerabilities, and yes, limitations of vision (psychological and spiritual, both). He found the paper Carver has those two men use—an old brown bag that once held onions—an unforgettably powerful symbol: the redemptive humility that enables an honesty of shared feeling that is rare, indeed, among many of us.

In Carver's often bleak world this student of privilege and promise, of high intellect and proven ambition, found a suggestive, even commanding ethical vision—the possibility of human understanding that comes with a candid acknowledgment of how it goes, really, in this or that home or place of work or neighborhood. Carver's characters are hurt, some badly, and they inevitably bleed, some badly—but that young reader of his kept returning oddly strengthened, even refreshed, from such territory to his own land of comfort and accomplishment:

> We're so guarded and sure of ourselves. We're busy winning every battle, so we don't know the price we pay, or what we lose—while climbing, or holding on fast to what we've got, where we are. My roommates say that Carver is "depressing"— and I answer, it's *so* "depressing" that they can't let Carver help them see how "depressing" some of our own ideas about what's important in life can be, if you stop and really think about what we want and how we've already learned to behave. Smugness, *that's* "depressing." The idea that you're the best, and that you should grab all you can, and if anyone is in the way, that's too bad for him, *that's* "depressing." I could go on and on!

So he did, too—he kept taking Carver's stories to heart, kept wondering, through them, about his own story: the plot ahead, the characters to appear, not to mention the nature of his own future character. He remembered a moment in *Middlemarch,* when Mr. Farebrother tells Dorothea this: "Character is not cut in marble—it is not something solid and unalterable. It is something living and changing and may become diseased as our bodies do." For him such words had all possible meaning: he was making decisions that were thoroughly ethical in nature—yet there seemed to be no public acknowledgement of that side of things as he went from class to class, as he spoke to college officials, to people in "career placement." Even as I was trying to analyze certain stories, show how they were constructed, urge their aesthetic virtues on my class, he was taken by their infectious moral vitality. He wrote a story himself in which the blind man from "Cathedral" meets the woman who "stands here ironing" in the Tillie Olsen story. Her work, too, had gotten to him, hit him hard, caused him to think of men and women and children to whom he'd otherwise have given little if any thought. Whitey in Olsen's "Hey Sailor, What Ship?" belonged, of course, to Carver's human scene, but the mother who looks back at her Depression-era life as a parent was someone not only wholly new to him, but, he felt, someone uniquely, tellingly, Olsen's own, and he made it his empathic business to let that mother live in his thoughts, to flourish in his imagination, to converse with him in ways that extended the story, gave it the additional life of a reader now become an authorial comrade of sorts to a particular short story writer. In one of his papers he called upon Degas's "Les Repasseuses," with its woman standing there, ironing, while another woman yawns and holds onto a bottle of wine—he had his version of Olsen's first person narrator look hard at that painting, done a century before her time, and wonder about the lives of those two women, what *they* thought as they did their work.

If at times students like him became all too self-aware and self-critical, courtesy of the stories they were reading, an exposure to Flannery O'Connor pushed such an inclination as far as it could possibly go—yet, paradoxically, helped provide a rescuing sense of proportion. Who, after all, living in an academic setting, and with the slightest inclination to self-criticism, can brush off O'Connor's concerted assaults on pretensions, and worse, a certain kind of intellectuality. In story after story she gives flesh to her much favored, derisive word "interleckchuls"—gives us their blind arrogance, their evasions and outright duplicities, and worst of all, maybe, the manipulative egoism that keeps them forever unable to see the harmful consequences of their own behavior. A reading of O'Connor's letters (in *The Habit of Being*) lets us know that she was thoroughly self-scrutinizing, that she knew whereof she spoke in the sense that her deeply felt Catholicism confronted her all the time with the very qualities she mocked and caricatured in her fictional characters. "She is harsh," my student kept saying as he contrasted O'Connor with Olsen or Carver—and her harshness both stirred him and set him on edge.

He much enjoyed the humbling of Mr. Head in "The Artificial Nigger"—intellect unmasked for all its potential dishonesty and more than occasional malice. He saw a similar vein explored in "Everything That Rises Must Converge," and of course, "The Lame Shall Enter First." That last story, a shrewd, unnerving version of the Biblical remonstrance "Physician, heal thyself!," especially seized his attention. O'Connor jabs knowingly at the assumptions and values of secularists for whom high performance on tests and examinations is not only evidence of a certain mental capability, but something much more—a sign of felt moral superiority. Paragraph by paragraph she strips bare the self-congratulatory side of us, her readers, who (like her) are quite delighted with our ability to spot and enjoy ironies, subtleties of action, thought, mood. For her, grace from the Lord is the only hope available—her searing and sour look at us provides no merely human redemptive possibility.

It is this reasoning that prompted my student to balk—to refuse, really, her insistence on divine intervention as the only possible resolution for our deeply flawed lives. "I understand her respect for sin as just about all-powerful, except for God's intervention through grace," I was told during an unforgettable conversation, during which O'Connor was both extolled and subjected to a withering critical analysis, and then this most arresting point, an ironic commentary on her use of irony:

> The trouble is, that she forgets that she herself, on her own as a storyteller, could confront all that "darkness" in us—doesn't that say something about what's possible? I guess I'm not sure O'Connor gives herself enough credit: She's the one who brings in one story, the Christian story, to the rescue of another one, her own! There's more "hope" in us than she'll allow—that's my take on her thinking. She tears us open, and gives us a full report on all the pathology, and then she

says that the situation is impossible, and death is right around the corner—unless God intervenes; and He does, sometimes, not always. But in those stories where that intervention takes place ["the action of mercy"], it's the author working herself and the rest of us out of a big hole, it's *her* "action." I have to keep reminding myself of that [line of analysis] or else I'll just shudder, and give up! I like O'Connor as a tough observer, but I like Olsen and Carver not because they're pie-in-the-sky optimists—they sure aren't!—but because they see us, at least sometimes, as capable of breaking through to the light, finding our dignity, our decency, on our own, or with someone's help, [such as] the blind man's.

When I think of what it means to read short stories, to teach them, to figure them out and write about them, to enjoy them and let them sink into one's consciousness, one's ongoing being, I keep remembering that student, needless to say, or others, such as those I have taught under circumstances far less favorable than those that inform a university class. All the time, the stories the writers construct connect in dozens and dozens of hard-to-predict, hard-to-know ways with other stories, those personal ones being built, day after day, by readers who choose to give their time and introspective ardor to one or another piece of fiction—each of which becomes, thereby, a ray of light, a sign, a reminder, a source of entertainment, a warning, a lesson, a moment's diversion, or a life's experience of rescue. We are, obviously, creatures of language, those who are equipped distinctively to ask and wonder, to try to sort out: creatures of consciousness thoroughly aware that there is an end to this gift of life, that dust does indeed return to dust, hence time is a hauntingly finite possession. No wonder, then, that we summon words to the task of self-explanation—an attempted explanation of what has been, what is, what might be, what ought to be. No wonder, too, we call upon words to represent ourselves, divert ourselves, humor ourselves, instruct ourselves, extend ourselves imaginatively, through stories and more stories, told to one another from childhood through our last days, and told to us on paper by certain men and women who have turned an aspect of their humanity into a professional calling.

I will always remember, in this regard, the advice I received from my favorite psychoanalytic supervisor, Alfred O. Ludwig, an internist turned psychiatrist who headed the Alcoholism Clinic at the Massachusetts General Hospital in Boston, where I took my residency, and where all the time men and women right out of Tillie Olsen's fiction and Raymond Carver's (and yes, more universally, Chekhov's or Tolstoy's) came for a breather of sorts in the midst of their exceedingly burdened, hurt, and fragile lives. "They talk a lot," I once remarked to Dr. Ludwig with annoyance: "alcoholics go on and on," I observed, and thereby they don't get to the point of things, meaning the point that I wanted: a psychological revelation, no less. How to get "there," I was asking my teacher by implication, how to cut through what in my mind were wandering, pointless digressions—the seeming torrent of banter, the illusions presented as factuality, the feint and bluff and braggadocio, the hoopla going nowhere? I was a tired "house officer" turning crabby, turning inward toward self-pity, turning away from his patients, not to mention his fellow human beings, turning to an older, much wiser physician and teacher out of more desperation that I realized at the moment. Dr. Ludwig, in turn, did not strike back at me, even as he heard me striking out at others—maybe striking out, period. Rather, he encouraged me to think of my patients as people desperately anxious to be heard, to be understood, and willing to go to almost any extent, in their conversations with me, to achieve that purpose. "They are storytellers," he pointed out, "like you and me." A pause, and then a few words more: "They're trying to get some place—get to you—just as you and I are doing the same as we talk, and what better way than through a report, an account of what took place! You and I have our own notion of what 'really' took place, of course, so we get impatient; but that's *our* story—about 'them,' and their stories!"

There was more, much more—and I welcomed his detours and asides while turning my back on those of certain patients: Flannery O'Connor's *hauteur,* evoked in all her fictions, being lived out over a thousand miles from Milledgeville, Georgia, in my own life. Yet, the equivalent of her often invoked "grace," so I thought, had arrived in another's willingness (that of Dr. Ludwig) to share a word or two, to construct, actually, an alternative take on things, a different story than the one I'd chosen unwittingly, wordlessly to uphold for myself in the course of my clinical work. In a sense, back then I was privy to a prefiguration of what would happen in my Cambridge office as I sat listening to that student some forty years later: as the young man had let me know, it is possible for us to reach out to one another, give one another a necessary boost—"the Lord working through us," my student said, even as he wondered whether O'Connor wouldn't approve of such a way of putting the matter. "God Himself is a story, one of our big ones, maybe our most important one," that student also declared—not in a truculent outburst of derision or flagrant doubt, but with an obvious solemnity that was meant to express reverence rather than indulgent narcissism. But our class, I reminded myself, was one in "literature" rather than theology, and I let the comment go by: back to the short story as something to enjoy, or as a guide, a companion on this life's journey, a way, really, of taking on the world—this one, of the here and now.

C. MICHAEL CURTIS

Publishers and Publishing

*T*hough publishing isn't—and shouldn't be—the primary measure of artistic worth, it goes a long way toward affirming one's status as a writer. It certainly provides a lubricant in the complicated business of bringing together the writer and his or her audience.

Ultimately, of course, the "validity" or excellence of a piece of writing is subjective, and no writer should be intimidated by critical standards that seem unduly rigid or limiting, or that rest on arguable assumptions. On the other hand, the people who decide what gets published will necessarily have decisive ideas about where value lies in arrangements of the written word. Within reason, the more writers can do to engage the interest and sympathy of these editors, the more their manuscript submissions will get fair readings and eventually make their way into print.

Some writers unintentionally reduce their chances of getting this sympathetic and attentive reading, often for reasons that, in a perfect world, would seem only marginally relevant to the serious business of editorial assessment. Manuscripts that are single-spaced, for example, or printed on both sides of the page, place a burden that gets in the way of friendly consideration. Similarly, narrow margins—which result in lines of type too wide for the eye to grasp without moving side to side—can interfere with attentive reading. Other potential obstacles are misspelled words, faulty punctuation or grammar, needless adjectives and adverbs, repeated use of ellipses, sentence fragments, non sequiturs—in short, any writing lapse or quirk that seems certain to be followed by others, and to disappoint even the most willing reader.

What most editors look for, in addition to a respect for the conventional strengths of orderly composition, is a sentence or two sufficiently complex in structure and idea to signify a serious mind at work. Editors look for an engaging sensibility, a writer with wit, imagination, and an appreciation for the benefits of a well-constructed sentence.

Eventually, of course, a fiction editor will look for fully developed characters, for plausible and distinctive dialogue, for themes (or at least variations of familiar themes) that seem fresh and perhaps even (though not necessarily) redemptive. Editors will normally want something to happen, unless the story is static by design and offers shrewdness or an eye for unexpected detail in place of narrative momentum and resolution.

Careful writers will not lose sleep over these matters, which tend to sort themselves out automatically. Even so, such writers need to keep an eye out for awkward repetitions, or for sentences that sprawl out of control.

With a well-honed manuscript, a helpfully phrased cover letter (of which, more later), and a stamped return envelope, a writer can reasonably expect sympathetic attention and timely response. If all goes well, the manuscript may win acceptance, and even a check.

The road to publication is long and bumpy, however, and a few of the roadblocks are worth a longer look.

A friend told me recently that she was struggling to recover from a letter of rejection she'd received from an editor at *The New Yorker*. Knowing that magazine's reputation for gentleness in such matters I asked for details. "He did say my story was 'nicely done,'" she admitted, "but he explained that *The New Yorker* wasn't taking that kind of story for the time being."

As someone who has been writing letters of rejection thirty or forty times a day for more than thirty-five years, I have considerable sympathy for my friend the writer—and an appreciation for the dilemma of "the editor," someone compelled to reject far more often than accept, and to manage relationships with writers that are wildly lopsided. The editor has almost obscenely exaggerated power—since the ratio of candidates to published stories is so enormous (at least 1000:1 at *The Atlantic Monthly*), and the emotional stake in acceptance or rejection is so huge on the writer's part.

I tried to soothe my writer friend by pointing out some obvious mitigating factors: the letter was, after all, more complimentary than assaultive; most stories, inevitably, have to be returned, in spite of their virtues; editors vary widely in their tastes and tolerances; rejection in one venue doesn't mean that others won't be receptive; some work is too demanding for general readers, and is better suited to the quarterlies and other periodicals whose readership, though small, is also well educated, in literary terms, and is more receptive to experimentation, testing of boundaries, deliberate challenge of the conventions of mainstream narrative.

The truth, however, is that publication in large commercial magazines offers far more material reward, in fee, potential audience size, and stature among literary high rollers, than does an appearance in a quarterly, no matter how honored by academic or literary professionals. The pain in rejection, therefore, is more than a test of authorial tenderness. It has also to do with the wish for fame and fortune, a conviction that the smiles of certain gods are measurably sunnier than the kindly benevolence of certain others. And to some extent, of course, this perception is roughly accurate. Publication in magazine A rather than magazine B may well multiply the chances of being noticed by literary agents looking for promising new clients, or book editors scouting for undiscovered talent. In an important sense, however, authentic gifts have a way, even if slow and meandering, of making themselves known to respectful and discerning audiences. Every magazine, no matter how rigorous in its screening and selection of candidates for publication, has a history of writers misjudged, talent unappreciated, opportunities for discovery overlooked.

Some writers are spotted early and spend years struggling to justify substantial but premature reputations. Others labor fruitfully in the vineyards, publishing their work in obscure magazines and small or antiestablishment publishing houses, and then emerge suddenly and spectacularly, most often because a careful reader has written the sort of detailed and appreciative review that encourages a long second look at writing not widely circulated or taken seriously.

An overriding truth about the business of publishing is that the "good" is permanently locked in a struggle for attention with the "bad." Much of the writing that pours onto the desks of literary editors at both the serious-minded but commercial general magazines and the smallest, most fiercely independent quarterlies is inept, undeveloped, amateurish, crazed, obscene, unintelligible, or some combination of the above. Sometimes the problem is developmental: the author may well have talent, but has little sense of form or is lazy about detail, mechanical or otherwise. Such writers may develop the discipline and controlled imagination necessary to engage the attention of serious readers. Others won't: they are like untrained athletes who haven't learned fundamentals, good practice habits, or how to place themselves realistically vis-à-vis the competition. Or they are handicapped by temperament or other cognitive shortcomings. Whatever the problem, their work must be assessed by readers who bring to every manuscript the hope that it will prove artful or publishable. This takes time, and can often lead to impatience, irritation, eventually to a resignation that gets in the way of attentiveness to the off-beat, slowly paced, loosely stitched, or otherwise idiosyncratic fiction offering. Fiction editors may read as many as forty to fifty stories a day, and the chances are that the ratio of good to bad will be roughly one to ten. Writers can do nothing about this, of course, but realism about the process may make living with it more comfortable.

HOW TO READ A REJECTION SLIP

Virtually all magazines have printed rejection slips. Some make their points succinctly, with little attempts to soften the blow. The basic message is straightforward: "We've decided not to publish your story." Some rejection forms make a half-hearted effort to explain away the obvious: "We're not reading fiction for the time being" or "another editor may think differently" (i.e., the problem may be ours and not yours). A few try diplomacy: "We're grateful for the chance to read your work." And others are mildly apologetic: "We're sorry that the quantity of manuscripts we consider makes it impossible to reply to each one personally." At bottom, however, the message is no more and likely no less than, simply, "No."

Some stories returned with form rejections may have intrigued an editor or two, or even been seriously considered for publication. The vast majority, however, have simply failed to make the cut—for reasons that will range from instantaneous and wholly justified discouragement to mild admiration. Either way, a writer ought to fight the impulse to read the rejection as a sign of repudiation, hostility, or proof of ineptitude.

Magazines that have a reputation for thoughtfulness in their selection of fiction, particularly magazines that—like *The Atlantic Monthly*—read all work submitted, whether sent by an agent, a writer, or some other friend of the court, receive many more manuscripts each day than the fiction editors can respond to individually. In a typical day, roughly 100 fiction manuscripts arrive at *The Atlantic Monthly.* Of those no more than a dozen or two are likely to be returned with a personal reply. Apart from the most pressing reason for this impersonal response—the absence of staff members who could undertake such a job—most editors would rather not explain how unimpressed they are by a story that wildly misses the mark. Nor do they want to take the time to think through and then articulate their reasons for deciding against a story whose first few sentences or paragraphs are grammatically unsound, visibly inept, or essentially incoherent. Why make explanations that can only wound? And why misrepresent your judgment by pretending admiration that isn't felt?

In short, little can safely be read into a form rejection, and the safest course, it seems to me, is to accept the verdict as gracefully as possible, and try other markets very quickly, so as to transfer emotional energy from the depleting slough of despond to the hopefulness that arises while a manuscript is "under consideration elsewhere." One writer I know took the further step of using his rejection forms as a form of interior decoration. He covered his bathroom door with them, and thus greeted each new one as an artistic challenge: he sought the most pleasing assemblage of typefaces, paper qualities, and manner of editorial apologetics.

Some magazines confuse the issue by using more than one rejection form. *The Atlantic Monthly,* for many years, sent a rejection slip printed in italics, conveying measured admiration for the work being returned and apologizing for the necessity of the printed form. Many writers who received this form (some of whom had long experience with the more cursory basic rejection) believed they were finally on the verge of an important breakthrough and would remind us with every submission that they were now among the chosen. Little could they have imagined that those italicized forms were intended, by a now departed editor, to be sent to the population groups who seemed most likely to expect special handling: the very old, the very young, prison inmates, mental patients, and others with an exaggerated sense of professional importance. Editors or others at *The New Yorker* have for years diluted the damaging potency of form rejection by adding, in pencil, the simple word "sorry." I'm certain that thousands of would-be contributors to *The New Yorker* have been heartened by that small note of personal regret, and have felt, rightly or wrongly, that an actual person had read their story submission and had felt right at home in it.

A significant step up from the rejection form is the personal letter, no matter how brief or general in its response. Fiction editors rarely write such letters unless they've seen writing of real quality, even in stories they don't want to publish. The exceptions: manuscripts from writers who seem to warrant a personal response by virtue of professional reputation, personal acquaintance, or documented volatility. Editors know, however, that once a writer hears personally from an editor that writer will expect personal communiqués from that day forward. As a consequence, the temptation to use form rejections is all but irresistible.

The personal letter may or may not offer detailed criticism or suggestions for the repair of "flawed" stories. One reason: some writers are fiercely protective of the quirkiness in their work and resist the idea that editorial resistance equates with authorial flaw. The editor is entitled to his or her opinion, such writers reason. But the "problem" may be less in the writing than in the limitations of the reader. From time to time this position is surely justified, and writers ought not to blithely accept criticisms of their stories that don't seem sensible or sensitive to their intentions. On the other hand, the editors are speaking for the sensibilities that determine what is chosen for publication and what is not, and their letters should be read with that practical object in mind—and not taken as definitive judgments of a story's worth, tactical logic, promise, or objective coherence. A balance is useful, however, between a writer's wholly understandable and necessary obligation to defend his or her work and the possibility that an editor's trained eye has spotted genuine flaws or has at least made intelligible the reason for rejection.

In most cases, the editor will have responded favorably to aspects of the work and is hoping that a revision, or another story by the same author, will lead to publication. The desirability of this stance cannot be overstated, and a wise writer will do all that is possible to nurture it—all that is possible, once again, without abandoning the writer's creative vision and purpose.

COVER LETTERS

Most short story submissions arrive accompanied by a cover letter, introducing the story and its author and affecting a sort of breaking of the ice, rather like a handshake greeting with a complete stranger. This introduction is a good idea, for the same reason that a brief, general greeting helps set the stage for other, more complicated social occasions. The absence of a cover letter signifies a disdain for interpersonal protocol, or an indifference that borders on the mechanical. I doubt that a publishable story has ever been turned away simply because its author failed to send a cover letter, but editors are as susceptible as anyone to the small gestures that convey friendliness or, in their absence, suggest an indifference seemingly bordering on contempt.

Even so, just as an overly aggressive or an inappropriately personal greeting can undermine a social transaction before it has a chance to develop, so a poorly conceived cover letter can discourage an editor from proceeding on to read the story to which it is attached.

Some mistakes are fundamental. Few editors like to have a story submission explained to them, and few experienced writers feel they can "explain" in a few short sentences what required the length of their narrative to express. Indeed, stories that can easily be summarized in a sentence or two may be little more than exercises extending or dramatizing the proposition imbedded in those sentences. In general, the more sophisticated and successful the writer, the more firmly he or she resists any invitation to encapsulate briefly stories that, to borrow from MacLeish, "must not mean, but be."

To make matters worse, writers—particularly beginning writers—are not always clear about the purposes or effects of their stories, and their cheerfully sculpted explanations may differ markedly from the conclusions likely to be drawn by a careful reader. Better by far to let the story speak for itself.

Another occasional error, usually made by beginners (and thus inadvertently damning—why advertise your relative lack of experience, when what you hope to do is convince an editor of your wisdom and mastery of craft?), is a reference to the response of other magazines to the story now being submitted, or, in extreme cases, a copy of the other magazine's rejection letter.

Although intended, no doubt, to suggest long and complicated involvement with the inner world of literary publishing, this history of rejection has several unintended consequences, none of them fortuitous. In addition to announcing yourself as a beginner (see above), your shared confidence permits a magazine editor to surmise at least the following:

His or her magazine (1) is well below the top of your list of preferred markets and (2) may even be a sort of "what's to lose" remote possibility, once you've exhausted the markets you think may be appropriate for your story.

The truth, of course, may be quite different. A writer's order of submission may have to do with personal acquaintance among editors, for example, or a willingness to honor a specific request for material from one editor or another. These aren't matters to be discussed in a cover letter, however, and the best solution is to keep a dignified silence about them.

In keeping with the above, a battered, coffee-stained, many times folded and unfolded manuscript reinforces the idea that a story has been making the rounds for years without success. Prickly editors may well feel, and be displeased by, the notion that their magazine is a court of last resort.

These matters aside, some writers believe their cover letters provide an opportunity to catch the eye of an editor with witticisms, evidence of substantial ego strength, or thinly disguised declarations of artistic independence. These messages do catch the eye of editors, but they're so predictably coupled with inept or artless manuscripts that their unhappy effect is to discourage further reading.

One writer, for example, sent me a cover letter with the following candid note:

> I have taken writing courses at [schools A, B, and C] but none of them have done me much good. Currently I teach at [school D], where they have been unable to nullify my contract. My publication list is unimpressive, and I am ugly.

This is hardly an in-your-face cover letter, and it conveys, at the least, a disarming humility. It does not, however, inspire an editor to read further.

Another, noticeably less self-effacing, writer accompanied a story submission with a letter that included the following

This [story one of a series] is enclosed for your reading satisfaction. You won't understand it, so don't even try. All you need to do is assess its value.

You must naturally assume that the less you understand of it, the better it is. All you need to determine is whether or not you can market this talent. That you are inept at judging its merit I already know from experience. That you will probably waste a lot of time and continue in your blindness, I already know. I think very little of your profession. People like you have been wasting my time for almost half my life now. Since I already know that the likelihood that you are qualified is extremely low, would you please do me the favor of responding in a timely fashion so that I may attempt some other method of gaining notoriety?

All this, from a writer unknown to us and submitting to *The Atlantic Monthly,* so far as we could tell, for the first time. This letter has the virtue of finely honed pugnacity, and it makes mildly interesting reading. But would any thoughtful reader expect the story attached to be inspiring or artfully imagined?

What should a good cover letter include? In my judgment it can provide at least two kinds of helpful information—helpful in the sense that it may dispose the editor to which it is addressed to give the accompanying story the benefit of the doubt: if the beginning is slow or eccentric, further reading may reward. The information that may fortify an editor's willingness to push on is this: (1) citations of stories published elsewhere, particularly in periodicals of comparable size and reputation; and (2) the note that the writer is or has been enrolled in a reputable MFA program, or has in some other way (residence at Bread Loaf or Sewanee, for example) demonstrated an interest in writing as a long-term endeavor, along with a willingness to be helped toward that end.

Virtually all editors of serious fiction realize that today's Iowa or Stanford or Johns Hopkins MFA student may be tomorrow's Raymond Carver, Flannery O'Connor, or Ethan Canin. These and other graduate writing programs generate a steady flow of talented, still-forming writers of fiction, and work from such programs tends to merit close readings. From the editor's perspective, even if stories from these programs are returned, a friendly and encouraging (ideally comprehensive) letter may pay dividends.

Beyond that sort of information, and ordinary civility, a cover letter ought to be brief and to the point. It should not be an impediment to respectful attention, and it may greatly increase a writer's opportunity to be read with seriousness and conditioned hopefulness.

QUARTERLIES VERSUS SLICKS

Once a fiction manuscript is ready for submission, where should it be sent, and what protocols should the writer observe? What kind of treatment can be expected? And should a writer start with the most competitive markets, then work down? Or choose the path of least resistance—a low circulation, less well-known quarterly—rather than face the likelihood of repeated rejection from the more esteemed magazines?

As luck would have it, some of the best known magazines are also the best paying, and one of these, *The New Yorker,* prints roughly fifty issues per year, and so can publish more fiction than even the literary-minded *The Atlantic Monthly, Harper's, Esquire,* and *GQ,* each a monthly that rarely averages more than one story per issue. Fees at *The New Yorker* arise out of calculations known only to its editors, but they seem to depend on frequency of publication in that magazine, length, and other factors, and range upward from a base of several thousand dollars. The monthlies hover slightly below or above $3,000 per story, as does *Playboy.* In the past, several women's magazines were strong fiction markets, but that seems to have changed, and only *Redbook* can now be said to look carefully for "literary" fiction, though *Redbook,* like other magazines with an overwhelmingly female readership, wants a youngish female point of view, accessible prose, and a relatively upbeat resolution. Conversely, *Playboy, Esquire, GQ,* and a number of even more specialized magazines are edited chiefly for male readers and seek a conspicuously masculine point of view in stories with a strong sense of event.

Publishing fiction in these large, slick, commercial magazines has the obvious advantage of significant financial return. They also reach a large number of readers, at least a portion of whom can be counted on to take literature seriously, to buy books, to help create an audience for essentially unknown writers. The fiction editors of these magazines tend to be, and to be known as, serious and attentive readers of fiction. Hence their judgments are often heeded and can become a factor in the wider world of publishing, as literary agents and book editors (who keep an eye on these magazines) try to decide who—among many claimants—is worth the investment of reading time and publishing investment.

On the down side is that competition for space in these magazines is intense. *The Atlantic Monthly* receives more than 12,000 stories each year, though it publishes only twelve to fifteen. *The New Yorker* no doubt receives still more candidates for its roughly fifty (the number seems to be shrinking slightly) annual fiction slots. So the odds are long, the quality of the competition is likely to be intimidating, and the chances of a swift decision are uncertain. A wait of several months is not unusual, and, inevitably, some manuscripts are mislaid, not closely read, or returned without comment—leaving the writer uncertain how he or she is faring in the scramble for respectful attention.

Unfortunately, the same problems occur when stories are sent to the alternative markets, though fewer manuscripts are in the mix and far greater tolerance of idiosyncrasy or not-yet-fully-developed talent is likely to be the rule.

In the first tier of so-called quarterlies (magazines published irregularly or at least no more than four times yearly, often sponsored and/or partially subsidized by a college or university, and typically edited by members of the English department at the sponsoring school) are magazines such as *DoubleTake, Story, Paris Review, Granta, Grand Street,* and a few others, which pay generous fees for fiction (in the $500 to $1,500 range), are edited by full-time, salaried professionals, and have a national, respectful readership. *Story,* once a major

player in the literary marketplace, faded from sight in the 1960s and 1970s and
has now been revitalized by a new editorial staff and dependable financing. Its
issues contain ten or more fiction listings, and are likely to include the work of
a number of able if relatively unknown talents.

All of these magazines are followed closely by agents, editors, and serious
readers, and, as a consequence, competition for space in these magazines is
formidable.

A second tier of quarterlies includes venerable publications such as *Georgia Review, Virginia Quarterly, Epoch, Prairie Schooner, Antaeus, Hudson
Review, Yale Review, Southwest Review, Northwest Review, Ploughshares, Agni,*
and others. These magazines have been around for years, typically since the
years immediately after World War II, when federal and state money was for a
few years available in the form of cultural seed money, and a number of serious-minded veterans found ways to make use of it.

These magazines reach a small readership, but it is loyal, well-read, and
patient with eccentricities that face resistance among editors at the larger magazines. Moreover, they're examined faithfully by those who nominate stories for
inclusion in the annual *Best American Short Stories* or *O. Henry Award* anthologies, and publication in any of them helps establish the credentials of a writer
seeking to sell a story collection or a novel.

A third tier of quarterlies includes just about every other small magazine
that publishes fiction, including at least a few well-funded newcomers like
Manoa, that specialize in the writing of minority cultures. Still others seek out,
more or less deliberately, work considered too scandalous or antinarrative for
representatives of a very broad mainstream. Many hundreds of these magazines
appear in bookstores and through subscriptions, though their existence is often
precarious. Publication in any of them is a plus, even if payment often is in kind
and readership is severely limited.

Whenever work is submitted, particularly in recent years, it ought to be
accompanied by a stamped, self-addressed return envelope. Even if you want
only news of a decision, you may not get one unless you send an SASE. And
don't expect a manuscript to be squeezed into a letter-sized envelope. If you
want the manuscript returned, send an appropriately sized—and stamped—
manila envelope.

SIMULTANEOUS SUBMISSIONS

Editors dislike simultaneous submissions, both because they offend the editor's
sense of exclusivity and because they invite the apprehension that valuable editorial decision-making time may prove wasted. Writers like them for an obvious reason: They reduce the time spent waiting for a decision. Since news of a
simultaneous submission may predispose an editor to give a manuscript short
shrift, I suggest a compromise. Send your manuscript to only one magazine at
a time, but after four to six weeks send an inquiry and declare, as pleasantly as
you can manage, that you'd like to feel free to submit your manuscript else-

where if you haven't heard anything in four more weeks, or less if you feel testy.

Few magazines are very efficient in reading and making decisions about manuscripts, and quarterlies—many of whose editors have full-time teaching or graduate student responsibilities elsewhere—are often the worst offenders. Try not to take delay personally, however. It rarely *is* personal, and friendly persistence on your part will loosen the log jam more frequently and equably than expressions of fury and indignation.

At the very least, if you feel compelled to send manuscripts to several magazines simultaneously, and you don't mind irritating an editor or two in the process, make sure you acknowledge what you're doing. To do otherwise is to invite a calamity that can only lead to hard feelings and is sure to contaminate your future relationships with all parties concerned.

Bear in mind that manuscripts are occasionally lost, no matter how scrupulously a magazine's editorial staff strives to manage the flow in and out. Make sure you keep a copy of anything you submit, anywhere, and allow at least a month or two to pass before worrying about misadventure.

At *The Atlantic Monthly,* most submissions that seem unsuited for publication are returned swiftly, often in a matter of days. The more promising manuscripts, however, are likely to be read by several editors, each of whom has many other chores, so the process is extended, often to an extent that can seem excruciating to the writer.

GENERAL CAUTIONS

A sensible writer will examine the contents of any magazine to which he or she wishes to send a manuscript. Take note of the length of stories there in print, and bear in mind that any typescript of more than twenty-five pages is going to seem "long" to a magazine editor. The absolute limit may vary from magazine to magazine (*Triquarterly* and *Paris Review,* for example, seem more patient with novella-length stories than most magazines), but thirty-five pages is an approximate outer limit for many, and a length of twelve to eighteen pages is far safer for many others.

Take note of language. Commercial magazines such as *The Atlantic Monthly* and *The New Yorker* have loosened up considerably in the past fifteen to twenty years, but still have a substantial readership (and editors) who resist what some call earthy frankness, and others call obscenity. Whatever one's views on the question, you waste time sending material to a magazine that can't publish it.

Bear in mind, as above, that some magazines want *only* stories told from a specified point of view, and involving characters of a certain age and type. All of this can be discerned by intelligent reading, and although you don't want to hamstring yourself by assuming too much about a magazine's likes and dislikes, you do yourself a favor by thinking about which, of the many available markets, will see your story as a good fit.

WHY PUBLISH

The value of a record of published work cannot be overstated. Introducing the work of a new writer is expensive and risky, regardless of the work's merit, and book publishers will always be more enthusiastic about a collection of stories, for example, if some or all of the stories have appeared previously in magazines, even small ones. Publication in a reputable quarterly means exposure, means the beginning of the development of an audience.

Publication is also a way of establishing one's credentials as a "professional," as someone whose work has been deemed publishable by one or more editors who are assumed to be choosy as well as students of the genre. As publication credits accumulate and if, ideally, they include one or more of the most reputable magazines or quarterlies, your chances improve of having your work read with more than the usual attention and patience. A careful reading does not ensure publication, of course, but it may well create a favorable impression with the editor in question, and heighten the likelihood that subsequent submissions will be read with interest and hopefulness.

Above all, don't let finished stories collect quietly in a desk drawer somewhere, out of misplaced modesty and a mistaken idea that stories can be placed individually once a book publisher agrees to publish them as a collection. The likelihood is that your window of opportunity will be small, probably twelve months or so. And you must bear in mind that most magazines, particularly the top of the line commercial magazines, want to publish stories *only* prior to book publication. Given the lead time of most monthlies (at any point in time *The Atlantic Monthly,* for example, is planning issues at least three months ahead, and may well have committed its fiction slots several months beyond that) that twelve month gap quickly shrinks to nine months. And if you factor in other considerations (magazines tend not to want to publish short stories at precisely the same time their competitors are publishing work by the same author, and some editors shy away from picking over work they may feel has already been judged "less successful" by other magazines), the problem of placing unpublished stories prior to book publication becomes all but unmanageable.

EDITORS

I doubt that any generalization about fiction editors is truly dependable or revealing. Apart from the obvious—an educated interest in short narrative forms—the most likely attributes will be something like the following:

- A capacity to read quickly and decisively. A fiction editor needs to know what he or she likes, and why, and must trust that judgment on an all but instinctive level. If that were not true, the chore of sorting through hundreds or thousands of manuscripts in search of publishable nuggets would become disorienting and insupportable.

- A liberal arts background, though not necessarily in English or literature, and not always arising out of a university education of particular distinction, or any formal higher education at all. Intellectual curiosity, however, is likely to be a conspicuous part of the mix.

- The ability and willingness to explain a story's shortcomings, as the editor perceives them, and to do so in understandable language and with, usually, admirable gentleness. A misanthrope simply couldn't survive the prickly diplomacy often required to negotiate between competing visions (the editor's and the author's) of a story about to be published. Nor could a reflexive grouch find ways to return dozens of stories each day without antagonizing or permanently wounding writers, many of whom take rejection personally.

As noted above, the message from editor to writer is often a mixed one. "We admire the story, for reasons we can enumerate, and we are confident it will be published. But not, alas, by us." A writer can hardly be blamed for wondering over such a response. But the alternatives—unexplained dismissal or disingenuousness—are not attractive or sustainable.

Fiction editors will have ideas about how a story can be improved, and at least some of these ideas will prove to be inspired. Others may seem (and may well be) merely meddlesome, or to stem from a failure to grasp nuances the writer has carefully considered. In the long run, the writer should have the last word, even if that means withdrawing a story rather than having it altered in ways that can't be borne.

Magazines that are sensitive to this tension send galleys to their authors, so that manuscript changes can be assessed and, if necessary, resisted. A fiction editor should be able to justify any such change, and writers should not hesitate to ask for that explanation. The changes, of course, may well be helpful; may tighten sentences that seem sprawling or wordy; may root out clumsy repetitions, or errors of grammar or syntax; may identify inconsistencies in detail, or questionable references that need shortening or alteration. The more skilled and attentive the editor, the more likely it is that troublesome references will be spotted and either eliminated or revised. I'd advise writers to be hopeful and open-minded in their dealing with fiction editors, but to resist changes that alter their meaning or undercut the distinctiveness of their language. The final product, simply, must be writing with which both editor and writer are content. Where that is not possible, the story ought to be withdrawn, or its purchase reconsidered.

PART 2

Short Stories

GUY DE MAUPASSANT

The String

Translated from the French by Ernest Boyd

Along all the roads around Goderville the peasants and their wives were coming towards the little town, for it was market-day. The men walked with plodding steps, their bodies bent forward at each thrust of their long bowed legs. They were deformed by hard work, by the pull of the heavy plough which raises the left shoulder and twists the torso, by the reaping of the wheat which forces the knees apart to get a firm stand, by all the slow and strenuous labors of life on the farm. Their blue smocks, starched, shining as if varnished, ornamented with a little design in white at the neck and wrists, puffed about their bony bodies, seemed like balloons ready to carry them off. From each smock a head, two arms, and two feet protruded.

Some led a cow or a calf at the end of a rope, and their wives, walking behind the animal, whipped its haunches with a leafy branch to hasten its progress. They carried on their arms large wicker-baskets, out of which here a chicken and there a duck thrust forth its head. The women walked with a quicker, livelier step than their husbands. Their spare, straight figures were wrapped in a scanty little shawl, pinned over their flat bosoms, and their heads were enveloped in a piece of white linen tightly pressed on the hair and surmounted by a cap.

Then a wagon passed, its nag's jerky trot shaking up and down two men seated side by side and a woman in the bottom of the vehicle, the latter holding on to the sides to lessen the stiff jolts.

The square of Goderville was filled with a milling throng of human beings and animals. The horns of the cattle, the rough-napped top-hats of the rich peasants, and the headgear of the peasant women stood out in the crowd. And the clamorous, shrill, shouting voices made a continuous and savage din dominated now and again by the robust lungs of some countryman's laugh, or the long lowing of a cow tied to the wall of a house.

The scene smacked of the stable, the dairy and the dung-heap, of hay and sweat, and gave forth that sharp, unpleasant odor, human and animal, peculiar to the people of the fields.

Maître Hauchecorne, of Bréauté, had just arrived at Goderville. He was directing his steps toward the square, when he perceived upon the ground a little piece of string. Maître Hauchecorne, economical like a true Norman, thought that everything useful ought to be picked up, and he stooped painfully, for he suffered from rheumatism. He took up the bit of string from the ground and was beginning to roll it carefully when he noticed Maître Malandain, the harness-maker, on the threshold of his door, looking at him. They had once had a quarrel on the subject of a halter, and they had remained on bad terms, being both good haters. Maître Hauchecorne was seized with a sort of shame to be seen thus by his enemy, picking a bit of string out of the dirt. He hid his find quickly under his smock, and slipped it into his trouser pocket; then he pretended to be still looking on the ground for something which he did not find, and he went towards the market, his head thrust forward, bent double by his pain.

He was soon lost in the noisy and slowly moving crowd, which was busy with interminable bargainings. The peasants looked at cows, went away, came back, perplexed, always in fear of being cheated, not daring to decide, watching the vendor's eye, ever trying to find the trick in the man and the flaw in the beast.

The women, having placed their great baskets at their feet, had taken out the poultry, which lay upon the ground, tied together by the feet, with terrified eyes and scarlet crests.

They listened to offers, stated their prices with a dry air and impassive face, or perhaps, suddenly deciding on some proposed reduction, shouted to the customer who was slowly going away: "All right, Maître Anthime, I'll let you have it for that."

Then little by little the square was deserted, the church bell rang out the hour of noon, and those who lived too far away went to the different inns.

At Jourdain's the great room was full of people eating, and the big yard was full of vehicles of all kinds, gigs, wagons, nondescript carts, yellow with dirt, mended and patched, some with their shafts rising to the sky like two arms, others with their shafts on the ground and their backs in the air.

Behind the diners seated at table, the immense fireplace, filled with bright flames, cast a lively heat on the backs of the row on the right. Three spits were turning on which were chickens, pigeons, and legs of mutton; and an appetizing odor of roast meat and gravy dripping over the nicely browned skin rose from the fireplace, lightening all hearts and making the mouth water.

All the aristocracy of the plough ate there, at Maître Jourdain's, tavern keeper and horse dealer, a clever fellow and well off.

The dishes were passed and emptied, as were the jugs of yellow cider. Everyone told his affairs, his purchases, and sales. They discussed the crops. The weather was favorable for the greens but rather damp for the wheat.

Suddenly the drum began to beat in the yard, before the house. Everybody rose, except a few indifferent persons, and ran to the door, or to the windows, their mouths still full, their napkins in their hands.

After the public crier had stopped beating his drum, he called out in a jerky voice, speaking his phrases irregularly:

"It is hereby made known to the inhabitants of Goderville, and in general to all persons present at the market, that there was lost this morning, on the road to Benzeville, between nine and ten o'clock, a black leather pocketbook containing five hundred francs and some business papers. The finder is requested to return same to the Mayor's office or to Maître Fortuné Houlbrèque of Manneville. There will be twenty francs' reward."

Then the man went away. The heavy roll of the drum and the crier's voice were again heard at a distance.

Then they began to talk of this event discussing the chances that Maître Houlbrèque had of finding or not finding his pocketbook.

And the meal concluded. They were finishing their coffee when the chief of the gendarmes appeared upon the threshold.

He inquired:

"Is Maître Hauchecorne, of Bréauté, here?"

Maître Hauchecorne, seated at the other end of the table, replied:

"Here I am."

And the officer resumed:

"Maître Hauchecorne, will you have the goodness to accompany me to the Mayor's office? The Mayor would like to talk to you."

The peasant, surprised and disturbed, swallowed at a draught his tiny glass of brandy, rose, even more bent than in the morning, for the first steps after each rest were specially difficult, and set out, repeating: "Here I am, here I am."

The Mayor was waiting for him, seated in an armchair. He was the local lawyer, a stout, solemn man, fond of pompous phrases.

"Maître Hauchecorne," said he, "you were seen this morning picking up, on the road to Benzeville, the pocketbook lost by Maître Houlbrèque, of Manneville."

The countryman looked at the Mayor in astonishment, already terrified by this suspicion resting on him without his knowing why.

"Me? Me? I picked up the pocketbook?"

"Yes, you, yourself."

"On my word of honor, I never heard of it."

"But you were seen."

"I was seen, me? Who says he saw me?"

"Monsieur Malandain, the harness-maker."

The old man remembered, understood, and flushed with anger.

"Ah, he saw me, the clodhopper, he saw me pick up this string, here, Mayor." And rummaging in his pocket he drew out the little piece of string.

But the Mayor, incredulous, shook his head.

"You will not make me believe, Maître Hauchecorne, that Monsieur Malandain, who is a man we can believe, mistook this string for a pocketbook."

The peasant, furious, lifted his hand, spat at one side to attest his honor, repeating:

"It is nevertheless God's own truth, the sacred truth. I repeat it on my soul and my salvation."

The Mayor resumed:

"After picking up the object, you went on staring, looking a long while in the mud to see if any piece of money had fallen out."

The old fellow choked with indignation and fear.

"How anyone can tell—how anyone can tell—such lies to take away an honest man's reputation! How can anyone——"

There was no use in his protesting, nobody believed him. He was confronted with Monsieur Malandain, who repeated and maintained his affirmation. They abused each other for an hour. At his own request, Maître Hauchecorne was searched. Nothing was found on him.

Finally the Mayor, very much perplexed, discharged him with the warning that he would consult the Public Prosecutor and ask for further orders.

The news had spread. As he left the Mayor's office, the old man was surrounded and questioned with a serious or bantering curiosity, in which there was no indignation. He began to tell the story of the string. No one believed him. They laughed at him.

He went along, stopping his friends, beginning endlessly his statement and his protestations, showing his pockets turned inside out, to prove that he had nothing.

They said:

"Ah, you old rascal!"

And he grew angry, becoming exasperated, hot and distressed at not being believed, not knowing what to do and endlessly repeating himself.

Night came. He had to leave. He started on his way with three neighbors to whom he pointed out the place where he had picked up the bit of string; and all along the road he spoke of his adventure.

In the evening he took a turn in the village of Bréauté, in order to tell it to everybody. He only met with incredulity.

It made him ill all night.

The next day about one o'clock in the afternoon, Marius Paumelle, a hired man in the employ of Maître Breton, husbandman at Ymauville, returned the pocketbook and its contents to Maître Houlbréque of Manneville.

This man claimed to have found the object in the road; but not knowing how to read, he had carried it to the house and given it to his employer.

The news spread through the neighborhood. Maître Hauchecorne was informed of it. He immediately went the circuit and began to recount his story completed by the happy climax. He triumphed.

"What grieved me so much was not the thing itself, as the lying. There is nothing so shameful as to be placed under a cloud on account of a lie."

He talked of his adventure all day long, he told it on the highway to people who were passing by, in the inn to people who were drinking there, and to persons coming out of church the following Sunday. He stopped strangers to tell them about it. He was calm now, and yet something disturbed him without his knowing exactly what it was. People seemed to wink at him while they listened. They did not seem convinced. He had the feeling that remarks were being made behind his back.

On Tuesday of the next week he went to the market at Goderville, urged solely by the necessity he felt of discussing the case.

Malandain, standing at his door, began to laugh on seeing him pass. Why?

He approached a farmer from Criquetot, who did not let him finish, and giving him a poke in the stomach said to his face:

"You clever rogue."

Then he turned his back on him.

Maître Hauchecorne was confused, why was he called a clever rogue?

When he was seated at the table, in Jourdain's tavern he commenced to explain "the affair."

A horse-dealer from Monvilliers called to him:

"Come, come, old sharper, that's an old trick; I know all about your piece of string!"

Hauchecorne stammered:

"But the pocketbook was found."

But the other man replied:

"That'll do to tell, pop. One man finds a thing, and another man brings it back. No one is any the wiser, so you get out of it."

The peasant stood choking. He understood. They accused him of having had the pocketbook returned by a confederate, by an accomplice.

He tried to protest. All the table began to laugh.

He could not finish his dinner and went away in the midst of jeers.

He went home ashamed and indignant, choking with anger and confusion, the more dejected for the fact that he with his Norman cunning was capable of doing what they had accused him of, and even of boasting of it as a good trick. His innocence seemed to him, in a confused way, impossible to prove, for his sharpness was well known. And he was stricken to the heart by the injustice of the suspicion.

Then he began to recount the adventure again, enlarging his story every day, adding each time new reasons, more energetic protestations, more solemn oaths which he formulated and prepared in his hours of solitude, his whole mind given up to the story of the string. The more complicated his defense and the more subtle his argument, the less he was believed.

"Those are lying excuses," people said behind his back.

He felt it, ate his heart out over it, and wore himself out with useless efforts. He was visibly wasting away.

The wags now made him tell about the string to amuse them, as they make a soldier who has been on a campaign tell about his battles. His mind, seriously affected, began to weaken.

Towards the end of December he took to his bed.

He died early in January, and in the delirium of his death struggles he continued to protest his innocence, and to repeat his story:

"A piece of string, a piece of string—look—here it is."

ANTON CHEKHOV

The Lady with the Pet Dog
Translated by Avrahm Yarmolinsky

I

A new person, it was said, had appeared on the esplanade: a lady with a pet dog. Dmitry Dmitrich Gurov, who had spent a fortnight at Yalta and had got used to the place, had also begun to take an interest in new arrivals. As he sat in Vernet's confectionery shop, he saw, walking on the esplanade, a fair-haired young woman of medium height, wearing a beret; a white Pomeranian was trotting behind her.

And afterwards he met her in the public garden and in the square several times a day. She walked alone, always wearing the same beret and always with the white dog; no one knew who she was and everyone called her simply "the lady with the pet dog."

"If she is here alone without husband or friends," Gurov reflected, "it wouldn't be a bad thing to make her acquaintance."

He was under forty, but he already had a daughter twelve years old, and two sons at school. They had found a wife for him when he was very young, a student in his second year, and by now she seemed half as old again as he. She was a tall, erect woman with dark eyebrows, stately and dignified and, as she said of herself, intellectual. She read a great deal, used simplified spelling in her letters, called her husband, not Dmitry, but Dimitry, while he privately considered her of limited intelligence, narrow-minded, dowdy, was afraid of her, and did not like to be at home. He had begun being unfaithful to her long ago—had been unfaithful to her often and, probably for that reason, almost always spoke ill of women, and when they were talked of in his presence used to call them "the inferior race."

It seemed to him that he had been sufficiently tutored by bitter experience to call them what he pleased, and yet he could not have lived without "the inferior race" for two days together. In the company of men he was bored and ill at ease, he was chilly and uncommunicative with them; but when he was among women he felt free, and knew what to speak to them about and how to comport himself; and even to be silent with them was no strain on him. In his appearance, in his character, in his whole make-up there was something attractive and elusive that disposed women in his favor and allured them. He knew that, and some force seemed to draw him to them, too.

Oft-repeated and really bitter experience had taught him long ago that with decent people—particularly Moscow people—who are irresolute and slow to move, every affair which at first seems a light and charming adventure inevitably grows into a whole problem of extreme complexity, and in the end a painful situation is created. But at every new meeting with an interesting woman this lesson of experience seemed to slip from his memory, and he was eager for life, and everything seemed so simple and diverting.

One evening while he was dining in the public garden the lady in the beret walked up without haste to take the next table. Her expression, her gait, her dress, and the way she did her hair told him that she belonged to the upper class, that she was married, that she was in Yalta for the first time and alone, and that she was bored there. The stories told of the immorality in Yalta are to a great extent untrue; he despised them, and knew that such stories were made up for the most part by persons who would have been glad to sin themselves if they had had the chance; but when the lady sat down at the next table three paces from him, he recalled these stories of easy conquests, of trips to the mountains, and the tempting thought of a swift, fleeting liaison, a romance with an unknown woman of whose very name he was ignorant, suddenly took hold of him.

He beckoned invitingly to the Pomeranian, and when the dog approached him, shook his finger at it. The Pomeranian growled; Gurov threatened it again.

The lady glanced at him and at once dropped her eyes.

"He doesn't bite," she said and blushed.

"May I give him a bone?" he asked; and when she nodded he inquired affably, "Have you been in Yalta long?"

"About five days."

"And I am dragging out the second week here."

There was a short silence.

"Time passes quickly, and yet it is so dull here!" she said, not looking at him.

"It's only the fashion to say it's dull here. A provincial will live in Belyov or Zhizdra and not be bored, but when he comes here it's 'Oh, the dullness! Oh, the dust!' One would think he came from Granada."

She laughed. Then both continued eating in silence, like strangers, but after dinner they walked together and there sprang up between them the light banter of people who are free and contented, to whom it does not matter where they go or what they talk about. They walked and talked of the strange light on the sea: the water was a soft, warm, lilac color, and there was a golden band of moonlight upon it. They talked of how sultry it was after a hot day. Gurov told her that he was a native of Moscow, that he had studied languages and literature at the university, but had a post in a bank; that at one time he had trained to become an opera singer but had given it up, that he owned two houses in Moscow. And he learned from her that she had grown up in Petersburg, but had lived in S——since her marriage two years previously, that she was going to stay in Yalta for about another month, and that her husband, who needed a rest, too, might perhaps come to fetch her. She was not certain whether her husband was a member of a Government Board or served on a Zemstvo Council,[1] and this amused her. And Gurov learned too that her name was Anna Sergeyevna.

Afterwards in his room at the hotel he thought about her—and was certain that he would meet her the next day. It was bound to happen. Getting into bed he recalled that she had been a schoolgirl only recently, doing lessons like his own daughter; he thought how much timidity and angularity there was still in her laugh and her manner of talking with a stranger. It must have been the first time in her life that she was alone in a setting in which she was followed, looked at, and spoken to for one secret purpose alone, which she could hardly fail to guess. He thought of her slim, delicate throat, her lovely gray eyes.

"There's something pathetic about her, though," he thought, and dropped off.

II

A week had passed since they had struck up an acquaintance. It was a holiday. It was close indoors, while in the street the wind whirled the dust about and blew people's hats off. One was thirsty all day, and Gurov often went into the restaurant and offered Anna Sergeyevna a soft drink or ice cream. One did not know what to do with oneself.

In the evening when the wind had abated they went out on the pier to watch the steamer come in. There were a great many people walking about the dock; they had come to welcome someone and they were carrying bunches of flowers. And two peculiarities of a festive Yalta crowd stood out: the elderly ladies were dressed like young ones and there were many generals.

Owing to the choppy sea, the steamer arrived late, after sunset, and it was a long time tacking about before it put in at the pier. Anna Sergeyevna peered at the steamer and the passengers through her lorgnette as though looking for acquaintances, and whenever she turned to Gurov her eyes were shining. She talked a great deal and asked questions jerkily, forgetting the next moment what she had asked; then she lost her lorgnette in the crush.

The festive crowd began to disperse; it was now too dark to see people's faces; there was no wind any more, but Gurov and Anna Sergeyevna still stood as though waiting to see someone else come off the steamer. Anna Sergeyevna was silent now, and sniffed her flowers without looking at Gurov.

"The weather has improved this evening," he said. "Where shall we go now? Shall we drive somewhere?"

She did not reply.

Then he looked at her intently, and suddenly embraced her and kissed her

---

[1]Country council.

on the lips, and the moist fragrance of her flowers enveloped him; and at once he looked round him anxiously, wondering if anyone had seen them.

"Let us go to your place," he said softly. And they walked off together rapidly.

The air in her room was close and there was the smell of the perfume she had bought at the Japanese shop. Looking at her, Gurov thought: "What encounters life offers!" From the past he preserved the memory of carefree, good-natured women whom love made gay and who were grateful to him for the happiness he gave them, however brief it might be; and of women like his wife who loved without sincerity, with too many words, affectedly, hysterically, with an expression that it was not love or passion that engaged them but something more significant; and of two or three others, very beautiful, frigid women, across whose faces would suddenly flit a rapacious expression—an obstinate desire to take from life more than it could give, and these were women no longer young, capricious, unreflecting, domineering, unintelligent, and when Gurov grew cold to them their beauty aroused his hatred, and the lace on their lingerie seemed to him to resemble scales.

But here there was the timidity, the angularity of inexperienced youth, a feeling of awkwardness; and there was a sense of embarrassment, as though someone had suddenly knocked at the door. Anna Sergeyevna, "the lady with the pet dog," treated what had happened in a peculiar way, very seriously, as though it were her fall—so it seemed, and this was odd and inappropriate. Her features drooped and faded, and her long hair hung down sadly on either side of her face; she grew pensive and her dejected pose was that of a Magdalene in a picture by an old master.

"It's not right," she said. "You don't respect me now, you first of all."

There was a watermelon on the table. Gurov cut himself a slice and began eating it without haste. They were silent for at least half an hour.

There was something touching about Anna Sergeyevna; she had the purity of a well-bred, naive woman who has seen little of life. The single candle burning on the table barely illumined her face, yet it was clear that she was unhappy.

"Why should I stop respecting you, darling?" asked Gurov. "You don't know what you're saying."

"God forgive me," she said, and her eyes filled with tears. "It's terrible."

"It's as though you were trying to exonerate yourself."

"How can I exonerate myself? No. I am a bad, low woman; I despise myself and I have no thought of exonerating myself. It's not my husband but myself I have deceived. And not only just now; I have been deceiving myself for a long time. My husband may be a good, honest man, but he is a flunkey! I don't know what he does, what his work is, but I know he is a flunkey! I was twenty when I married him. I was tormented by curiosity; I wanted something better. 'There must be a different sort of life,' I said to myself. I wanted to live! To live, to live! Curiosity kept eating at me—you don't understand it, but I swear to God I could no longer control myself; something was going on in me; I could not be held back. I told my husband I was ill, and came here. And here I have been walking about as though in a daze, as though I were mad; and now I have become a vulgar, vile woman whom anyone may despise."

Gurov was already bored with her; he was irritated by her naive tone, by her repentance, so unexpected and so out of place, but for the tears in her eyes he might have thought she was joking or play-acting.

"I don't understand, my dear," he said softly. "What do you want?"

She hid her face on his breast and pressed close to him.

"Believe me, believe me, I beg you," she said, "I love honesty and purity, and sin is loathsome to me; I don't know what I'm doing. Simple people say, 'The Evil One has led me astray.' And I may say of myself now that the Evil One has led me astray."

"Quiet, quiet," he murmured.

He looked into her fixed, frightened eyes, kissed her, spoke to her softly and affectionately, and by degrees she calmed down, and her gaiety returned; both began laughing.

Afterwards when they went out there was not a soul on the esplanade. The town with its cypresses looked quite dead, but the sea was still sounding as it broke upon the beach; a single launch was rocking on the waves and on it a lantern was blinking sleepily.

They found a cab and drove to Oreanda.

"I found out your surname in the hall just now: it was written on the board—von Dideritz," said Gurov. "Is your husband German?"

"No; I believe his grandfather was German, but he is Greek Orthodox himself."

At Oreanda they sat on a bench not far from the church, looked down at the sea, and were silent. Yalta was barely visible through the morning mist; white clouds rested motionlessly on the mountaintops. The leaves did not stir on the trees, cicadas twanged, and the monotonous muffled sound of the sea that rose from below spoke of the peace, the eternal sleep awaiting us. So it rumbled below when there was no Yalta, no Oreanda here; so it rumbles now, and it will rumble as indifferently and as hollowly when we are no more. And in this constancy, in this complete indifference to the life and death of each of us, there lies, perhaps, a pledge of our eternal salvation, of the unceasing advance of life upon earth, of unceasing movement towards perfection. Sitting beside a young woman who in the dawn seemed so lovely, Gurov, soothed and spellbound by these magical surroundings—the sea, the mountains, the clouds, the wide sky—thought how everything is really beautiful in this world when one reflects: everything except what we think or do ourselves when we forget the higher aims of life and our own human dignity.

A man strolled up to them—probably a guard—looked at them, and walked away. And this detail, too, seemed so mysterious and beautiful. They saw a steamer arrive from Feodosia, its lights extinguished in the glow of dawn.

"There is dew on the grass," said Anna Sergeyevna, after a silence.

"Yes, it's time to go home."

They returned to the city.

Then they met every day at twelve o'clock on the esplanade, lunched and dined together, took walks, admired the sea. She complained that she slept badly, that she had palpitations, asked the same questions, troubled now by jealousy and now by the fear that he did not respect her sufficiently. And often in the square or the public garden, when there was no one near them, he suddenly drew her to him and kissed her passionately. Complete idleness, these kisses in broad daylight exchanged furtively in dread of someone's seeing them, the heat, the smell of the sea, and the continual flitting before his eyes of idle, well-dressed, well-fed people, worked a complete change in him; he kept telling Anna Sergeyevna how beautiful she was, how seductive, was urgently passionate; he would not move a step away from her, while she was often pensive and continually pressed him to confess that he did not respect her, did not love her in the least, and saw in her nothing but a common woman. Almost every evening rather late they drove somewhere out of town, to Oreanda or to the waterfall; and the excursion was always a success, the scenery invariably impressed them as beautiful and magnificent.

They were expecting her husband, but a letter came from him saying that he had eye-trouble, and begging his wife to return home as soon as possible. Anna Sergeyevna made haste to go.

"It's a good thing I am leaving," she said to Gurov. "It's the hand of Fate!"

She took a carriage to the railway station, and he went with her. They were driving the whole day. When she had taken her place in the express, and when the second bell had rung, she said, "Let me look at you once more—let me look at you again. Like this."

She was not crying but was so sad that she seemed ill and her face was quivering.

"I shall be thinking of you—remembering you," she said. "God bless you; be happy. Don't remember evil against me. We are parting forever—it has to be, for we ought never to have met. Well, God bless you."

The train moved off rapidly, its lights soon vanished, and a minute later there was no sound of it, as though everything had conspired to end as quickly as possible that sweet trance, that madness. Left alone on the platform, and gazing into the dark distance, Gurov listened to the twang of the grasshoppers and the hum of the telegraph wires, feeling as though he had just waked up. And he reflected, musing, that there had now been another episode or adventure in his life, and it, too, was at an end, and nothing was left of it but a memory. He was moved, sad, and slightly remorseful: this young woman whom he would never meet again had not been happy with him; he had been warm and affectionate with her, but yet in his manner, his tone, and his caresses there had been a shade of light irony, the slightly coarse arrogance of a happy male who was, besides, almost twice her age. She had constantly called him kind, exceptional, high-minded; obviously he had seemed to her different from what he really was, so he had involuntarily deceived her.

Here at the station there was already a scent of autumn in the air; it was a chilly evening.

"It is time for me to go north, too," thought Gurov as he left the platform. "High time!"

III

At home in Moscow the winter routine was already established; the stoves were heated, and in the morning it was still dark when the children were having breakfast and getting ready for school, and the nurse would light the lamp for a short time. There were frosts already. When the first snow falls, on the first day the sleighs are out, it is pleasant to see the white earth, the white roofs; one draws easy, delicious breaths, and the season brings back the days of one's youth. The old limes and birches, white with hoar-frost, have a good-natured look; they are closer to one's heart than cypresses and palms, and near them one no longer wants to think of mountains and the sea.

Gurov, a native of Moscow, arrived there on a fine frosty day, and when he put on his fur coat and warm gloves and took a walk along Petrovka, and when on Saturday night he heard the bells ringing, his recent trip and the places he had visited lost all charm for him. Little by little he became immersed in Moscow life, greedily read three newspapers a day, and declared that he did not read the Moscow papers on principle. He already felt a longing for restaurants, clubs, formal dinners, anniversary celebrations, and it flattered him to entertain distinguished lawyers and actors, and to play cards with a professor at the physicians' club. He could eat a whole portion of meat stewed with pickled cabbage and served in a pan, Moscow style.

A month or so would pass and the image of Anna Sergeyevna, it seemed to him, would become misty in his memory, and only from time to time he would dream of her with her touching smile as he dreamed of others. But more than a month went by, winter came into its own, and everything was still clear in his memory as though he had parted from Anna Sergeyevna only yesterday. And his memories glowed more and more vividly. When in the evening stillness the voices of his children preparing their lessons reached his study, or when he listened to a song or to an organ playing in a restaurant, or when the storm howled in the chimney, suddenly everything would rise up in his memory; what had happened on the pier and the early morning with the mist on the mountains, and the steamer coming from Feodosia, and the kisses. He would pace about his room a long time, remembering and smiling; then his memories passed into reveries, and in his imagination the past would mingle with what was to come. He did not dream of Anna Sergeyevna, but she followed him about everywhere and watched him. When he shut his eyes he saw her before him as though she were there in the flesh, and she seemed to him lovelier, younger, tenderer than she had been, and he imagined himself a finer man than he had been in Yalta. Of evenings she peered out at him from the bookcase, from the fireplace, from the corner—he heard her breathing, the caressing rustle of her clothes. In the street he followed the women with his eyes, looking for someone who resembled her.

Already he was tormented by a strong desire to share his memories with someone. But in his home it was impossible to talk of his love, and he had no one to talk to outside; certainly he could not confide in his tenants or in anyone at the bank. And what was there to talk about? He hadn't loved her then, had he? Had there been anything beautiful, poetical, edifying, or simply interesting in his relations with Anna Sergeyevna? And he was forced to talk vaguely of love, of women, and no one guessed what he meant; only his wife would twitch her black eyebrows and say, "The part of a philanderer does not suit you at all, Dimitry."

One evening, coming out of the physicians' club with an official with whom he had been playing cards, he could not resist saying:

"If you only knew what a fascinating woman I became acquainted with at Yalta!"

The official got into his sledge and was driving away, but turned suddenly and shouted:

"Dmitry Dmitrich!"

"What is it?"

"You were right this evening: the sturgeon was a bit high."

These words, so commonplace, for some reason moved Gurov to indignation, and struck him as degrading and unclean. What savage manners, what mugs! What stupid nights, what dull, humdrum days! Frenzied gambling, gluttony, drunkenness, continual talk always about the same thing! Futile pursuits and conversations always about the same topics take up the better part of one's time, the better part of one's strength, and in the end there is left a life clipped and wingless, an absurd mess, and there is no escaping or getting away from it—just as though one were in a madhouse or a prison.

Gurov, boiling with indignation, did not sleep all night. And he had a headache all the next day. And the following nights too he slept badly; he sat up in bed, thinking, or paced up and down his room. He was fed up with his children, fed up with the bank; he had no desire to go anywhere or to talk of anything.

In December during the holidays he prepared to take a trip and told his wife he was going to Petersburg to do what he could for a young friend—and he set off for S——. What for? He did not know, himself. He wanted to see Anna Sergeyevna and talk with her, to arrange a rendezvous if possible.

He arrived at S—— in the morning, and at the hotel took the best room, in which the floor was covered with gray army cloth, and on the table there was an inkstand, gray with dust and topped by a figure on horseback, its hat in its raised hand and its head broken off. The porter gave him the necessary information: von Dideritz lived in a house of his own on Staro-Goncharnaya Street, not far from the hotel: he was rich and lived well and kept his own horses; everyone in the town knew him. The porter pronounced the name: "Dridiritz."

Without haste Gurov made his way to Staro-Goncharnaya Street and found the house. Directly opposite the house stretched a long gray fence studded with nails.

"A fence like that would make one run away," thought Gurov, looking now at the fence, now at the windows of the house.

He reflected: this was a holiday, and the husband was apt to be at home. And in any case, it would be tactless to go into the house and disturb her. If he were to send her a note, it might fall into her husband's hands, and that might spoil everything. The best thing was to rely on chance. And he kept walking up and down the street and along the fence, waiting for the chance. He saw a beggar go in at the gate and heard the dogs attack him; then an hour later he heard a piano, and the sound came to him faintly and indistinctly. Probably it was Anna Sergeyevna playing. The front door opened suddenly, and an old woman came out, followed by the familiar white Pomeranian. Gurov was on the point of calling to the dog, but his heart began beating violently, and in his excitement he could not remember the Pomeranian's name.

He kept walking up and down, and hated the gray fence more and more, and by now he thought irritably that Anna Sergeyevna had forgotten him, and was perhaps already diverting herself with another man, and that that was very natural in a young woman who from morning till night had to look at that damn fence. He went back to his hotel room and sat on the couch for a long while, not knowing what to do, then he had dinner and a long nap.

"How stupid and annoying all this is!" he thought when he woke and looked at the dark windows: it was already evening. "Here I've had a good sleep for some reason. What am I going to do at night?"

He sat on the bed, which was covered with a cheap gray blanket of the kind seen in hospitals, and he twitted himself in his vexation:

"So there's your lady with the pet dog. There's your adventure. A nice place to cool your heels in."

That morning at the station a playbill in large letters had caught his eye. *The Geisha* was to be given for the first time. He thought of this and drove to the theater.

"It's quite possible that she goes to first nights," he thought.

The theater was full. As in all provincial theaters, there was a haze above the chandelier, the gallery was noisy and restless; in the front row, before the beginning of the performance the local dandies were standing with their hands clasped behind their backs; in the Governor's box the Governor's daughter, wearing a boa, occupied the front seat, while the Governor himself hid modestly behind the portiere and only his hands were visible; the curtain swayed; the orchestra was a long time tuning up. While the audience was coming in and taking their seats, Gurov scanned the faces eagerly.

Anna Sergeyevna, too, came in. She sat down in the third row, and when Gurov looked at her his heart contracted, and he understood clearly that in the whole world there was no human being so near, so precious, and so important to him; she, this little, undistinguished woman, lost in a provincial crowd, with a vulgar lorgnette in her hand, filled his whole life now, was his sorrow and his joy, the only happiness that he now desired for himself, and to the sounds of the bad orchestra, of the miserable local violins, he thought how lovely she was. He thought and dreamed.

A young man with small side-whiskers, very tall and stooped, came in with Anna Sergeyevna and sat down beside her; he nodded his head at every step and seemed to be bowing continually. Probably this was the husband whom at Yalta, in an access of bitter feeling, she had called a flunkey. And there really was in his lanky figure, his side-whiskers, his small bald patch, something of a flunkey's retiring manner; his smile was mawkish, and in his buttonhole there was an academic badge like a waiter's number.

During the first intermission the husband went out to have a smoke; she remained in her seat. Gurov, who was also sitting in the orchestra, went up to her and said in a shaky voice, with a forced smile:

"Good evening!"

She glanced at him and turned pale, then looked at him again in horror, unable to believe her eyes, and gripped the fan and the lorgnette tightly together in her hands, evidently trying to keep herself from fainting. Both were silent. She was sitting, he was standing, frightened by her distress and not daring to take a seat beside her. The violins and the flute that were being tuned up sang out. He suddenly felt frightened: it seemed as if all the people in the boxes were looking at them. She got up and went hurriedly to the exit; he followed her, and both of them walked blindly along the corridors and up and down stairs, and figures in the uniforms prescribed for magistrates, teachers, and officials of the Department of Crown Lands, all wearing badges, flitted before their eyes, as did also ladies, and fur coats on hangers; they were conscious of drafts and the smell of stale tobacco. And Gurov, whose heart was beating violently, thought:

"Oh, Lord! Why are these people here and this orchestra!"

And at that instant he suddenly recalled how when he had seen Anna Sergeyevna off at the station he had said to himself that all was over between them and that they would never meet again. But how distant the end still was!

On the narrow, gloomy staircase over which it said "To the Amphitheatre," she stopped.

"How you frightened me!" she said, breathing hard, still pale and stunned. "Oh, how you frightened me! I am barely alive. Why did you come? Why?"

"But do understand, Anna, do understand—" he said hurriedly, under his breath. "I implore you, do understand—"

She looked at him with fear, with entreaty, with love; she looked at him intently, to keep his features more distinctly in her memory.

"I suffer so," she went on, not listening to him. "All this time I have been thinking of nothing but you; I live only by the thought of you. And I wanted to forget, to forget; but why, oh, why have you come?"

On the landing above them two high school boys were looking down and smoking, but it was all the same to Gurov; he drew Anna Sergeyevna to him and began kissing her face and hands.

"What are you doing, what are you doing!" she was saying in horror, pushing him away. "We have lost our senses. Go away today; go away at once—I conjure you by all that is sacred, I implore you—People are coming this way!"

Someone was walking up the stairs.

"You must leave," Anna Sergeyevna went on in a whisper. "Do you hear, Dmitry Dmitrich? I will come and see you in Moscow. I have never been happy; I am unhappy now, and I never, never shall be happy, never! So don't make me suffer still more! I swear I'll come to Moscow. But now let us part. My dear, good, precious one, let us part!"

She pressed his hand and walked rapidly downstairs, turning to look round at him, and from her eyes he could see that she really was unhappy. Gurov stood for a while, listening, then when all grew quiet, he found his coat and left the theater.

IV

And Anna Sergeyevna began coming to see him in Moscow. Once every two or three months she left S——telling her husband that she was going to consult a doctor about a woman's ailment from which she was suffering—and her husband did and did not believe her. When she arrived in Moscow she would stop at the Slavyansky Bazar Hotel, and at once send a man in a red cap to Gurov. Gurov came to see her, and no one in Moscow knew of it.

Once he was going to see her in this way on a winter morning (the messenger had come the evening before and not found him in). With him walked his daughter, whom he wanted to take to school; it was on the way. Snow was coming down in big wet flakes.

"It's three degrees above zero,[2] and yet it's snowing," Gurov was saying to his daughter. "But this temperature prevails only on the surface of the earth; in the upper layers of the atmosphere there is quite a different temperature."

"And why doesn't it thunder in winter, papa?"

He explained that, too. He talked, thinking all the while that he was on his way to a rendezvous, and no living soul knew of it, and probably no one would ever know. He had two lives, an open one, seen and known by all who needed to know it, full of conventional truth and conventional falsehood, exactly like the lives of his friends and acquaintances; and another life that went on in secret. And through some strange, perhaps accidental, combination of circumstances, everything that was of interest and importance to him, everything that was essential to him, everything about which he felt sincerely and did not deceive himself, everything that constituted the core of his life, was going on concealed from others; while all that was false, the shell in which he hid to cover the truth—his work at the bank, for instance, his discussions at the club, his references to the "inferior race," his appearances at anniversary celebrations with his wife—all that went on in the open. Judging others by himself, he did not believe what he saw, and always fancied that every man led his real, most interesting life under cover of secrecy as under cover of night. The personal life of every individual is based on secrecy, and perhaps it is partly for that reason that civilized man is so nervously anxious that personal privacy should be respected.

Having taken his daughter to school, Gurov went on to the Slavyansky Bazar Hotel. He took off his fur coat in the lobby, went upstairs, and knocked gently at the door. Anna Sergeyevna, wearing his favorite gray dress, exhausted by the journey and by waiting, had been expecting him since the previous

---

[2]On the Celsius scale—about thirty-seven degrees Fahrenheit.

evening. She was pale, and looked at him without a smile, and he had hardly entered when she flung herself on his breast. That kiss was a long, lingering one, as though they had not seen one another for two years.

"Well, darling, how are you getting on there?" he asked. "What news?"

"Wait; I'll tell you in a moment—I can't speak."

She could not speak; she was crying. She turned away from him, and pressed her handkerchief to her eyes.

"Let her have her cry; meanwhile I'll sit down," he thought, and he seated himself in an armchair.

Then he rang and ordered tea, and while he was having his tea she remained standing at the window with her back to him. She was crying out of sheer agitation, in the sorrowful consciousness that their life was so sad; that they could only see each other in secret and had to hide from people like thieves! Was it not a broken life?

"Come, stop now, dear!" he said.

It was plain to him that this love of theirs would not be over soon, that the end of it was not in sight. Anna Sergeyevna was growing more and more attached to him. She adored him, and it was unthinkable to tell her that their love was bound to come to an end some day; besides, she would not have believed it!

He went up to her and took her by the shoulders, to fondle her and say something diverting, and at that moment he caught sight of himself in the mirror.

His hair was already beginning to turn gray. And it seemed odd to him that he had grown so much older in the last few years, and lost his looks. The shoulders on which his hands rested were warm and heaving. He felt compassion for this life, still so warm and lovely, but probably already about to begin to fade and wither like his own. Why did she love him so much? He always seemed to women different from what he was, and they loved in him not himself, but the man whom their imagination created and whom they had been eagerly seeking all their lives; and afterwards, when they saw their mistake, they loved him nevertheless. And not one of them had been happy with him. In the past he had met women, come together with them, parted from them, but he had never once loved; it was anything you please, but not love. And only now when his head was gray he had fallen in love, really, truly—for the first time in his life.

Anna Sergeyevna and he loved each other as people do who are very close and intimate, like man and wife, like tender friends; it seemed to them that Fate itself had meant them for one another, and they could not understand why he had a wife and she a husband; and it was as though they were a pair of migratory birds, male and female, caught and forced to live in different cages. They forgave each other what they were ashamed of in their past, they forgave everything in the present, and felt that this love of theirs had altered them both.

Formerly in moments of sadness he had soothed himself with whatever logical arguments came into his head, but now he no longer cared for logic; he felt profound compassion, he wanted to be sincere and tender.

"Give it up now, my darling," he said. "You've had your cry; that's enough. Let us have a talk now, we'll think up something."

Then they spent a long time taking counsel together, they talked of how to avoid the necessity for secrecy, for deception, for living in different cities, and not seeing one another for long stretches of time. How could they free themselves from these intolerable fetters?

"How? How?" he asked, clutching his head. "How?"

And it seemed as though in a little while the solution would be found, and then a new and glorious life would begin; and it was clear to both of them that the end was still far off, and that what was to be most complicated and difficult for them was only just beginning.

ERNEST HEMINGWAY

Hills Like White Elephants

The hills across the valley of the Ebro were long and white. On this side there was no shade and no trees and the station was between two lines of rails in the sun. Close against the side of the station there was the warm shadow of the building and a curtain, made of strings of bamboo beads, hung across the open door into the bar, to keep out flies. The American and the girl with him sat at a table in the shade, outside the building. It was very hot and the express from Barcelona would come in forty minutes. It stopped at this junction for two minutes and went on to Madrid.

"What should we drink?" the girl asked. She had taken off her hat and put it on the table.

"It's pretty hot," the man said.

"Let's drink beer."

"*Dos cervezas,*" the man said into the curtain.

"Big ones?" a woman asked from the doorway.

"Yes. Two big ones."

The woman brought two glasses of beer and two felt pads. She put the felt pads and the beer glasses on the table and looked at the man and the girl. The girl was looking off at the line of hills. They were white in the sun and the country was brown and dry.

"They look like white elephants," she said.

"I've never seen one," the man drank his beer.

"No, you wouldn't have."

"I might have," the man said. "Just because you say I wouldn't have doesn't prove anything."

The girl looked at the bead curtain. "They've painted something on it," she said. "What does it say?"

"Anis del Toro. It's a drink,"

"Could we try it?"

The man called "Listen" through the curtain. The woman came out from the bar.

"Four reales."

"We want two Anis del Toro."

"With water?"

145

"Do you want it with water?"

"I don't know," the girl said. "Is it good with water?"

"It's all right."

"You want them with water?" asked the woman.

"Yes, with water."

"It tastes like licorice," the girl said and put the glass down.

"That's the way with everything."

"Yes," said the girl. "Everything tastes of licorice. Especially all the things you've waited so long for, like absinthe."

"Oh, cut it out."

"You started it," the girl said. "I was being amused. I was having a fine time."

"Well, let's try and have a fine time."

"All right. I was trying. I said the mountains looked like white elephants. Wasn't that bright?"

"That was bright."

"I wanted to try this new drink: That's all we do, isn't it—look at things and try new drinks?"

"I guess so."

The girl looked across at the hills.

"They're lovely hills," she said. "They don't really look like white elephants. I just meant the coloring of their skin through the trees."

"Should we have another drink?"

"All right."

The warm wind blew the bead curtain against the table.

"The beer's nice and cool," the man said.

"It's lovely," the girl said.

"It's really an awfully simple operation, Jig," the man said. "It's not really an operation at all."

The girl looked at the ground the table legs rested on.

"I know you wouldn't mind it, Jig. It's really not anything. It's just to let the air in."

The girl did not say anything.

"I'll go with you and I'll stay with you all the time. They just let the air in and then it's all perfectly natural."

"Then what will we do afterward?"

"We'll be fine afterward. Just like we were before."

"What makes you think so?"

"That's the only thing that bothers us. It's the only thing that's made us unhappy."

The girl looked at the bead curtain, put her hand out, and took hold of two of the strings of beads.

"And you think then we'll be all right and be happy."

"I know we will. You don't have to be afraid. I've known lots of people that have done it."

"So have I," said the girl. "And afterward they were all so happy."

"Well," the man said, "if you don't want to you don't have to. I wouldn't have you do it if you didn't want to. But I know it's perfectly simple."

"And you really want to?"

"I think it's the best thing to do. But I don't want you to do it if you don't really want to."

"And if I do it you'll be happy and things will be like they were and you'll love me?"

"I love you now. You know I love you."

"I know. But if I do it, then it will be nice again if I say things are like white elephants, and you'll like it?"

"I'll love it. I love it now but I just can't think about it. You know how I get when I worry."

"If I do it you won't ever worry?"

"I won't worry about that because it's perfectly simple."

"Then I'll do it. Because I don't care about me."

"What do you mean?"

"I don't care about me."

"Well, I care about you."

"Oh, yes. But I don't care about me. And I'll do it and then everything will be fine."

"I don't want you to do it if you feel that way."

The girl stood up and walked to the end of the station. Across, on the other side, were fields of grain and trees along the banks of the Ebro. Far away, beyond the river, were mountains. The shadow of a cloud moved across the field of grain and she saw the river through the trees.

"And we could have all this," she said, "And we could have everything and every day we make it more impossible."

"What did you say?"

"I said we could have everything."

"We can have everything."

"No, we can't."

"We can have the whole world."

"No, we can't."

"We can go everywhere."

"No, we can't. It isn't ours any more."

"It's ours."

"No, it isn't. And once they take it away, you never get it back."

"But they haven't taken it away."

"We'll wait and see."

"Come on back in the shade," he said. "You mustn't feel that way."

"I don't feel any way," the girl said. "I just know things."

"I don't want you to do anything that you don't want to do—"

"Nor that isn't good for me," she said. "I know. Could we have another beer?"

"All right. But you've got to realize——"

"I realize," the girl said. "Can't we maybe stop talking?"

They sat down at the table and the girl looked across at the hills on the dry side of the valley and the man looked at her and at the table.

"You've got to realize," he said, "that I don't want you to do it if you don't want to. I'm perfectly willing to go through with it if it means anything to you."

"Doesn't it mean anything to you? We could get along."

"Of course it does. But I don't want anybody but you. I don't want any one else. And I know it's perfectly simple."

"Yes, you know it's perfectly simple."

"It's all right for you to say that, but I do know it."

"Would you do something for me now?"

"I'd do anything for you."

"Would you please please please please please please please stop talking?"

He did not say anything but looked at the bags against the wall of the station. There were labels on them from all the hotels where they had spent nights.

"But I don't want you to," he said, "I don't care anything about it."

"I'll scream," the girl said.

The woman came out through the curtains with two glasses of beer and put them down on the damp felt pads. "The train comes in five minutes," she said.

"What did she say?" asked the girl.

"That the train is coming in five minutes."

The girl smiled brightly at the woman, to thank her.

"I'd better take the bags over to the other side of the station," the man said. She smiled at him.

"All right. Then come back and we'll finish the beer."

He picked up the two heavy bags and carried them around the station to the other tracks. He looked up the tracks but could not see the train. Coming back, he walked through the barroom, where people waiting for the train were drinking. He drank an Anis at the bar and looked at the people. They were all waiting reasonably for the train. He went out through the bead curtain. She was sitting at the table and smiled at him.

"Do you feel better?" he asked.

"I feel fine," she said. "There's nothing wrong with me. I feel fine."

TILLIE OLSEN

I Stand Here Ironing

I stand here ironing, and what you asked me moves tormented back and forth with the iron.

"I wish you would manage the time to come in and talk with me about your daughter. I'm sure you can help me understand her. She's a youngster who needs help and whom I'm deeply interested in helping."

"Who needs help." . . . Even if I came, what good would it do? You think because I am her mother I have a key, or that in some way you could use me as a key? She has lived for nineteen years. There is all that life that has happened outside of me, beyond me.

And when is there time to remember, to sift, to weigh, to estimate, to total? I will start and there will be an interruption and I will have to gather it all together again. Or I will become engulfed with all I did or did not do, with what should have been and what cannot be helped.

She was a beautiful baby. The first and only one of our five that was beautiful at birth. You do not guess how new and uneasy her tenancy in her now-loveliness. You did not know her all those years she was thought homely, or see her poring over her baby pictures, making me tell her over and over how beautiful she had been—and would be, I would tell her—and was now, to the seeing eye. But the seeing eyes were few or nonexistent. Including mine.

I nursed her. They feel that's important nowadays, I nursed all the children, but with her, with all the fierce rigidity of first motherhood, I did like the books then said. Though her cries battered me to trembling and my breasts ached with swollenness, I waited till the clock decreed.

Why do I put that first? I do not even know if it matters, or if it explains anything.

She was a beautiful baby. She blew shining bubbles of sound. She loved motion, loved light, loved color and music and textures. She would lie on the floor in her blue overalls patting the surface so hard in ecstasy her hands and feet would blur. She was a miracle to me, but when she was eight months old I had to leave her daytimes with the woman downstairs to whom she was no miracle at all, for I worked or looked for work and for Emily's father, who "could no longer endure" (he wrote in his good-bye note) "sharing want with us."

I was nineteen. It was pre-relief, pre-WPA world of the depression. I would start running as soon as I got off the streetcar, running up the stairs, the place smelling sour, and awake or asleep to startle awake, when she saw me she would break into a clogged weeping that could not be comforted, a weeping I can hear yet.

After a while I found a job hashing at night so I could be with her days, and it was better. But it came to where I had to bring her to his family and leave her.

It took a long time to raise the money for her fare back. Then she got chicken pox and I had to wait longer. When she finally came, I hardly knew her, walking quick and nervous like her father, looking like her father, thin, and dressed in a shoddy red that yellowed her skin and glared at the pock-marks. All the baby loveliness gone.

She was two. Old enough for nursery school they said, and I did not know then what I know now—the fatigue of the long day, and the lacerations of group life in the kinds of nurseries that are only parking places for children.

Except that it would have made no difference if I had known. It was the only place there was. It was the only way we could be together, the only way I could hold a job.

And even without knowing, I knew. I knew the teacher that was evil because all these years it has curdled into my memory, the little boy hunched in the corner, her rasp, "why aren't you outside, because Alvin hits you? that's no reason, go out, scaredy." I knew Emily hated it even if she did not clutch and implore "don't go Mommy" like the other children, mornings.

She always had a reason why we should stay home. Momma, you look sick. Momma, I feel sick. Momma, the teachers aren't there today, they're sick. Momma, we can't go, there was a fire last night. Momma, it's a holiday today, no school, they told me.

But never a direct protest, never rebellion. I think of our others in their three-, four-year-oldness—the explosions, the tempers, the denunciations, the demands—and I feel suddenly ill. I put the iron down. What in me demanded that goodness in her? And what was the cost, the cost to her of such goodness?

The old man living in the back once said in his gentle way: "You should smile at Emily more when you look at her." What *was* in my face when I looked at her? I loved her. There were all the acts of love.

It was only with the others I remembered what he said, and it was the face of joy, and not of care or tightness or worry I turned to them—too late for Emily. She does not smile easily, let alone almost always as her brothers and sisters do. Her face is closed and sombre, but when she wants, how fluid. You must have seen it in her pantomimes, you spoke of her rare gift for comedy on the stage that rouses laughter out of the audience so dear they applaud and applaud and do not want to let her go.

Where does it come from, that comedy? There was none of it in her when she came back to me that second time, after I had to send her away again. She had a new daddy now to learn to love, and I think perhaps it was a better time.

Except when we left her alone nights, telling ourselves she was old enough.

"Can't you go some other time, Mommy, like tomorrow?" she would ask. "Will it be just a little while you'll be gone? Do you promise?"

The time we came back, the front door open, the clock on the floor in the hall. She rigid awake. "It wasn't just a little while. I didn't cry. Three times I called you, just three times, and then I ran downstairs to open the door so you could come faster. The clock talked loud. I threw it away, it scared me what it talked."

She said the clock talked loud again that night I went to the hospital to have Susan. She was delirious with the fever that comes before red measles, but she was fully conscious all the week I was gone and the week after we were home when she could not come near the new baby or me.

She did not get well. She stayed skeleton thin, not wanting to eat, and night after night she had nightmares. She would call for me, and I would rouse from exhaustion to sleepily call back: "You're all right, darling, go to sleep, it's just a dream," and if she still called, in a sterner voice, "now go to sleep, Emily, there's nothing to hurt you." Twice, only twice, when I had to get up for Susan anyhow, I went in to sit with her.

Now when it is too late (as if she would let me hold her and comfort her like I do the others) I get up and go to her at once at her moan or restless stirring. "Are you awake, Emily? Can I get you something?" And the answer is always the same: "No, I'm all right, go back to sleep, Mother."

They persuaded me at the clinic to send her away to a convalescent home in the country where "she can have the kind of food and care you can't manage for her, and you'll be free to concentrate on the new baby." They still send children to that place. I see pictures on the society page of sleek young women planning affairs to raise money for it, or dancing at the affairs, or decorating Easter eggs or filling Christmas stockings for the children.

They never have a picture of the children so I do not know if the girls still wear those gigantic red bows and the ravaged looks on the every other Sunday when parents can come to visit "unless otherwise notified"—as we were notified the first six weeks.

Oh it is a handsome place, green lawns and tall trees and fluted flower beds. High up on the balconies of each cottage the children stand, the girls in their red bows and white dresses, the boys in white suits and giant red ties. The parents stand below shrieking up to be heard and the children shriek down to be heard, and between them the invisible wall "Not To Be Contaminated by Parental Germs or Physical Affection."

There was a tiny girl who always stood hand in hand with Emily. Her parents never came. One visit she was gone. "They moved her to Rose Cottage," Emily shouted in explanation. "They don't like you to love anybody here."

She wrote once a week, the labored writing of a seven-year-old. "I am fine. How is the baby. If I write my leter nicly I will have a star. Love." There never was a star. We wrote every other day, letters she could never hold or keep but only hear read—once. "We simply do not have room for children to keep any personal possessions," they patiently explained when we pieced one Sunday's shrieking together to plead how much it would mean to Emily, who loved so to keep things, to be allowed to keep her letters and cards.

Each visit she looked frailer. "She isn't eating," they told us.

(They had runny eggs for breakfast or mush with lumps, Emily said later, I'd hold it in my mouth and not swallow. Nothing ever tasted good, just when they had chicken.)

It took us eight months to get her released home, and only the fact that she gained back so little of her seven lost pounds convinced the social worker.

I used to try to hold and love her after she came back, but her body would stay stiff, and after a while she'd push away. She ate little. Food sickened her, and I think much of life too. Oh she had physical lightness and brightness, twinkling by on skates, bouncing like a ball up and down up and down over the jump rope, skimming over the hill; but these were momentary.

She fretted about her appearance, thin and dark and foreign-looking at a time when every little girl was supposed to look or thought she should look a chubby blonde replica of Shirley Temple. The doorbell sometimes rang for her, but no one seemed to come and play in the house or to be a best friend. Maybe because we moved so much.

There was a boy she loved painfully through two school semesters. Months later she told me how she had taken pennies from my purse to buy him candy. "Licorice was his favorite and I brought him some every day, but he still liked Jennifer better'n me. Why, Mommy?" The kind of question for which there is no answer.

School was a worry for her. She was not glib or quick in a world where glibness and quickness were easily confused with ability to learn. To her overworked and exasperated teachers she was an overconscientious "slow learner" who kept trying to catch up and was absent entirely too often.

I let her be absent, though sometimes the illness was imaginary. How different from my now-strictness about attendance with the others. I wasn't working. We had a new baby. I was home anyhow. Sometimes, after Susan grew old enough, I would keep her home from school, too, to have them all together.

Mostly Emily had asthma, and her breathing, harsh and labored, would fill the house with a curiously tranquil sound. I would bring the two old dresser mirrors and her boxes of collections to her bed. She would select beads and single earrings, bottle tops and shells, dried flowers and pebbles, old postcards and scraps, all sorts of oddments; then she and Susan would play Kingdom, setting up landscapes and furniture, peopling them with action.

Those were the only times of peaceful companionship between her and Susan. I have edged away from it, that poisonous feeling between them, that terrible balancing of hurts and needs I had to do between the two, and did so badly, those earlier years.

Oh there were conflicts between the others too, each one human, needing, demanding, hurting, taking—but only between Emily and Susan, no, Emily toward Susan that corroding resentment. It seems so obvious on the surface, yet it is not obvious; Susan, the second child, Susan, golden- and curly-haired and chubby, quick and articulate and assured, everything in appearance and manner Emily was not; Susan, not able to resist Emily's precious things, losing or sometimes clumsily breaking them; Susan telling jokes and riddles to company for applause while Emily sat silent (to say to me later: that was *my* riddle, Mother, I told it to Susan); Susan, who for all the five years' difference in age was just a year behind Emily in developing physically.

I am glad for that slow physical development that widened the difference between her and her contemporaries, though she suffered over it. She was too vulnerable for that terrible world of youthful competition, of preening and parading, of constant measuring of yourself against every other, of envy, "If I had that copper hair," "If I had that skin. . . ." She tormented herself enough about not looking like the others, there was enough of unsureness, the having to be conscious of words before you speak, the constant caring—what are they thinking of me? without having it all magnified by the merciless physical drives.

Ronnie is calling. He is wet and I change him. It is rare there is such a cry now. That time of motherhood is almost behind me when the ear is not one's own but must always be racked and listening for the child cry, the child call. We sit for a while and I hold him, looking out over the city spread in charcoal with its soft aisles of light. "*Shoogily,*" he breathes and curls closer. I carry him back to bed, asleep. *Shoogily.* A funny word, a family word, inherited from Emily, invented by her to say: *comfort.*

In this and other ways she leaves her seal, I say aloud. And startle at my saying it. What do I mean? What did I start to gather together, to try and make coherent? I was at the terrible, growing years. War years. I do not remember them well. I was working, there were four smaller ones now, there was not time for her. She had to help be a mother, and housekeeper, and shopper. She had to get her seal. Mornings of crisis and near hysteria trying to get lunches packed, hair combed, coats and shoes found, everyone to school or Child Care on time, the baby ready for transportation. And always the paper scribbled on by a smaller one, the book looked at by Susan then mislaid, the homework not done. Running out to that huge school where she was one, she was lost, she was a drop; suffering over the unpreparedness, stammering and unsure in her classes.

There was so little time left at night after the kids were bedded down. She would struggle over books, always eating (it was in those years she developed her enormous appetite that is legendary in our family) and I would be ironing, or preparing food for the next day, or writing V-mail to Bill, or tending the baby. Sometimes, to make me laugh, or out of her despair, she would imitate happenings or types at school.

I think I said once: "Why don't you do something like this in the school amateur show?" One morning she phoned me at work, hardly understandable through the weeping: "Mother, I did it. I won, I won; they gave me first prize; they clapped and clapped and wouldn't let me go."

Now suddenly she was Somebody, and as imprisoned in her difference as she had been in anonymity.

She began to be asked to perform at other high schools, even in colleges, then at city and statewide affairs. The first one we went to, I only recognized her that first moment when thin, shy, she almost drowned herself into the curtains. Then: Was this Emily? The control, the command, the convulsing and deadly clowning, the spell, then the roaring, stamping audience, unwilling to let this rare and precious laughter out of their lives.

Afterwards: You ought to do something about her with a gift like that—but without money or knowing how, what does one do? We have left it all to her, and the gift has so often eddied inside, clogged and clotted, as been used and growing.

She is coming. She runs up the stairs two at a time with her light graceful step, and I know she is happy tonight. Whatever it was that occasioned your call did not happen today.

"Aren't you ever going to finish the ironing, Mother? Whistler painted his mother in a rocker. I'd have to paint mine standing over an ironing board." This is one of her communicative nights and she tells me everything and nothing as she fixes herself a plate of food out of the icebox.

She is so lovely. Why did you want me to come in at all? Why were you concerned? She will find her way.

She starts up the stairs to bed. "Don't get me up with the rest in the morning." "But I thought you were having midterms." "Oh, those," she comes back in, kisses me, and says quite lightly, "in a couple of years when we'll all be atom-dead they won't matter a bit."

She has said it before. She *believes* it. But because I have been dredging the past, and all that compounds a human being is so heavy and meaningful in me, I cannot endure it tonight.

I will never total it all. I will never come in to say: She was a child seldom smiled at. Her father left me before she was a year old. I had to work her first six years when there was work, or I sent her home and to his relatives. There were years she had care she hated. She was dark and thin and foreign-looking in a world where the prestige went to blondeness and curly hair and dimples, she was slow where glibness was prized. She was a child of anxious, not proud, love. We were poor and could not afford for her the soil of easy growth. I was a young mother, I was a distracted mother. There were other children pushing up, demanding. Her younger sister seemed all that she was not. There were years she did not want me to touch her. She kept too much in herself, her life was such she had to keep too much in herself. My wisdom came too late. She has much to her and probably little will come of it. She is a child of her age, of depression, of war, of fear.

Let her be. So all that is in her will not bloom but in how many does it? There is still enough left to live by. Only help her to know—help make it so there is cause for her to know—that she is more than this dress on the ironing board, helpless before the iron.

WILLIAM FAULKNER

A Rose for Emily

I

When Miss Emily Grierson died, our whole town went to her funeral: the men through a sort of respectful affection for a fallen monument, the women mostly out of curiosity to see the inside of her house, which no one save an old manservant—a combined gardener and cook—had seen in at least ten years.

It was a big, squarish frame house that had once been white, decorated with cupolas and spires and scrolled balconies in the heavily lightsome style of the seventies, set on what had once been our most select street. But garages and cotton gins had encroached and obliterated even the august names of that neighborhood; only Miss Emily's house was left, lifting its stubborn and coquettish decay above the cotton wagons and the gasoline pumps—an eyesore among eyesores. And now Miss Emily had gone to join the representatives of those august names where they lay in the cedar-bemused cemetery among the ranked and anonymous graves of Union and Confederate soldiers who fell at the battle of Jefferson.

Alive, Miss Emily had been a tradition, a duty, and a care; a sort of hereditary obligation upon the town, dating from that day in 1894 when Colonel Sartoris, the mayor—he who fathered the edict that no Negro woman should appear on the streets without an apron—remitted her taxes, the dispensation dating from the death of her father on into perpetuity. Not that Miss Emily would have accepted charity. Colonel Sartoris invented an involved tale to the effect that Miss Emily's father had loaned money to the town, which the town, as a matter of business, preferred this way of repaying. Only a man of Colonel Sartoris' generation and thought could have invented it, and only a woman could have believed it.

When the next generation, with its more modern ideas, became mayors and aldermen, this arrangement created some little dissatisfaction. On the first of the year they mailed her a tax notice. February came, and there was no reply. They wrote her a formal letter, asking her to call at the sheriff's office at her convenience. A week later the mayor wrote her himself, offering to call or to send his car for her, and received in reply a note on paper of an archaic shape, in a thin, flowing calligraphy in faded ink, to the effect that she no longer went out at all. The tax notice was also enclosed, without comment.

They called a special meeting of the Board of Aldermen. A deputation waited upon her, knocked at the door through which no visitor had passed since she ceased giving china-painting lessons eight or ten years earlier. They were admitted by the old Negro into a dim hall from which a stairway mounted into still more shadow. It smelled of dust and disuse—a close, dank smell. The Negro led them into the parlor. It was furnished in heavy, leather-covered furniture. When the Negro opened the blinds of one window, they could see that the leather was cracked; and when they sat down, a faint dust rose sluggishly about their thighs, spinning with slow motes in the single sun-ray. On a tarnished gilt easel before the fireplace stood a crayon portrait of Miss Emily's father.

They rose when she entered—a small, fat woman in black, with a thin gold chain descending to her waist and vanishing into her belt, leaning on an ebony cane with a tarnished gold head. Her skeleton was small and spare; perhaps that was why what would have been merely plumpness in another was obesity in her. She looked bloated, like a body long submerged in motionless water, and of that pallid hue. Her eyes, lost in the fatty ridges of her face, looked like two small pieces of coal pressed into a lump of dough as they moved from one face to another while the visitors stated their errand.

She did not ask them to sit. She just stood in the door and listened quietly until the spokesman came to a stumbling halt. Then they could hear the invisible watch ticking at the end of the gold chain.

Her voice was dry and cold. "I have no taxes in Jefferson. Colonel Sartoris explained it to me. Perhaps one of you can gain access to the city records and satisfy yourselves."

"But we have. We are the city authorities, Miss Emily. Didn't you get a notice from the sheriff, signed by him?"

"I received a paper, yes," Miss Emily said. "Perhaps he considers himself the sheriff. . . . I have no taxes in Jefferson."

"But there is nothing on the books to show that, you see. We must go by the—"

"See Colonel Sartoris. I have no taxes in Jefferson."

"But, Miss Emily—"

"See Colonel Sartoris." (Colonel Sartoris had been dead almost ten years.) "I have no taxes in Jefferson. Tobe!" The Negro appeared. "Show these gentlemen out."

II

So she vanquished them, horse and foot, just as she had vanquished their fathers thirty years before about the smell. That was two years after her father's death and a short time after her sweetheart—the one we believed would marry her—had deserted her. After her father's death she went out very little; after her sweetheart went away, people hardly saw her at all. A few of the ladies had the temerity to call, but were not received, and the only sign of life about the place was the Negro man—a young man then—going in and out with a market basket.

"Just as if a man—any man—could keep a kitchen properly," the ladies said; so they were not surprised when the smell developed. It was another link between the gross, teeming world and the high and mighty Griersons.

A neighbor, a woman, complained to the mayor, Judge Stevens, eighty years old.

"But what will you have me do about it, madam?" he said.

"Why, send her word to stop it," the woman said. "Isn't there a law?"

"I'm sure that won't be necessary," Judge Stevens said. "It's probably just a snake or a rat that nigger of hers killed in the yard. I'll speak to him about it."

The next day he received two more complaints, one from a man who came in diffident deprecation. "We really must do something about it, Judge. I'd be the last one in the world to bother Miss Emily, but we've got to do something." That night the Board of Aldermen met—three graybeards and one younger man, a member of the rising generation.

"It's simple enough," he said. "Send her word to have her place cleaned up. Give her a certain time to do it in, and if she don't. . . ."

"Dammit, sir," Judge Stevens said, "will you accuse a lady to her face of smelling bad?"

So the next night, after midnight, four men crossed Miss Emily's lawn and slunk about the house like burglars, sniffing along the base of the brickwork and at the cellar openings while one of them performed a regular sowing motion with his hand out of a sack slung from his shoulder. They broke open the cellar door and sprinkled lime there, and in all the outbuildings. As they recrossed the lawn, a window that had been dark was lighted and Miss Emily sat in it, the light behind her, and her upright torso motionless as that of an idol. They crept quietly across the lawn and into the shadow of the locusts that lined the street. After a week or two the smell went away.

That was when people had begun to feel really sorry for her. People in our town, remembering how old lady Wyatt, her great-aunt, had gone completely crazy at last, believed that the Griersons held themselves a little too high for what they really were. None of the young men were quite good enough for Miss Emily and such. We had long thought of them as a tableau, Miss Emily a slender figure in white in the background, her father a spraddled silhouette in the foreground, his back to her and clutching a horsewhip, the two of them framed by the backflung front door. So when she got to be thirty and was still single, we were not pleased exactly, but vindicated; even with insanity in the family she wouldn't have turned down all of her chances if they had really materialized.

When her father died, it got about that the house was all that was left to her; and in a way, people were glad. At last they could pity Miss Emily. Being left alone, and a pauper, she had become humanized. Now she too would know the old thrill and the old despair of a penny more or less.

The day after his death all the ladies prepared to call at the house and offer condolence and aid, as is our custom. Miss Emily met them at the door, dressed as usual and with no trace of grief on her face. She told them that her father was not dead. She did that for three days, with the ministers calling on her, and the doctors, trying to persuade her to let them dispose of the body. Just as they were about to resort to law and force, she broke down, and they buried her father quickly.

We did not say she was crazy then. We believed she had to do that. We remembered all the young men her father had driven away, and we knew that with nothing left, she would have to cling to that which had robbed her, as people will.

III

She was sick for a long time. When we saw her again, her hair was cut short, making her look like a girl, with a vague resemblance to those angels in colored church windows—sort of tragic and serene.

The town had just let the contracts for paving the sidewalks, and in the summer after her father's death they began the work. The construction company came with niggers and mules and machinery, and a foreman named Homer Barron, a Yankee—a big, dark, ready man, with a big voice and eyes lighter than his face. The little boys would follow in groups to hear him cuss the niggers, and the niggers singing in time to the rise and fall of picks. Pretty soon he knew everybody in town. Whenever you heard a lot of laughing anywhere about the square, Homer Barron would be in the center of the group. Presently, we began to see him and Miss Emily on Sunday afternoons driving in the yellow-wheeled buggy and the matched team of bays from the livery stable.

At first we were glad that Miss Emily would have an interest, because the ladies all said, "Of course a Grierson would not think seriously of a Northerner, a day laborer." But there were still others, older people, who said that even grief could not cause a real lady to forget *noblesse oblige*—without calling it *noblesse oblige*. They just said, "Poor Emily. Her kinsfolk should come to her." She had some kin in Alabama; but years ago her father had fallen out with them over the estate of old lady Wyatt, the crazy woman, and there was no communication between the two families. They had not even been represented at the funeral.

And as soon as the old people said, "Poor Emily," the whispering began. "Do you suppose it's really so?" they said to one another. "Of course it is. What else could. . . ." This behind their hands; rustling of craned silk and satin behind jalousies closed upon the sun of Sunday afternoon as the thin swift clop-clop-clop of the matched team passed: "Poor Emily."

She carried her head high enough—even when we believed that she was fallen. It was as if she demanded more than ever the recognition of her dignity as the last Grierson; as if it had wanted that touch of earthiness to reaffirm her imperviousness. Like when she bought the rat poison, the arsenic. That was over a year after they had begun to say "Poor Emily," and while the two female cousins were visiting her.

"I want some poison," she said to the druggist. She was over thirty then, still a slight woman, though thinner than usual, with cold, haughty black eyes in a face the flesh of which was strained across the temples and about the eye-sockets as you imagine a lighthouse-keeper's face ought to look. "I want some poison," she said.

"Yes, Miss Emily. What kind? For rats and such? I'd recom——"

"I want the best you have. I don't care what kind."

The druggist named several. "They'll kill anything up to an elephant. But what you want is——"

"Arsenic," Miss Emily said. "Is that a good one?"

"Is . . . arsenic? Yes, ma'am. But what you want——"

"I want arsenic."

The druggist looked down at her. She looked back at him, erect, her face like a strained flag. "Why, of course," the druggist said. "If that's what you want. But the law requires you to tell what you are going to use it for."

Miss Emily just stared at him, her head tilted back in order to look him eye for eye, until he looked away and went and got the arsenic and wrapped it up. The Negro delivery boy brought her the package; the druggist didn't come back. When she opened the package at home there was written on the box, under the skull and bones: "For rats."

IV

So the next day we all said, "She will kill herself"; and we said it would be the best thing. When she had first begun to be seen with Homer Barron, we had said, "She will marry him." Then we said, "She will persuade him yet," because Homer himself had remarked—he liked men, and it was known that he drank with the younger men in the Elks' Club—that he was not a marrying man. Later we said, "Poor Emily" behind the jalousies as they passed on Sunday afternoon in the glittering buggy, Miss Emily with her head high and Homer Barron with his hat cocked and a cigar in his teeth, reins and whip in a yellow glove.

Then some of the ladies began to say that it was a disgrace to the town and a bad example to the young people. The men did not want to interfere, but at last the ladies forced the Baptist minister—Miss Emily's people were Episcopal—to call upon her. He would never divulge what happened during that interview, but he refused to go back again. The next Sunday they again drove about the streets, and the following day the minister's wife wrote to Miss Emily's relations in Alabama.

So she had blood-kin under her roof again and we sat back to watch developments. At first nothing happened. Then we were sure that they were to be married. We learned that Miss Emily had been to the jeweler's and ordered a man's toilet set in silver, with the letters H.B. on each piece. Two days later we learned that she had bought a complete outfit of men's clothing, including a nightshirt, and we said, "They are married." We were really glad. We were glad because the two female cousins were even more Grierson than Miss Emily had ever been.

So we were not surprised when Homer Barron—the streets had been finished some time since—was gone. We were a little disappointed that there was not a public blowing-off, but we believed that he had gone on to prepare for Miss Emily's coming, or to give her a chance to get rid of the cousins. (By that time it was a cabal, and we were all Miss Emily's allies to help circumvent the cousins.) Sure enough, after another week they departed. And, as we had expected all along, within three days Homer Barron was back in town. A neighbor saw the Negro man admit him at the kitchen door at dusk one evening.

And that was the last we saw of Homer Barron. And of Miss Emily for some time. The Negro man went in and out with the market basket, but the front door remained closed. Now and then we would see her at the window for a moment, as the men did that night when they sprinkled the lime, but for almost six months she did not appear on the streets. Then we knew that this was to be expected too; as if that quality of her father which had thwarted her woman's life so many times had been too virulent and too furious to die.

When we next saw Miss Emily, she had grown fat and her hair was turning gray. During the next few years it grew grayer and grayer until it attained an even pepper-and-salt iron-gray, when it ceased turning. Up to the day of her death at seventy-four it was still that vigorous iron-gray, like the hair of an active man.

From that time on her front door remained closed, save during a period of six or seven years, when she was about forty, during which she gave lessons in china-painting. She fitted up a studio in one of the downstairs rooms, where the daughters and granddaughters of Colonel Sartoris' contemporaries were sent to her with the same regularity and in the same spirit that they were sent to church on Sundays with a twenty-five-cent piece for the collection plate. Meanwhile her taxes had been remitted.

Then the newer generation became the backbone and the spirit of the town, and the painting pupils grew up and fell away and did not send their children to her with boxes of color and tedious brushes and pictures cut from the ladies' magazines. The front door closed upon the last one and remained closed for good. When the town got free postal delivery, Miss Emily alone refused to let them fasten the metal numbers above her door and attach a mailbox to it. She would not listen to them.

Daily, monthly, yearly we watched the Negro grow grayer and more stooped, going in and out with the market basket. Each December we sent her a tax notice, which would be returned by the post office a week later, unclaimed. Now and then we would see her in one of the downstairs windows—she had evidently shut up the top floor of the house—like the carven torso of an idol in a niche, looking or not looking at us, we could never tell which. Thus she passed from generation to generation—dear, inescapable, impervious, tranquil, and perverse.

And so she died. Fell ill in the house filled with dust and shadows, with only a doddering Negro man to wait on her. We did not even know she was sick; we had long since given up trying to get any information from the Negro. He talked to no one, probably not even to her, for his voice had grown harsh and rusty, as if from disuse.

She died in one of the downstairs rooms, in a heavy walnut bed with a curtain, her gray head propped on a pillow yellow and moldy with age and lack of sunlight.

V

The Negro met the first of the ladies at the front door and let them in, with their hushed, sibilant voices and their quick, curious glances, and then he disappeared. He walked right through the house and out the back and was not seen again.

The two female cousins came at once. They held the funeral on the second day, with the town coming to look at Miss Emily beneath a mass of bought flowers, with the crayon face of her father musing profoundly above the bier and the ladies sibilant and macabre; and the very old men—some in their brushed Confederate uniforms—on the porch and the lawn, talking of Miss Emily as if she had been a contemporary of theirs, believing that they had danced with her and courted her perhaps, confusing time with its mathematical progression, as the old do, to whom all the past is not a diminishing road but, instead, a huge meadow which no winter ever quite touches, divided from them now by the narrow bottleneck of the most recent decade of years.

Already we knew that there was one room in that region above stairs which no one had seen in forty years, and which would have to be forced. They waited until Miss Emily was decently in the ground before they opened it.

The violence of breaking down the door seemed to fill this room with pervading dust. A thin, acrid pall as of the tomb seemed to lie everywhere upon this room decked and furnished as for a bridal: upon the valance curtains of faded rose color, upon the rose-shaded lights, upon the dressing table, upon the delicate array of crystal and the man's toilet things backed with tarnished silver, silver so tarnished that the monogram was obscured. Among them lay a collar and tie, as if they had just been removed, which, lifted, left upon the surface a pale crescent in the dust. Upon a chair hung the suit, carefully folded; beneath it the two mute shoes and the discarded socks.

The man himself lay in the bed.

For a long while we just stood there, looking down at the profound and fleshless grin. The body had apparently once lain in the attitude of an embrace, but now the long sleep that outlasts love, that conquers even the grimace of love, had cuckolded him. What was left of him, rotted beneath what was left of the nightshirt, had become inextricable from the bed in which he lay; and upon him and upon the pillow beside him lay that even coating of the patient and biding dust.

Then we noticed that in the second pillow was the indentation of a head. One of us lifted something from it, and leaning forward, that faint and invisible dust dry and acrid in the nostrils, we saw a long strand of iron-gray hair.

The Chrysanthemums

*T*he high grey-flannel fog of winter closed off the Salinas Valley from the sky and from all the rest of the world. On every side it sat like a lid on the mountains and made of the great valley a closed pot. On the broad, level land floor the gang plows bit deep and left the black earth shining like metal where the shares had cut. On the foothill ranches across the Salinas River, the yellow stubble fields seemed to be bathed in pale cold sunshine, but there was no sunshine in the valley now in December. The thick willow scrub along the river flamed with sharp and positive yellow leaves.

It was a time of quiet and of waiting. The air was cold and tender. A light wind blew up from the southwest so that the farmers were mildly hopeful of a good rain before long; but fog and rain do not go together.

Across the river, on Henry Allen's foothill ranch there was little work to be done, for the hay was cut and stored and the orchards were plowed up to receive the rain deeply when it should come. The cattle on the higher slopes were becoming shaggy and rough-coated.

Elisa Allen, working in her flower garden, looked down across the yard and saw Henry, her husband, talking to two men in business suits. The three of them stood by the tractor shed, each man with one foot on the side of the little Fordson. They smoked cigarettes and studied the machine as they talked.

Elisa watched them for a moment and then went back to her work. She was thirty-five. Her face was lean and strong and her eyes were as clear as water. Her figure looked blocked and heavy in her gardening costume, a man's black hat pulled low down over her eyes, clod-hopper shoes, a figured print dress almost completely covered by a big corduroy apron with four big pockets to hold the snips, the trowel and scratcher, the seeds, and the knife she worked with. She wore heavy leather gloves to protect her hands while she worked.

She was cutting down the old year's chrysanthemum stalks with a pair of short and powerful scissors. She looked down toward the men by the tractor shed now and then. Her face was eager and mature and handsome; even her work with the scissors was overeager, overpowerful. The chrysanthemum stems seemed too small and easy for her energy.

She brushed a cloud of hair out of her eyes with the back of her glove, and left a smudge of earth on her cheek in doing it. Behind her stood the neat white farm house with red geraniums close-banked around it as high as the windows. It was a hard-swept looking little house with hard-polished windows, and a clean mud-mat on the front steps.

Elisa cast another glance toward the tractor shed. The strangers were getting into their Ford coupe. She took off a glove and put her strong fingers down into the forest of new green chrysanthemum sprouts that were growing around the old roots. She spread the leaves and looked down among the close-growing stems. No aphids were there, no sowbugs or snails or cutworms. Her terrier fingers destroyed such pests before they could get started.

Elisa started at the sound of her husband's voice. He had come near quietly, and he leaned over the wire fence that protected her flower garden from cattle and dogs and chickens.

"At it again," he said. "You've got a strong new crop coming."

Elisa straightened her back and pulled on the gardening glove again. "Yes. They'll be strong this coming year." In her tone and on her face there was a little smugness.

"You've got a gift with things," Henry observed. "Some of those yellow chrysanthemums you had this year were ten inches across. I wish you'd work out in the orchard and raise some apples that big."

Her eyes sharpened. "Maybe I could do it, too. I've a gift with things, all right. My mother had it. She could stick anything in the ground and make it grow. She said it was having planters' hands that knew how to do it."

"Well, it sure works with flowers," he said.

"Henry, who were those men you were talking to?"

"Why, sure, that's what I came to tell you. They were from the Western Meat Company. I sold thirty head of three-year-old steers. Got nearly my own price, too."

"Good," she said. "Good for you."

"And I thought," he continued, "I thought how it's Saturday afternoon, and we might go into Salinas for dinner at a restaurant, and then to a picture show— to celebrate, you see."

"Good," she repeated. "Oh, yes. That will be good."

Henry put on his joking tone. "There's fights tonight. How'd you like to go to the fights?"

"Oh, no," she said breathlessly. "No, I wouldn't like fights."

"Just fooling, Elisa. We'll go to a movie. Let's see. It's two now. I'm going to take Scotty and bring down those steers from the hill. It'll take us maybe two hours. We'll go in town about five and have dinner at the Cominos Hotel. Like that?"

"Of course I'll like it. It's good to eat away from home."

"All right, then. I'll go get up a couple of horses."

She said, "I'll have plenty of time to transplant some of these sets, I guess."

She heard her husband calling Scotty down by the barn. And a little later she saw the two men ride up the pale yellow hillside in search of the steers.

There was a little square sandy bed kept for rooting the chrysanthemums.

With her trowel she turned the soil over and over, and smoothed it and patted it firm. Then she dug ten parallel trenches to receive the sets. Back at the chrysanthemum bed she pulled out the little crisp shoots, trimmed off the leaves at each one with her scissors, and laid it on a small orderly pile.

A squeak of wheels and plod of hoofs came from the road. Elisa looked up. The country road ran along the dense bank of willows and cottonwoods that bordered the river, and up this road came a curious vehicle, curiously drawn. It was an old spring-wagon, with a round canvas top on it like the corner of a prairie schooner. It was drawn by an old bay horse and a little grey-and-white burro. A big stubble-bearded man sat between the cover flaps and drove the crawling team. Underneath the wagon, between the hind wheels, a lean and rangy mongrel dog walked sedately. Words were painted on the canvas, in clumsy, crooked letters. "Pots, pans, knives, sisors, lawn mores, Fixed." Two rows of articles, and the triumphantly definitive "Fixed" below. The black paint had run down in little sharp points beneath each letter.

Elisa, squatting on the ground, watched to see the crazy, loose-jointed wagon pass by. But it didn't pass. It turned into the farm road in front of her house, crooked old wheels skirling and squeaking. The rangy dog darted from between the wheels and ran ahead. Instantly the two ranch shepherds flew out at him. Then all three stopped, and with stiff and quivering tails, with taut straight legs, with ambassadorial dignity, they slowly circled, sniffing daintily. The caravan pulled up to Elisa's wire fence and stopped. Now the newcomer dog, feeling outnumbered, lowered his tail and retired under the wagon with raised hackles and bared teeth.

The man on the seat called out, "That's a bad dog in a fight when he gets started."

Elisa laughed. "I see he is. How soon does he generally get started?"

The man caught up her laughter and echoed it heartily. "Sometimes not for weeks and weeks," he said. He climbed stiffly down, over the wheel. The horse and the donkey dropped like unwatered flowers.

Elisa saw that he was a very big man. Although his hair and beard were greying, he did not look old. His worn black suit was wrinkled and spotted with grease. The laughter had disappeared from his face and eyes the moment his laughing voice ceased. His eyes were dark, and they were full of the brooding that gets in the eyes of teamsters and of sailors. The calloused hands he rested on the wire fence were cracked, and every crack was a black line. He took off his battered hat.

"I'm off my general road, ma'am," he said. "Does this dirt road cut over across the river to the Los Angeles highway?"

Elisa stood up and shoved the thick scissors in her apron pocket. "Well, yes, it does, but it winds around and then fords the river. I don't think your team could pull through the sand."

He replied with some asperity, "It might surprise you what them beasts can pull through."

"When they get started?" she asked.

He smiled for a second. "Yes. When they get started."

"Well," said Elisa, "I think you'll save time if you go back to the Salinas road and pick up the highway there."

He drew a big finger down the chicken wire and made it sing. "I ain't in any hurry, ma'am. I go from Seattle to San Diego and back every year. Takes all my time. About six months each way. I aim to follow nice weather."

Elisa took off her gloves and stuffed them in the apron pocket with the scissors. She touched the under edge of her man's hat, searching for fugitive hairs. "That sounds like a nice kind of a way to live," she said.

He leaned confidentially over the fence. "Maybe you noticed the writing on my wagon. I mend pots and sharpen knives and scissors. You got any of them things to do?"

"Oh, no," she said, quickly. "Nothing like that." Her eyes hardened with resistance.

"Scissors is the worst thing," he explained. "Most people just ruin scissors trying to sharpen 'em, but I know how. I got a special tool. It's a little bobbit kind of thing, and patented. But it sure does the trick."

"No. My scissors are all sharp."

"All right, then. Take a pot," he continued earnestly, "a bent pot, or a pot with a hole. I can make it like new so you don't have to buy no new ones. That's a savings for you."

"No," she said shortly. "I tell you I have nothing like that for you to do."

His face fell to an exaggerated sadness. His voice took on a whining undertone. "I ain't had a thing to do today. Maybe I won't have no supper tonight. You see I'm off my regular road. I know folks on the highway clear from Seattle to San Diego. They save their things for me to sharpen up because they know I do it so good and save them money."

"I'm sorry," Elisa said irritably. "I haven't anything for you to do."

His eyes left her face and fell to searching the ground. They roamed about until they came to the chrysanthemum bed where she had been working. "What's them plants, ma'am?"

The irritation and resistance melted from Elisa's face. "Oh, those are chrysanthemums, giant whites and yellows. I raise them every year, bigger than anybody around here."

"Kind of a long-stemmed flower? Looks like a quick puff of colored smoke?" he asked.

"That's it. What a nice way to describe them."

"They smell kind of nasty till you get used to them," he said.

"It's a good bitter smell," she retorted, "not nasty at all."

He changed his tone quickly, "I like the smell myself."

"I had ten-inch-blooms this year," she said.

The man leaned farther over the fence. "Look, I know a lady down the road a piece, has got the nicest garden you ever seen. Got nearly every kind of flower but no chrysanthemums. Last time I was mending a copper-bottom washtub for her (that's a hard job but I do it good), she said to me, 'If you ever run acrost some nice chrysanthemums I wish you'd try to get me a few seeds.' That's what she told me."

Elisa's eyes grew alert and eager. "She couldn't have known much about chrysanthemums. You *can* raise them from seed, but it's much easier to root the little sprouts you see there."

"Oh," he said. "I s'pose I can't take none to her, then."

"Why yes you can," Elisa cried. "I can put some in damp sand, and you can carry them right along with you. They'll take root in the pot if you keep them damp. And then she can transplant them."

"She'd sure like to have some, ma'am. You say they're nice ones?"

"Beautiful," she said. "Oh, beautiful." Her eyes shone. She tore off the battered hat and shook out her dark pretty hair. "I'll put them in a flower pot, and you can take them right with you. Come into the yard."

While the man came through the picket gate Elisa ran excitedly along the geranium-bordered path to the back of the house. And she returned carrying a big red flower pot. The gloves were forgotten now. She kneeled on the ground by the starting bed and dug up the sandy soil with her fingers and scooped it into the bright new flower pot. Then she picked up the little pile of shoots she had prepared. With her strong fingers she pressed them into the sand and tamped around them with her knuckles. The man stood over her. "I'll tell you what to do," she said. "You remember so you can tell the lady."

"Yes, I'll try to remember."

"Well, look. These will take root in about a month. Then she must set them out, about a foot apart in good rich earth like this, see?" She lifted a handful of dark soil for him to look at. "They'll grow fast and tall. Now remember this: In July tell her to cut them down, about eight inches from the ground."

"Before they bloom?" he asked.

"Yes, before they bloom." Her face was tight with eagerness. "They'll grow right up again. About the last of September the buds will start."

She stopped and seemed perplexed. "It's the budding that takes the most care," she said hesitantly. "I don't know how to tell you." She looked deep into his eyes, searchingly. Her mouth opened a little, and she seemed to be listening. "I'll try to tell you," she said. "Did you ever hear of planting hands?"

"Can't say I have, ma'am."

"Well, I can only tell you what it feels like. It's when you're picking off the buds you don't want. Everything goes right down into your fingertips. You watch your fingers work. They do it themselves. You can feel how it is. They pick and pick the buds. They never make a mistake. They're with the plant. Do you see? Your fingers and the plant. You can feel that, right up your arm. They know. They never make a mistake. You can feel it. When you're like that you can't do anything wrong. Do you see that? Can you understand that?"

She was kneeling on the ground looking up at him. Her breast swelled passionately.

The man's eyes narrowed. He looked away self-consciously. "Maybe I know," he said. "Sometimes in the night in the wagon there—"

Elisa's voice grew husky. She broke in on him, "I've never lived as you do, but I know what you mean. When the night is dark—why, the stars are sharp-pointed, and there's quiet. Why, you rise up and up! Every pointed star gets driven into your body. It's like that. Hot and sharp and—lovely."

Kneeling there, her hand went out toward his legs in the greasy black trousers. Her hesitant fingers almost touched the cloth. Then her hand dropped to the ground. She crouched low like a fawning dog.

He said, "It's nice, just like you say. Only when you don't have no dinner, it ain't."

She stood up then, very straight, and her face was ashamed. She held the flower pot out to him and placed it gently in his arms. "Here. Put it in your wagon, on the seat, where you can watch it. Maybe I can find something for you to do."

At the back of the house she dug in the can pile and found two old and battered aluminum saucepans. She carried them back and gave them to him. "Here, maybe you can fix these."

His manner changed. He became professional. "Good as new I can fix them." At the back of his wagon he set a little anvil, and out of an oily tool box dug a small machine hammer. Elisa came through the gate to watch him while he pounded out the dents in the kettles. His mouth grew sure and knowing. At a difficult part of the work he sucked his underlip.

"You sleep right in the wagon?" Elisa asked.

"Right in the wagon, ma'am. Rain or shine I'm dry as a cow in there."

"It must be nice," she said. "It must be very nice. I wish women could do such things."

"It ain't the right kind of a life for a woman."

Her upper lip raised a little, showing her teeth. "How do you know? How can you tell?" she said.

"I don't know, ma'am," he protested. "Of course I don't know. Now here's your kettles, done. You don't have to buy no new ones."

"How much?"

"Oh, fifty cents'll do. I keep my prices down and my work good. That's why I have all them satisfied customers up and down the highway."

Elisa brought him a fifty-cent piece from the house and dropped it in his hand. "You might be surprised to have a rival some time. I can sharpen scissors, too. And I can beat the dents out of little pots. I could show you what a woman might do."

He put his hammer back in the oily box and shoved the little anvil out of sight. "It would be a lonely life for a woman, ma'am, and a scarey life, too, with animals creeping under the wagon all night." He climbed over the singletree, steadying himself with a hand on the burro's white rump. He settled himself in the seat, picked up the lines. "Thank you kindly, ma'am," he said. "I'll do like you told me; I'll go back and catch the Salinas road."

"Mind," she called, "if you're long in getting there, keep the sand damp."

"Sand, ma'am? . . . Sand? Oh, sure. You mean around the chrysanthemums. Sure I will." He clucked his tongue. The beasts leaned luxuriously into their collars. The mongrel dog took his place between the back wheels. The wagon turned and crawled out the entrance road and back the way it had come, along the river.

Elisa stood in front of her wire fence watching the slow progress of the caravan. Her shoulders were straight, her head thrown back, her eyes half-closed, so that the scene came vaguely into them. Her lips moved silently, forming the words "Good-bye—good-bye." Then she whispered, "That's a bright direction. There's a glowing there." The sound of her whisper startled her. She shook herself free and looked about to see whether anyone had been listening. Only the dogs had heard. They lifted their heads toward her from their sleeping in the dust, and then stretched out their chins and settled asleep again. Elisa turned and ran hurriedly into the house.

In the kitchen she reached behind the stove and felt the water tank. It was full of hot water from the noonday cooking. In the bathroom she tore off her soiled clothes and flung them into the corner. And then she scrubbed herself with a little block of pumice, legs and thighs, loins and chest and arms, until her skin was scratched and red. When she had dried herself she stood in front of a mirror in her bedroom and looked at her body. She tightened her stomach and threw out her chest. She turned and looked over her shoulder at her back.

After a while she began to dress, slowly. She put on her newest underclothing and her nicest stockings and the dress which was the symbol of her prettiness. She worked carefully on her hair, penciled her eyebrows and rouged her lips.

Before she was finished she heard the little thunder of hoofs and the shouts of Henry and his helper as they drove the red steers into the corral. She heard the gate bang shut and set herself for Henry's arrival.

His step sounded on the porch. He entered the house calling, "Elisa, where are you?"

"In my room, dressing. I'm not ready. There's hot water for your bath. Hurry up. It's getting late."

When she heard him splashing in the tub, Elisa laid his dark suit on the bed, and shirt and socks and tie beside it. She stood his polished shoes on the floor beside the bed. Then she went to the porch and sat primly and stiffly down. She looked toward the river road where the willow-line was still yellow with frosted leaves so that under the high grey fog they seemed a thin band of sunshine. This was the only color in the grey afternoon. She sat unmoving for a long time. Her eyes blinked rarely.

Henry came banging out of the door, shoving his tie inside his vest as he came. Elisa stiffened and her face grew tight. Henry stopped short and looked at her. "Why—why, Elisa. You look so nice!"

"Nice? You think I look nice? What do you mean by 'nice'?"

Henry blundered on. "I don't know. I mean you look different, strong and happy."

"I am strong? Yes, strong. What do you mean 'strong'?"

He looked bewildered. "You're playing some kind of a game," he said helplessly. "It's a kind of a play. You look strong enough to break a calf over your knee, happy enough to eat it like a watermelon."

For a second she lost her rigidity. "Henry! Don't talk like that. You didn't know what you said." She grew complete again. "I'm strong," she boasted, "I never knew before how strong."

Henry looked down toward the tractor shed, and when he brought his eyes back to her, they were his own again. "I'll get out the car. You can put on your coat while I'm starting."

Elisa went into the house. She heard him drive to the gate and idle down his motor, and then she took a long time to put on her hat. She pulled it here and pressed it there. When Henry turned the motor off she slipped into her coat and went out.

The little roadster bounced along on the dirt road by the river, raising the birds and driving the rabbits into the brush. Two cranes flapped heavily over the willow-line and dropped into the river-bed.

Far ahead on the road Elisa saw a dark speck. She knew.

She tried not to look as they passed it, but her eyes would not obey. She whispered to herself sadly, "He might have thrown them off the road. That wouldn't have been much trouble, not very much. But he kept the pot," she explained. "He had to keep the pot. That's why he couldn't get them off the road."

The roadster turned a bend and she saw the caravan ahead. She swung full around toward her husband so she could not see the little covered wagon and the mismatched team as the car passed them.

In a moment it was over. The thing was done. She did not look back.

She said loudly, to be heard above the motor. "It will be good, tonight, a good dinner."

"Now you're changed again," Henry complained. He took one hand from the wheel and patted her knee. "I ought to take you in to dinner oftener. It would be good for both of us. We get so heavy out on the ranch."

"Henry," she asked, "could we have wine at dinner?"

"Sure we could. Say! That will be fine."

She was silent for a while; then she said, "Henry, at those prize fights, do the men hurt each other very much?"

"Sometimes a little, not often. Why?"

"Well, I've read how they break noses, and blood runs down their chests. I've read how the fighting gloves get heavy and soggy with blood."

He looked around at her. "What's the matter, Elisa? I didn't know you read things like that." He brought the car to a stop, then turned to the right over the Salinas River bridge.

"Do any women ever go to the fights?" she asked.

"Oh, sure, some. What's the matter Elisa? Do you want to go? I don't think you'd like it, but I'll take you if you really want to go."

She relaxed limply in the seat. "Oh, no. No. I don't want to go. I'm sure I don't." Her face was turned away from him. "It will be enough if we can have wine. It will be plenty." She turned up her coat collar so he could not see that she was crying weakly—like an old woman.

FLANNERY O'CONNOR

Everything That Rises Must Converge

*H*er doctor had told Julian's mother that she must lose twenty pounds on account of her blood pressure, so on Wednesday nights Julian had to take her downtown on the bus for a reducing class at the Y. The reducing class was designed for working girls over fifty, who weighed from 165 to 200 pounds. His mother was one of the slimmer ones, but she said ladies did not tell their age or weight. She would not ride the buses by herself at night since they had been integrated, and because the reducing class was one of her few pleasures, necessary for her health, and *free*, she said Julian could at least put himself out to take her, considering all she did for him. Julian did not like to consider all she did for him, but every Wednesday night he braced himself and took her.

She was almost ready to go, standing before the hall mirror, putting on her hat, while he, his hands behind him, appeared pinned to the door frame, waiting like Saint Sebastian for the arrows to begin piercing him. The hat was new and had cost her seven dollars and a half. She kept saying, "Maybe I shouldn't have paid that for it. No, I shouldn't have. I'll take it off and return it tomorrow. I shouldn't have bought it."

Julian raised his eyes to heaven. "Yes, you should have bought it," he said. "Put it on and let's go." It was a hideous hat. A purple velvet flap came down on one side of it and stood up on the other; the rest of it was green and looked like a cushion with the stuffing out. He decided it was less comical than jaunty and pathetic. Everything that gave her pleasure was small and depressed him.

She lifted the hat one more time and set it down slowly on top of her head. Two wings of gray hair protruded on either side of her florid face, but her eyes, sky-blue, were as innocent and untouched by experience as they must have been when she was ten. Were it not that she was a widow who had struggled fiercely to feed and clothe and put him through school and who was supporting him still, "until he got on his feet," she might have been a little girl that he had to take to town.

"It's all right, it's all right," he said. "Let's go." He opened the door himself and started down the walk to get her going. The sky was a dying violet and the

houses stood out darkly against it, bulbous liver-colored monstrosities of a uni-
form ugliness though no two were alike. Since this had been a fashionable
neighborhood forty years ago, his mother persisted in thinking they did well to
have an apartment in it. Each house had a narrow collar of dirt around it in
which sat, usually, a grubby child. Julian walked with his hands in his pockets,
his head down and thrust forward, and his eyes glazed with the determination
to make himself completely numb during the time he would be sacrificed to
her pleasure.

The door closed and he turned to find the dumpy figure, surmounted by
the atrocious hat, coming toward him. "Well," she said, "you only live once and
paying a little more for it, I at least won't meet myself coming and going."

"Some day I'll start making money," Julian said gloomily—he knew he
never would— "and you can have one of those jokes whenever you take the
fit." But first they would move. He visualized a place where the nearest neighbor would be three miles away on either side.

"I think you're doing fine," she said, drawing on her gloves. "You've only
been out of school a year. Rome wasn't built in a day."

She was one of the few members of the Y reducing class who arrived in
hat and gloves and who had a son who had been to college. "It takes time,"
she said, "and the world is in such a mess. This hat looked better on me than
any of the others, though when she brought it out I said. 'Take that thing back.
I wouldn't have it on my head,' and she said, 'Now wait till you see it on,' and
when she put it on me, I said, 'We-ull,' and she said, 'If you ask me, that hat
does something for you and you do something for the hat, and besides,' she
said, 'with that hat, you won't meet yourself coming and going.'"

Julian thought he could have stood his lot better if she had been selfish, if
she had been an old hag who drank and screamed at him. He walked along,
saturated in depression, as if in the midst of his martyrdom he had lost his faith.
Catching sight of his long, hopeless, irritated face, she stopped suddenly with
a grief-stricken look, and pulled back on his arm. "Wait on me," she said. "I'm
going back to the house and take this thing off and tomorrow I'm going to
return it. I was out of my head. I can pay the gas bill with the seven-fifty."

He caught her arm in a vicious grip. "You are not going to take it back," he
said. "I like it."

"Well," she said, "I don't think I ought . . ."

"Shut up and enjoy it," he muttered, more depressed than ever.

"With the world in the mess it's in," she said, "it's a wonder we can enjoy
anything. I tell you, the bottom rail is on the top."

Julian sighed.

"Of course," she said, "if you know who you are, you can go anywhere."
She said this every time he took her to the reducing class. "Most of them in it
are not our kind of people," she said, "but I can be gracious to anybody. I know
who I am."

"They don't give a damn for your graciousness," Julian said savagely.
"Knowing who you are is good for one generation only. You haven't the fog-
giest idea where you stand now or who you are."

She stopped and allowed her eyes to flash at him. "I most certainly do know who I am," she said, "and if you don't know who you are, I'm ashamed of you."

"Oh hell," Julian said.

"Your great-grandfather was a former governor of this state," she said "Your grandfather was a prosperous landowner. Your grandmother was a Godhigh."

"Will you look around you," he said tensely, "and see where you are now?" and he swept his arm jerkily out to indicate the neighborhood, which the growing darkness at least made less dingy.

"You remain what you are," she said. "Your great-grandfather had a plantation and two hundred slaves."

"There are no more slaves," he said irritably.

"They were better off when they were," she said. He groaned to see that she was off on that topic. She rolled onto it every few days like a train on an open track. He knew every stop, every junction, every swamp along the way, and knew the exact point at which her conclusion would roll majestically into the station: "It's ridiculous. It's simply not realistic. They should rise, yes, but on their own side of the fence."

"Let's skip it," Julian said.

"The ones I feel sorry for," she said, "are the ones that are half white. They're tragic."

"Will you skip it?"

"Suppose we were half white. We would certainly have mixed feelings."

"I have mixed feelings now," he groaned.

"Well let's talk about something pleasant," she said. "I remember going to Grandpa's when I was a little girl. Then the house had double stairways that went up to what was really the second floor—all the cooking was done on the first. I used to like to stay down in the kitchen on account of the way the walls smelled. I would sit with my nose pressed against the plaster and take deep breaths. Actually the place belonged to the Godhighs but your grandfather Chestny paid the mortgage and saved it for them. They were in reduced circumstances," she said, "but reduced or not, they never forgot who they were."

"Doubtless that decayed mansion reminded them," Julian muttered. He never spoke of it without contempt or thought of it without longing. He had seen it once when he was a child before it had been sold. The double stairways had rotted and had been torn down. Negroes were living in it. But it remained in his mind as his mother had known it. It appeared in his dreams regularly. He would stand on the wide porch, listening to the rustle of oak leaves, then wander through the high-ceilinged hall into the parlor that opened onto it and gaze at the worn rugs and faded draperies. It occurred to him that it was he, not she, who could have appreciated it. He preferred its threadbare elegance to anything he could name and it was because of it that all the neighborhoods they had lived in had been a torment to him—whereas she had hardly known the difference. She called her insensitivity "being adjustable."

"And I remember the old darky who was my nurse, Caroline. There was no better person in the world. I've always had a great respect for my colored friends," she said. "I'd do anything in the world for them and they'd . . ."

"Will you for God's sake get off that subject?" Julian said. When he got on a bus by himself, he made it a point to sit down beside a Negro, in reparation as it were for his mother's sins.

"You're mighty touchy tonight," she said. "Do you feel all right?"

"Yes I feel all right," he said. "Now lay off."

She pursed her lips. "Well, you certainly are in a vile humor," she observed. "I just won't speak to you at all."

They had reached the bus stop. There was no bus in sight and Julian, his hands still jammed in his pockets and his head thrust forward, scowled down the empty street. The frustration of having to wait on the bus as well as ride on it began to creep up his neck like a hot hand. The presence of his mother was borne in upon him as she gave a pained sigh. He looked at her bleakly. She was holding herself very erect under the preposterous hat, wearing it like a banner of her imaginary dignity. There was in him an evil urge to break her spirit. He suddenly unloosened his tie and pulled it off and put it in his pocket.

She stiffened. "Why must you look like *that* when you take me to town?" she said. "Why must you deliberately embarrass me?"

"If you'll never learn where you are," he said, "you can at least learn where I am."

"You look like a—thug," she said.

"Then I must be one," he murmured.

"I'll just go home," she said. " I will not bother you. If you can't do a little thing like that for me . . ."

Rolling his eyes upward, he put his tie back on. "Restored to my class," he muttered. He thrust his face toward her and hissed, "True culture is in the mind, the *mind*," he said, and tapped his head, "the mind."

"It's in the heart," she said, "and in how you do things and how you do things is because of who you *are*."

"Nobody in the damn bus cares who you are."

"I care who I am," she said icily.

The lighted bus appeared on top of the next hill and as it approached, they moved out into the street to meet it. He put his hand under her elbow and hoisted her up on the creaking step. She entered with a little smile, as if she were going into a drawing room where everyone had been waiting for her. While he put in the tokens, she sat down on one of the broad front seats for three which faced the aisle. A thin woman with protruding teeth and long yellow hair was sitting on the end of it. His mother moved up beside her and left room for Julian beside herself. He sat down and looked at the floor across the aisle where a pair of thin feet in red and white canvas sandals were planted.

His mother immediately began a general conversation meant to attract anyone who felt like talking. "Can it get any hotter?" she said and removed from her purse a folding fan, black with a Japanese scene on it, which she began to flutter before her.

"I reckon it might could," the woman with the protruding teeth said, "but I know for a fact my apartment couldn't get no hotter."

"It must get the afternoon sun," his mother said. She sat forward and looked up and down the bus. It was half filled. Everybody was white. "I see we have the bus to ourselves," she said. Julian cringed.

"For a change," said the woman across the aisle, the owner of the red and white canvas sandals. "I come on one the other day and they were thick as fleas—up front and all through."

"The world is in a mess everywhere," his mother said. "I don't know how we've let it get in this fix."

"What gets my goat is all those boys from good families stealing automobile tires," the woman with the protruding teeth said. "I told my boy, I said you may not be rich but you been raised right and if I ever catch you in any such mess, they can send you on to the reformatory. Be exactly where you belong."

"Training tells," his mother said. "Is your boy in high school?"

"Ninth grade," the woman said.

"My son just finished college last year. He wants to write but he's selling typewriters until he gets started," his mother said.

The woman leaned forward and peered at Julian. He threw her such a malevolent look that she subsided against the seat. On the floor across the aisle there was an abandoned newspaper. He got up and got it and opened it out in front of him. His mother discreetly continued the conversation in a lower tone but the woman across the aisle said in a loud voice, "Well that's nice. Selling typewriters is close to writing. He can go right from one to the other."

"I tell him," his mother said, "that Rome wasn't built in a day."

Behind the newspaper Julian was withdrawing into the inner compartment of his mind where he spent most of his time. This was a kind of mental bubble in which he established himself when he could not bear to be part of what was going on around him. From it he could see out and judge but in it he was safe from any kind of penetration from without. It was the only place where he felt free of the general idiocy of his fellows. His mother had never entered it but from it he could see her with absolute clarity.

The old lady was clever enough and he thought that if she had started from any of the right premises, more might have been expected of her. She lived according to the laws of her own fantasy world, outside of which he had never seen her set foot. The law of it was to sacrifice herself for him after she had first created the necessity to do so by making a mess of things. If he had permitted her sacrifices, it was only because her lack of foresight had made them necessary. All of her life had been a struggle to act like a Chestny without the Chestny goods, and to give him everything she thought a Chestny ought to have; but since, said she, it was fun to struggle, why complain? And when you had won, as she had won, what fun to look back on the hard times! He could not forgive her that she had enjoyed the struggle and that she thought *she* had won.

What she meant when she said she had won was that she had brought him up successfully and had sent him to college and that he had turned out so well—good looking (her teeth had gone unfilled, so that his could be straightened), intelligent (he realized he was too intelligent to be a success), and with a future ahead of him (there was of course no future ahead of him). She excused his gloominess on the grounds that he was still growing up and his radical ideas on his lack of practical experience. She said he didn't yet know a thing about "life," that he hadn't even entered the real world—when already he was as disenchanted with it as a man of fifty.

The further irony of all this was that in spite of her, he had turned out so well. In spite of going to only a third-rate college, he had, on his own initiative, come out with a first-rate education; in spite of growing up dominated by a small mind, he had ended up with a large one; in spite of all her foolish views, he was free of prejudice and unafraid to face facts. Most miraculous of all, instead of being blinded by love for her as she was for him, he had cut himself emotionally free of her and could see her with complete objectivity. He was not dominated by his mother.

The bus stopped with a sudden jerk and shook him from his meditation. A woman from the back lurched forward with little steps and barely escaped falling in his newspaper as she righted herself. She got off and a large Negro got on. Julian kept his paper lowered to watch. It gave him a certain satisfaction to see injustice in daily operation. It confirmed his view that with a few exceptions there was no one worth knowing within a radius of three hundred miles. The Negro was well dressed and carried a briefcase. He looked round and then sat down on the other end of the seat where the woman with the red and white canvas sandals was sitting. He immediately unfolded a newspaper and obscured himself behind it. Julian's mother's elbow at once prodded insistently into his ribs. "Now you see why I won't ride on these buses by myself," she whispered.

The woman with the red and white canvas sandals had risen at the same time the Negro sat down and had gone further back in the bus and taken the seat of the woman who had got off. His mother leaned forward and cast her an approving look.

Julian rose, crossed the aisle, and sat down in the place of the woman with the canvas sandals. From this position, he looked serenely across at his mother. Her face had turned an angry red. He stared at her, making his eyes the eyes of a stranger. He felt his tension suddenly lift as if he had openly declared war on her.

He would have liked to get in conversation with the Negro and to talk with him about art or politics or any subject that would be above the comprehension of those around them, but the man remained entrenched behind his paper. He was either ignoring the change of seating or had never noticed it. There was no way for Julian to convey his sympathy.

His mother kept her eyes fixed reproachfully on his face. The woman with the protruding teeth was looking at him avidly as if he were a type of monster new to her.

"Do you have a light?" he asked the Negro.

Without looking away from his paper, the man reached in his pocket and handed him a packet of matches.

"Thanks," Julian said. For a moment he held the matches foolishly. A NO SMOKING sign looked down upon him from over the door. This alone would not have deterred him; he had no cigarettes. He had quit smoking some months before because he could not afford it. "Sorry," he muttered and handed back the matches. The Negro lowered the paper and gave him an annoyed look. He took the matches and raised the paper again.

His mother continued to gaze at him but she did not take the advantage of his momentary discomfort. Her eyes retained their battered look. Her face seemed to be unnaturally red, as if her blood pressure had risen. Julian allowed no glimmer of sympathy to show on his face. Having got the advantage, he wanted desperately to keep it and carry it through. He would have liked to teach her a lesson that would last her a while, but there seemed no way to continue the point. The Negro refused to come out from behind his paper.

Julian folded his arms and looked stolidly before him, facing her but as if he did not see her, as if he had ceased to recognize her existence. He visualized a scene in which, the bus having reached their stop, he would remain in his seat and when she said, "Aren't you going to get off?" he would look at her as a stranger who had rashly addressed him. The corner they got off on was usually deserted, but it was well lighted and it would not hurt her to walk by herself the four blocks to the Y. He decided to wait until the time came and then decide whether or not he would let her get off by herself. He would have to be at the Y at ten to bring her back, but he could leave her wondering if he was going to show up. There was no reason for her to think she could always depend on him.

He retired again into the high-ceilinged room sparsely settled with large pieces of antique furniture. His soul expanded momentarily but then he became aware of his mother across from him and the vision shriveled. He studied her coldly. Her feet in little pumps dangled like a child's and did not quite reach the floor. She was training on him an exaggerated look of reproach. He felt completely detached from her. At that moment he could with pleasure have slapped her as he would have slapped a particularly obnoxious child in his charge.

He began to imagine various unlikely ways by which he could teach her a lesson. He might make friends with some distinguished Negro professor or lawyer and bring him home to spend the evening. He would be entirely justified but her blood pressure would rise to 300. He could not push her to the extent of making her have a stroke, and moreover, he had never been successful at making any Negro friends. He had tried to strike up an acquaintance on the bus with some of the better types, with ones that looked like professors or ministers or lawyers. One morning he had sat down next to a distinguished-looking dark brown man who had answered his questions with a sonorous solemnity but who had turned out to be an undertaker. Another day he had sat down beside a cigar-smoking Negro with a diamond ring on his finger, but after a few stilted pleasantries, the Negro had rung the buzzer and risen, slipping two lottery tickets into Julian's hand as he climbed over him to leave.

He imagined his mother lying desperately ill and his being able to secure only a Negro doctor for her. He toyed with that idea for a few minutes and then dropped it for a momentary vision of himself participating as a sympathizer in a sit-in demonstration. This was possible but he did not linger with it. Instead, he approached the ultimate horror. He brought home a beautiful suspiciously Negroid woman. Prepare yourself, he said. There is nothing you can do about it. This is the woman I've chosen. She's intelligent, dignified, even good, and she's suffered and she hasn't thought it *fun*. Now persecute us, go ahead and persecute us. Drive her out of here, but remember, you're driving me too. His eyes were narrowed and through the indignation he had generated, he saw his mother across the aisle, purplefaced, shrunken to the dwarf-like proportions of her moral nature, sitting like a mummy beneath the ridiculous banner of her hat.

He was tilted out of his fantasy again as the bus stopped. The door opened with a sucking hiss and out of the dark a large, gaily dressed, sullen-looking colored woman got on with a little boy. The child, who might have been four, had on a short plaid suit and a Tyrolean hat with a blue feather in it. Julian hoped that he would sit down beside him and that the woman would push in beside his mother. He could think of no better arrangement.

As she waited for her tokens, the woman was surveying the seating possibilities—he hoped with the idea of sitting where she was least wanted. There was something familiar-looking about her but Julian could not place what it was. She was a giant of a woman. Her face was set not only to meet opposition but to seek it out. The downward tilt of her large lower lip was like a warning sign: DON'T TAMPER WITH ME. Her bulging figure was encased in a green crepe dress and her feet overflowed in red shoes. She had on a hideous hat. A purple velvet flap came down on one side of it and stood up on the other; the rest of it was green and looked like a cushion with the stuffing out. She carried a mammoth red pocketbook that bulged throughout as if it were stuffed with rocks.

To Julian's disappointment, the little boy climbed up on the empty seat beside his mother. His mother lumped all children, black and white, into the common category, "cute," and she thought little Negroes were on the whole cuter than little white children. She smiled at the little boy as he climbed on the seat.

Meanwhile the woman was bearing down upon the empty seat beside Julian. To his annoyance, she squeezed herself into it. He saw his mother's face change as the woman settled herself next to him and he realized with satisfaction that this was more objectionable to her than it was to him. Her face seemed almost gray and there was a look of dull recognition in her eyes, as if suddenly she had sickened at some awful confrontation. Julian saw that it was because she and the woman had, in a sense, swapped sons. Though his mother would not realize the symbolic significance of this, she would feel it. His amusement showed plainly on his face.

The woman next to him muttered something unintelligible to herself. He was conscious of a kind of bristling next to him, muted growling like that of an angry cat. He could not see anything but the red pocketbook upright on the bulging green thighs. He visualized the woman as she had stood waiting for her tokens—the ponderous figure, rising from the red shoes upward over the solid hips, the mammoth bosom, the haughty face, to the green and purple hat.

His eyes widened.

The vision of the two hats, identical, broke upon him with the radiance of a brilliant sunrise. His face was suddenly lit with joy. He could not believe that Fate had thrust upon his mother such a lesson. He gave a loud chuckle so that she would look at him and see that he saw. She turned her eyes on him slowly. The blue in them seemed to have turned a bruised purple. For a moment he had an uncomfortable sense of her innocence, but it lasted only a second before principle rescued him. Justice entitled him to laugh. His grin hardened until it said to her as plainly as if he were saying aloud: Your punishment exactly fits your pettiness. This should teach you a permanent lesson.

Her eyes shifted to the woman. She seemed unable to bear looking at him and to find the woman preferable. He became conscious again of the bristling presence at his side. The woman was rumbling like a volcano about to become active. His mother's mouth began to twitch slightly at one corner. With a sinking heart, he saw incipient signs of recovery on her face and realized that this was going to strike her suddenly as funny and was going to be no lesson at all. She kept her eyes on the woman and an amused smile came over her face as if the woman were a monkey that had stolen her hat. The little Negro was looking up at her with large fascinated eyes. He had been trying to attract her attention for some time.

"Carver," the woman said suddenly. "Come heah!"

When he saw that the spotlight was on him at last, Carver drew his feet up and turned himself toward Julian's mother and giggled.

"Carver!" the woman said. "You heah me? Come Heah!"

Carver slid down from the seat but remained squatting with his back against the base of it, his head turned slowly around toward Julian's mother, who was smiling at him. The woman reached a hand across the aisle and snatched him to her. He righted himself and hung backwards on her knees, grinning at Julian's mother. "Isn't he cute?" Julian's mother said to the woman with the protruding teeth.

"I reckon he is," the woman said without conviction.

The Negress yanked him upright but he eased out of her grip and shot across the aisle and scrambled, giggling wildly, onto the seat beside his love.

"I think he likes me," Julian's mother said, and smiled at the woman. It was the smile she used when she was being particularly gracious to an inferior. Julian saw everything lost. The lesson had rolled off her like rain on a roof.

The woman stood up and yanked the little boy off the seat as if she were snatching him from contagion. Julian could feel the rage in her at having no weapon like his mother's smile. She gave the child a sharp slap across his leg. He howled once and then thrust his head into her stomach and kicked his feet against her shins. "Behave," she said vehemently.

The bus stopped and the Negro who had been reading the newspaper got off. The woman moved over and set the little boy down with a thump between herself and Julian. She held him firmly by the knee. In a moment he put his hands in front of his face and peeped at Julian's mother through his fingers.

"I see yoooooooo!" she said and put her hand in front of her face and peeped at him.

The woman slapped his hand down. "Quit yo' foolishness," she said, "before I knock the living Jesus out of you!"

Julian was thankful that the next stop was theirs. He reached up and pulled the cord. The woman reached up and pulled it at the same time. Oh my God, he thought. He had the terrible intuition that when they got off the bus together, his mother would open her purse and give the little boy a nickel. The gesture would be as natural to her as breathing. The bus stopped and the woman got up and lunged to the front, dragging the child, who wished to stay on, after her. Julian and his mother got up and followed. As they neared the door, Julian tried to relieve her of her pocketbook.

"No," she murmured, "I want to give the little boy a nickel."

"No!" Julian hissed. "No!"

She smiled down at the child and opened her bag. The bus door opened and the woman picked him up by the arm and descended with him, hanging at her hip. Once in the street she set him down and shook him.

Julian's mother had to close her purse while she got down the bus step but as soon as her feet were on the ground, she opened it again and began to rummage inside. "I can't find but a penny," she whispered, "but it looks like a new one."

"Don't do it!" Julian said fiercely between his teeth. There was a streetlight on the corner and she hurried to get under it so that she could better see into her pocketbook. The woman was heading off rapidly down the street with the child still hanging backward on her hand.

"Oh little boy!" Julian's mother called and took a few quick steps and caught up with them just beyond the lamppost. "Here's a bright new penny for you," and she held out the coin, which shone bronze in the dim light.

The huge woman turned and for a moment stood, her shoulders lifted and her face frozen with frustrated rage, and stared at Julian's mother. Then all at once she seemed to explode like a piece of machinery that had been given one ounce of pressure too much. Julian saw the black fist swing out with the red pocketbook. He shut his eyes and cringed as he heard the woman shout, "He don't take nobody's pennies!" When he opened his eyes, the woman was disappearing down the street with the little boy staring wide-eyed over her shoulder. Julian's mother was sitting on the sidewalk.

"I told you not to do that," Julian said angrily. "I told you not to do that!"

He stood over her for a minute, gritting his teeth. Her legs were stretched out in front of her and her hat was on her lap. He squatted down and looked her in the face. It was totally expressionless. "You got exactly what you deserved," he said. "Now get up."

He picked up her pocketbook and put what had fallen out back in it. He picked the hat up off her lap. The penny caught his eye on the sidewalk and he picked that up and let it drop before her eyes into the purse. Then he stood up and leaned over and held his hands out to pull her up. She remained immobile. He sighed. Rising above them on either side were black apartment buildings, marked with irregular rectangles of light. At the end of the block a man came out of a door and walked off in the opposite direction. "All right," he said, "suppose somebody happens by and wants to know why you're sitting on the sidewalk?"

She took the hand and, breathing hard, pulled heavily up on it and then stood for a moment, swaying slightly as if the spots of light in the darkness were circling around her. Her eyes, shadowed and confused, finally settled on his face. He did not try to conceal his irritation. "I hope this teaches you a lesson," he said. She leaned forward and her eyes raked his face. She seemed trying to determine his identity. Then, as if she found nothing familiar about him, she started off with a headlong movement in the wrong direction.

"Aren't you going to the Y?" he asked.

"Home," she muttered.

"Well, are we walking?"

For answer she kept going. Julian followed along, his hands behind him. He saw no reason to let the lesson she had had go without backing it up with an explanation of its meaning. She might as well be made to understand what had happened to her. "Don't think that was just an uppity Negro woman," he said. "That was the whole colored race which will no longer take your condescending pennies. That was your black double. She can wear the same hat as you, and to be sure," he added gratuitously (because he thought it was funny), "it looked better on her than it did on you. What all this means," he said, "is that the old world is gone. The old manners are obsolete and your graciousness is not worth a damn." He thought bitterly of the house that had been lost for him. "You aren't who you think you are," he said.

She continued to plow ahead, paying no attention to him. Her hair had come undone on one side. She dropped her pocketbook and took no notice. He stopped and picked it up and handed it to her but she did not take it.

"You needn't act as if the world had come to an end," he said, "because it hasn't. From now on you've got to live in a new world and face a few realities for a change. Buck up," he said, "it won't kill you."

She was breathing fast.

"Let's wait on the bus," he said.

"Home," she said thickly.

"I hate to see you behave like this," he said. "Just like a child. I should be able to expect more of you." He decided to stop where he was and make her stop and wait for a bus. "I'm not going any farther," he said, stopping. "We're going on the bus."

She continued to go on as if she had not heard him. He took a few steps and caught her arm and stopped her. He looked into her face and caught his breath. He was looking into a face he had never seen before. "Tell Grandpa to come get me," she said.

He stared, stricken.

"Tell Caroline to come get me," she said.

Stunned, he let her go and she lurched forward again, walking as if one leg were shorter than the other. A tide of darkness seemed to be sweeping her from him. "Mother!" he cried. "Darling, sweetheart, wait!" Crumpling, she fell to the pavement. He dashed forward and fell at her side, crying, "Mamma, Mamma!" He turned her over. Her face was fiercely distorted. One eye, large and staring, moved slightly to the left as if it had become unmoored. The other remained fixed on him, raked his face again, found nothing, and closed.

"Wait here, wait here!" he cried and jumped up and began to run for help toward a cluster of lights he saw in the distance ahead of him. "Help, help!" he shouted, but his voice was thin, scarcely a thread of sound. The lights drifted farther away the faster he ran and his feet moved numbly as if they carried him nowhere. The tide of darkness seemed to sweep him back to her, postponing from moment to moment his entry into the world of guilt and sorrow.

Sonny's Blues

I read about it in the paper, in the subway, on my way to work. I read it, and I couldn't believe it, and I read it again. Then perhaps I just stared at it, at the newsprint spelling out his name, spelling out the story. I stared at it in the swinging lights of the subway car, and in the faces and bodies of the people, and in my own face, trapped in the darkness which roared outside.

It was not to be believed and I kept telling myself that, as I walked from the subway station to the high school. And at the same time I couldn't doubt it. I was scared, scared for Sonny. He became real to me again. A great block of ice got settled in my belly and kept melting there slowly all day long, while I taught my classes algebra. It was a special kind of ice. It kept melting, sending trickles of ice water all up and down my veins, but it never got less. Sometimes it hardened and seemed to expand until I felt my guts were going to come spilling out or that I was going to choke or scream. This would always be at a moment when I was remembering some specific thing Sonny had once said or done.

When he was about as old as the boys in my classes his face had been bright and open, there was a lot of copper in it; and he'd had wonderfully direct brown eyes, and great gentleness and privacy. I wondered what he looked like now. He had been picked up, the evening before, in a raid on an apartment downtown, for peddling and using heroin.

I couldn't believe it: but what I mean by that is that I couldn't find any room for it anywhere inside me. I had kept it outside me for a long time. I hadn't wanted to know. I had had suspicions, but I didn't name them, I kept putting them away. I told myself that Sonny was wild, but he wasn't crazy. And he'd always been a good boy, he hadn't ever turned hard or evil or disrespectful, the way kids can, so quick, so quick, especially in Harlem. I didn't want to believe that I'd ever see my brother going down, coming to nothing, all that light in his face gone out, in the condition I'd already seen so many others. Yet it had happened and here I was, talking about algebra to a lot of boys who might, every one of them for all I knew, be popping off needles every time they went to the head. Maybe it did more for them than algebra could.

I was sure that the first time Sonny had ever had horse, he couldn't have been much older than these boys were now. These boys, now, were living as we'd been living then, they were growing up with a rush and their heads bumped abruptly against the low ceiling of their actual possibilities. They were filled with rage. All they really knew were two darknesses, the darkness of their lives, which was now closing in on them, and the darkness of the movies, which had blinded them to that other darkness, and in which they now, vindictively, dreamed, at once more together than they were at any other time, and more alone.

When the last bell rang, the last class ended, I let out my breath. It seemed I'd been holding it for all that time. My clothes were wet—I may have looked as though I'd been sitting in a steam bath, all dressed up, all afternoon. I sat alone in the classroom a long time. I listened to the boys outside, downstairs, shouting and cursing and laughing. Their laughter struck me for perhaps the first time. It was not the joyous laughter which—God knows why—one associates with children. It was mocking and insular, its intent to denigrate. It was disenchanted, and in this, also, lay the authority of their curses. Perhaps I was listening to them because I was thinking about my brother and in them I heard my brother. And myself.

One boy was whistling a tune, at once very complicated and very simple, it seemed to be pouring out of him as though he were a bird, and it sounded very cool and moving through all that harsh, bright air, only just holding its own through all those other sounds.

I stood up and walked over to the window and looked down into the courtyard. It was the beginning of the spring and the sap was rising in the boys. A teacher passed through them every now and again, quickly, as though he or she couldn't wait to get out of that courtyard, to get those boys out of their sight and off their minds. I started collecting my stuff. I thought I'd better get home and talk to Isabel.

The courtyard was almost deserted by the time I got downstairs. I saw this boy standing in the shadow of a doorway, looking just like Sonny. I almost called his name. Then I saw that it wasn't Sonny, but somebody we used to know, a boy from around our block. He'd been Sonny's friend. He'd never been mine, having been too young for me, and, anyway, I'd never liked him. And now, even though he was a grown-up man, he still hung around that block, still spent hours on the street corners, was always high and raggy. I used to run into him from time to time and he'd often work around to asking me for a quarter or fifty cents. He always had some real good excuse, too, and I always gave it to him, I don't know why.

But now, abruptly, I hated him. I couldn't stand the way he looked at me, partly like a dog, partly like a cunning child. I wanted to ask him what the hell he was doing in the school courtyard.

He sort of shuffled over to me, and he said, "I see you got the papers. So you already know about it."

"You mean about Sonny? Yes, I already know about it. How come they didn't get you?"

He grinned. It made him repulsive and it also brought to mind what he'd looked like as a kid. "I wasn't there. I stay away from them people."

"Good for you." I offered him a cigarette and I watched him through the smoke. "You come all the way down here just to tell me about Sonny?"

"That's right." He was sort of shaking his head and his eyes looked strange, as though they were about to cross. The bright sun deadened his damp dark brown skin and it made his eyes look yellow and showed up the dirt in his kinked hair. He smelled funky. I moved a little away from him and I said, "Well, thanks. But I already know about it and I got to get home."

"I'll walk you a little ways," he said. We started walking. There were a couple of kids still loitering in the courtyard and one of them said goodnight to me and looked strangely at the boy beside me.

"What're you going to do?" he asked me. "I mean, about Sonny?"

"Look. I haven't seen Sonny for over a year. I'm not sure I'm going to do anything. Anyway, what the hell *can* I do?"

"That's right," he said quickly, "ain't nothing you can do. Can't much help old Sonny no more, I guess."

It was what I was thinking and so it seemed to me he had no right to say it.

"I'm surprised at Sonny, though," he went on—he had a funny way of talking, he looked straight ahead as though he were talking to himself—"I thought Sonny was a smart boy, I thought he was too smart to get hung."

"I guess he thought so too," I said sharply, "and that's how he got hung. And now about you? You're pretty goddamn smart, I bet."

Then he looked directly at me, just for a minute. "I ain't smart," he said. "If I was smart, I'd have reached for a pistol a long time ago."

"Look. Don't tell *me* your sad story, if it was up to me, I'd give you one." Then I felt guilty—guilty, probably, for never having supposed that the poor bastard *had* a story of his own, much less a sad one, and I asked, quickly, "What's going to happen to him now?"

He didn't answer this. He was off by himself some place. "Funny thing," he said, and from his tone we might have been discussing the quickest way to get to Brooklyn, "when I saw the papers this morning, the first thing I asked myself was if I had anything to do with it. I felt sort of responsible."

I began to listen more carefully. The subway station was on the corner, just before us, and I stopped. He stopped, too. We were in front of a bar and he ducked slightly, peering in, but whoever he was looking for didn't seem to be there. The juke box was blasting away with something black and bouncy and I half watched the barmaid as she danced her way from the juke box to her place behind the bar. And I watched her face as she laughingly responded to something someone said to her, still keeping time to the music. When she smiled one saw the little girl, one sensed the doomed, still-struggling woman beneath the battered face of the semi-whore.

"I never *give* Sonny nothing," the boy said finally, "but a long time ago I come to school high and Sonny asked me how it felt." He paused, I couldn't bear to watch him, I watched the barmaid, and I listened to the music which seemed to be causing the pavement to shake. "I told him it felt great." The music stopped, the barmaid paused and watched the juke box until the music began again. "It did."

All this was carrying me some place I didn't want to go. I certainly didn't want to know how it felt. It filled everything, the people, the houses, the music, the dark, quicksilver barmaid, with menace; and this menace was their reality.

"What's going to happen to him now?" I asked again.

"They'll send him away some place and they'll try to cure him." He shook his head. "Maybe he'll even think he's kicked the habit. Then they'll let him loose"—he gestured, throwing his cigarette into the gutter. "That's all."

"What do you mean, that's *all?*"

But I knew what he meant.

"I *mean,* that's *all.*" He turned his head and looked at me, pulling down the corners of his mouth. "Don't you know what I mean?" he asked, softly.

"How the hell *would* I know what you mean?" I almost whispered it, I don't know why.

"That's right," he said to the air, "how would *he* know what I mean?" He turned toward me again, patient and calm, and yet I somehow felt him shaking, shaking as though he were going to fall apart. I felt that ice in my guts again, the dread I'd felt all afternoon; and again I watched the barmaid, moving about the bar, washing glasses, and singing. "Listen. They'll let him out and then it'll just start all over again. That's what I mean."

"You mean—they'll let him out. And then he'll just start working his way back in again. You mean he'll never kick the habit. Is that what you mean?"

"That's right," he said, cheerfully. "*You* see what I mean."

"Tell me," I said at last, "why does he want to die? He must want to die, he's killing himself, why does he want to die?"

He looked at me in surprise. He licked his lips. "He don't want to die. He wants to live. Don't nobody want to die, ever."

Then I wanted to ask him—too many things. He could not have answered, or if he had, I could not have borne the answers. I started walking. "Well, I guess it's none of my business."

"It's going to be rough on old Sonny," he said. We reached the subway station. "This is your station?" he asked. I nodded. I took one step down. "Damn!" he said, suddenly. I looked up at him. He grinned again. "Damn it if I didn't leave all my money home. You ain't got a dollar on you, have you? Just for a couple of days, is all."

All at once something inside gave and threatened to come pouring out of me. I didn't hate him any more. I felt that in another moment I'd start crying like a child.

"Sure," I said. "Don't sweat." I looked in my wallet and didn't have a dollar, I only had a five. "Here," I said. "That hold you?"

He didn't look at it—he didn't want to look at it. A terrible closed look came over his face, as though he were keeping the number on the bill a secret from him and me. "Thanks," he said, and now he was dying to see me go. "Don't worry about Sonny. Maybe I'll write him or something."

"Sure," I said. "You do that. So long."

"Be seeing you," he said. I went on down the steps.

And I didn't write Sonny or send him anything for a long time. When I finally did, it was just after my little girl died, he wrote me back a letter which made me feel like a bastard.

Here's what he said:

> Dear brother,
>
> You don't know how much I needed to hear from you. I wanted to write you many a time but I dug how much I must have hurt you and so I didn't write. But now I feel like a man who's been trying to climb up out of some deep, real deep and funky hole and just saw the sun up there, outside. I got to get outside.
>
> I can't tell you much about how I got here. I mean I don't know how to tell you. I guess I was afraid of something or I was trying to escape from something and you know I have never been very strong in the head (smile). I'm glad Mama and Daddy are dead and can't see what's happened to their son and I swear if I'd known what I was doing I would never have hurt you so, you and a lot of other fine people who were nice to me and who believed in me.
>
> I don't want you to think it had anything to do with me being a musician. It's more than that. Or maybe less than that. I can't get anything straight in my head down here and I try not to think about what's going to happen to me when I get outside again. Sometime I think I'm going to flip and *never* get outside and sometime I think I'll come straight back. I tell you one thing, though, I'd rather blow my brains out than go through this again. But that's what they all say, so they tell me. If I tell you when I'm coming to New York and if you could meet me, I sure would appreciate it. Give my love to Isabel and the kids and I was sure sorry to hear about little Gracie. I wish I could be like Mama and say the Lord's will be done, but I don't know it seems to me that trouble is the one thing that never does get stopped and I don't know what good it does to blame it on the Lord. But maybe it does some good if you believe it.
>
> Your brother,
Sonny

Then I kept in constant touch with him and I sent him whatever I could and I went to meet him when he came back to New York. When I saw him many things I thought I had forgotten came flooding back to me. This was because I had begun, finally, to wonder about Sonny, about the life that Sonny lived inside. This life, whatever it was, had made him older and thinner and it had deepened the distant stillness in which he had always moved. He looked very unlike my baby brother. Yet, when he smiled, when we shook hands, the baby brother I'd never known looked out from the depths of his private life, like an animal waiting to be coaxed into the light.

"How you been keeping?" he asked me.

"All right. And you?"

"Just fine." He was smiling all over his face. "It's good to see you again."

"It's good to see you."

The seven years' difference in our ages lay between us like a chasm: I wondered if these years would ever operate between us as a bridge. I was remembering, and it made it hard to catch my breath, that I had been there when he

was born; and I had heard the first words he had ever spoken. When he started
to walk, he walked from our mother straight to me. I caught him just before he
fell when he took the first steps he ever took in this world.

"How's Isabel?"

"Just fine. She's dying to see you."

"And the boys?"

"They're fine, too. They're anxious to see their uncle."

"Oh, come on. You know they don't remember me."

"Are you kidding? Of course they remember you."

He grinned again. We got into a taxi. We had a lot to say to each other, far
too much to know how to begin.

As the taxi began to move, I asked, "You still want to go to India?"

He laughed. "You still remember that. Hell, no. This place is Indian enough
for me."

"It used to belong to them," I said.

And he laughed again. "They damn sure knew what they were doing when
they got rid of it."

Years ago, when he was around fourteen, he'd been all hipped on the idea
of going to India. He read books about people sitting on rocks, naked, in all
kinds of weather, but mostly bad, naturally, and walking barefoot through hot
coals and arriving at wisdom. I used to say that it sounded to me as though they
were getting away from wisdom as fast as they could. I think he sort of looked
down on me for that.

"Do you mind," he asked, "if we have the driver drive alongside the park?
On the west side—I haven't seen the city in so long."

"Of course not," I said. I was afraid that I might sound as though I were
humoring him, but I hoped he wouldn't take it that way.

So we drove along, between the green of the park and the stony, lifeless
elegance of hotels and apartment buildings, toward the vivid, killing streets of
our childhood. These streets hadn't changed, though housing projects jutted up
out of them now like rocks in the middle of a boiling sea. Most of the houses
in which we had grown up had vanished, as had the stores from which we had
stolen, the basements in which we had first tried sex, the rooftops from which
we had hurled tin cans and bricks. But houses exactly like the houses of our
past yet dominated the landscape, boys exactly like the boys we once had been
found themselves smothering in these houses, came down into the streets for
light and air and found themselves encircled by disaster. Some escaped the
trap, most didn't. Those who got out always left something of themselves
behind, as some animals amputate a leg and leave it in the trap. It might be
said, perhaps, that I had escaped, after all, I was a school teacher; or that Sonny
had, he hadn't lived in Harlem for years. Yet, as the cab moved uptown through
streets which seemed, with a rush, to darken with dark people, and as I covertly
studied Sonny's face, it came to me that what we both were seeking through
our separate cab windows was that part of ourselves which had been left
behind. It's always at the hour of trouble and confrontation that the missing
member aches.

We hit 110th Street and started rolling up Lenox Avenue. And I'd known this avenue all my life, but it seemed to me again, as it had seemed on the day I'd first heard about Sonny's trouble, filled with a hidden menace which was its very breath of life.

"We almost there," said Sonny.

"Almost." We were both too nervous to say anything more.

We live in a housing project. It hasn't been up long. A few days after it was up it seemed uninhabitably new, now, of course, it's already rundown. It looks like a parody of the good, clean, faceless life—God knows the people who live in it do their best to make it a parody. The beat-looking grass lying around isn't enough to make their lives green, the hedges will never hold out the streets, and they know it. The big windows fool no one, they aren't big enough to make space out of no space. They don't bother with the windows, they watch the TV screen instead. The playground is most popular with the children who don't play at jacks, or skip rope, or roller skate, or swing, and they can be found in it after dark. We moved in partly because it's not too far from where I teach, and partly for the kids; but it's really just like the houses in which Sonny and I grew up. The same things happen, they'll have the same things to remember. The moment Sonny and I started into the house I had the feeling that I was simply bringing him back into the danger he had almost died trying to escape.

Sonny has never been talkative. So I don't know why I was sure he'd be dying to talk to me when supper was over the first night. Everything went fine, the oldest boy remembered him, and the youngest boy liked him, and Sonny had remembered to bring something for each of them; and Isabel, who is really much nicer than I am, more open and giving, had gone to a lot of trouble about dinner and was genuinely glad to see him. And she's always been able to tease Sonny in a way that I haven't. It was nice to see her face so vivid again and to hear her laugh and watch her make Sonny laugh. She wasn't, or, anyway, she didn't seem to be, at all uneasy or embarrassed. She chatted as though there were no subject which had to be avoided and she got Sonny past his first, faint stiffness. And thank God she was there, for I was filled with that icy dread again. Everything I did seemed awkward to me, and everything I said sounded freighted with hidden meaning. I was trying to remember everything I'd heard about dope addiction and I couldn't help watching Sonny for signs. I wasn't doing it out of malice. I was trying to find out something about my brother. I was dying to hear him tell me he was safe.

"Safe!" my father grunted, whenever Mama suggested trying to move to a neighborhood which might be safer for children. "Safe, hell! Ain't no place safe for kids, nor nobody."

He always went on like this, but he wasn't, ever, really as bad as he sounded, not even on weekends, when he got drunk. As a matter of fact, he was always on the lookout for "something a little better," but he died before he found it. He died suddenly, during a drunken weekend in the middle of the war, when Sonny was fifteen. He and Sonny hadn't ever got on too well. And this was partly because Sonny was the apple of his father's eye. It was because he loved Sonny so much and was frightened for him, that he was always fighting with him. It doesn't do any good to fight with Sonny. Sonny just moves back, inside himself, where he can't be reached. But the principal reason that they never hit it off is that they were so much alike. Daddy was big and rough and loud-talking, just the opposite of Sonny, but they both had—that same privacy.

Mama tried to tell me something about this, just after Daddy died. I was home on leave from the army.

This was the last time I ever saw my mother alive. Just the same, this picture gets all mixed up in my mind with pictures I had of her when she was younger. The way I always see her is the way she used to be on a Sunday afternoon, say, when the old folks were talking after the big Sunday dinner. I always see her wearing pale blue. She'd be sitting on the sofa. And my father would be sitting in the easy chair, not far from her. And the living room would be full of church folks and relatives. There they sit, in chairs all around the living room, and the night is creeping up outside, but nobody knows it yet. You can see the darkness growing against the windowpanes and you hear the street noises every now and again, or maybe the jangling beat of a tambourine from one of the churches close by, but it's real quiet in the room. For a moment nobody's talking, but every face looks darkening, like the sky outside. And my mother rocks a little from the waist, and my father's eyes are closed. Everyone is looking at something a child can't see. For a minute they've forgotten the children. Maybe a kid is lying on the rug, half asleep. Maybe somebody's got a kid in his lap and is absent-mindedly stroking the kid's head. Maybe there's a kid, quiet and big-eyed, curled up in a big chair in the corner. The silence, the darkness coming, and the darkness in the faces frightens the child obscurely. He hopes that the hand which strokes his forehead will never stop—will never die. He hopes that there will never come a time when the old folks won't be sitting around the living room, talking about where they've come from, and what they've seen, and what's happened to them and their kinfolk.

But something deep and watchful in the child knows that this is bound to end, is already ending. In a moment someone will get up and turn on the light. Then the old folks will remember the children and they won't talk any more that day. And when light fills the room, the child is filled with darkness. He knows that everytime this happens he's moved just a little closer to that darkness outside. The darkness outside is what the old folks have been talking about. It's what they've come from. It's what they endure. The child knows that they won't talk any more because if he knows too much about what's happened to *them,* he'll know too much too soon, about what's going to happen to *him.*

The last time I talked to my mother, I remember I was restless. I wanted to get out and see Isabel. We weren't married then and we had a lot to straighten out between us.

There Mama sat, in black, by the window. She was humming an old church song, *Lord, you brought me from a long ways off.* Sonny was out somewhere. Mama kept watching the streets.

"I don't know," she said, "if I'll ever see you again, after you go off from here. But I hope you'll remember the things I tried to teach you."

"Don't talk like that," I said, and smiled. "You'll be here a long time yet."

She smiled, too, but she said nothing. She was quiet for a long time. And I said, "Mama, don't you worry about nothing. I'll be writing all the time, and you be getting the checks. . . ."

"I want to talk to you about your brother," she said, suddenly. "If anything happens to me he ain't going to have nobody to look out for him."

"Mama," I said, "ain't nothing going to happen to you *or* Sonny. Sonny's all right. He's a good boy and he's got good sense."

"It ain't a question of his being a good boy," Mama said, "nor of his having good sense. It ain't only the bad ones, nor yet the dumb ones that gets sucked under." She stopped, looking at me. "Your Daddy once had a brother," she said, and she smiled in a way that made me feel she was in pain. "You didn't never know that, did you?"

"No," I said, "I never knew that," and I watched her face.

"Oh, yes," she said, "your Daddy had a brother." She looked out of the window again. "I know you never saw your Daddy cry. But *I* did—many a time, through all these years."

I asked her, "What happened to his brother? How come nobody's ever talked about him?"

This was the first time I ever saw my mother look old.

"His brother got killed," she said, "when he was just a little younger than you are now. I knew him. He was a fine boy. He was maybe a little full of the devil, but he didn't mean nobody no harm."

Then she stopped and the room was silent, exactly as it had sometimes been on those Sunday afternoons. Mama kept looking out into the streets.

"He used to have a job in the mill," she said, "and, like all young folks, he just liked to perform on Saturday nights. Saturday nights, him and your father would drift around to different places, go to dances and things like that, or just sit around with people they knew, and your father's brother would sing, he had a fine voice, and play along with himself on his guitar. Well, this particular Saturday night, him and your father was coming home from some place, and they were both a little drunk and there was a moon that night, it was bright like day. Your father's brother was feeling kind of good, and he was whistling to himself, and he had his guitar slung over his shoulder. They was coming down a hill and beneath them was a road that turned off from the highway. Well, your father's brother, being always kind of frisky, decided to run down this hill, and he did, with that guitar banging and clanging behind him, and he ran across the road, and he was making water behind a tree. And your father was sort of amused at him and he was still coming down the hill, kind of slow. Then he heard a car motor and that same minute his brother stepped from behind the tree, into the road, in the moonlight. And he started to cross the road. And your father started to run down the hill, he says he don't know why. This car was full of white men. They was all drunk, and when they seen your father's brother they let out a great whoop and holler and they aimed the car straight at him. They was having fun, they just wanted to scare him, the way they do sometimes, you know. But they was drunk. And I guess the boy, being drunk, too, and scared, kind of lost his head. By the time he jumped it was too late. Your father says he heard his brother scream when the car rolled over him, and he heard the wood of that guitar when it give, and he heard them strings go flying, and he heard them white men shouting, and the car kept on a-going and it ain't stopped till this day. And, time your father got down the hill, his brother weren't nothing but blood and pulp."

Tears were gleaming on my mother's face. There wasn't anything I could say.

"He never mentioned it," she said, "because I never let him mention it before you children. Your Daddy was like a crazy man that night and for many a night thereafter. He says he never in his life seen anything as dark as that road after the lights of that car had gone away. Weren't nothing, weren't nobody on that road, just your Daddy and his brother and that busted guitar. Oh, yes. Your Daddy never did really get right again. Till the day he died he weren't sure but that every white man he saw was the man that killed his brother."

She stopped and took out her handkerchief and dried her eyes and looked at me.

"I ain't telling you all this," she said, "to make you scared or bitter or to make you hate nobody. I'm telling you this because you got a brother. And the world ain't changed."

I guess I didn't want to believe this. I guess she saw this in my face. She turned away from me, toward the window again, searching those streets.

"But I praise my Redeemer," she said at last, "that He called your Daddy home before me. I ain't saying it to throw no flowers at myself, but, I declare, it keeps me from feeling too cast down to know I helped your father get safely through this world. Your father always acted like he was the roughest, strongest man on earth. And everybody took him to be like that. But if he hadn't had *me* there—to see his tears!"

She was crying again. Still, I couldn't move. I said, "Lord, Lord, Mama, I didn't know it was like that."

"Oh, honey," she said, "there's a lot that you don't know. But you are going to find it out." She stood up from the window and came over to me. "You got to hold on to your brother," she said, "and don't let him fall, no matter what it looks like is happening to him and no matter how evil you gets with him. You going to be evil with him many a time. But don't you forget what I told you, you hear?"

"I won't forget," I said. "Don't you worry, I won't forget. I won't let nothing happen to Sonny."

My mother smiled as though she were amused at something she saw in my face. Then, "You may not be able to stop nothing from happening. But you got to let him know you's *there*."

Two days later I was married, and then I was gone. And I had a lot of things on my mind and I pretty well forgot my promise to Mama until I got shipped home on a special furlough for her funeral.

And, after the funeral, with just Sonny and me alone in the empty kitchen, I tried to find out something about him.

"What do you want to do?" I asked him.

"I'm going to be a musician," he said.

For he had graduated, in the time I had been away, from dancing to the juke box to finding out who was playing what, and what they were doing with it, and he had bought himself a set of drums.

"You mean, you want to be a drummer?" I somehow had the feeling that being a drummer might be all right for other people but not for my brother Sonny.

"I don't think," he said, looking at me very gravely, "that I'll ever be a good drummer. But I think I can play a piano."

I frowned. I'd never played the role of the older brother quite so seriously before, had scarcely ever, in fact, *asked* Sonny a damn thing. I sensed myself in the presence of something I didn't really know how to handle, didn't understand. So I made my frown a little deeper as I asked: "What kind of musician do you want to be?"

He grinned. "How many kinds do you think there are?"

"Be *serious*," I said.

He laughed, throwing his head back, and then looked at me. "I *am* serious."

"Well, then, for Christ's sake, stop kidding around and answer a serious question. I mean, do you want to be a concert pianist, you want to play classical music and all that, or—or what?" Long before I finished he was laughing again. "For Christ's *sake*, Sonny!"

He sobered, but with difficulty. "I'm sorry. But you sound so—*scared!*" and he was off again.

"Well, you may think it's funny now, baby, but it's not going to be so funny when you have to make your living at it, let me tell you *that*." I was furious because I knew he was laughing at me and I didn't know why.

"No," he said, very sober now, and afraid, perhaps, that he'd hurt me, "I don't want to be a classical pianist. That isn't what interests me. I mean"—he paused, looking hard at me, as though his eyes would help me to understand, and then gestured helplessly, as though perhaps his hand would help—"I mean, I'll have a lot of studying to do, and I'll have to study *everything,* but, I mean, I want to play *with*—jazz musicians." He stopped. "I want to play jazz," he said.

Well, the word had never before sounded as heavy, as real, as it sounded that afternoon in Sonny's mouth. I just looked at him and I was probably frowning a real frown by this time. I simply couldn't see why on earth he'd want to spend his time hanging around nightclubs, clowning around on bandstands, while people pushed each other around a dance floor. It seemed—beneath him, somehow. I had never thought about it before, had never been forced to, but I suppose I had always put jazz musicians in a class with what Daddy called "good-time people."

"Are you *serious?*"

"Hell, *yes,* I'm serious."

He looked more helpless than ever, and annoyed, and deeply hurt.

I suggested, helpfully: "You mean—like Louis Armstrong?"

His face closed as though I'd struck him. "No. I'm not talking about none of that old-time, down home crap."

"Well, look, Sonny, I'm sorry, don't get mad. I just don't altogether get it, that's all. Name somebody—you know, a jazz musician you admire."

"Bird."

"Who?"

"Bird! Charlie Parker! Don't they teach you nothing in the goddamn army?"

I lit a cigarette. I was surprised and then a little amused to discover that I was trembling. "I've been out of touch," I said. "You'll have to be patient with me. Now. Who's this Parker character?"

"He's just one of the greatest jazz musicians alive," said Sonny, sullenly, his hands in his pockets, his back to me. "Maybe *the* greatest," he added, bitterly, "that's probably why *you* never heard of him."

"All right," I said, "I'm ignorant. I'm sorry. I'll go out and buy all the cat's records right away, all right?"

"It don't," said Sonny, with dignity, "make any difference to me. I don't care what you listen to. Don't do me no favors."

I was beginning to realize that I'd never seen him so upset before. With another part of my mind I was thinking that this would probably turn out to be one of those things kids go through and that I shouldn't make it seem important by pushing it too hard. Still, I didn't think it would do any harm to ask: "Doesn't all this take a lot of time? Can you make a living at it?"

He turned back to me and half leaned, half sat, on the kitchen table. "Everything takes time," he said, "and—well, yes, sure, I can make a living at it. But what I don't seem to be able to make you understand is that it's the only thing I want to do."

"Well, Sonny," I said, gently, "you know people can't always do exactly what they *want* to do—"

"*No,* I don't know that," said Sonny, surprising me. "I think people *ought* to do what they want to do, what else are they alive for?"

"You getting to be a big boy," I said desperately, "it's time you started thinking about your future."

"I'm thinking about my future," said Sonny, grimly. "I think about it all the time."

I gave up. I decided, if he didn't change his mind, that we could always talk about it later. "In the meantime," I said, "you got to finish school." We had already decided that he'd have to move in with Isabel and her folks. I knew this wasn't the ideal arrangement because Isabel's folks are inclined to be dicty and they hadn't especially wanted Isabel to marry me. But I didn't know what else to do. "And we have to get you fixed up at Isabel's."

There was a long silence. He moved from the kitchen table to the window. "That's a terrible idea. You know it yourself."

"Do you have a *better* idea?"

He just walked up and down the kitchen for a minute. He was as tall as I was. He had started to shave. I suddenly had the feeling that I didn't know him at all.

He stopped at the kitchen table and picked up my cigarettes. Looking at me with a kind of mocking, amused defiance, he put one between his lips. "You mind?"

"You smoking already?"

He lit the cigarette and nodded, watching me through the smoke. "I just wanted to see if I'd have the courage to smoke in front of you." He grinned and blew a great cloud of smoke to the ceiling. "It was easy." He looked at my face. "Come on, now. I bet you was smoking at my age, tell the truth."

I didn't say anything but the truth was on my face, and he laughed. But now there was something very strained in his laugh. "Sure. And I bet that ain't all you was doing."

He was frightening me a little. "Cut the crap," I said. "We already decided that you was going to go and live at Isabel's. Now what's got into you all of a sudden?"

"*You* decided it," he pointed out. "*I* didn't decide nothing." He stopped in front of me, leaning against the stove, arms loosely folded. "Look, brother. I don't want to stay in Harlem no more, I really don't." He was very earnest. He looked at me, then over toward the kitchen window. There was something in his eyes I'd never seen before, some thoughtfulness, some worry all his own. He rubbed the muscle of one arm. "It's time I was getting out of here."

"Where do you want to *go*, Sonny?"

"I want to join the army. Or the navy, I don't care. If I say I'm old enough, they'll believe me."

Then I got mad. It was because I was so scared. "You must be crazy. You goddamn fool, what the hell do you want to go and join the *army* for?"

"I just told you. To get out of Harlem."

"Sonny, you haven't even finished *school*. And if you really want to be a musician, how do you expect to study if you're in the *army*?"

He looked at me, trapped, and in anguish. "There's ways. I might be able to work out some kind of deal. Anyway, I'll have the G.I. Bill when I come out."

"*If* you come out." We stared at each other. "Sonny, please. Be reasonable. I know the setup is far from perfect. But we got to do the best we can."

"I ain't learning nothing in school," he said. "Even when I go." He turned away from me and opened the window and threw his cigarette out into the narrow alley. I watched his back. "At least, I ain't learning nothing you'd want me to learn." He slammed the window so hard I thought the glass would fly out, and turned back to me. "And I'm sick of the stink of these garbage cans!"

"Sonny," I said, "I know how you feel. But if you don't finish school now, you're going to be sorry later that you didn't." I grabbed him by the shoulders. "And you only got another year. It ain't so bad. And I'll come back and I swear I'll help you do *whatever* you want to do. Just try to put up with it till I come back. Will you please do that? For me?"

He didn't answer and he wouldn't look at me.

"Sonny. You hear me?"

He pulled away. "I hear you. But you never hear anything *I* say."

I didn't know what to say to that. He looked out of the window and then back at me. "OK," he said, and sighed. "I'll try."

Then I said, trying to cheer him up a little, "They got a piano at Isabel's. You can practice on it."

And as a matter of fact, it did cheer him up for a minute. "That's right," he said to himself. "I forgot that." His face relaxed a little. But the worry, the thoughtfulness, played on it still, the way shadows play on a face which is staring into the fire.

But I thought I'd never hear the end of that piano. At first, Isabel would write me, saying how nice it was that Sonny was so serious about his music and how, as soon as he came in from school, or wherever he had been when he was supposed to be at school, he went straight to that piano and stayed there until suppertime. And, after supper, he went back to that piano and stayed there until everybody went to bed. He was at the piano all day Saturday and all day Sunday. Then he bought a record player and started playing records. He'd play one record over and over again, all day long sometimes, and he'd improvise along with it on the piano. Or he'd play one section of the record, one chord, one change, one progression, then he'd do it on the piano. Then back to the record. Then back to the piano.

Well, I really don't know how they stood it. Isabel finally confessed that it wasn't like living with a person at all, it was like living with sound. And the sound didn't make any sense to her, didn't make any sense to any of them—naturally. They began, in a way, to be afflicted by this presence that was living in their home. It was as though Sonny were some sort of god, or monster. He moved in an atmosphere which wasn't like theirs at all. They fed him and he ate, he washed himself, he walked in and out of their door; he certainly wasn't nasty or unpleasant or rude, Sonny isn't any of those things; but it was as though he were all wrapped up in some cloud, some fire, some vision all his own; and there wasn't any way to reach him.

At the same time, he wasn't really a man yet, he was still a child, and they had to watch out for him in all kinds of ways. They certainly couldn't throw him out. Neither did they dare to make a great scene about that piano because even they dimly sensed, as I sensed, from so many thousands of miles away, that Sonny was at that piano playing for his life.

But he hadn't been going to school. One day a letter came from the school board and Isabel's mother got it—there had, apparently, been other letters but Sonny had torn them up. This day, when Sonny came in, Isabel's mother showed him the letter and asked where he'd been spending his time. And she finally got it out of him that he'd been down in Greenwich Village, with musicians and other characters, in a white girl's apartment. And this scared her and she started to scream at him and what came up, once she began—though she denies it to this day—was what sacrifices they were making to give Sonny a decent home and how little he appreciated it.

Sonny didn't play the piano that day. By evening, Isabel's mother had calmed down but then there was the old man to deal with, and Isabel herself. Isabel says she did her best to be calm but she broke down and started crying. She says she just watched Sonny's face. She could tell, by watching him, what was happening with him. And what was happening was that they penetrated his cloud, they had reached him. Even if their fingers had been a thousand times more gentle than human fingers ever are, he could hardly help feeling that they had stripped him naked and were spitting on that nakedness. For he also had to see that his presence, that music, which was life or death to him, had been torture for them and that they had endured it, not at all for his sake, but only for mine. And Sonny couldn't take that. He can take it a little better today than he could then but he's still not very good at it and, frankly, I don't know anybody who is.

The silence of the next few days must have been louder than the sound of all the music ever played since time began. One morning, before she went to work, Isabel was in his room for something and she suddenly realized that all of his records were gone. And she knew for certain that he was gone. And he was. He went as far as the navy would carry him. He finally sent me a postcard from some place in Greece and that was the first I knew that Sonny was still alive. I didn't see him any more until we were both back in New York and the war had long been over.

He was a man by then, of course, but I wasn't willing to see it. He came by the house from time to time, but we fought almost every time we met. I didn't like the way he carried himself, loose and dreamlike all the time, and I didn't like his friends, and his music seemed to be merely an excuse for the life he led. It sounded just that weird and disordered.

Then we had a fight, a pretty awful fight, and I didn't see him for months. By and by I looked him up, where he was living, in a furnished room in the Village, and I tried to make it up. But there were lots of people in the room and Sonny just lay on his bed, and he wouldn't come downstairs with me, and he treated these other people as though they were his family and I weren't. So I got mad and then he got mad, and then I told him that he might just as well be dead as live the way he was living. Then he stood up and he told me not to worry about him any more in life, that he *was* dead as far as I was concerned. Then he pushed me to the door and the other people looked on as though nothing were happening, and he slammed the door behind me. I stood in the hallway, staring at the door. I heard somebody laugh in the room and then the tears came to my eyes. I started down the steps, whistling to keep from crying, I kept whistling to myself, *You going to need me, baby, one of these cold, rainy days.*

I read about Sonny's trouble in the spring. Little Grace died in the fall. She was a beautiful little girl. But she only lived a little over two years. She died of polio and she suffered. She had a slight fever for a couple of days, but it didn't seem like anything and we just kept her in bed. And we would certainly have called the doctor, but the fever dropped, she seemed to be all right. So we thought it had just been a cold. Then, one day, she was up, playing, Isabel was in the kitchen fixing lunch for the two boys when they'd come in from school, and she heard Grace fall down in the living room. When you have a lot of children you don't always start running when one of them falls, unless they start screaming or something. And, this time, Grace was quiet. Yet, Isabel says that when she heard that *thump* and then that silence, something happened in her to make her afraid. And she ran to the living room and there was little Grace on the floor, all twisted up, and the reason she hadn't screamed was that she couldn't get her breath. And when she did scream, it was the worst sound, Isabel says, that she'd ever heard in all her life, and she still hears it sometimes in her dreams. Isabel will sometimes wake me up with a low, moaning, strangled sound and I have to be quick to awaken her and hold her to me and where Isabel is weeping against me seems a mortal wound.

I think I may have written Sonny the very day that little Grace was buried. I was sitting in the living room in the dark, by myself, and I suddenly thought of Sonny. My trouble made his real.

One Saturday afternoon, when Sonny had been living with us, or, anyway, been in our house, for nearly two weeks, I found myself wandering aimlessly about the living room, drinking from a can of beer, and trying to work up the courage to search Sonny's room. He was out, he was usually out whenever I was home, and Isabel had taken the children to see their grandparents. Suddenly I was standing still in front of the living room window, watching Seventh Avenue. The idea of searching Sonny's room made me still. I scarcely dared to admit to myself what I'd be searching for. I didn't know what I'd do if I found it. Or if I didn't.

On the sidewalk across from me, near the entrance to a barbecue joint, some people were holding an old-fashioned revival meeting. The barbecue cook, wearing a dirty white apron, his conked hair reddish and metallic in the pale sun, and a cigarette between his lips, stood in the doorway, watching them. Kids and older people paused in their errands and stood there, along with some older men and a couple of very tough-looking women who watched everything that happened on the avenue, as though they owned it, or were maybe owned by it. Well, they were watching this, too. The revival was being carried on by three sisters in black, and a brother. All they had were their voices and their Bibles and a tambourine. The brother was testifying and while he testified two of the sisters stood together, seeming to say, amen, and the third sister walked around with the tambourine outstretched and a couple of people dropped coins into it. Then the brother's testimony ended and the sister who had been taking up the collection dumped the coins into her palm and transferred them to the pocket of her long black robe. Then she raised both hands, striking the tambourine against the air, and then against one hand, and she started to sing. And the two other sisters and the brother joined in.

It was strange, suddenly, to watch, though I had been seeing these street meetings all my life. So, of course, had everybody else down there. Yet, they paused and watched and listened and I stood still at the window. *"Tis the old ship of Zion,"* they sang, and the sister with the tambourine kept a steady, jangling beat, *"it has rescued many a thousand!"* Not a soul under the sound of their voices was hearing this song for the first time, not one of them had been rescued. Nor had they seen much in the way of rescue work being done around them. Neither did they especially believe in the holiness of the three sisters and the brother, they knew too much about them, knew where they lived, and how. The woman with the tambourine, whose voice dominated the air, whose face was bright with joy, was divided by very little from the woman who stood watching her, a cigarette between her heavy, chapped lips, her hair a cuckoo's nest, her face scarred and swollen from many beatings, and her black eyes glittering like coal. Perhaps they both knew this, which was why, when, as rarely, they addressed each other, they addressed each other as Sister. As the singing filled the air the watching, listening faces underwent a change, the eyes focusing on something within; the music seemed to soothe a poison out of them; and time seemed, nearly, to fall away from the sullen, belligerent, battered faces, as though they were fleeing back to their first condition, while dreaming of their last. The barbecue cook half shook his head and smiled, and dropped his cigarette and disappeared into his joint. A man fumbled in his pockets for change and stood holding it in his hand impatiently, as though he had just remembered a pressing appointment further up the avenue. He looked furious. Then I saw Sonny, standing on the edge of the crowd. He was carrying a wide, flat notebook with a green cover, and it made him look, from where I was standing, almost like a schoolboy. The coppery sun brought out the copper in his skin, he was very faintly smiling, standing very still. Then the singing stopped, the tambourine turned into a collection plate again. The furious man dropped in his coins and vanished, so did a couple of the women, and Sonny dropped some change in the plate, looking directly at the woman with a little smile. He started across the avenue, toward the house. He has a slow, loping walk, something like the way Harlem hipsters walk, only he's imposed on this his own half-beat. I had never really noticed it before.

I stayed at the window, both relieved and apprehensive. As Sonny disappeared from my sight, they began singing again. And they were still singing when his key turned in the lock.

"Hey," he said.

"Hey, yourself. You want some beer?"

"No. Well, maybe." But he came up to the window and stood beside me, looking out. "What a warm voice," he said.

They were singing *If I could only hear my mother pray again!*

"Yes," I said, "and she can sure beat that tambourine."

"But what a terrible song," he said, and laughed. He dropped his notebook on the sofa and disappeared into the kitchen. "Where's Isabel and the kids?"

"I think they went to see their grandparents. You hungry?"

"No." He came back into the living room with his can of beer. "You want to come some place with me tonight?"

I sensed, I don't know how, that I couldn't possibly say no. "Sure. Where?"

He sat down on the sofa and picked up his notebook and started leafing through it. "I'm going to sit in with some fellows in a joint in the Village."

"You mean, you're going to play, tonight?"

"That's right." He took a swallow of his beer and moved back to the window. He gave me a sidelong look. "If you can stand it."

"I'll try," I said.

He smiled to himself and we both watched as the meeting across the way broke up. The three sisters and the brother, heads bowed, were singing *God be with you till we meet again*. The faces around them were very quiet. Then the song ended. The small crowd dispersed. We watched the three women and the lone man walk slowly up the avenue.

"When she was singing before," said Sonny, abruptly, "her voice reminded me for a minute of what heroin feels like sometimes—when it's in your veins. It makes you feel sort of warm and cool at the same time. And distant. And—and sure." He sipped his beer, very deliberately not looking at me. I watched his face. "It makes you feel—in control. Sometimes you've got to have that feeling."

"Do you?" I sat down slowly in the easy chair.

"Sometimes." He went to the sofa and picked up his notebook again. "Some people do."

"In order," I asked, "to play?" And my voice was very ugly, full of contempt and anger.

"Well"—he looked at me with great, troubled eyes, as though, in fact, he hoped his eyes would tell me things he could never otherwise say—"they *think* so. And *if* they think so—!"

"And what do *you* think?" I asked.

He sat on the sofa and put his can of beer on the floor. "I don't know," he said, and I couldn't be sure if he were answering my question or pursuing his thoughts. His face didn't tell me. "It's not so much to *play*. It's to *stand* it, to be able to make it at all. On any level." He frowned and smiled: "In order to keep from shaking to pieces."

"But these friends of yours," I said, "they seem to shake themselves to pieces pretty goddamn fast."

"Maybe." He played with the notebook. And something told me that I should curb my tongue, that Sonny was doing his best to talk, that I should listen. "But of course you only know the ones that've gone to pieces. Some don't—or at least they haven't *yet* and that's just about all *any* of us can say." He paused. "And then there are some who just live, really, in hell, and they know it and they see what's happening and they go right on. I don't know." He sighed, dropped the notebook, folded his arms. "Some guys, you can tell from the way they play, they on something *all* the time. And you can see that, well, it makes something real for them. But of course," he picked up his beer from the floor and sipped it and put the can down again, "they *want* to, too, you've got to see that. Even some of them that say they don't—*some*, not all."

"And what about you?" I asked—I couldn't help it. "What about you? Do *you* want to?"

He stood up and walked to the window and remained silent for a long time. Then he sighed. "Me," he said. Then: "While I was downstairs before, on my way here, listening to that woman sing, it struck me all of a sudden how much suffering she must have had to go through—to sing like that. It's *repulsive* to think you have to suffer that much."

I said: "But there's no way not to suffer—is there, Sonny?"

"I believe not," he said and smiled, "but that's never stopped anyone from trying." He looked at me. "Has it?" I realized, with this mocking look, that there stood between us, forever, beyond the power of time or forgiveness, the fact that I had held silence—so long!—when he had needed human speech to help him. He turned back to the window. "No, there's no way not to suffer. But you try all kinds of ways to keep from drowning in it, to keep on top of it, and to make it seem—well, like *you*. Like you did something, all right, and now you're suffering for it. You know?" I said nothing. "Well you know," he said, impatiently, "why *do* people suffer? Maybe it's better to do something to give it a reason, *any* reason."

"But we just agreed," I said "that there's no way not to suffer. Isn't it better, then, just to—take it?"

"But nobody just takes it," Sonny cried, "that's what I'm telling you! *Everybody* tries not to. You're just hung up on the *way* some people try—it's not *your* way!"

The hair on my face began to itch, my face felt wet. "That's not true," I said, "that's not true. I don't give a damn what other people do, I don't even care how they suffer. I just care how *you* suffer." And he looked at me. "Please believe me," I said, "I don't want to see you—die—trying not to suffer."

"I won't," he said, flatly, "die trying not to suffer. At least, not any faster than anybody else."

"But there's no need," I said, trying to laugh, "is there? in killing yourself."

I wanted to say more, but I couldn't. I wanted to talk about will power and how life could be—well, beautiful. I wanted to say that it was all within; but was it? or, rather, wasn't that exactly the trouble? And I wanted to promise that I would never fail him again. But it would all have sounded—empty words and lies.

So I made the promise to myself and prayed that I would keep it.

"It's terrible sometimes, inside," he said, "that's what's the trouble. You walk these streets, black and funky and cold, and there's not really a living ass to talk to, and there's nothing shaking, and there's no way of getting it out—that storm inside. You can't talk it and you can't make love with it, and when you finally try to get with it and play it, you realize *nobody's* listening. So *you've* got to listen. You got to find a way to listen."

And then he walked away from the window and sat on the sofa again, as though all the wind had suddenly been knocked out of him. "Sometimes you'll do *anything* to play, even cut your mother's throat." He laughed and looked at me. "Or your brother's." Then he sobered. "Or your own." Then: "Don't worry. I'm all right now and I think I'll *be* all right. But I can't forget—where I've been. I don't mean just the physical place I've been, I mean where I've *been*. And *what* I've been."

"What have you been, Sonny?" I asked.

He smiled—but sat sideways on the sofa, his elbow resting on the back, his fingers playing with his mouth and chin, not looking at me. "I've been something I didn't recognize, didn't know I could be. Didn't know anybody could be." He stopped, looking inward, looking helplessly young, looking old. "I'm not talking about it now because I feel *guilty* or anything like that—maybe it would be better if I did, I don't know. Anyway, I can't really talk about it. Not to you, not to anybody," and now he turned and faced me. "Sometimes, you know, and it was actually when I was most *out* of the world, I felt that I was in it, that I was *with* it, really, and I could play or I didn't really have to *play,* it just came out of me, it was there. And I don't know how I played, thinking about it now, but I know I did awful things, those times, sometimes, to people. Or it wasn't that I *did* anything to them—it was that they weren't real." He picked up the beer can; it was empty; he rolled it between his palms: "And other times—well, I needed a fix, I needed to find a place to lean, I needed to clear a space to *listen*—and I couldn't find it, and I—went crazy, I did terrible things to *me,* I was terrible *for* me." He began pressing the beer can between his hands, I watched the metal begin to give. It glittered, as he played with it, like a knife, and I was afraid he would cut himself, but I said nothing. "Oh well. I can never tell you. I was all by myself at the bottom of something, stinking and sweating and crying and shaking, and I smelled it, you know? *my* stink, and I thought I'd die if I couldn't get away from it and yet, all the same, I knew that everything I was doing was just locking me in with it. And I didn't know," he paused, still flattening the beer can, "I didn't know, I still *don't* know, something kept telling me that maybe it was good to smell your own stink, but I didn't think that *that* was what I'd been trying to do—and—who can stand it?" and he abruptly dropped the ruined beer can, looking at me with a small, still smile, and then rose, walking to the window as though it were the lodestone rock. I watched his face, he watched the avenue. "I couldn't tell you when Mama died—but the reason I wanted to leave Harlem so bad was to get away from drugs. And then, when I ran away, that's what I was running from—really. When I came back, nothing had changed, *I* hadn't changed, I was just—older." And he stopped, drumming with his fingers on the windowpane. The sun had vanished, soon darkness would fall. I watched his face. "It can come again," he said, almost as though speaking to himself. Then he turned to me. "It can come again," he repeated. "I just want you to know that."

"All right," I said, at last. "So it can come again. All right."

He smiled, but the smile was sorrowful. "I had to try to tell you," he said.

"Yes," I said. "I understand that."

"You're my brother," he said, looking straight at me, and not smiling at all.

"Yes," I repeated, "yes. I understand that."

He turned back to the window, looking out. "All that hatred down there," he said, "all that hatred and misery and love. It's a wonder it doesn't blow the avenue apart."

We went to the only nightclub on a short, dark street, downtown. We squeezed through the narrow, chattering, jam-packed bar to the entrance of the big room, where the bandstand was. And we stood there for a moment, for the lights were very dim in this room and we couldn't see. Then, "Hello, boy," said a voice and an enormous black man, much older than Sonny or myself, erupted out of all that atmospheric lighting and put an arm around Sonny's shoulder. "I been sitting right here," he said, "waiting for you."

He had a big voice, too, and heads in the darkness turned toward us.

Sonny grinned and pulled a little away, and said, "Creole, this is my brother. I told you about him."

Creole shook my hand. "I'm glad to meet you, son," he said, and it was clear that he was glad to meet me *there,* for Sonny's sake. And he smiled, "You got a real musician in *your* family," and he took his arm from Sonny's shoulder and slapped him, lightly, affectionately, with the back of his hand.

"Well. Now I've heard it all," said a voice behind us. This was another musician, and a friend of Sonny's, a coal-black, cheerful-looking man, built close to the ground. He immediately began confiding to me, at the top of his lungs, the most terrible things about Sonny, his teeth gleaming like a lighthouse and his laugh coming up out of him like the beginning of an earthquake. And it turned out that everyone at the bar knew Sonny, or almost everyone; some were musicians, working there, or nearby, or not working, some were simply hangers-on, and some were there to hear Sonny play. I was introduced to all of them and they were all very polite to me. Yet, it was clear that, for them, I was only Sonny's brother. Here, I was in Sonny's world. Or, rather: his kingdom. Here, it was not even a question that his veins bore royal blood.

They were going to play soon and Creole installed me, by myself, at a table in a dark corner. Then I watched them, Creole, and the little black man, and Sonny, and the others, while they horsed around, standing just below the bandstand. The light from the bandstand spilled just a little short of them and, watching them laughing and gesturing and moving about, I had the feeling that they, nevertheless, were being most careful not to step into that circle of light too suddenly: that if they moved into the light too suddenly, without thinking, they would perish in flame. Then, while I watched, one of them, the small, black man, moved into the light and crossed the bandstand and started fooling around with his drums. Then—being funny and being, also, extremely ceremonious—Creole took Sonny by the arm and led him to the piano. A woman's voice called Sonny's name and a few hands started clapping. And Sonny, also being funny and being ceremonious, and so touched, I think, that he could have cried, but neither hiding it nor showing it, riding it like a man, grinned, and put both hands to his heart and bowed from the waist.

Creole then went to the bass fiddle and a lean, very bright-skinned brown man jumped up on the bandstand and picked up his horn. So there they were, and the atmosphere on the bandstand and in the room began to change and tighten. Someone stepped up to the microphone and announced them. Then there were all kinds of murmurs. Some people at the bar shushed others. The waitress ran around, frantically getting in the last orders, guys and chicks got closer to each other, and the lights on the bandstand, on the quartet, turned to a kind of indigo. Then they all looked different there. Creole looked about him for the last time, as though he were making certain that all his chickens were in the coop, and then he—jumped and struck the fiddle. And there they were.

All I know about music is that not many people ever really hear it. And even then, on the rare occasions when something opens within, and the music enters, what we mainly hear, or hear corroborated, are personal, private, vanishing evocations. But the man who creates the music is hearing something else, is dealing with the roar rising from the void and imposing order on it as it hits the air. What is evoked in him, then, is of another order, more terrible because it has no words, and triumphant, too, for that same reason. And his triumph, when he triumphs, is ours. I just watched Sonny's face. His face was troubled, he was working hard, but he wasn't with it. And I had the feeling that, in a way, everyone on the bandstand was waiting for him, both waiting for him and pushing him along. But as I began to watch Creole, I realized that it was Creole who held them all back. He had them on a short rein. Up there, keeping the beat with his whole body, wailing on the fiddle, with his eyes half closed, he was listening to everything, but he was listening to Sonny. He was having a dialogue with Sonny. He wanted Sonny to leave the shoreline and strike out for the deep water. He was Sonny's witness that deep water and drowning were not the same thing—he had been there, and he knew. And he wanted Sonny to know. He was waiting for Sonny to do the things on the keys which would let Creole know that Sonny was in the water.

And, while Creole listened, Sonny moved, deep within, exactly like someone in torment. I had never before thought of how awful the relationship must be between the musician and his instrument. He has to fill it, this instrument, with the breath of life, his own. He has to make it do what he wants it to do. And a piano is just a piano. It's made out of so much wood and wires and little hammers and big ones, and ivory. While there's only so much you can do with it, the only way to find this out is to try; to try and make it do everything.

And Sonny hadn't been near a piano for over a year. And he wasn't on much better terms with his life, not the life that stretched before him now. He and the piano stammered, started one way, got scared, stopped; started another way, panicked, marked time, started again; then seemed to have found a direction, panicked again, got stuck. And the face I saw on Sonny I'd never seen before. Everything had been burned out of it, and, at the same time, things usually hidden were being burned in, by the fire and fury of the battle which was occurring in him up there.

Yet, watching Creole's face as they neared the end of the first set, I had the feeling that something had happened, something I hadn't heard. Then they finished, there was scattered applause, and then, without an instant's warning, Creole started into something else, it was almost sardonic, it was *Am I Blue*. And, as though he commanded, Sonny began to play. Something began to happen. And Creole let out the reins. The dry, low, black man said something awful on the drums, Creole answered, and the drums talked back. Then the horn insisted, sweet and high, slightly detached perhaps, and Creole listened, commenting now and then, dry, and driving, beautiful and calm and old. Then they all came together again, and Sonny was part of the family again. I could tell this from his face. He seemed to have found, right there beneath his fingers, a damn brand-new piano. It seemed that he couldn't get over it. Then, for awhile, just being happy with Sonny, they seemed to be agreeing with him that brand-new pianos certainly were a gas.

Then Creole stepped forward to remind them that what they were playing was the blues. He hit something in all of them, he hit something in me, myself, and the music tightened and deepened, apprehension began to beat the air. Creole began to tell us what the blues were all about. They were not about anything very new. He and his boys up there were keeping it new, at the risk of ruin, destruction, madness, and death, in order to find new ways to make us listen. For, while the tale of how we suffer, and how we are delighted, and how we may triumph is never new, it always must be heard. There isn't any other tale to tell, it's the only light we've got in all this darkness.

And this tale, according to that face, that body, those strong hands on those strings, has another aspect in every country, and a new depth in every generation. Listen, Creole seemed to be saying, listen. Now these are Sonny's blues. He made the little black man on the drums know it, and the bright, brown man on the horn. Creole wasn't trying any longer to get Sonny in the water. He was wishing him Godspeed. Then he stepped back, very slowly, filling the air with the immense suggestion that Sonny speak for himself.

Then they all gathered around Sonny and Sonny played. Every now and again one of them seemed to say, amen. Sonny's fingers filled the air with life, his life. But that life contained so many others. And Sonny went all the way back, he really began with the spare, flat statement of the opening phrase of the song. Then he began to make it his. It was very beautiful because it wasn't hurried and it was no longer a lament. I seemed to hear with what burning he had made it his, with what burning we had yet to make it ours, how we could cease lamenting. Freedom lurked around us and I understood, at last, that he could help us to be free if we would listen, that he would never be free until we did. Yet, there was no battle in his face now. I heard what he had gone through, and would continue to go through until he came to rest in earth. He had made it his: that long line, of which we knew only Mama and Daddy. And he was giving it back, as everything must be given back, so that, passing through death, it can live forever. I saw my mother's face again, and felt, for the first time, how the stones of the road she had walked on must have bruised her feet. I saw the moonlit road where my father's brother died. And it brought something else back to me, and carried me past it. I saw my little girl again and felt Isabel's tears again, and I felt my own tears begin to rise. And I was yet aware that this was only a moment, that the world waited outside, as hungry as a tiger, and that trouble stretched above us, longer than the sky.

Then it was over. Creole and Sonny let out their breath, both soaking wet, and grinning. There was a lot of applause and some of it was real. In the dark, the girl came by and I asked her to take drinks to the bandstand. There was a long pause, while they talked up there in the indigo light and after awhile I saw the girl put a Scotch and milk on top of the piano for Sonny. He didn't seem to notice it, but just before they started playing again, he sipped from it and looked toward me, and nodded. Then he put it back on top of the piano. For me, then, as they began to play again, it glowed and shook above my brother's head like the very cup of trembling.

CYNTHIA OZICK

The Shawl

Stella, cold, cold, the coldness of hell. How they walked on the roads together, Rosa with Magda curled up between sore breasts, Magda wound up in the shawl. Sometimes Stella carried Magda. But she was jealous of Magda. A thin girl of fourteen, too small, with thin breasts of her own, Stella wanted to be wrapped in a shawl, hidden away, asleep, rocked by the march, a baby, a round infant in arms. Magda took Rosa's nipple, and Rosa never stopped walking, a walking cradle. There was not enough milk; sometimes Magda sucked air; then she screamed. Stella was ravenous. Her knees were tumors on sticks, her elbows chicken bones.

Rosa did not feel hunger; she felt light, not like someone walking but like someone in a faint, in trance, arrested in a fit, someone who is already a floating angel, alert and seeing everything, but in the air, not there, not touching the road. As if teetering on the tips of her fingernails. She looked into Magda's face through a gap in the shawl: a squirrel in a nest, safe, no one could reach her inside the little house of the shawl's windings. The face, very round, a pocket mirror of a face: but it was not Rosa's bleak complexion, dark like cholera, it was another kind of face altogether, eyes blue as air, smooth feathers of hair nearly as yellow as the Star sewn into Rosa's coat. You could think she was one of *their* babies.

Rosa, floating, dreamed of giving Magda away in one of the villages. She could leave the line for a minute and push Magda into the hands of any woman on the side of the road. But if she moved out of line they might shoot. And even if she fled the line for half a second and pushed the shawl-bundle at a stranger, would the woman take it? She might be surprised, or afraid; she might drop the shawl, and Magda would fall out and strike her head and die. The little round head. Such a good child, she gave up screaming, and sucked now only for the taste of the drying nipple itself. The neat grip of the tiny gums. One mite of a tooth tip sticking up in the bottom gum, how shining, an elfin tombstone of white marble, gleaming there. Without complaining, Magda relinquished Rosa's teats, first the left, then the right; both were cracked, not a sniff of milk. The duct crevice extinct, a dead volcano, blind eye, chill hole, so Magda took the corner of the shawl and milked it instead. She sucked and sucked, flooding the threads with wetness. The shawl's good flavor, milk of linen.

It was a magic shawl, it could nourish an infant for three days and three nights. Magda did not die, she stayed alive, although very quiet. A peculiar smell, of cinnamon and almonds, lifted out of her mouth. She held her eyes open every moment, forgetting how to blink or nap, and Rosa and sometimes Stella studied their blueness. On the road they raised one burden of a leg after another and studied Magda's face. "Aryan," Stella said, in a voice grown as thin as a string; and Rosa thought how Stella gazed at Magda like a young cannibal. And the time that Stella said "Aryan," it sounded to Rosa as if Stella had really said, "Let us devour her."

But Magda lived to walk. She lived that long, but she did not walk very well, partly because she was only fifteen months old, and partly because the spindles of her legs could not hold up her fat belly. It was fat with air, full and round. Rosa gave almost all her food to Magda, Stella gave nothing; Stella was ravenous, a growing child herself, but not growing much. Stella did not menstruate. Rosa did not menstruate. Rosa was ravenous, but also not; she learned from Magda how to drink the taste of a finger in one's mouth. They were in a place without pity, all pity was annihilated in Rosa, she looked at Stella's bones without pity. She was sure that Stella was waiting for Magda to die so she could put her teeth into the little thighs.

Rosa knew Magda was going to die very soon; she should have been dead already, but she had been buried away deep inside the magic shawl, mistaken there for the shivering mound of Rosa's breasts; Rosa clung to the shawl as if it covered only herself. No one took it away from her. Magda was mute. She never cried. Rosa hid her in the barracks, under the shawl, but she knew that one day someone would inform; or one day someone, not even Stella, would steal Magda to eat her. When Magda began to walk Rosa knew that Magda was going to die very soon, something would happen. She was afraid to fall asleep; she slept with the weight of her thigh on Magda's body; she was afraid she would smother Magda under her thigh. The weight of Rosa was becoming less and less, Rosa and Stella were slowly turning into air.

Magda was quiet, but her eyes were horribly alive, like blue tigers. She watched. Sometimes she laughed—it seemed a laugh, but how could it be? Magda had never seen anyone laugh. Still, Magda laughed at her shawl when the wind blew its corners, the bad wind with pieces of black in it, that made Stella's and Rosa's eyes tear. Magda's eyes were always clear and tearless. She watched like a tiger. She guarded her shawl. No one could touch it; only Rosa could touch it. Stella was not allowed. The shawl was Magda's own baby, her pet, her little sister. She tangled herself up in it and sucked on one of the corners when she wanted to be very still.

Then Stella took the shawl away and made Magda die.

Afterward Stella said: "I was cold."

And afterward she was always cold, always. The cold went into her heart: Rosa saw that Stella's heart was cold. Magda flopped onward with her little pencil legs scribbling this way and that, in search of the shawl; the pencils faltered at the barracks opening, where the light began. Rosa saw and pursued. But already Magda was in the square outside the barracks, in the jolly light. It was the roll-call arena. Every morning Rosa had to conceal Magda under the shawl against a wall of the barracks and go out and stand in the arena with Stella and hundreds of others, sometimes for hours, and Magda, deserted, was quiet under the shawl, sucking on her corner. Every day Magda was silent, and so she did not die. Rosa saw that today Magda was going to die, and at the same time a fearful joy ran in Rosa's two palms, her fingers were on fire, she was astonished, febrile: Magda, in the sunlight, swaying on her pencil legs, was howling. Ever since the drying up of Rosa's nipples, ever since Magda's last scream on the road, Magda had been devoid of any syllable; Magda was a mute. Rosa believed that something had gone wrong with her vocal cords, with her windpipe, with the cave of her larynx; Magda was defective, without a voice; perhaps she was deaf; there might be something amiss with her intelligence; Magda was dumb. Even the laugh that came when the ash-stippled wind made a clown out of Magda's shawl was only the air-blown showing of her teeth. Even when the lice, head lice and body lice, crazed her so that she became as wild as one of the big rats that plundered the barracks at daybreak looking for carrion, she rubbed and scratched and kicked and bit and rolled without a whimper. But now Magda's mouth was spilling a long viscous rope of clamor.

"Maaaa—"

It was the first noise Magda had ever sent out from her throat since the drying up of Rosa's nipples.

"Maaaa . . . aaa!"

Again! Magda was wavering in the perilous sunlight of the arena, scribbling on such pitiful little bent shins. Rosa saw. She saw that Magda was grieving the loss of her shawl, she saw that Magda was going to die. A tide of commands hammered in Rosa's nipples: Fetch, get, bring! But she did not know which to go after first, Magda or the shawl. If she jumped out into the arena to snatch Magda up, the howling would not stop, because Magda would still not have the shawl; but if she ran back into the barracks to find the shawl, and if she found it, and if she came after Magda holding it and shaking it, then she would get Magda back, Magda would put the shawl in her mouth and turn dumb again.

Rosa entered the dark. It was easy to discover the shawl. Stella was heaped under it, asleep in her thin bones. Rosa tore the shawl free and flew—she could fly, she was only air—into the arena. The sunheat murmured of another life, of butterflies in summer. The light was placid, mellow. On the other side of the steel fence, far away, there were green meadows speckled with dandelions and deep-colored violets; beyond them, even farther, innocent tiger lilies, tall, lifting their orange bonnets. In the barracks they spoke of "flowers," of "rain": excrement, thick turd-braids, and the slow stinking maroon waterfall that slunk down from the upper bunks, the stink mixed with a bitter fatty floating smoke that greased Rosa's skin. She stood for an instant at the margin of the arena. Sometimes the electricity inside the fence would seem to hum; even Stella said it was only an imagining, but Rosa heard real sounds in the wire: grainy sad voices. The farther she was from the fence, the more clearly the voices crowded at her. The lamenting voices strummed so convincingly, so passionately, it was impossible to suspect them of being phantoms. The voices told her to hold up the shawl, high; the voices told her to shake it, to whip with it, to unfurl it like a flag. Rosa lifted, shook, whipped, unfurled. Far off, very far, Magda leaned across her air-fed belly, reaching out with the rods of her arms. She was high up, elevated, riding someone's shoulder. But the shoulder that carried Magda was not coming toward Rosa and the shawl, it was drifting away, the speck of Magda was moving more and more into the smoky distance. Above the shoulder a helmet glinted. A light tapped the helmet and sparkled it into a goblet. Below the helmet a black body like a domino and a pair of black boots hurled themselves in the direction of the electrified fence. The electric voices began to chatter wildly. "Maamaa, maaamaaa," they all hummed together. How far Magda was from Rosa now, across the whole square, past a dozen barracks, all the way on the other side! She was no bigger than a moth.

All at once Magda was swimming through the air. The whole of Magda traveled through loftiness. She looked like a butterfly touching a silver vine. And the moment Magda's feathered round head and her pencil legs and balloonish belly and zigzag arms splashed against the fence, the steel voices went mad in their growling, urging Rosa to run and run to the spot where Magda had fallen from her flight against the electrified fence; but of course Rosa did not obey them. She only stood, because if she ran they would shoot, and if she tried to pick up the sticks of Magda's body they would shoot, and if she let the wolf's screech ascending now through the ladder of her skeleton break out, they would shoot; so she took Magda's shawl and filled her own mouth with it, stuffed it in and stuffed it in, until she was swallowing up the wolf's screech and tasting the cinnamon and almond depth of Magda's saliva; and Rosa drank Magda's shawl until it dried.

JOHN UPDIKE

A & P

*I*n walks these three girls in nothing but bathing suits. I'm in the third checkout slot, with my back to the door, so I don't see them until they're over by the bread. The one that caught my eye first was the one in the plaid green two-piece. She was a chunky kid, with a good tan and a sweet broad soft-looking can with those two crescents of white just under it, where the sun never seems to hit, at the top of the backs of her legs. I stood there with my hand on a box of HiHo crackers trying to remember if I rang it up or not. I ring it up again and the customer starts giving me hell. She's one of these cash-register-watchers, a witch about fifty with rouge on her cheekbones and no eyebrows, and I know it made her day to trip me up. She'd been watching cash registers for fifty years and probably never seen a mistake before.

By the time I got her feathers smoothed and her goodies into a bag—she gives me a little snort in passing, if she'd been born at the right time they would have burned her over in Salem—by the time I get her on her way the girls had circled around the bread and were coming back, without a pushcart, back my way along the counters, in the aisle between the checkouts and the Special bins. They didn't even have shoes on. There was this chunky one, with the two-piece—it was bright green and the seams on the bra were still sharp and her belly was still pretty pale so I guessed she just got it (the suit)—there was this one, with one of those chubby berry-faces, the lips all bunched together under her nose, this one, and a tall one, with black hair that hadn't quite frizzed right, and one of these sunburns right across under the eyes, and a chin that was too long—you know, the kind of girl other girls think is very "striking" and "attractive" but never quite makes it, as they very well know, which is why they like her so much—and then the third one, that wasn't quite so tall. She was the queen. She kind of led them, the other two peeking around and making their shoulders round. She didn't look around, not this queen, she just walked straight on slowly, on these long white prima-donna legs. She came down a little hard on her heels, as if she didn't walk in her bare feet that much, putting down her heels and then letting the weight move along to her toes as if she was testing the floor with every step, putting a little deliberate extra action into it. You never know for sure how girls' minds work (do you really think it's a mind in there or just a little buzz like a bee in a glass jar?) but you got the idea she had talked the other two into coming in here with her, and now she was showing them how to do it, walk slow and hold yourself straight.

She had on a kind of dirty-pink—beige maybe, I don't know—bathing suit with a little nubble all over it, and what got me, the straps were down. They were off her shoulders looped loose around the cool tops of her arms, and I guess as a result the suit had slipped a little on her, so all around the top of the cloth there was this shining rim. If it hadn't been there you wouldn't have known there could have been anything whiter than those shoulders. With the straps pushed off, there was nothing between the top of the suit and the top of her head except just *her,* this clean bare plane of the top of her chest down from the shoulder bones like a dented sheet of metal tilted in the light. I mean, it was more than pretty.

She had sort of oaky hair that the sun and salt had bleached, done up in a bun that was unravelling, and a kind of prim face. Walking into the A & P with your straps down, I suppose it's the only kind of face you can have. She held her head so high her neck, coming up out of those white shoulders, looked kind of stretched, but I didn't mind. The longer her neck was, the more of her there was.

She must have felt in the corner of her eye me and over my shoulder Stokesie in the second slot watching, but she didn't tip. Not this queen. She kept her eyes moving across the racks, and stopped, and turned so slow it made my stomach rub the inside of my apron, and buzzed to the other two, who kind of huddled against her for relief, and then they all three of them went up the cat-and-dog-food-breakfast-cereal-macaroni-rice-raisins-season-ings-spreads-spaghetti-soft-drinks-crackers-and-cookies aisle. From the third slot I look straight up this aisle to the meat counter, and I watched them all the way. The fat one with the tan sort of fumbled with the cookies, but on second thought she put the package back. The sheep pushing their carts down the aisle—the girls were walking against the usual traffic (not that we have one-way signs or anything)—were pretty hilarious. You could see them, when Queenie's white shoulders dawned on them, kind of jerk, or hop, or hiccup, but their eyes snapped back to their own baskets and on they pushed. I bet you could set off dynamite in an A & P and the people would by and large keep reaching and checking oatmeal off their lists and muttering "Let me see, there was a third thing, began with A, asparagus, no, ah, yes, applesauce!" or what-ever it is they do mutter. But there was no doubt, this jiggled them. A few houseslaves in pin curlers even looked around after pushing their carts past to make sure what they had seen was correct.

You know, it's one thing to have a girl in a bathing suit down on the beach, where what with the glare nobody can look at each other much anyway, and another thing in the cool of the A & P, under the fluorescent lights, against all those stacked packages, with her feet paddling along naked over our check-board green-and-cream rubber-tile floor.

"Oh Daddy," Stokesie said beside me. "I feel so faint."

"Darling," I said. "Hold me tight." Stokesie's married, with two babies chalked up on his fuselage already, but as far as I can tell that's the only difference. He's twenty-two, and I was nineteen this April.

"Is it done?" he asks, the responsible married man finding his voice. I forgot to say he thinks he's going to be manager some sunny day, maybe in 1990 when it's called the Great Alexandrov and Petrooshki Tea Company or something.

What he meant was, our town is five miles from a beach, with a big summer colony out on the Point, but we're right in the middle of town, and the women generally put on a shirt or shorts or something before they get out of the car into the street. And anyway these are usually women with six children and varicose veins mapping their legs and nobody, including them, could care less. As I say, we're right in the middle of town, and if you stand at our front doors you can see two banks and the Congregational church and the newspaper store and three real-estate offices and about twenty-seven old freeloaders tearing up Central Street because the sewer broke again. It's not as if we're on the Cape; we're north of Boston and there's people in this town haven't seen the ocean for twenty years.

The girls had reached the meat counter and were asking McMahon something. He pointed, they pointed, and they shuffled out of sight behind a pyramid of Diet Delight peaches. All that was left for us to see was old McMahon patting his mouth and looking after them sizing up their joints. Poor kids, I began to feel sorry for them, they couldn't help it.

Now here comes the sad part of the story, at least my family says it's sad, but I don't think it's so sad myself. The store's pretty empty, it being Thursday afternoon, so there was nothing much to do except lean on the register and wait for the girls to show up again. The whole store was like a pinball machine and I didn't know which tunnel they'd come out of. After a while they come around out of the far aisle, around the light bulbs, records at discount of the Caribbean Six or Tony Martin Sings or some such gunk you wonder they waste the wax on, sixpacks of candy bars, and plastic toys done up in cellophane that fall apart when a kid looks at them anyway. Around they come, Queenie still leading the way, and holding a little gray jar in her hand. Slots Three through Seven are unmanned and I could see her wondering between Stokes and me, but Stokesie with his usual luck draws an old party in baggy gray pants who stumbles up with four giant cans of pineapple juice (what do these bums *do* with all that pineapple juice? I've often asked myself) so the girls come to me. Queenie puts down the jar and I take it into my fingers icy cold. Kingfish Fancy Herring Snacks in Pure Sour Cream: 49¢. Now her hands are empty, not a ring or a bracelet, bare as God made them, and I wonder where the money's coming from. Still with that prim look she lifts a folded dollar bill out of the hollow at the center of her nubbled pink top. The jar went heavy in my hand. Really, I thought that was so cute.

Then everybody's luck begins to run out. Lengel comes in from haggling with a truck full of cabbages on the lot and is about to scuttle into that door marked MANAGER behind which he hides all day when the girls touch his eye.

Lengel's pretty dreary, teaches Sunday school and the rest, but he doesn't miss that much. He comes over and says, "Girls, this isn't the beach."

Queenie blushes, though maybe it's just a brush of sunburn I was noticing for the first time, now that she was so close. "My mother asked me to pick up a jar of herring snacks." Her voice kind of startled me, the way voices do when you see the people first, coming out so flat and dumb yet kind of tony, too, the way it ticked over "pick up" and "snacks." All of a sudden I slid right down her voice into her living room. Her father and the other men were standing around in ice-cream coats and bow ties and the women were in sandals picking up herring snacks on toothpicks off a big glass plate and they were all holding drinks the color of water with olives and sprigs of mint in them. When my parents have somebody over they get lemonade and if it's a real racy affair Schlitz in tall glasses with "They'll Do It Every Time" cartoons stencilled on.

"That's all right," Lengel said. "But this isn't the beach." His repeating this struck me as funny, as if it had just occurred to him, and he had been thinking all these years the A & P was a great big sand dune and he was the head lifeguard. He didn't like my smiling—as I say he doesn't miss much—but he concentrates on giving the girls that sad Sunday-school–superintendent stare.

Queenie's blush is no sunburn now, and the plump one in plaid, that I liked better from the back—a really sweet can—pipes up, "We weren't doing any shopping. We just came in for the one thing."

"That makes no difference," Lengel tells her, and I could see from the way his eyes went that he hadn't noticed she was wearing a two-piece before. "We want you decently dressed when you come in here."

"We *are* decent," Queenie says suddenly, her lower lip pushing, getting sore now that she remembers her place, a place from which the crowd that runs the A & P must look pretty crummy. Fancy Herring Snacks flashed in her very blue eyes.

"Girls, I don't want to argue with you. After this come in here with your shoulders covered. It's our policy." He turns his back. That's policy for you. Policy is what the kingpins want. What the others want is juvenile delinquency.

All this while, the customers had been showing up with their carts but, you know, sheep, seeing a scene, they had all bunched up on Stokesie, who shook open a paper bag as gently as peeling a peach, not wanting to miss a word. I could feel in the silence everybody getting nervous, most of all Lengel, who asks me, "Sammy, have you rung up their purchase?"

I thought and said "No" but it wasn't about that I was thinking. I go through the punches, 4, 9, GROC, TOT—it's more complicated than you think, and after you do it often enough, it begins to make a little song, that you hear words to, in my case "Hello (*bing*) there, you (*gung*) hap-py *pee*-pul (*splat*)!"—the *splat* being the drawer flying out. I uncrease the bill, tenderly as you may imagine, it just having come from between the two smoothest scoops of vanilla I had ever known were there, and pass a half and a penny into her narrow pink palm, and nestle the herrings in a bag and twist its neck and hand it over, all the time thinking.

The girls, and who'd blame them, are in a hurry to get out, so I say "I quit" to Lengel enough for them to hear, hoping they'll stop and watch me, their unsuspected hero. They keep right on going, into the electric eye; the door flies open and they flicker across the lot to their car, Queenie and Plaid and Big Tall Goony-Goony (not that as raw material she was so bad), leaving me with Lengel and a kink in his eyebrow.

"Did you say something, Sammy?"

"I said I quit."

"I thought you did."

"You didn't have to embarrass them."

"It was they who were embarrassing us."

I started to say something that came out "Fiddle-de-doo." It's a saying of my grandmother's, and I know she would have been pleased.

"I don't think you know what you're saying," Lengel said.

"I know you don't," I said. "But I do." I pull the bow at the back of my apron and start shrugging it off my shoulders. A couple customers that had been heading for my slot begin to knock against each other, like scared pigs in a chute.

Lengel sighs and begins to look very patient and old and gray. He's been a friend of my parents for years. "Sammy, you don't want to do this to your Mom and Dad," he tells me. It's true, I don't. But it seems to me that once you begin a gesture it's fatal not to go through with it. I fold the apron, "Sammy" stitched in red on the pocket, and put it on the counter, and drop the bow tie on top of it. The bow tie is theirs, if you've ever wondered. "You'll feel this for the rest of your life," Lengel says, and I know that's true, too, but remembering how he made that pretty girl blush makes me so scrunchy inside I punch the No Sale tab and the machine whirs "pee-pul" and the drawer splats out. One advantage to this scene taking place in summer, I can follow this up with a clean exit, there's no fumbling around getting your coat and galoshes, I just saunter into the electric eye in my white shirt that my mother ironed the night before, and the door heaves itself open, and outside the sunshine is skating around on the asphalt.

I look around for my girls, but they're gone, of course. There wasn't anybody but some young married screaming with her children about some candy they didn't get by the door of a powder-blue Falcon station wagon. Looking back in the big windows, over the bags of peat moss and aluminum lawn furniture stacked on the pavement, I could see Lengel in my place in the slot, checking the sheep through. His face was dark gray and his back stiff, as if he'd just had an injection of iron, and my stomach kind of fell as I felt how hard the world was going to be to me hereafter.

RAYMOND CARVER

Cathedral

*T*his blind man, an old friend of my wife's, he was on his way to spend the night. His wife had died. So he was visiting the dead wife's relatives in Connecticut. He called my wife from his in-laws'. Arrangements were made. He would come by train, a five-hour trip, and my wife would meet him at the station. She hadn't seen him since she worked for him one summer in Seattle ten years ago. But she and the blind man had kept in touch. They made tapes and mailed them back and forth. I wasn't enthusiastic about his visit. He was no one I knew. And his being blind bothered me. My idea of blindness came from the movies. In the movies, the blind moved slowly and never laughed. Sometimes they were led by seeing-eye dogs. A blind man in my house was not something I looked forward to.

That summer in Seattle she had needed a job. She didn't have any money. The man she was going to marry at the end of the summer was in officers' training school. He didn't have any money, either. But she was in love with the guy, and he was in love with her, etc. She'd seen something in the paper: HELP WANTED—*Reading to Blind Man,* and a telephone number. She phoned and went over, was hired on the spot. She'd worked with this blind man all summer. She read stuff to him, case studies, reports, that sort of thing. She helped him organize his little office in the county social-service department. They'd become good friends, my wife and the blind man. How do I know these things? She told me. And she told me something else. On her last day in the office, the blind man asked if he could touch her face. She agreed to this. She told me he touched his fingers to every part of her face, her nose—even her neck! She never forgot it. She even tried to write a poem about it. She was always trying to write a poem. She wrote a poem or two every year, usually after something really important had happened to her.

When we first started going out together, she showed me the poem. In the poem, she recalled his fingers and the way they had moved around over her face. In the poem, she talked about what she had felt at the time, about what went through her mind when the blind man touched her nose and lips. I can remember I didn't think much of the poem. Of course, I didn't tell her that. Maybe I just don't understand poetry. I admit it's not the first thing I reach for when I pick up something to read.

Anyway, this man who'd first enjoyed her favors, the officer-to-be, he'd been her childhood sweetheart. So okay. I'm saying that at the end of the summer she let the blind man run his hands over her face, said goodbye to him, married her childhood etc., who was now a commissioned officer, and she moved away from Seattle. But they'd kept in touch, she and the blind man. She made the first contact after a year or so. She called him up one night from an Air Force base in Alabama. She wanted to talk. They talked. He asked her to send him a tape and tell him about her life. She did this. She sent the tape. On the tape, she told the blind man about her husband and about their life together in the military. She told the blind man she loved her husband but she didn't like it where they lived and she didn't like it that he was a part of the military-industrial thing. She told the blind man she'd written a poem and he was in it. She told him that she was writing a poem about what it was like to be an Air Force officer's wife. The poem wasn't finished yet. She was still writing it. The blind man made a tape. He sent her the tape. She made a tape. This went on for years. My wife's officer was posted to one base and then another. She sent tapes from Moody AFB, McGuire, McConnell, and finally Travis, near Sacramento, where one night she got to feeling lonely and cut off from people she kept losing in that moving-around life. She got to feeling she couldn't go it another step. She went in and swallowed all the pills and capsules in the medicine chest and washed them down with a bottle of gin. Then she got into a hot bath and passed out.

But instead of dying, she got sick. She threw up. Her officer—why should he have a name? he was the childhood sweetheart, and what more does he want?—came home from somewhere, found her, and called the ambulance. In time, she put it all on a tape and sent the tape to the blind man. Over the years, she put all kinds of stuff on tapes and sent the tapes off lickety-split. Next to writing a poem every year, I think it was her chief means of recreation. On one tape, she told the blind man she'd decided to live away from her officer for a time. On another tape, she told him about her divorce. She and I began going out, and of course she told her blind man about it. She told him everything, or so it seemed to me. Once she asked me if I'd like to hear the latest tape from the blind man. This was a year ago. I was on the tape, she said. So I said okay, I'd listen to it. I got us drinks and we settled down in the living room. We made ready to listen. First she inserted the tape into the player and adjusted a couple of dials. Then she pushed a lever. The tape squeaked and someone began to talk in this loud voice. She lowered the volume. After a few minutes of harmless chitchat, I heard my own name in the mouth of this stranger, this blind man I didn't even know! And then this: "From all you've said about him, I can only conclude—" But we were interrupted, a knock at the door, something, and we didn't ever get back to the tape. Maybe it was just as well. I'd heard all I wanted to.

Now this same blind man was coming to sleep in my house.

"Maybe I could take him bowling," I said to my wife. She was at the draining board doing scalloped potatoes. She put down the knife she was using and turned around.

"If you love me," she said, "you can do this for me. If you don't love me, okay. But if you had a friend, any friend, and the friend came to visit, I'd make him feel comfortable." She wiped her hands with the dish towel.

"I don't have any blind friends," I said.

"You don't have *any* friends," she said. "Period. Besides," she said, "god-damn it, his wife's just died! Don't you understand that? The man's lost his wife!"

I didn't answer, She'd told me a little about the blind man's wife. Her name was Beulah. Beulah! That's a name for a colored woman.

"Was his wife Negro?" I asked.

"Are you crazy?" my wife said. "Have you just flipped or something?" She picked up a potato. I saw it hit the floor, then roll under the stove. "What's wrong with you?" she said. "Are you drunk?"

"I'm just asking," I said.

Right then my wife filled me in with more detail than I cared to know. I made a drink and sat at the kitchen table to listen. Pieces of the story began to fall into place.

Beulah had gone to work for the blind man the summer after my wife had stopped working for him. Pretty soon Beulah and the blind man had them-selves a church wedding. It was a little wedding—who'd want to go to such a wedding in the first place?—just the two of them, plus the minister and the min-ister's wife. But it was a church wedding just the same. It was what Beulah had wanted, he'd said. But even then Beulah must have been carrying the cancer in her glands. After they had been inseparable for eight years—my wife's word, *inseparable*—Beulah's health went into a rapid decline. She died in a Seattle hospital room, the blind man sitting beside the bed and holding on to her hand. They'd married, lived and worked together, slept together—had sex, sure—and then the blind man had to bury her. All this without his having ever seen what the goddamned woman looked like. It was beyond my understanding. Hearing this, I felt sorry for the blind man for a little bit. And then I found myself think-ing what a pitiful life this woman must have led. Imagine a woman who could never see herself as she was seen in the eyes of her loved one. A woman who could go on day after day and never receive the smallest compliment from her beloved. A woman whose husband could never read the expression on her face, be it misery or something better. Someone who could wear makeup or not—what difference to him? She could, if she wanted, wear green eye-shadow around one eye, a straight pin in her nostril, yellow slacks and purple shoes, no matter. And then to slip off into death, the blind man's hand on her hand, his blind eyes streaming tears—I'm imagining now—her last thought maybe this: that he never even knew what she looked like, and she on an express to the grave. Robert was left with a small insurance policy and half of a twenty-peso Mexican coin. The other half of the coin went into the box with her. Pathetic.

So when the time rolled around, my wife went to the depot to pick him up. With nothing to do but wait—sure, I blamed him for that—I was having a drink and watching the TV when I heard the car pull into the drive. I got up from the sofa with my drink and went to the window to have a look.

I saw my wife laughing as she parked the car. I saw her get out of the car and shut the door. She was still wearing a smile. Just amazing. She went around to the other side of the car to where the blind man was already starting to get out. This blind man, feature this, he was wearing a full beard! A beard on a blind man! Too much, I say. The blind man reached into the back seat and dragged out a suitcase. My wife took his arm, shut the car door, and, talking all the way, moved him down the drive and then up the steps to the front porch. I turned off the TV. I finished my drink, rinsed the glass, dried my hands. Then I went to the door.

My wife said, "I want you to meet Robert. Robert, this is my husband. I've told you all about him." She was beaming. She had this blind man by his coat sleeve.

The blind man let go of his suitcase and up came his hand.

I took it. He squeezed hard, held my hand, and then he let it go.

"I feel like we've already met," he boomed.

"Likewise," I said. I didn't know what else to say. Then I said, "Welcome. I've heard a lot about you." We began to move then, a little group, from the porch into the living room, my wife guiding him by the arm. The blind man was carrying his suitcase in his other hand. My wife said things like, "To your left here, Robert. That's right. Now watch it, there's a chair. That's it. Sit down right here. This is the sofa. We just bought this sofa two weeks ago."

I started to say something about the old sofa. I'd liked that old sofa. But I didn't say anything. Then I wanted to say something else, small-talk, about the scenic ride along the Hudson. How going *to* New York, you should sit on the right-hand side of the train, and coming *from* New York, the left-hand side.

"Did you have a good train ride," I said. "Which side of the train did you sit on, by the way?"

"What a question, which side!" my wife said. "What's it matter which side?" she said.

"I just asked," I said.

"Right side," the blind man said. "I hadn't been on a train in nearly forty years. Not since I was a kid. With my folks. That's been a long time. I'd nearly forgotten the sensation. I have winter in my beard now," he said. "So I've been told, anyway. Do I look distinguished, my dear?" the blind man said to my wife.

"You look distinguished, Robert," she said. "Robert," she said. "Robert, it's just so good to see you."

My wife finally took her eyes off the blind man and looked at me. I had the feeling she didn't like what she saw. I shrugged.

I've never met, or personally known, anyone who was blind. This blind man was late forties, a heavy-set, balding man with stooped shoulders, as if he carried a great weight there. He wore brown slacks, brown shoes, a light-brown shirt, a tie, a sports coat. Spiffy. He also had this full beard. But he didn't use a cane and he didn't wear dark glasses. I'd always thought dark glasses were a must for the blind. Fact was, I wished he had a pair. At first glance, his eyes looked like anyone else's eyes. But if you look close, there was something different about them. Too much white in the iris, for one thing, and the pupils seemed to move around in the sockets without his knowing it or being able to stop it. Creepy. As I stared at his face, I saw the left pupil turn in toward his nose while the other made an effort to keep in one place. But it was only an effort, for that eye was on the roam without his knowing it or wanting it to be.

I said, "Let me get you a drink. What's your pleasure? We have a little of everything. It's one of our pastimes."

"Bub, I'm a Scotch man myself," he said fast enough in this big voice.

"Right," I said. Bub! "Sure you are, I knew it."

He let his fingers touch his suitcase, which was sitting alongside the sofa. He was taking his bearings. I didn't blame him for that.

"I'll move that up to your room," my wife said.

"No, that's fine," the blind man said loudly. "It can go up when I go up."

"A little water with the Scotch?" I said.

"Very little," he said.

"I knew it," I said.

He said, "Just a tad. The Irish actor, Barry Fitzgerald? I'm like that fellow. When I drink water, Fitzgerald said, I drink water. When I drink whiskey, I drink whiskey." My wife laughed. The blind man brought his hand up under his beard. He lifted his beard slowly and let it drop.

I did the drinks, three big glasses of Scotch with a splash of water in each. Then we made ourselves comfortable and talked about Robert's travels. First the long flight from the West Coast to Connecticut, we covered that. Then from Connecticut up here by train. We had another drink concerning that leg of the trip.

I remembered having read somewhere that the blind didn't smoke because, as speculation had it, they couldn't see the smoke they exhaled. I thought I knew that much and that much only about blind people. But this blind man smoked his cigarette down to the nubbin and then lit another one. This blind man filled his ashtray and my wife emptied it.

When we sat down at the table for dinner, we had another drink. My wife heaped Robert's plate with cube steak, scalloped potatoes, green beans. I buttered him up two slices of bread. I said, "Here's bread and butter for you." I swallowed some of my drink. "Now let us pray," I said, and the blind man lowered his head. My wife looked at me, her mouth agape. "Pray the phone won't ring and the food doesn't get cold," I said.

We dug in. We ate everything there was to eat on the table. We ate like there was no tomorrow. We didn't talk. We ate. We scarfed. We grazed that table. We were into serious eating. The blind man had right away located his foods, he knew just where everything was on his plate. I watched with admiration as he used his knife and fork on the meat. He'd cut two pieces of meat, fork the meat into his mouth, and then go all out for the scalloped potatoes, the beans next, and then he'd tear off a hunk of buttered bread and eat that. He'd follow this up with a big drink of milk. It didn't seem to bother him to use his fingers once in a while, either.

We finished everything, including half a strawberry pie. For a few moments, we sat as if stunned. Sweat beaded on our faces. Finally, we got up from the table and left the dirty plates. We didn't look back. We took ourselves into the living room and sank into our places again. Robert and my wife sat on the sofa. I took the big chair. We had us two or three more drinks while they talked about the major things that had come to pass for them in the past ten years. For the most part, I just listened. Now and then I joined in. I didn't want him to think I'd left the room, and I didn't want her to think I was feeling left out. They talked of things that had happened to them—to them!—these past ten years. I waited in vain to hear my name on my wife's sweet lips: "And then my dear husband came into my life"—something like that. But I heard nothing of the sort. More talk of Robert. Robert had done a little of every-thing, it seemed, a regular blind jack-of-all-trades. But most recently he and his wife had had an Amway distributorship, from which, I gathered, they'd earned their living, such as it was. The blind man was also a ham radio operator. He talked in his loud voice about conversations he'd had with fellow operators in Guam, in the Philippines, in Alaska, and even in Tahiti. He said he'd have a lot of friends there if he ever wanted to go visit those places. From time to time, he'd turn his blind face toward me, put his hand under his beard, ask me some-thing. How long had I been in my present position? (Three years.) Did I like my work? (I didn't.) Was I going to stay with it? (What were the options?) Finally, when I thought he was beginning to run down, I got up and turned on the TV.

My wife looked at me with irritation. She was heading toward a boil. Then she looked at the blind man and said, "Robert, do you have a TV?"

The blind man said, "My dear, I have two TVs. I have a color set and a black-and-white thing, an old relic. It's funny, but if I turn the TV on, and I'm always turning it on, I turn on the color set. It's funny, don't you think?"

I didn't know what to say to that. I had absolutely nothing to say to that. No opinions. So I watched the news program and tried to listen to what the announcer was saying.

"This is a color TV," the blind man said. "Don't ask me how, but I can tell."

"We traded up a while ago," I said.

The blind man had another taste of his drink. He lifted his beard, sniffed it, and let it fall. He leaned forward on the sofa. He positioned his ashtray on the coffee table, then put the lighter to his cigarette. He leaned back on the sofa and crossed his legs at the ankles.

My wife covered her mouth, and then she yawned. She stretched. She said, "I think I'll go upstairs and put on my robe. I think I'll change into something else. Robert, you make yourself comfortable," she said.

"I'm comfortable," the blind man said.

"I want you to feel comfortable in this house," she said.

"I am comfortable," the blind man said.

After she'd left the room, he and I listened to the weather report and then to the sports roundup. By that time, she'd been gone so long I didn't know if she was going to come back. I thought she might have gone to bed. I wished she'd come back downstairs. I didn't want to be left alone with a blind man. I asked him if he wanted another drink, and he said sure. Then I asked if he wanted to smoke some dope with me. I said I'd just rolled a number. I hadn't, but I planned to do so in about two shakes.

"I'll try some with you," he said.

"Damn right," I said. "That's the stuff."

I got our drinks and sat down on the sofa with him. Then I rolled us two fat numbers. I lit one and passed it. I brought it to his fingers. He took it and inhaled.

"Hold it as long as you can," I said. I could tell he didn't know the first thing.

My wife came back downstairs wearing her pink robe and her pink slippers.

"What do I smell?" she said.

"We thought we'd have us some cannabis," I said.

My wife gave me a savage look. Then she looked at the blind man and said, "Robert, I didn't know you smoked."

He said, "I do now, my dear. There's a first time for everything. But I don't feel anything yet."

"This stuff is pretty mellow," I said. "This stuff is mild. It's dope you can reason with," I said. "It doesn't mess you up."

"Not much it doesn't, bub," he said, and laughed.

My wife sat on the sofa between the blind man and me. I passed her the number. She took it and toked and then passed it back to me. "Which way is this going?" she said. Then she said, "I shouldn't be smoking this. I can hardly keep my eyes open as it is. That dinner did me in. I shouldn't have eaten so much."

"It was the strawberry pie," the blind man said. "That's what did it," he said, and he laughed his big laugh. Then he shook his head.

"There's more strawberry pie," I said.

"Do you want some more, Robert?" my wife said.

"Maybe in a little while," he said.

We gave our attention to the TV. My wife yawned again. She said, "Your bed is made up when you feel like going to bed, Robert. I know you must have had a long day. When you're ready to go to bed, say so." She pulled his arm. "Robert?"

He came to and said, "I've had a real nice time. This beats tapes, doesn't it?"

I said. "Coming at you," and I put the number between his fingers. He inhaled, held the smoke, and then let it go. It was like he'd been doing it since he was nine years old.

"Thanks, bub," he said. "But I think this is all for me. I think I'm beginning to feel it," he said. He held the burning roach out for my wife.

"Same here," she said. "Ditto. Me, too." She took the roach and passed it to me. "I may just sit here for a while between you two guys with my eyes closed. But don't let me bother you, okay? Either one of you. If it bothers you, say so. Otherwise, I may just sit here with my eyes closed until you're ready to go to bed," she said. "Your bed's made up, Robert, when you're ready. It's right next to our room at the top of the stairs. We'll show you up when you're ready. You wake me up now, you guys, if I fall asleep." She said that and then she closed her eyes and went to sleep.

The news program ended. I got up and changed the channel. I sat back down on the sofa. I wished my wife hadn't pooped out. Her head lay across the back of the sofa, her mouth open. She'd turned so that her robe had slipped away from her legs, exposing a juicy thigh. I reached to draw her robe back over her, and it was then that I glanced at the blind man. What the hell! I flipped the robe open again.

"You say when you want some strawberry pie," I said.

"I will," he said.

I said, "Are you tired? Do you want me to take you up to your bed? Are you ready to hit the hay?"

"Not yet," he said. "No, I'll stay up with you, bub. If that's all right. I'll stay up until you're ready to turn in. We haven't had a chance to talk. Know what I mean? I feel like me and her monopolized the evening." He lifted his beard and he let it fall. He picked up his cigarettes and his lighter.

"That's all right," I said. Then I said, "I'm glad for the company."

And I guess I was. Every night I smoked dope and stayed up as long as I could before I fell asleep. My wife and I hardly ever went to bed at the same time. When I did go to sleep, I had these dreams. Sometimes I'd wake up from one of them, my heart going crazy.

Something about the church and the Middle Ages was on the TV. Not your run-of-the-mill TV fare. I wanted to watch something else. I turned to the other channels. But there was nothing on them, either. So I turned back to the first channel and apologized.

"Bub, it's all right," the blind man said. "It's fine with me. Whatever you want to watch is okay. I'm always learning something. Learning never ends. It won't hurt me to learn something tonight. I got ears," he said.

We didn't say anything for a time. He was leaning forward with his head turned at me, his right ear aimed in the direction of the set. Very disconcerting. Now and then his eyelids drooped and then they snapped open again. Now and then he put his fingers into his beard and tugged, like he was thinking about something he was hearing on the television.

On the screen, a group of men wearing cowls was being set upon and tormented by men dressed in skeleton costumes and men dressed as devils. The men dressed as devils wore devil masks, horns, and long tails. This pageant was part of a procession. The Englishman who was narrating the thing said it took place in Spain once a year. I tried to explain to the blind man what was happening.

"Skeletons," he said. "I know about skeletons," he said, and he nodded.

The TV showed this one cathedral. Then there was a long, slow look at another one. Finally, the picture switched to the famous one in Paris, with its flying buttresses and its spires reaching up to the clouds. The camera pulled away to show the whole of the cathedral rising above the skyline.

There were times when the Englishman who was telling the thing would shut up, would simply let the camera move around over the cathedrals. Or else the camera would tour the countryside, men in fields walking behind oxen. I waited as long as I could. Then I felt I had to say something. I said, "They're showing the outside of this cathedral now. Gargoyles. Little statues carved to look like monsters. Now I guess they're in Italy. Yeah, they're in Italy. There's paintings on the walls of this one church."

"Are those fresco paintings, bub?" he asked, and he sipped from his drink.

I reached for my glass. But it was empty. I tried to remember what I could remember. "You're asking me are those frescoes?" I said. "That's a good question. I don't know."

The camera moved to a cathedral outside Lisbon. The differences in the Portuguese cathedral compared with the French and Italian were not that great. But they were there. Mostly the interior stuff. Then something occurred to me, and I said, "Something has occurred to me. Do you have any idea what a cathedral is? What they look like, that is? Do you follow me? If somebody says cathedral to you, do you have any notion what they're talking about? Do you know the difference between that and a Baptist church, say?"

He let the smoke dribble from his mouth. "I know they took hundreds of workers fifty or a hundred years to build," he said. "I just heard the man say that, of course. I know generations of the same families worked on a cathedral. I heard him say that too. The men who began their life's work on them, they never lived to see the completion of their work. In that wise, bub, they're no different from the rest of us, right?" He laughed. Then his eyelids drooped again. His head nodded. He seemed to be snoozing. Maybe he was imagining himself in Portugal. The TV was showing another cathedral now. This one was in Germany. The Englishman's voice droned on. "Cathedrals," the blind man said. He sat up and rolled his head back and forth. "If you want the truth, bub, that's about all I know. What I just said. What I heard him say. But maybe you could describe one to me? I wish you'd do it. I'd like that. If you want to know, I really don't have a good idea."

I stared hard at the shot of the cathedral on the TV. How could I even begin to describe it? But say my life depended on it. Say my life was being threatened by an insane guy who said I had to do it or else.

I stared some more at the cathedral before the picture flipped off into the countryside. There was no use. I turned to the blind man and said, "To begin with, they're very tall." I was looking around the room for clues. "They reach way up. Up and up. Toward the sky. They're so big, some of them, they have to have these supports. To help hold them up, so to speak. These supports are called buttresses. They remind me of viaducts, for some reason. But maybe you don't know viaducts, either? Sometimes the cathedrals have devils and such carved into the front. Sometimes lords and ladies. Don't ask me why this is," I said.

He was nodding. The whole upper part of his body seemed to be moving back and forth.

"I'm not doing so good, am I?" I said.

He stopped nodding and leaned forward on the edge of the sofa. As he listened to me, he was running his fingers through his beard. I wasn't getting through to him, I could see that. But he waited for me to go on just the same. He nodded, like he was trying to encourage me. I tried to think what else to say. "They're really big," I said. "They're massive. They're built of stone. Marble, too, sometimes. In those olden days, when they built cathedrals, men wanted to be close to God. In those olden days, God was an important part of everyone's life. You could tell this from their cathedral-building. I'm sorry," I said, "but it looks like that's the best I can do for you. I'm just no good at it."

"That's all right, bub," the blind man said. "Hey, listen. I hope you don't mind my asking you. Can I ask you something? Let me ask you a simple question, yes or no. I'm just curious and there's no offense. You're my host. But let me ask if you are in any way religious? You don't mind my asking?"

I shook my head. He couldn't see that, though. A wink is the same as a nod to a blind man. "I guess I don't believe in it. In anything. Sometimes it's hard. You know what I'm saying?"

"Sure I do," he said.

"Right," I said.

The Englishman was still holding forth. My wife sighed in her sleep. She drew a long breath and went on with her sleeping.

"You'll have to forgive me," I said. "But I can't tell you what a cathedral looks like. It just isn't in me to do it. I can't do any more than I've done."

The blind man sat very still, his head down, as he listened to me.

I said, "The truth is, cathedrals don't mean anything special to me. Nothing. Cathedrals. They're something to look at on late-night TV. That's all they are."

It was then that the blind man cleared his throat. He brought something up. He took a handkerchief from his back pocket. Then he said, "I get it, bub. It's okay. It happens. Don't worry about it," he said. "Hey, listen to me. Will you do me a favor? I got an idea. Why don't you find us some heavy paper? And a pen. We'll do something. We'll draw one together. Get us a pen and some heavy paper. Go on, bub, get the stuff," he said.

So I went upstairs. My legs felt like they didn't have any strength in them. They felt like they did after I'd done some running. In my wife's room, I looked around. I found some ballpoints in a little basket on her table. And then I tried to think where to look for the kind of paper he was talking about.

Downstairs, in the kitchen, I found a shopping bag with onion skins in the bottom of the bag. I emptied the bag and shook it. I brought it into the living room and sat down with it near his legs. I moved some things, smoothed the wrinkles from the bag, spread it out on the coffee table.

The blind man got down from the sofa and sat next to me on the carpet.

He ran his fingers over the paper. He went up and down the sides of the paper. The edges, even the edges. He fingered the corners.

"All right," he said. "All right, let's do her."

He found my hand, the hand with the pen. He closed his hand over my hand. "Go ahead, bub, draw," he said. "Draw. You'll see. I'll follow along with you. It'll be okay. Just begin now like I'm telling you. You'll see. Draw," the blind man said.

So I began. First I drew a box that looked like a house. It could have been the house I lived in. Then I put a roof on it. At either end of the roof, I drew spires. Crazy.

"Swell," he said. "Terrific. You're doing fine," he said.

"Never thought anything like this could happen in your lifetime, did you, bub? Well, it's a strange life, we all know that. Go on now. Keep it up."

I put in windows with arches. I drew flying buttresses. I hung great doors. I couldn't stop. The TV station went off the air. I put down the pen and closed and opened my fingers. The blind man felt round over the paper. He moved the tips of his fingers over the paper, all over what I had drawn, and he nodded.

"Doing fine," the blind man said.

I took up the pen again, and he found my hand. I kept at it. I'm no artist. But I kept drawing just the same.

My wife opened up her eyes and gazed at us. She sat up on the sofa, her robe hanging open. She said, "What are you doing? Tell me, I want to know."

I didn't answer her.

The blind man said, "We're drawing a cathedral. Me and him are working on it. Press hard," he said to me. "That's right. That's good," he said. "Sure. You got it, bub. I can tell. You didn't think you could. But you can, can't you? You're cooking with gas now. You know what I'm saying? We're going to really have us something here in a minute. How's the old arm?" he said. "Put some people in there now. What's a cathedral without people?"

My wife said, "What's going on? Robert, what are you doing? What's going on?"

"It's all right," he said to her. "Close your eyes now," the blind man said to me.

I did it. I closed them just like he said.

"Are they closed? he said. "Don't fudge."

"They're closed," I said.

"Keep them that way," he said. He said. "Don't stop now. Draw."

So we kept on with it. His fingers rode my fingers as my hand went over the paper. It was like nothing else in my life up to now.

Then he said, "I think that's it. I think you got it," he said. "Take a look. What do you think?"

But I had my eyes closed. I thought I'd keep them that way for a little longer. I thought it was something I ought to do.

"Well?" he said. "Are you looking?"

My eyes were still closed. I was in my house. I knew that. But I didn't feel like I was inside anything.

"It's really something," I said.

Saint Marie

MARIE LAZARRE

So when I went there, I knew the dark fish must rise. Plumes of radiance had soldered on me. No reservation girl had ever prayed so hard. There was no use in trying to ignore me any longer. I was going up there on the hill with the black robe women. They were not any lighter than me. I was going up there to pray as good as they could. Because I don't have that much Indian blood. And they never thought they'd have a girl from this reservation as a saint they'd have to kneel to. But they'd have me. And I'd be carved in pure gold. With ruby lips. And my toenails would be little pink ocean shells, which they would have to stoop down off their high horse to kiss.

I was ignorant. I was near age fourteen. The length of sky is just about the size of my ignorance. Pure and wide. And it was just that—the pure and wideness of my ignorance—that got me up the hill to Sacred Heart Convent and brought me back down alive. For maybe Jesus did not take my bait, but them Sisters tried to cram me right down whole.

You ever see a walleye strike so bad the lure is practically out its back end before you reel it in? That is what they done with me. I don't like to make that low comparison, but I have seen a walleye do that once. And it's the same attempt as Sister Leopolda made to get me in her clutch.

I had the mail-order Catholic soul you get in a girl raised out in the bush, whose only thought is getting into town. For Sunday Mass is the only time my father brought his children in except for school, when we were harnessed. Our soul went cheap. We were so anxious to get there we would have walked in on our hands and knees. We just craved going to the store, slinging bottle caps in the dust, making fool eyes at each other. And of course we went to church.

Where they have the convent is on top of the highest hill, so that from its windows the Sisters can be looking into the marrow of the town. Recently a windbreak was planted before the bar "for the purposes of tornado insurance." Don't tell me that. That poplar stand was put up to hide the drinkers as they get the transformation. As they are served into the beast of their burden. While they're drinking, that body comes upon them, and then they stagger or crawl out the bar door, pulling a weight they can't move past the poplars. They don't want no holy witness to their fall.

Anyway, I climbed. That was a long-ago day. There was a road then for wagons that wound in ruts to the top of the hill where they had their buildings of painted brick. Gleaming white. So white the sun glanced off in dazzling display to set forms whirling behind your eyelids. The face of God you could hardly look at. But that day it drizzled, so I could look all I wanted. I saw the homelier side. The cracked whitewash and swallows nesting in the busted ends of eaves. I saw the boards sawed the size of broken windowpanes and the fruit trees, stripped. Only the tough wild rhubarb flourished. Goldenrod rubbed up their walls. It was a poor convent. I didn't see that then but I know that now. Compared to others it was humble, ragtag, out in the middle of no place. It was the end of the world to some. Where the maps stopped. Where God had only half a hand in the creation. Where the Dark One had put in thick bush, liquor, wild dogs, and Indians.

I heard later that the Sacred Heart Convent was a catchall place for nuns that don't get along elsewhere. Nuns that complain too much or lose their mind. I'll always wonder now, after hearing that, where they picked up Sister Leopolda. Perhaps she had scarred someone else, the way she left a mark on me. Perhaps she was just sent around to test her Sisters' faith, here and there, like the spot-checker in a factory. For she was the definite most-hard trial to anyone's endurance, even when they started out with veils of wretched love upon their eyes.

I was that girl who thought the black hem of her garment would help me rise. Veils of love which was only hate petrified by longing—that was me. I was like those bush Indians who stole the holy black hat of a Jesuit and swallowed little scraps of it to cure their fevers. But the hat itself carried smallpox and was killing them with belief. Veils of faith! I had this confidence in Leopolda. She was different. The other Sisters had long ago gone blank and given up on Satan. He slept for them. They never noticed his comings and goings. But Leopolda kept track of him and knew his habits, minds he burrowed in, deep spaces where he hid. She knew as much about him as my grandma, who called him by other names and was not afraid.

In her class, Sister Leopolda carried a long oak pole for opening high windows. It had a hook made of iron on one end that could jerk a patch of your hair out or throttle you by the collar—all from a distance. She used this deadly hook-pole for catching Satan by surprise. He could have entered without your knowing it—through your lips or your nose or any one of your seven openings—and gained your mind. But she would see him. That pole would brain you from behind. And he would gasp, dazzled, and take the first thing she offered, which was pain.

She had a stringer of children who could only breathe if she said the word. I was the worst of them. She always said the Dark One wanted me most of all, and I believed this. I stood out. Evil was a common thing I trusted. Before sleep sometimes he came and whispered conversation in the old language of the bush. I listened. He told me things he never told anyone but Indians. I was privy to both worlds of his knowledge. I listened to him, but I had confidence in Leopolda. She was the only one of the bunch he even noticed.

There came a day, though, when Leopolda turned the tide with her hookpole.

It was a quiet day with everyone working at their desks, when I heard him. He had sneaked into the closets in the back of the room. He was scratching around, tasting crumbs in our pockets, stealing buttons, squirting his dark juice in the linings and the boots. I was the only one who heard him, and I got bold. I smiled. I glanced back and smiled and looked up at her sly to see if she had noticed. My heart jumped. For she was looking straight at me. And she sniffed. She had a big stark bony nose stuck to the front of her face for smelling out brimstone and evil thoughts. She had smelled him on me. She stood up. Tall, pale, a blackness leading into the deeper blackness of the slate wall behind her. Her oak pole had flown into her grip. She had seen me glance at the closet. Oh, she knew. She knew just where he was. I watched her watch him in her mind's eye. The whole class was watching now. She was staring, sizing, following his scuffle. And all of a sudden she tensed down, posed on her bent kneesprings, cocked her arm back. She threw the oak pole singing over my head, through my braincloud. It cracked through the thin wood door of the back closet, and the heavy pointed hook drove through his heart. I turned. She'd speared her own black rubber overboot where he'd taken refuge in the tip of her darkest toe.

Something howled in my mind. Loss and darkness. I understood. I was to suffer for my smile.

He rose up hard in my heart. I didn't blink when the pole cracked. My skull was tough. I didn't flinch when she shrieked in my ear. I only shrugged at the flowers of hell. He wanted me. More than anything he craved me. But then she did the worst. She did what broke my mind to her. She grabbed me by the collar and dragged me, feet flying, through the room and threw me in the closet with her dead black overboot. And I was there. The only light was a crack beneath the door. I asked the Dark One to enter into me and boost my mind. I asked him to restrain my tears, for they was pushing behind my eyes. But he was afraid to come back there. He was afraid of her sharp pole. And I was afraid of Leopolda's pole for the first time, too. And I felt the cold hook in my heart. How it could crack through the door at any minute and drag me out, like a dead fish on a gaff, drop me on the floor like a gutshot squirrel.

I was nothing. I edged back to the wall as far as I could. I breathed the chalk dust. The hem of her full black cloak cut against my cheek. He had left me. Her spear could find me any time. Her keen ears would aim the hook into the beat of my heart.

What was that sound?

It filled the closet, filled it up until it spilled over, but I did not recognize the crying wailing voice as mine until the door cracked open, brightness, and she hoisted me to her camphor-smelling lips.

"He *wants* you," she said. "That's the difference. I give you love."

Love. The black hook. The spear singing through the mind. I saw that she had tracked the Dark One to my heart and flushed him out into the open. So now my heart was an empty nest where she could lurk.

Well, I was weak. I was weak when I let her in, but she got a foothold there. Hard to dislodge as the year passed. Sometimes I felt him—the brush of dim wings—but only rarely did his voice compel. It was between Marie and Leopolda now, and the struggle changed. I began to realize I had been on the wrong track with the fruits of hell. The real way to overcome Leopolda was this: I'd get to heaven first. And then, when I saw her coming, I'd shut the gate. She'd be out! That is why, besides the bowing and the scraping I'd be dealt, I wanted to sit on the altar as a saint.

To this end, I went up on the hill. Sister Leopolda was the consecrated nun who had sponsored me to come there.

"You're not vain," she said. "You're too honest, looking into the mirror, for that. You're not smart. You don't have the ambition to get clear. You have two choices. One, you can marry a no-good Indian, bear his brats, die like a dog. Or two, you can give yourself to God."

"I'll come up there," I said, "but not because of what you think."

I could have had any damn man on the reservation at the time. And I could have made him treat me like his own life. I looked good. And I looked white. But I wanted Sister Leopolda's heart. And here was the thing: sometimes I wanted her heart in love and admiration. Sometimes. And sometimes I wanted her heart to roast on a black stick.

She answered the back door where they had instructed me to call. I stood there with my bundle. She looked me up and down.

"All right," she said finally. "Come in."

She took my hand. Her fingers were like a bundle of broom straws, so thin and dry, but the strength of them was unnatural. I couldn't have tugged loose if she was leading me into rooms of white-hot coal. Her strength was a kind of perverse miracle, for she got it from fasting herself thin. Because of this hunger practice her lips were a wounded brown and her skin deadly pale. Her eye sockets were two deep lashless hollows in a taut skull. I told you about the nose already. It stuck out far and made the place her eyes moved even deeper, as if she stared out the wrong end of a gun barrel. She took the bundle from my hands and threw it in the corner.

"You'll be sleeping behind the stove, child."

It was immense, like a great furnace. There was a small cot close behind it.

"Looks like it could get warm there," I said.

"Hot. It does."

"Do I get a habit?"

I wanted something like the thing she wore. Flowing black cotton. Her face was strapped in white bandages, and a sharp crest of starched white cardboard hung over her forehead like a glaring beak. If possible, I wanted a bigger, longer, whiter beak than hers.

"No," she said, grinning her great skull grin. "You don't get one yet. Who knows, you might not like us. Or we might not like you."

But she had loved me, or offered me love. And she had tried to hunt the Dark One down. So I had this confidence.

"I'll inherit your keys from you," I said.

She looked at me sharply, and her grin turned strange. She hissed, taking in her breath. Then she turned to the door and took a key from her belt. It was a giant key, and it unlocked the larder where the food was stored.

Inside there was all kinds of good stuff. Things I'd tasted only once or twice in my life. I saw sticks of dried fruit, jars of orange peel, spice like cinnamon. I saw tins of crackers with ships painted on the side. I saw pickles. Jars of herring and the rind of pigs. There was cheese, a big brown block of it from the thick milk of goats. And besides that there was the everyday stuff, in great quantities, the flour and the coffee.

It was the cheese that got to me. When I saw it my stomach hollowed. My tongue dripped. I loved that goat-milk cheese better than anything I'd ever ate. I stared at it. The rich curve in the buttery cloth.

"When you inherit my keys," she said sourly, slamming the door in my face, "you can eat all you want of the priest's cheese."

Then she seemed to consider what she'd done. She looked at me. She took the key from her belt and went back, sliced a hunk off, and put it in my hand.

"If you're good you'll taste this cheese again. When I'm dead and gone," she said.

Then she dragged out the big sack of flour. When I finished that heaven stuff she told me to roll my sleeves up and begin doing God's labor. For a while we worked in silence, mixing up the dough and pounding it out on stone slabs.

"God's work," I said after a while. "If this is God's work, then I've done it all my life."

"Well, you've done it with the Devil in your heart then," she said. "Not God."

"How do you know?" I asked. But I knew she did. And I wished I had not brought up the subject.

"I see right into you like a clear glass," she said. "I always did."

"You don't know it," she continued after a while, "but he's come around here sulking. He's come around here brooding. You brought him in. He knows the smell of me, and he's going to make a last ditch try to get you back. Don't let him." She glared over at me. Her eyes were cold and lighted. "Don't let him touch you. We'll be a long time getting rid of him."

So I was careful. I was careful not to give him an inch. I said a rosary, two rosaries, three, underneath my breath. I said the Creed. I said every scrap of Latin I knew while we punched the dough with our fists. And still, I dropped the cup. It rolled under that monstrous iron stove, which was getting fired up for baking.

And she was on me. She saw he'd entered my distraction.

"Our good cup," she said. "Get it out of there, Marie."

I reached for the poker to snag it out from beneath the stove. But I had a sinking feel in my stomach as I did this. Sure enough, her long arm darted past me like a whip. The poker lighted in her hand.

"Reach," she said. "Reach with your arm for that cup. And when your flesh is hot, remember that the flames you feel are only one fraction of the heat you will feel in his hellish embrace."

She always did things this way, to teach you lessons. So I wasn't surprised. It was playacting, anyway, because a stove isn't very hot underneath right along the floor. They aren't made that way. Otherwise a wood floor would burn. So I said yes and got down on my stomach and reached under. I meant to grab it quick and jump up again, before she could think up another lesson, but here it happened. Although I groped for the cup, my hand closed on nothing. That cup was nowhere to be found. I heard her step toward me, a slow step. I heard the creak of thick shoe leather, the little *plat* as the folds of her heavy skirts met, a trickle of fine sand sifting, somewhere, perhaps in the bowels of her, and I was afraid. I tried to scramble up, but her foot came down lightly behind my ear, and I was lowered. The foot came down more firmly at the base of my neck, and I was held.

"You're like I was," she said. "He wants you very much."

"He doesn't want me no more," I said. "He had his fill. I got the cup!"

I heard the valve opening, the hissed intake of breath, and knew that I should not have spoke.

"You lie," she said. "You're cold. There is a wicked ice forming in your blood. You don't have a shred of devotion for God. Only wild cold dark lust. I know it. I know how you feel. I see the beast . . . the beast watches me out of your eyes sometimes. Cold."

The urgent scrape of metal. It took a moment to know from where. Top of the stove. Kettle. Lessons. She was steadying herself with the iron poker. I could feel it like pure certainty, driving into the wood floor. I would not remind her of pokers. I heard the water as it came, tipped from the spout, cooling as it fell but still scalding as it struck. I must have twitched beneath her foot, because she steadied me, and then the poker nudged up beside my arm as if to guide. "To warm your cold ash heart," she said. I felt how patient she would be. The water came. My mind went dead blank. Again. I could only think the kettle would be cooling slowly in her hand. I could not stand it. I bit my lip so as not to satisfy her with a sound. She gave me more reason to keep still.

"I will boil him from your mind if you make a peep," she said, "by filling up your ear."

Any sensible fool would have run back down the hill the minute Leopolda let them up from under her heel. But I was snared in her black intelligence by then. I could not think straight. I had prayed so hard I think I broke a cog in my mind. I prayed while her foot squeezed my throat. While my skin burst. I prayed even when I heard the wind come through, shrieking in the busted bird nests. I didn't stop when pure light fell, turning slowly behind my eyelids. God's face. Even that did not disrupt my continued praise. Words came. Words came from nowhere and flooded my mind.

Now I could pray much better than any one of them. Than all of them full force. This was proved. I turned to her in a daze when she let me up. My thoughts were gone, and yet I remember how surprised I was. Tears glittered in her eyes, deep down, like the sinking reflection in a well.

"It was so hard, Marie," she gasped. Her hands were shaking. The kettle clattered against the stove. "But I have used all the water up now. I think he is gone."

"I prayed," I said foolishly. "I prayed very hard."

"Yes," she said. "My dear one, I know."

We sat together quietly because we had no more words. We let the dough rise and punched it down once. She gave me a bowl of mush, unlocked the sausage from a special cupboard, and took that in to the Sisters. They sat down the hall, chewing their sausage, and I could hear them. I could hear their teeth bite through their bread and meat. I couldn't move. My shirt was dry but the cloth stuck to my back, and I couldn't think straight. I was losing the sense to understand how her mind worked. She'd gotten past me with her poker and I would never be a saint. I despaired. I felt I had no inside voice, nothing to direct me, no darkness, no Marie. I was about to throw that cornmeal mush out to the birds and make a run for it, when the vision rose up blazing in my mind.

I was rippling gold. My breasts were bare and my nipples flashed and winked. Diamonds tipped them. I could walk through panes of glass. I could walk through windows. She was at my feet, swallowing the glass after each step I took. I broke through another and another. The glass she swallowed ground and cut until her starved insides were only a subtle dust. She coughed. She coughed a cloud of dust. And then she was only a black rag that flapped off, snagged in bob wire, hung there for an age, and finally rotted into the breeze.

I saw this, mouth hanging open, gazing off into the flagged boughs of trees.

"Get up!" she cried. "Stop dreaming. It is time to bake."

Two other Sisters had come in with her, wide women with hands like paddles. They were evening and smoothing out the firebox beneath the great jaws of the oven.

"Who is this one?" they asked Leopolda. "Is she yours?"

"She is mine," said Leopolda. "A very good girl."

"What is your name?" one asked me.

"Marie."

"Marie. Star of the Sea."

"She will shine," said Leopolda, "when we have burned off the dark corrosion."

The others laughed, but uncertainly. They were mild and sturdy French, who did not understand Leopolda's twisted jokes, although they muttered respectfully at things she said. I knew they wouldn't believe what she had done with the kettle. There was no question. So I kept quiet.

"*Elle est docile,*" they said approvingly as they left to starch the linens.

"Does it pain?" Leopolda asked me as soon as they were out the door.

I did not answer. I felt sick with the hurt.

"Come along," she said.

The building was wholly quiet now. I followed her up the narrow staircase into a hall of little rooms, many doors. Her cell was the quietest, at the very end. Inside, the air smelled stale, as if the door had not been opened for years. There was a crude straw mattress, a tiny bookcase with a picture of Saint Francis hanging over it, a ragged palm, a stool for sitting on, a crucifix. She told me to remove my blouse and sit on the stool. I did so. She took a pot of salve from the bookcase and began to smooth it upon my burns. Her hands made slow, wide circles, stopping the pain. I closed my eyes. I expected to see blackness. Peace. But instead the vision reared up again. My chest was still tipped with diamonds. I was walking through windows. She was chewing up the broken litter I left behind.

"I am going," I said. "Let me go."

But she held me down.

"Don't go," she said quickly. "Don't. We have just begun."

I was weakening. My thoughts were whirling pitifully. The pain had kept me strong, and as it left me I began to forget it; I couldn't hold on. I began to wonder if she'd really scalded me with the kettle. I could not remember. To remember this seemed the most important thing in the world. But I was losing the memory. The scalding. The pouring. It began to vanish. I felt like my mind was coming off its hinge, flapping in the breeze, hanging by the hair of my own pain. I wrenched out of her grip.

"He was always in you," I said. "Even more than in me. He wanted you even more. And now he's got you. Get thee behind me!"

I shouted that, grabbed my shirt, and ran through the door throwing it on my body. I got down the stairs and into the kitchen, even, but no matter what I told myself, I couldn't get out the door. It wasn't finished. And she knew I would not leave. Her quiet step was immediately behind me.

"We must take the bread from the oven now," she said.

She was pretending nothing happened. But for the first time I had gotten through some chink she'd left in her darkness. Touched some doubt. Her voice was so low and brittle it cracked off at the end of her sentence.

"Help me, Marie," she said slowly.

But I was not going to help her, even though she had calmly buttoned the back of my shirt up and put the big cloth mittens in my hands for taking out the loaves. I could have bolted for it then. But I didn't. I knew that something was nearing completion. Something was about to happen. My back was a wall of singing flame. I was turning. I watched her take the long fork in one hand, to tap the loaves. In the other hand she gripped the black poker to hook the pans.

"Help me," she said again, and I thought, Yes, this is part of it. I put the mittens on my hands and swung the door open on its hinges. The oven gaped. She stood back a moment, letting the first blast of heat rush by. I moved behind her. I could feel the heat at my front and at my back. Before, behind. My skin was turning to beaten gold. It was coming quicker than I thought. The oven was like the gate of a personal hell. Just big enough and hot enough for one person, and that was her. One kick and Leopolda would fly in headfirst. And that would be one-millionth of the heat she would feel when she finally collapsed in his hellish embrace.

Saints know these numbers.

She bent forward with her fork held out. I kicked her with all my might. She flew in. But the outstretched poker hit the back wall first, so she rebounded. The oven was not so deep as I had thought.

There was a moment when I felt a sort of thin, hot disappointment, as when a fish slips off the line. Only I was the one going to be lost. She was fearfully silent. She whirled. Her veil had cutting edges. She had the poker in one hand. In the other she held that long sharp fork she used to tap the delicate crusts of loaves. Her face turned upside down on her shoulders. Her face turned blue. But saints are used to miracles. I felt no trace of fear.

If I was going to be lost, let the diamonds cut! Let her eat ground glass!

"Bitch of Jesus Christ!" I shouted. "Kneel and beg! Lick the floor!"

That was when she stabbed me through the hand with the fork, then took the poker up alongside my head, and knocked me out.

It must have been a half an hour later when I came around. Things were so strange. So strange I can hardly tell it for delight at the remembrance. For when I came around this was actually taking place. I was being worshiped. I had somehow gained the altar of a saint.

I was laying back on the stiff couch in the Mother Superior's office. I looked around me. It was as though my deepest dream had come to life. The Sisters of the convent were kneeling to me. Sister Bonaventure. Sister Dympna. Sister Cecilia Saint-Claire. The two French with hands like paddles. They were down on their knees. Black capes were slung over some of their heads. My name was buzzing up and down the room, like a fat autumn fly lighting on the tips of their tongues between Latin, humming up the heavy blood-dark curtains, circling their little cosseted heads. Marie! Marie! A girl thrown in a closet. Who was afraid of a rubber overboot. Who was half overcome. A girl who came in the back door where they threw their garbage. Marie! Who never found the cup. Who had to eat their cold mush. Marie! Leopolda had her face buried in her knuckles. Saint Marie of the Holy Slops! Saint Marie of the Bread Fork! Saint Marie of the Burnt Back and Scalded Butt!

I broke out and laughed.

They looked up. All holy hell burst loose when they saw I'd woke. I still did not understand what was happening. They were watching, talking, but not to me.

"The marks . . ."

"She has her hand closed."

"*Je ne peux pas voir.*"

I was not stupid enough to ask what they were talking about. I couldn't tell why I was laying in white sheets. I couldn't tell why they were praying to me. But I'll tell you this: it seemed entirely natural. It was me. I lifted up my hand as in my dream. It was completely limp with sacredness.

"Peace be with you."

My arm was dried blood from the wrist down to the elbow. And it hurt. Their faces turned like flat flowers of adoration to follow that hand's movements. I let it swing through the air, imparting a saint's blessing. I had practiced. I knew exactly how to act.

They murmured. I heaved a sigh, and a golden beam of light suddenly broke through the clouded window and flooded down directly on my face. A stroke of perfect luck! They had to be convinced.

Leopolda still knelt in the back of the room. Her knuckles were crammed halfway down her throat. Let me tell you, a saint has senses honed keen as a wolf. I knew that she was over my barrel now. How it happened did not matter. The last thing I remembered was how she flew from the oven and stabbed me. That one thing was most certainly true.

"Come forward, Sister Leopolda." I gestured with my heavenly wound. Oh, it hurt. It bled when I reopened the slight heal. "Kneel beside me," I said.

She kneeled, but her voice box evidently did not work, for her mouth opened, shut, opened, but no sound came out. My throat clenched in noble delight I had read of as befitting a saint. She could not speak. But she was beaten. It was in her eyes. She stared at me now with all the deep hate of the wheel of devilish dust that rolled wild within her emptiness.

"What is it you want to tell me?" I asked. And at last she spoke.

"I have told my Sisters of your passion," she managed to choke out. "How the stigmata . . . the marks of the nails . . . appeared in your palm and you swooned at the holy vision. . . ."

"Yes," I said curiously.

And then, after a moment, I understood.

Leopolda had saved herself with her quick brain. She had witnessed a miracle. She had hid the fork and told this to the others. And of course they believed her, because they never knew how Satan came and went or where he took refuge.

"I saw it from the first," said the large one who put the bread in the oven. "Humility of the spirit. So rare in these girls."

"I saw it too," said the other one with great satisfaction. She sighed quietly. "If only it was me."

Leopolda was kneeling bolt upright, face blazing and twitching, a barely held fountain of blasting poison.

"Christ has marked me," I agreed.

I smiled the saint's smirk into her face. And then I looked at her. That was my mistake.

For I saw her kneeling there. Leopolda with her soul like a rubber overboot. With her face of a starved rat. With the desperate eyes drowning in the deep wells of her wrongness. There would be no one else after me. And I would leave. I saw Leopolda kneeling within the shambles of her love.

My heart had been about to surge from my chest with the blackness of my joyous heat. Now it dropped. I pitied her. I pitied her. Pity twisted in my stomach like that hook-pole was driven through me. I was caught. It was a feeling more terrible than any amount of boiling water and worse than being forked. Still, still, I could not help what I did. I had already smiled in a saint's mealy forgiveness. I heard myself speaking gently.

"Receive the dispensation of my sacred blood," I whispered.

But there was no heart in it. No joy when she bent to touch the floor. No dark leaping. I fell back into the white pillows. Blank dust was whirling through the light shafts. My skin was dust. Dust my lips. Dust the dirty spoons on the ends of my feet.

Rise up! I thought. Rise up and walk! There is no limit to this dust!

The Things They Carried

F irst Lieutenant Jimmy Cross carried letters from a girl named Martha, a junior at Mount Sebastian College in New Jersey. They were not love letters, but Lieutenant Cross was hoping, so he kept them folded in plastic at the bottom of his rucksack. In the late afternoon, after a day's march, he would dig his foxhole, wash his hands under a canteen, unwrap the letters, hold them with the tips of his fingers, and spend the last hour of light pretending. He would imagine romantic camping trips into the White Mountains in New Hampshire. He would sometimes taste the envelope flaps, knowing her tongue had been there. More than anything, he wanted Martha to love him as he loved her, but the letters were mostly chatty, elusive on the matter of love. She was a virgin, he was almost sure. She was an English major at Mount Sebastian, and she wrote beautifully about her professors and roommates and midterm exams, about her respect for Chaucer and her great affection for Virginia Woolf. She often quoted lines of poetry; she never mentioned the war, except to say, Jimmy, take care of yourself. The letters weighed ten ounces. They were signed "Love, Martha," but Lieutenant Cross understood that "Love" was only a way of signing and did not mean what he sometimes pretended it meant. At dusk, he would carefully return the letters to his rucksack. Slowly, a bit distracted, he would get up and move among his men, checking the perimeter, then at full dark he would return to his hole and watch the night and wonder if Martha was a virgin.

The things they carried were largely determined by necessity. Among the necessities or near necessities were P-38 can openers, pocket knives, heat tabs, wrist watches, dog tags, mosquito repellent, chewing gum, candy, cigarettes, salt tablets, packets of Kool-Aid, lighters, matches, sewing kits, Military Payment Certificates, C rations, and two or three canteens of water. Together, these items weighed between fifteen and twenty pounds, depending upon a man's habits or rate of metabolism. Henry Dobbins, who was a big man, carried extra rations; he was especially fond of canned peaches in heavy syrup over pound cake. Dave Jensen, who practiced field hygiene, carried a tooth-brush, dental floss, and several hotel-size bars of soap he'd stolen on R&R in Sydney, Australia. Ted Lavender, who was scared, carried tranquilizers until he was shot in the head outside the village of Than Khe in mid-April. By necessity, and because it was SOP,[1] they all carried steel helmets that weighed five pounds including the liner

---

[1]Standard operating procedure.

and camouflage cover. They carried the standard fatigue jackets and trousers. Very few carried underwear. On their feet they carried jungle boots—2.1 pounds—and Dave Jensen carried three pairs of socks and a can of Dr. Scholl's foot powder as a precaution against trench foot. Until he was shot, Ted Lavender carried six or seven ounces of premium dope, which for him was a necessity. Mitchell Sanders, the RTO,[2] carried condoms. Norman Bowker carried a diary. Rat Kiley carried comic books. Kiowa, a devout Baptist, carried an illustrated New Testament that had been presented to him by his father, who taught Sunday school in Oklahoma City, Oklahoma. As a hedge against bad times, however, Kiowa also carried his grandmother's distrust of the white man, his grandfather's old hunting hatchet. Necessity dictated. Because the land was mined and booby-trapped, it was SOP for each man to carry a steel-centered, nylon-covered flak jacket, which weighed 6.7 pounds, but which on hot days seemed much heavier. Because you could die so quickly, each man carried at least one large compress bandage, usually in the helmet band for easy access. Because the nights were cold, and because the monsoons were wet, each carried a green plastic poncho that could be used as a rain-coat or ground sheet or makeshift tent. With its quilted liner, the poncho weighed almost two pounds, but it was worth every ounce. In April, for instance, when Ted Lavender was shot, they used his poncho to wrap him up, then to carry him across the paddy, then to lift him into the chopper that took him away.

They were called legs or grunts.

To carry something was to "hump" it, as when Lieutenant Jimmy Cross humped his love for Martha up the hills and through the swamps. In its intransitive form, "to hump" meant "to walk," or "to march," but it implied burdens far beyond the intransitive.

Almost everyone humped photographs. In his wallet, Lieutenant Cross carried two photographs of Martha. The first was a Kodachrome snapshot signed "Love," though he knew better. She stood against a brick wall. Her eyes were gray and neutral, her lips slightly open as she stared straight-on at the camera. At night, sometimes, Lieutenant Cross wondered who had taken the picture, because he knew she had boyfriends, because he loved her so much, and because he could see the shadow of the picture taker spreading out against the brick wall. The second photograph had been clipped from the 1968 Mount Sebastian yearbook. It was an action shot—women's volleyball—and Martha was bent horizontal to the floor, reaching, the palms of her hands in sharp focus, the tongue taut, the expression frank and competitive. There was no visible sweat. She wore white gym shorts. Her legs, he thought, were almost certainly the legs of a virgin, dry and without hair, the left knee cocked and carrying her entire weight, which was just over one hundred pounds. Lieutenant Cross remembered touching that left knee. A dark theater, he remembered, and the movie was *Bonnie and Clyde,* and Martha wore a tweed skirt, and during the final scene, when he touched her knee, she turned and looked at him in a sad, sober way that made him pull his hand back, but he would always remem-

[2]Radiotelephone operator.

ber the feel of the tweed skirt and the knee beneath it and the sound of the gunfire that killed Bonnie and Clyde, how embarrassing it was, how slow and oppressive. He remembered kissing her good night at the dorm door. Right then, he thought, he should've done something brave. He should've carried her up the stairs to her room and tied her to the bed and touched that left knee all night long. He should've risked it. Whenever he looked at the photographs, he thought of new things he should've done.

What they carried was partly a function of rank, partly of field specialty.

As a first lieutenant and platoon leader, Jimmy Cross carried a compass, maps, code books, binoculars, and a .45-caliber pistol that weighed 2.9 pounds fully loaded. He carried a strobe light and the responsibility for the lives of his men.

As an RTO, Mitchell Sanders carried the PRC-25 radio, a killer, twenty-six pounds with its battery.

As a medic, Rat Kiley carried a canvas satchel filled with morphine and plasma and malaria tablets and surgical tape and comic books and all the things a medic must carry, including M&M's for especially bad wounds, for a total weight of nearly twenty pounds.

As a big man, therefore a machine gunner, Henry Dobbins carried the M-60, which weighed twenty-three pounds unloaded, but which was almost always loaded. In addition, Dobbins carried between ten and fifteen pounds of ammunition draped in belts across his chest and shoulders.

As PFCs or Spec 4s, most of them were common grunts and carried the standard M-16 gas-operated assault rifle. The weapon weighed 7.5 pounds unloaded, 8.2 pounds with its full twenty-round magazine. Depending on numerous factors, such as topography and psychology, the riflemen carried anywhere from twelve to twenty magazines, usually in cloth bandoliers, adding on another 8.4 pounds at minimum, fourteen pounds at maximum. When it was available, they also carried M-16 maintenance gear—rods and steel brushes and swabs and tubes of LSA oil—all of which weighed about a pound. Among the grunts, some carried the M-79 grenade launcher, 5.9 pounds unloaded, a reasonably light weapon except for the ammunition, which was heavy. A single round weighed ten ounces. The typical load was twenty-five rounds. But Ted Lavender, who was scared, carried thirty-four rounds when he was shot and killed outside Than Khe, and he went down under an exceptional burden, more than twenty pounds of ammunition, plus the flak jacket and helmet and rations and water and toilet paper and tranquilizers and all the rest, plus the unweighed fear. He was dead weight. There was no twitching or flopping. Kiowa, who saw it happen, said it was like watching a rock fall, or a big sandbag or something— just boom, then down—not like the movies where the dead guy rolls around and does fancy spins and goes ass over teakettle—not like that, Kiowa said, the poor bastard just flat-fuck fell. Boom. Down. Nothing else. It was a bright morning in mid-April. Lieutenant Cross felt the pain. He blamed himself. They stripped off Lavender's canteens and ammo, all the heavy things, and Rat Kiley said the obvious, the guy's dead, and Mitchell Sanders used his radio to report one U.S. KIA[3] and to request a chopper. Then they wrapped Lavender in his poncho. They carried him out to a dry paddy, established security, and sat smoking the dead man's dope until the chopper came. Lieutenant Cross kept to himself. He pictured Martha's smooth young face, thinking he loved her more than anything, more than his men, and now Ted Lavender was dead because he loved her so much and could not stop thinking about her. When the dust-off arrived, they carried Lavender aboard. Afterward they burned Than Khe. They marched until dusk, then dug their holes, and that night Kiowa kept explaining how you had to be there, how fast it was, how the poor guy just dropped like so much concrete. Boom-down, he said. Like cement.

In addition to the three standard weapons—the M-60, M-16, and M-79—they carried whatever presented itself, or whatever seemed appropriate as a means of killing or staying alive. They carried catch-as-catch-can. At various times, in various situations, they carried M-14s and CAR-15s and Swedish Ks and grease guns and captured AK-47s and Chi-Coms and RPGs and Simonov carbines and black-market Uzis and .38-caliber Smith & Wesson handguns and 66 mm LAWs and shotguns and silencers and blackjacks and bayonets and C-4 plastic explosives. Lee Strunk carried a slingshot; a weapon of last resort, he called it. Mitchell Sanders carried brass knuckles. Kiowa carried his grandfather's feathered hatchet. Every third or fourth man carried a Claymore antipersonnel mine—3.5 pounds with its firing device. They all carried fragmentation grenades—fourteen ounces each. They all carried at least one M-18 colored smoke grenade—twenty-four ounces. Some carried CS or tear-gas grenades. Some carried white-phosphorus grenades. They carried all they could bear, and then some, including a silent awe for the terrible power of the things they carried.

In the first week of April, before Lavender died, Lieutenant Jimmy Cross received a good-luck charm from Martha. It was a simple pebble, an ounce at most. Smooth to the touch, it was a milky-white color with flecks of orange and violet, oval-shaped, like a miniature egg. In the accompanying letter, Martha wrote that she had found the pebble on the Jersey shoreline, precisely where the land touched water at high tide, where things came together but also separated. It was this separate-but-together quality, she wrote, that had inspired her to pick up the pebble and to carry it in her breast pocket for several days, where it seemed weightless, and then to send it through the mail, by air, as a token of her truest feelings for him. Lieutenant Cross found this romantic. But he wondered what her truest feelings were, exactly, and what she meant by separate-but-together. He wondered how the tides and waves had come into play on that afternoon along the Jersey shoreline when Martha saw the pebble and bent down to rescue it from geology. He imagined bare feet. Martha was a poet, with the poet's sensibilities, and her feet would be brown and bare, the toenails unpainted, the eyes chilly and somber like the ocean in March, and

---

[3]Killed in action.

though it was painful, he wondered who had been with her that afternoon. He imagined a pair of shadows moving along the strip of sand where things came together but also separated. It was phantom jealousy, he knew, but he couldn't help himself. He loved her so much. On the march, through the hot days of early April, he carried the pebble in his mouth, turning it with his tongue, tasting sea salts and moisture. His mind wandered. He had difficulty keeping his attention on the war. On occasion he would yell at his men to spread out the column, to keep their eyes open, but then he would slip away into daydreams, just pretending, walking barefoot along the Jersey shore, with Martha, carrying nothing. He would feel himself rising. Sun and waves and gentle winds, all love and lightness.

What they carried varied by mission.

When a mission took them to the mountains, they carried mosquito netting, machetes, canvas tarps, and extra bug juice.

If a mission seemed especially hazardous, or if it involved a place they knew to be bad, they carried everything they could. In certain heavily mined AOs,[4] where the land was dense with Toe Poppers and Bouncing Betties, they took turns humping a twenty-eight-pound mine detector. With its headphones and big sensing plate, the equipment was a stress on the lower back and shoulders, awkward to handle, often useless because of the shrapnel in the earth, but they carried it anyway, partly for safety, partly for the illusion of safety.

On ambush, or other night missions, they carried peculiar little odds and ends. Kiowa always took along his New Testament and a pair of moccasins for silence. Dave Jensen carried night-sight vitamins high in carotin. Lee Strunk carried his slingshot; ammo, he claimed, would never be a problem. Rat Kiley carried brandy and M&M's. Until he was shot, Ted Lavender carried the starlight scope, which weighed 6.3 pounds with its aluminum carrying case. Henry Dobbins carried his girlfriend's pantyhose wrapped around his neck as a comforter. They all carried ghosts. When dark came, they would move out single file across the meadows and paddies to their ambush coordinates, where they would quietly set up the Claymores and lie down and spend the night waiting.

Other missions were more complicated and required special equipment. In mid-April, it was their mission to search out and destroy the elaborate tunnel complexes in the Than Khe area south of Chu Lai. To blow the tunnels, they carried one-pound blocks of pentrite high explosives, four blocks to a man, sixty-eight pounds in all. They carried wiring, detonators, and battery-powered clackers. Dave Jensen carried earplugs. Most often, before blowing the tunnels, they were ordered by higher command to search them, which was considered bad news, but by and large they just shrugged and carried out orders. Because he was a big man, Henry Dobbins was excused from tunnel duty. The others would draw numbers. Before Lavender died there were seventeen men in the platoon, and whoever drew the number seventeen would strip off his gear and crawl in head first with a flashlight and Lieutenant Cross's .45-caliber pistol. The

---

[4]Areas of operations.

rest of them would fan out as security. They would sit down or kneel, not facing the hole, listening to the ground beneath them, imagining cobwebs and
ghosts, whatever was down there—the tunnel walls squeezing in—how the
flashlight seemed impossibly heavy in the hand and how it was tunnel vision in
the very strictest sense, compression in all ways, even time, and how you had
to wiggle in—ass and elbows—a swallowed-up feeling—and how you found
yourself worrying about odd things—will your flashlight go dead? Do rats carry
rabies? If you screamed, how far would the sound carry? Would your buddies
hear it? Would they have the courage to drag you out? In some respects, though
not many, the waiting was worse than the tunnel itself. Imagination was a killer.

On April 16, when Lee Strunk drew the number seventeen, he laughed and
muttered something and went down quickly. The morning was hot and very
still. Not good, Kiowa said. He looked at the tunnel opening, then out across a
dry paddy toward the village of Than Khe. Nothing moved. No clouds or birds
or people. As they waited, the men smoked and drank Kool-Aid, not talking
much, feeling sympathy for Lee Strunk but also feeling the luck of the draw.
You win some, you lose some, said Mitchell Sanders, and sometimes you settle for a rain check. It was a tired line and no one laughed.

Henry Dobbins ate a tropical chocolate bar. Ted Lavender popped a tran-
quilizer and went off to pee.

After five minutes, Lieutenant Jimmy Cross moved to the tunnel, leaned
down, and examined the darkness. Trouble, he thought—a cave-in maybe. And
then suddenly, without willing it, he was thinking about Martha. The stresses
and fractures, the quick collapse, the two of them buried alive under all that
weight. Dense, crushing love. Kneeling, watching the hole, he tried to concentrate on Lee Strunk and the war, all the dangers, but his love was too much for
him, he felt paralyzed, he wanted to sleep inside her lungs and breathe her
blood and be smothered. He wanted her to be a virgin and not a virgin, all at
once. He wanted to know her. Intimate secrets—why poetry? Why so sad? Why
the grayness in her eyes? Why so alone? Not lonely, just alone—riding her bike
across campus or sitting off by herself in the cafeteria. Even dancing, she
danced alone—and it was the aloneness that filled him with love. He remembered telling her that one evening. How she nodded and looked away. And
how, later, when he kissed her, she received the kiss without returning it, her
eyes wide open, not afraid, not a virgin's eyes, just flat and uninvolved.

Lieutenant Cross gazed at the tunnel. But he was not there. He was buried
with Martha under the white sand at the Jersey shore. They were pressed
together, and the pebble in his mouth was her tongue. He was smiling. Vaguely,
he was aware of how quiet the day was, the sullen paddies, yet he could not
bring himself to worry about matters of security. He was beyond that. He was
just a kid at war, in love. He was twenty-two years old. He couldn't help it.

A few moments later Lee Strunk crawled out of the tunnel. He came up
grinning, filthy but alive. Lieutenant Cross nodded and closed his eyes while
the others clapped Strunk on the back and made jokes about rising from the
dead.

Worms, Rat Kiley said. Right out of the grave. Fuckin' zombie.

The men laughed. They all felt great relief.

Spook City, said Mitchell Sanders.

Lee Strunk made a funny ghost sound, a kind of moaning, yet very happy, and right then, when Strunk made that high happy moaning sound, when he went *Ahhooooo,* right then Ted Lavender was shot in the head on his way back from peeing. He lay with his mouth open. The teeth were broken. There was a swollen black bruise under his left eye. The cheekbone was gone. Oh shit, Rat Kiley said, the guy's dead. The guy's dead, he kept saying, which seemed profound—the guy's dead. I mean really.

The things they carried were determined to some extent by superstition. Lieutenant Cross carried his good-luck pebble. Dave Jensen carried a rabbit's foot. Norman Bowker, otherwise a very gentle person, carried a thumb that had been presented to him as a gift by Mitchell Sanders. The thumb was dark brown, rubbery to the touch, and weighed four ounces at most. It had been cut from a VC corpse, a boy of fifteen or sixteen. They'd found him at the bottom of an irrigation ditch, badly burned, flies in his mouth and eyes. The boy wore black shorts and sandals. At the time of his death he had been carrying a pouch of rice, a rifle, and three magazines of ammunition.

You want my opinion, Mitchell Sanders said, there's a definite moral here.

He put his hand on the dead boy's wrist. He was quiet for a time, as if counting a pulse, then he patted the stomach, almost affectionately, and used Kiowa's hunting hatchet to remove the thumb.

Henry Dobbins asked what the moral was.

Moral?

You know. *Moral.*

Sanders wrapped the thumb in toilet paper and handed it across to Norman Bowker. There was no blood. Smiling, he kicked the boy's head, watched the flies scatter, and said, It's like with that old TV show—Paladin. Have gun, will travel.

Henry Dobbins thought about it.

Yeah, well, he finally said. I don't see no moral.

There it *is,* man.

Fuck off.

They carried USO stationery and pencils and pens. They carried Sterno, safety pins, trip flares, signal flares, spools of wire, razor blades, chewing tobacco, liberated joss sticks and statuettes of the smiling Buddha, candles, grease pencils, *The Stars and Stripes,* fingernail clippers, Psy Ops[5] leaflets, bush hats, bolos, and much more. Twice a week, when the resupply choppers came in, they carried hot chow in green Mermite cans and large canvas bags filled with iced beer and soda pop. They carried plastic water containers, each with a two-gallon capacity. Mitchell Sanders carried a set of starched tiger fatigues for special occasions. Henry Dobbins carried Black Flag insecticide. Dave

[5]Psychological operations.

Jensen carried empty sandbags that could be filled at night for added protection. Lee Strunk carried tanning lotion. Some things they carried in common. Taking turns, they carried the big PRC-77 scrambler radio, which weighed thirty pounds with its battery. They shared the weight of memory. They took up what others could no longer bear. Often, they carried each other, the wounded or weak. They carried infections. They carried chess sets, basketballs, Vietnamese-English dictionaries, insignia of rank, Bronze Stars and Purple Hearts, plastic cards imprinted with the Code of Conduct. They carried diseases, among them malaria and dysentery. They carried lice and ringworm and leeches and paddy algae and various rots and molds. They carried the land itself—Vietnam, the place, the soil—a powdery orange-red dust that covered their boots and fatigues and faces. They carried the sky. The whole atmosphere, they carried it, the humidity, the monsoons, the stink of fungus and decay, all of it, they carried gravity. They moved like mules. By daylight they took sniper fire, at night they were mortared, but it was not battle, it was just the endless march, village to village, without purpose, nothing won or lost. They marched for the sake of the march. They plodded along slowly, dumbly, leaning forward against the heat, unthinking, all blood and bone, simple grunts, soldiering with their legs, toiling up the hills and down into the paddies and across the rivers and up again and down, just humping, one step and then the next and then another, but no volition, no will, because it was automatic, it was anatomy, and the war was entirely a matter of posture and carriage, the hump was everything, a kind of inertia, a kind of emptiness, a dullness of desire and intellect and conscience and hope and human sensibility. Their principles were in their feet. Their calculations were biological. They had no sense of strategy or mission. They searched the villages without knowing what to look for, not caring, kicking over jars of rice, frisking children and old men, blowing tunnels, sometimes setting fires and sometimes not, then forming up and moving on to the next village, then other villages, where it would always be the same. They carried their own lives. The pressures were enormous. In the heat of early afternoon, they would remove their helmets and flak jackets, walking bare, which was dangerous but which helped ease the strain. They would often discard things along the route of march. Purely for comfort, they would throw away rations, blow their Claymores and grenades, no matter, because by nightfall the resupply choppers would arrive with more of the same, then a day or two later still more, fresh watermelons and crates of ammunition and sunglasses and woolen sweaters—the resources were stunning—sparklers for the Fourth of July, colored eggs for Easter. It was the great American war chest—the fruits of science, the smokestacks, the canneries, the arsenals at Hartford, the Minnesota forests, the machine shops, the vast fields of corn and wheat—they carried like freight trains; they carried it on their backs and shoulders—and for all the ambiguities of Vietnam, all the mysteries and unknowns, there was at least the single abiding certainty that they would never be at a loss for things to carry.

After the chopper took Lavender away, Lieutenant Jimmy Cross led his men into the village of Than Khe. They burned everything. They shot chickens and dogs, they trashed the village well, they called in artillery and watched the wreckage, then they marched for several hours through the hot afternoon, and then at dusk, while Kiowa explained how Lavender died, Lieutenant Cross found himself trembling.

He tried not to cry. With his entrenching tool, which weighed five pounds, he began digging a hole in the earth.

He felt shame. He hated himself. He had loved Martha more than his men, and as a consequence Lavender was now dead, and this was something he would have to carry like a stone in his stomach for the rest of the war.

All he could do was dig. He used his entrenching tool like an ax, slashing, feeling both love and hate, and then later, when it was full dark, he sat at the bottom of his foxhole and wept. It went on for a long while. In part, he was grieving for Ted Lavender, but mostly it was for Martha, and for himself, because she belonged to another world, which was not quite real, and because she was a junior at Mount Sebastian College in New Jersey, a poet and a virgin and uninvolved, and because he realized she did not love him and never would.

Like cement, Kiowa whispered in the dark. I swear to God—boom-down. Not a word.

I've heard this, said Norman Bowker.

A pisser, you know? Still zipping himself up. Zapped while zipping.

All right, fine. That's enough.

Yeah, but you had to see it, the guy just—

I *heard,* man. Cement. So why not shut the fuck *up?*

Kiowa shook his head sadly and glanced over at the hole where Lieutenant Jimmy Cross sat watching the night. The air was thick and wet. A warm, dense fog had settled over the paddies and there was the stillness that precedes rain.

After a time Kiowa sighed.

One thing for sure, he said. The Lieutenant's in some deep hurt. I mean that crying jag—the way he was carrying on—it wasn't fake or anything, it was real heavy-duty hurt. The man cares.

Sure, Norman Bowker said.

Say what you want, the man does care.

We all got problems.

Not Lavender.

No, I guess not, Bowker said. Do me a favor, though.

Shut up?

That's a smart Indian. Shut up.

Shrugging, Kiowa pulled off his boots. He wanted to say more, just to lighten up his sleep, but instead he opened his New Testament and arranged it beneath his head as a pillow. The fog made things seem hollow and unattached. He tried not to think about Ted Lavender, but then he was thinking how fast it was, no drama, down and dead, and how it was hard to feel anything except surprise. It seemed un-Christian. He wished he could find some great sadness, or even anger, but the emotion wasn't there and he couldn't make it happen. Mostly he felt pleased to be alive. He liked the smell of the New Testament under his cheek, the leather and ink and paper and glue, whatever the chemicals were. He liked hearing the sounds of night. Even his fatigue, it felt fine, the stiff muscles and the prickly awareness of his own body, a floating feeling. He enjoyed not being dead. Lying there, Kiowa admired Lieutenant Jimmy Cross's capacity for grief. He wanted to share the man's pain, he wanted to care as Jimmy Cross cared. And yet when he closed his eyes, all he could think was Boom-down, and all he could feel was the pleasure of having his boots off and the fog curling in around him and the damp soil and the Bible smells and the plush comfort of night.

After a moment Norman Bowker sat up in the dark.

What the hell, he said. You want to talk, *talk*. Tell it to me.

Forget it.

No, man, go on. One thing I hate, it's a silent Indian.

For the most part they carried themselves with poise, a kind of dignity. Now and then, however, there were times of panic, when they squealed or wanted to squeal but couldn't, when they twitched and made moaning sounds and covered their heads and said Dear Jesus and flopped around on the earth and fired their weapons blindly and cringed and sobbed and begged for the noise to stop and went wild and made stupid promises to themselves and to God and to their mothers and fathers, hoping not to die. In different ways, it happened to all of them. Afterward, when the firing ended, they would blink and peek up. They would touch their bodies, feeling shame, then quickly hiding it. They would force themselves to stand. As if in slow motion, frame by frame, the world would take on the old logic—absolute silence, then the wind, then sunlight, then voices. It was the burden of being alive. Awkwardly, the men would reassemble themselves, first in private, then in groups, becoming soldiers again. They would repair the leaks in their eyes. They would check for casualties, call in dust-offs, light cigarettes, try to smile, clear their throats and spit and begin cleaning their weapons. After a time someone would shake his head and say, No lie, I almost shit my pants, and someone else would laugh, which meant it was bad, yes, but the guy had obviously not shit his pants, it wasn't that bad, and in any case nobody would ever do such a thing and then go ahead and talk about it. They would squint into the dense, oppressive sunlight. For a few moments, perhaps, they would fall silent, lighting a joint and tracking its passage from man to man, inhaling, holding in the humiliation. Scary stuff, one of them might say. But then someone else would grin or flick his eyebrows and say, Roger-dodger, almost cut me a new asshole, *almost*.

There were numerous such poses. Some carried themselves with a sort of wistful resignation, others with pride or stiff soldierly discipline or good humor or macho zeal. They were afraid of dying but they were even more afraid to show it.

They found jokes to tell.

They used a hard vocabulary to contain the terrible softness. *Greased,* they'd say. *Offed, lit up, zapped while zipping.* It wasn't cruelty, just stage presence. They were actors and the war came at them in 3-D. When someone died, it wasn't quite dying, because in a curious way it seemed scripted, and because they had their lines mostly memorized, irony mixed with tragedy, and because they called it by other names, as if to encyst and destroy the reality of death itself. They kicked corpses. They cut off thumbs. They talked grunt lingo. They told stories about Ted Lavender's supply of tranquilizers, how the poor guy didn't feel a thing, how incredibly tranquil he was.

There's a moral here, said Mitchell Sanders.

They were waiting for Lavender's chopper, smoking the dead man's dope.

The moral's pretty obvious, Sanders said, and winked. Stay away from drugs. No joke, they'll ruin your day every time.

Cute, said Henry Dobbins.

Mind-blower, get it? Talk about wiggy—nothing left, just blood and brains.

They made themselves laugh.

There it is, they'd say, over and over, as if the repetition itself were an act of poise, a balance between crazy and almost crazy, knowing without going. There it is, which meant be cool, let it ride, because oh yeah, man, you can't change what can't be changed, there it is, there it absolutely and positively and fucking well *is*.

They were tough.

They carried all the emotional baggage of men who might die. Grief, terror, love, longing—these were intangibles, but the intangibles had their own mass and specific gravity, they had tangible weight. They carried shameful memories. They carried the common secret of cowardice barely restrained, the instinct to run or freeze or hide, and in many respects this was the heaviest burden of all, for it could never be put down, it required perfect balance and perfect posture. They carried their reputations. They carried the soldier's greatest fear, which was the fear of blushing. Men killed, and died, because they were embarrassed not to. It was what had brought them to the war in the first place, nothing positive, no dreams of glory or honor, just to avoid the blush of dishonor. They died so as not to die of embarrassment. They crawled into tunnels and walked point and advanced under fire. Each morning, despite the unknowns, they made their legs move. They endured. They kept humping. They did not submit to the obvious alternative, which was simply to close the eyes and fall. So easy, really. Go limp and tumble to the ground and let the muscles unwind and not speak and not budge until your buddies picked you up and lifted you into the chopper that would roar and dip its nose and carry you off to the world. A mere matter of falling, yet no one ever fell. It was not courage, exactly; the object was not valor. Rather, they were too frightened to be cowards.

By and large they carried these things inside, maintaining the masks of composure. They sneered at sick call. They spoke bitterly about guys who had found release by shooting off their own toes or fingers. Pussies, they'd say. Candyasses. It was fierce, mocking talk, with only a trace of envy or awe, but even so, the image played itself out behind their eyes.

They imagined the muzzle against flesh. They imagined the quick, sweet pain, then the evacuation to Japan, then a hospital with warm beds and cute geisha nurses.

They dreamed of freedom birds.

At night, on guard, staring into the dark, they were carried away by jumbo jets. They felt the rush of takeoff. *Gone!* they yelled. And then velocity, wings and engines, a smiling stewardess—but it was more than a plane, it was a real bird, a big sleek silver bird with feathers and talons and high screeching. They were flying. The weights fell off, there was nothing to bear. They laughed and held on tight, feeling the cold slap of wind and altitude, soaring, thinking *It's over, I'm gone!*—they were naked, they were light and free—it was all lightness, bright and fast and buoyant, light as light, a helium buzz in the brain, a giddy bubbling in the lungs as they were taken up over the clouds and the war, beyond duty, beyond gravity and mortification and global entanglements—*Sin loi!*[6] they yelled, *I'm sorry, motherfuckers, but I'm out of it, I'm goofed, I'm on a space cruise, I'm gone!*—and it was a restful, disencumbered sensation, just riding the light waves, sailing that big silver freedom bird over the mountains and oceans, over America, over the farms and great sleeping cities and cemeteries and highways and the golden arches of McDonald's. It was flight, a kind of fleeing, a kind of falling, falling higher and higher, spinning off the edge of the earth and beyond the sun and through the vast, silent vacuum where there were no burdens and where everything weighed exactly nothing. *Gone!* they screamed, *I'm sorry but I'm gone!* And so at night, not quite dreaming, they gave themselves over to lightness, they were carried, they were purely borne.

On the morning after Ted Lavender died, First Lieutenant Jimmy Cross crouched at the bottom of his foxhole and burned Martha's letters. Then he burned the two photographs. There was a steady rain falling, which made it difficult, but he used heat tabs and Sterno to build a small fire, screening it with his body, holding the photographs over the tight blue flame with the tips of his fingers.

He realized it was only a gesture. Stupid, he thought. Sentimental, too, but mostly just stupid.

Lavender was dead. You couldn't burn the blame.

Besides, the letters were in his head. And even now, without photographs, Lieutenant Cross could see Martha playing volleyball in her white gym shorts and yellow T-shirt. He could see her moving in the rain.

When the fire died out, Lieutenant Cross pulled his poncho over his shoulders and ate breakfast from a can.

There was no great mystery, he decided.

In those burned letters Martha had never mentioned the war, except to say, Jimmy, take care of yourself. She wasn't involved. She signed the letters "Love," but it wasn't love, and all the fine lines and technicalities did not matter.

The morning came up wet and blurry. Everything seemed part of everything else, the fog and Martha and the deepening rain.

[6]"Sorry about that!"

It was a war, after all.

Half smiling, Lieutenant Jimmy Cross took out his maps. He shook his head hard, as if to clear it, then bent forward and began planning the day's march. In ten minutes, or maybe twenty, he would rouse the men and they would pack up and head west, where the maps showed the country to be green and inviting. They would do what they had always done. The rain might add some weight, but otherwise it would be one more day layered upon all the other days.

He was realistic about it. There was that new hardness in his stomach.

No more fantasies, he told himself.

Henceforth, when he thought about Martha, it would be only to think that she belonged elsewhere. He would shut down the daydreams. This was not Mount Sebastian, it was another world, where there were no pretty poems or midterm exams, a place where men died because of carelessness and gross stupidity. Kiowa was right. Boom-down, and you were dead, never partly dead.

Briefly, in the rain, Lieutenant Cross saw Martha's gray eyes gazing back at him.

He understood.

It was very sad, he thought. The things men carried inside. The things men did or felt they had to do.

He almost nodded at her, but didn't.

Instead he went back to his maps. He was now determined to perform his duties firmly and without negligence. It wouldn't help Lavender, he knew that, but from this point on he would comport himself as a soldier. He would dispose of his good-luck pebble. Swallow it, maybe, or use Lee Strunk's slingshot, or just drop it along the trail. On the march he would impose strict field discipline. He would be careful to send out flank security, to prevent straggling or bunching up, to keep his troops moving at the proper pace and at the proper interval. He would insist on clean weapons. He would confiscate the remainder of Lavender's dope. Later in the day, perhaps, he would call the men together and speak to them plainly. He would accept the blame for what had happened to Ted Lavender. He would be a man about it. He would look them in the eyes, keeping his chin level, and he would issue the new SOPs in a calm, impersonal tone of voice, an officer's voice, leaving no room for argument or discussion. Commencing immediately, he'd tell them, they would no longer abandon equipment along the route of march. They would police up their acts. They would get their shit together, and keep it together, and maintain it neatly and in good working order.

He would not tolerate laxity. He would show strength, distancing himself.

Among the men there would be grumbling, of course, and maybe worse, because their days would seem longer and their loads heavier, but Lieutenant Cross reminded himself that his obligation was not to be loved but to lead. He would dispense with love; it was not now a factor. And if anyone quarreled or complained, he would simply tighten his lips and arrange his shoulders in the correct command posture. He might give a curt little nod. Or he might not. He might just shrug and say Carry on, then they would saddle up and form into a column and move out toward the villages of Than Khe.

JOYCE CAROL OATES

Heat

*I*t was midsummer, the heat rippling above the macadam roads. Cicadas screaming out of the trees and the sky like pewter, glaring.

The days were the same day, like the shallow mud-brown river moving always in the same direction but so slow you couldn't see it. Except for Sunday: Church in the morning, then the fat Sunday newspaper, the color comics and newsprint on your fingers.

Rhea and Rhoda Kunkel went flying on their rusted old bicycles, down the long hill toward the railroad yard, Whipple's Ice, the scrubby pastureland where dairy cows grazed. They'd stolen six dollars from their own grandmother who loved them. They were eleven years old, they were identical twins, they basked in their power.

Rhea and Rhoda Kunkel: it was always Rhea-and-Rhoda, never Rhoda-and-Rhea, I couldn't say why. You just wouldn't say the names that way. Not even the teachers at school would say them that way.

We went to see them in the funeral parlor where they were waked, we were made to. The twins in twin caskets, white, smooth, gleaming, perfect as plastic, with white satin lining puckered like the inside of a fancy candy box. And the waxy white lilies, and the smell of talcum powder and perfume. The room was crowded, there was only one way in and out.

Rhea and Rhoda were the same girl, they'd wanted it that way.

Only looking from one to the other could you see they were two.

The heat was gauzy, you had to push your way through like swimming. On their bicycles Rhea and Rhoda flew through it hardly noticing, from their grandmother's place on Main Street to the end of South Main where the paved road turned to gravel leaving town. That was the summer before seventh grade, when they died. Death was coming for them but they didn't know.

They thought the same thoughts sometimes at the same moment, had the same dream and went all day trying to remember it, bringing it back like something you'd be hauling out of the water on a tangled line. We watched them, we were jealous. None of us had a twin. Sometimes they were serious and sometimes, remembering, they shrieked and laughed like they were being killed. They stole things out of desks and lockers but if you caught them they'd hand them right back, it was like a game.

There were three floor fans in the funeral parlor that I could see, tall whirring fans with propellor blades turning fast to keep the warm air moving. Strange little gusts came from all directions making your eyes water. By this time Roger Whipple was arrested, taken into police custody. No one had hurt him. He would never stand trial, he was ruled mentally unfit, he would never be released from confinement.

He died there, in the state psychiatric hospital, years later, and was brought back home to be buried, the body of him I mean. His earthly remains.

Rhea and Rhoda Kunkel were buried in the same cemetery, the First Methodist. The cemetery is just a field behind the church.

In the caskets the dead girls did not look like anyone we knew really. They were placed on their backs with their eyes closed, and their mouths, the way you don't always in life when you're sleeping. Their faces were too small. Every eyelash showed, too perfect. Like angels everyone was saying and it was strange it was *so*. I stared and stared.

What had been done to them, the lower parts of them, didn't show in the caskets.

Roger Whipple worked for his father at Whipple's Ice. In the newspaper it stated he was nineteen, he'd gone to DeWitt Clinton until he was sixteen, my mother's friend Sadie taught there and remembered him from the special education class. A big slow sweet-faced boy with these big hands and feet, thighs like hams. A shy gentle boy with good manners and a hushed voice.

He wasn't simpleminded exactly, like the others in that class. He was watchful, he held back.

Roger Whipple in overalls squatting in the rear of his father's truck, one of his older brothers drove. There would come the sound of the truck in the driveway, the heavy block of ice smelling of cold, ice tongs over his shoulder. He was strong, round-shouldered like an older man. Never staggered or grunted. Never dropped anything. Pale washed-looking eyes lifting out of a big face, a soft mouth wanting to smile. We giggled and looked away. They said he'd never been the kind to hurt even an animal, all the Whipples swore.

Sucking ice, the cold goes straight into your jaws and deep into the bone.

People spoke of them as the Kunkel twins. Mostly nobody tried to tell them apart. Homely corkscrew-twisty girls you wouldn't know would turn up so quiet and solemn and almost beautiful, perfect little dolls' faces with the freckles powdered over, touches of rouge on the cheeks and mouths. I was tempted to whisper to them, kneeling by the coffins. Hey Rhea! Hey Rhoda! Wake *up!*

They had loud slip-sliding voices that were the same voice. They weren't shy. They were always first in line. One behind you and one in front of you and you'd better be wary of some trick. Flamey-orange hair and the bleached-out skin that goes with it, freckles like dirty raindrops splashed on their faces. Sharp green eyes they'd bug out until you begged them to stop.

Places meant to be serious, Rhea and Rhoda had a hard time sitting still. In church, in school, a sideways glance between them could do it. Jamming their knuckles into their mouths, choking back giggles. Sometimes laughing escaped through their fingers like steam hissing. Sometimes it came out like snorting and then none of us could hold back. The worst time was in assembly, the principal up there telling us that Miss Flagler had died, we would all miss her. Tears shining in the woman's eyes behind her goggle-glasses and one of the twins gave a breathless little snort, you could feel it like flames running down the whole row of girls, none of us could hold back.

Sometimes the word "tickle" was enough to get us going, just that word.

I never dreamt about Rhea and Rhoda so strange in their caskets sleeping out in the middle of a room where people could stare at them, shed tears and pray over them. I never dream about actual things, only things I don't know. Places I've never been, people I've never seen. Sometimes the person I am in the dream isn't me. Who it is, I don't know.

Rhea and Rhoda bounced up the drive behind Whipple's Ice. They were laughing like crazy and didn't mind the potholes jarring their teeth, or the clouds of dust. If they'd had the same dream the night before, the hot sunlight erased it entirely.

When death comes for you you sometimes know and sometimes don't.

Roger Whipple was by himself in the barn, working. Kids went down there to beg him for ice to suck or throw around or they'd tease him, not out of meanness but for something to do. It was slow, the days not changing in the summer, heat sometimes all night long. He was happy with children that age, he was that age himself in his head, sixth grade learning abilities as the newspaper stated though he could add and subtract quickly. Other kinds of arithmetic gave him trouble.

People were saying afterward he'd always been strange. Watchful like he was, those thick soft lips. The Whipples did wrong, to let him run loose.

They said he'd always been a good gentle boy, went to Sunday school and sat still there and never gave anybody any trouble. He collected Bible cards, he hid them away under his mattress for safekeeping. Mr. Whipple started in early, disciplining him the way you might discipline a big dog or a horse. Not letting the creature know he has any power to be himself exactly. Not giving him the opportunity to test his will.

Neighbors said the Whipples worked him like a horse in fact. The older brothers were the most merciless. And why they all wore coveralls, heavy denim and long legs on days so hot, nobody knew. The thermometer above the First Midland Bank read 98°F. on noon of that day, my mother said.

Nights afterward my mother would hug me before I went to bed. Pressing my face hard against her breasts and whispering things I didn't hear, like praying to Jesus to love and protect *her* little girl and keep *her* from harm but I didn't hear, I shut my eyes tight and endured it. Sometimes we prayed together, all of us or just my mother and me kneeling by my bed. Even then I knew she was a good mother, there was this girl she loved as her daughter that was me and loved more than that girl deserved. There was nothing I could do about it.

Mrs. Kunkel would laugh and roll her eyes over the twins. In that house they were "double trouble"—you'd hear it all the time like a joke on the radio that keeps coming back. I wonder did she pray with them too. I wonder would they let her.

In the long night you forget about the day, it's like the other side of the world. Then the sun is there, and the heat. You forget.

We were running through the field behind school, a place where people dumped things sometimes and there was a dead dog there, a collie with beautiful fur but his eyes were gone from the sockets and the maggots had got him where somebody tried to lift him with her foot and when Rhea and Rhoda saw they screamed a single scream and hid their eyes.

They did nice things—gave their friends candy bars, nail polish, some novelty key chains they'd taken from somewhere, movie stars' pictures framed in plastic. In the movies they'd share a box of popcorn not noticing where one or the other of them left off and a girl who wasn't any sister of theirs sat.

Once they made me strip off my clothes where we'd crawled under the Kunkel's veranda. This was a large hollowed-out space where the earth dropped away at one end, you could sit without bumping your head, it was cool and smelled of dirt and stone. Rhea said all of a sudden, Strip! and Rhoda said at once, Strip!—come on! So it happened. They wouldn't let me out unless I took off my clothes, my shirt and shorts, yes and my panties too. Come *on* they said whispering and giggling, they were blocking the way out so I had no choice. I was scared but I was laughing too. This is to show our power over you, they said. But they stripped too just like me.

You have power over others you don't realize until you test it.

Under the Kunkels' veranda we stared at each other but we didn't touch each other. My teeth chattered because what if somebody saw us ? Some boy, or Mrs. Kunkel herself? I was scared but I was happy too. Except for our faces, their face and mine, we could all be the same girl.

The Kunkel family lived in one side of a big old clapboard house by the river, you could hear the trucks rattling on the bridge, shifting their noisy gears on the hill. Mrs. Kunkel had eight children, Rhea and Rhoda were the youngest. Our mothers wondered why Mrs. Kunkel had let herself go—she had a moon-shaped pretty face but her hair was frizzed ratty, she must have weighed two hundred pounds, sweated and breathed so hard in the warm weather. They'd known her in school. Mr. Kunkel worked construction for the county. Summer evenings after work he'd be sitting on the veranda drinking beer, flicking cigarette butts out into the yard, you'd be fooled almost thinking they were fireflies. He went barechested in the heat, his upper body dark like stained wood. Flat little purplish nipples inside his chest hair the girls giggled to see. Mr. Kunkel teased us all, he'd mix Rhea and Rhoda up the way he'd mix the rest of us up like it was too much trouble to keep names straight.

Mr. Kunkel was in police custody, he didn't even come to the wake. Mrs. Kunkel was there in rolls of chin fat that glistened with sweat and tears, the makeup on her face was caked and discolored so you were embarrassed to look. It scared me, the way she grabbed me as soon as my parents and I came in. Hugging me against her big balloon breasts sobbing and all the strength went out of me, I couldn't push away.

The police had Mr. Kunkel, for his own good they said. He'd gone to the Whipples, though the murderer had been taken away, saying he would kill anybody he could get his hands on, the old man, the brothers. They were all responsible he said, his little girls were dead. Tear them apart with his bare hands he said but he had a tire iron.

Did it mean anything special, or was it just an accident, Rhea and Rhoda had taken six dollars from their grandmother an hour before? Because death was coming for them, it had to happen one way or another.

If you believe in God you believe that. And if you don't believe in God it's obvious.

Their grandmother lived upstairs over a shoe store downtown, an apartment looking out on Main Street. They'd bicycle down there for something to do and she'd give them grape juice or lemonade and try to keep them a while, a lonely old lady but she was nice, she was always nice to me, it was kind of nasty of Rhea and Rhoda to steal from her but they were like that. One was in the kitchen talking with her and without any plan or anything the other went to use the bathroom then slipped into her bedroom, got the money out of her purse like it was something she did every day of the week, that easy. On the stairs going down to the street Rhoda whispered to Rhea what did you *do?* knowing Rhea had done something she hadn't ought to have done but not knowing what it was or anyway how much money it was. They started in poking each other, trying to hold the giggles back until they were safe away.

On their bicycles they stood high on the pedals, coasting, going down the hill but not using their brakes. *What did you do! Oh what did you do!*

Rhea and Rhoda always said they could never be apart. If one didn't know exactly where the other was that one could die. Or the other could die. Or both.

Once they'd gotten some money from somewhere, they wouldn't say where, and paid for us all to go to the movies. And ice cream afterward too.

You could read the newspaper articles twice through and still not know what he did. Adults talked about it for a long time but not so we could hear. I thought probably he'd used an ice pick. Or maybe I heard somebody guess that who didn't know any more than me.

We liked it that Rhea and Rhoda had been killed, and all the stuff in the paper, and everybody talking about it, but we didn't like it that they were dead, we missed them.

Later, in the tenth grade, the Kaufmann twins moved into our school district. Doris and Diane. But it wasn't the same thing.

Roger Whipple said he didn't remember any of it. Whatever he did, he didn't remember. At first everybody thought he was lying then they had to accept it as true, or true in some way, doctors from the state hospital examined him. He said over and over he hadn't done anything and he didn't remember the twins there that afternoon but he couldn't explain why their bicycles were where they were at the foot of his stairway and he couldn't explain why he'd taken a bath in the middle of the day. The Whipples admitted that wasn't a practice of Roger's or of any of them, ever, a bath in the middle of the day.

Roger Whipple was a clean boy, though. His hands always scrubbed so you actually noticed, swinging the block of ice off the truck and, inside the kitchen, helping to set it in the ice box. They said he'd go crazy if he got bits of straw under his nails from the ice house or inside his clothes. He'd been taught to shave and he shaved every morning without fail, they said the sight of the beard growing in, the scratchy feel of it, seemed to scare him.

A few years later his sister Linda told us how Roger was built like a horse. She was our age, a lot younger than him, she made a gesture toward her crotch so we'd know what she meant. She'd happened to see him a few times she said, by accident.

There he was squatting in the dust laughing, his head lowered watching Rhea and Rhoda circle him on their bicycles. It was a rough game where the twins saw how close they could come to hitting him, brushing him with the bike fenders and he'd lunge out not seeming to notice if his fingers hit the spokes, it was all happening so fast you maybe wouldn't feel pain. Out back of the ice house where the yard blended in with the yard of the old railroad depot next door that wasn't used any more. It was burning hot in the sun, dust rose in clouds behind the girls. Pretty soon they got bored with the game though Roger Whipple even in his heavy overalls wanted to keep going. He was red-faced with all the excitement, he was a boy who loved to laugh and didn't have much chance. Rhea said she was thirsty, she wanted some ice, so Roger Whipple scrambled right up and went to get a big bag of ice cubes!—he hadn't any more sense than that.

They sucked on the ice cubes and fooled around with them. He was panting and lolling his tongue pretending to be a dog and Rhea and Rhoda cried, Here doggie! Here doggie-doggie! tossing ice cubes at Roger Whipple he tried to catch in his mouth. That went on for a while. In the end the twins just dumped the rest of the ice onto the dirt then Roger Whipple was saying he had some secret things that belonged to his brother Eamon he could show them. Hidden under his bed mattress, would they like to see what the things were?

He wasn't one who could tell Rhea from Rhoda or Rhoda from Rhea. There was a way some of us knew, the freckles on Rhea's face were a little darker than Rhoda's. Rhea's eyes were just a little darker than Rhoda's. But you'd have to see the two side by side with no clowning around to know.

Rhea said okay, she'd like to see the secret things. She let her bike fall where she was straddling it.

Roger Whipple said he could only take one of them upstairs to his room at a time, he didn't say why.

Okay said Rhea. Of the Kunkel twins Rhea always had to be first.

She'd been born first, she said. Weighed a pound or two more.

Roger Whipple's room was in a strange place—on the second floor of the Whipple house above an unheated storage space that had been added after the main part of the house was built. There was a way of getting to the room from the outside, up a flight of rickety wood stairs. That way Roger could get in and out of his room without going through the rest of the house. People said the Whipples had him live there like some animal, they didn't want him tramping through the house but they denied it. The room had an inside door too.

Roger Whipple weighed about one-hundred ninety pounds that day. In the hospital he swelled up like a balloon, people said, bloated from the drugs, his skin was soft and white as bread dough and his hair fell out. He was an old man when he died aged thirty-one.

Exactly why he died, the Whipples never knew. The hospital just told them his heart had stopped in his sleep.

Rhoda shaded her eyes watching her sister running up the stairs with Roger Whipple behind her and felt the first pinch of fear, that something was wrong, or was going to be wrong. She called after them in a whining voice that she wanted to come along too, she didn't want to wait down there all alone, but Rhea just called back to her to be quiet and wait her turn, so Rhoda waited, kicking at the ice cubes melting in the dirt, and after a while she got restless and shouted up to them—the door was shut, the shade on the window was drawn—saying she was going home, damn them she was sick of waiting she said and she was going home. But nobody came to the door or looked out the window, it was like the place was empty. Wasps had built one of those nests that look like mud in layers under the eaves and the only sound was wasps.

Rhoda bicycled toward the road so anybody who was watching would think she was going home, she was thinking she hated Rhea! hated her damn twin sister! wished she was dead and gone, God damn her! She was going home and the first thing she'd tell their mother was that Rhea had stolen six dollars from Grandma: she had it in her pocket right that moment.

The Whipple house was an old farmhouse they'd tried to modernize by putting on red asphalt siding meant to look like brick. Downstairs the rooms were big and drafty, upstairs they were small, some of them unfinished and with bare floorboards, like Roger Whipple's room which people would afterward say based on what the police said was like an animal's pen, nothing in it but a bed shoved into a corner and some furniture and boxes and things Mrs. Whipple stored there.

Of the Whipples—there were seven in the family still living at home—only Mrs. Whipple and her daughter Iris were home that afternoon. They said they hadn't heard a sound except for kids playing in the back, they swore it.

Rhoda was bent on going home and leaving Rhea behind but at the end of the driveway something made her turn her bicycle wheel back . . . so if you were watching you'd think she was just cruising around for something to do, a red-haired girl with whitish skin and freckles, skinny little body, pedaling fast, then slow, then coasting, then fast again, turning and dipping and criss-crossing her path, talking to herself as if she was angry. She hated Rhea! She was furious at Rhea! But feeling sort of scared too and sickish in the pit of her belly knowing that she and Rhea shouldn't be in two places, something might happen to one of them or to both. Some things you know.

So she pedaled back to the house. Laid her bike down in the dirt next to Rhea's. The bikes were old hand-me-downs, the kickstands were broken. But their daddy had put on new Goodyear tires for them at the start of the summer and he'd oiled them too.

You never would see just one of the twins' bicycles anywhere, you always saw both of them laid down on the ground and facing in the same direction with the pedals in about the same position.

Rhoda peered up at the second floor of the house, the shade drawn over the window, the door still closed. She called out Rhea? Hey Rhea? starting up the stairs making a lot of noise so they'd hear her, pulling on the railing as if to break it the way a boy would. Still she was scared. But making noise like that and feeling so disgusted and mad helped her get stronger, and there was Roger Whipple with the door open staring down at her flush-faced and sweaty as if he was scared too. He seemed to have forgotten her. He was wiping his hands on his overalls. He just stared, a lemony light coming up in his eyes.

Afterward he would say he didn't remember anything—didn't remember anything. Big as a grown man but round-shouldered so it was hard to judge how tall he was, or how old. His straw-colored hair falling in his eyes and his fingers twined together as if he was praying or trying with all his strength to keep his hands still. He didn't remember anything about the twins or anything in his room or in the ice house afterward but he cried a lot, he acted scared and guilty and sorry, they decided he shouldn't be put on trial, there was no point to it.

Mrs. Whipple kept to the house afterward, never went out not even to church or grocery shopping. She died of cancer just before Roger died, she'd loved him she said, she always said none of it had been his fault really, he wasn't the kind of boy even to hurt an animal, he'd loved kittens especially and was a good sweet obedient boy and religious too and whatever happened it must have been because those girls were teasing him, he'd had a lifetime of being teased and taunted by children, his heart broken by all the abuse, and something must have snapped that day, that was all.

The Whipples were the ones, though, who called the police. Mr. Whipple found the girls' bodies back in the ice house hidden under some straw and canvas.

He found them around nine that night, with a flashlight. He knew, he said. The way Roger was acting, and the fact the Kunkel girls were missing, word had gotten out. He knew but he didn't know what he knew or what he would find. Roger taking a bath like that in the middle of the day and washing his hair too and shaving for the second time and not answering when his mother spoke to him, just sitting there staring at the floor as if he was listening to something no one else could hear. He knew, Mr. Whipple said. The hardest minute of his life was in the ice house lifting that canvas to see what was under it.

He took it hard too, he never recovered. He hadn't any choice but to think what a lot of people thought—it had been his fault. He was an old-time Methodist, he took all that seriously, but none of it helped him. Believed Jesus Christ was his personal savior and He never stopped loving Roger or turned His face from him and if Roger did truly repent in his heart he would be saved and they would be reunited in Heaven, all the Whipples reunited. He believed, but none of it helped in his life.

The ice house is still there but boarded up and derelict, the Whipples' ice business ended long ago. Strangers live in the house and the yard is littered with rusting hulks of cars and pickup trucks. Some Whipples live scattered around the country but none in town. The old train depot is still there too.

After I'd been married some years I got involved with this man, I won't say his name, his name is not a name I say, but we would meet back there sometimes, back in that old lot that's all weeds and scrub trees. Wild as kids and on the edge of being drunk. I was crazy for this guy, I mean crazy like I could hardly think of anybody but him or anything but the two of us making love the way we did, with him deep inside me I wanted it never to stop just fuck and fuck and fuck I'd whisper to him and this went on for a long time, two or three years then ended the way these things do and looking back on it I'm not able to recognize that woman as if she was someone not even not-me but a crazy woman I would despise, making so much of such a thing, risking her marriage and her kids finding out and her life being ruined for such a thing, my God. The things people do.

It's like living out a story that has to go on its way.

Behind the ice house in his car I'd think of Rhea and Rhoda and what happened that day upstairs in Roger Whipple's room. And the funeral parlor with the twins like dolls laid out and their eyes like dolls' eyes too that shut when you tilt them back. One night when I wasn't asleep but wasn't awake either I saw my parents standing in the doorway of my bedroom watching me and I knew their thoughts, how they were thinking of Rhea and Rhoda and of me their daughter wondering how they could keep me from harm and there was no clear answer.

In his car in his arms I'd feel my mind drift. After we'd made love or at least after the first time. And I saw Rhoda Kunkel hesitating on the stairs a few steps down from Roger Whipple. I saw her white-faced and scared but deciding to keep going anyway, pushing by Roger Whipple to get inside the room, to find Rhea, she had to brush against him where he was standing as if he meant to block her but not having the nerve exactly to block her and he was smelling of his body and breathing hard but not in imitation of any dog now, not with his tongue flopping and lolling to make them laugh. Rhoda was asking where was Rhea?—she couldn't see well at first in the dark little cubbyhole of a room because the sunshine had been so bright outside.

Roger Whipple said Rhea had gone home. His voice sounded scratchy as if it hadn't been used in some time. She'd gone home he said and Rhoda said right away that Rhea wouldn't go home without her and Roger Whipple came toward her saying yes she did, yes she *did* as if he was getting angry she wouldn't believe him. Rhoda was calling, Rhea? Where are you? Stumbling against something on the floor tangled with the bedclothes.

Behind her was this big boy saying again and again yes she did, yes she *did,* his voice rising but it would never get loud enough so that anyone would hear and come save her.

I wasn't there, but some things you know.

ROBERT BOSWELL

The Darkness of Love

THE DARKNESS OF LOVE, IN WHOSE SWEATING MEMORY ALL ERROR
IS FORCED.

—Amiri Baraka

DAY 1

When Handle woke at ten in the morning, he got up and walked to the far window. Hung over, he half expected the sound of traffic or the fading drone of an airliner as he lifted the window. He had lived in the city for so long that even after two weeks in Tennessee, he found the quiet of the green countryside severe and foreign. Trees just appeared outside his window, new, each morning. He had come to escape the city, but his dreams returned him each night to New York, sometimes in a patrol car but most often on his feet, in an alley, running after a bone-skinny black boy who would suddenly turn, knife in his hand, and Handle would wake, startled that the boy's face was his, a younger face, but essentially his.

Handle dressed in the corduroy jeans he'd bought for the trip and pulled a blue T-shirt with white lettering over his head. His wife had given him the shirt, which read HANDLE WITH CARE. He walked back to look at the trees again. Wind through the leaves sounded like people speaking, and the sound of voices made him feel more at home. He closed the window quietly, as if the noise would disturb the trees, the grass, or his in-laws, who, he was sure, had been awake for hours.

As he turned from the window to his unmade bed, he pictured his wife stealing a few minutes' extra sleep, waiting for him to kiss her neck and shake her awake. The image of her brown body against the white sheets sparked a memory—a night before they were married. He had promised to meet her in the lobby of an auditorium and was running late. In the dim lights of the smoke-filled lobby, he'd had trouble finding her. Finally he spotted her across the room, leaning against the wall opposite him. That was the memory: Marilyn, tall, thin, dark against the white stucco wall, wearing a thick beige coat fringed with fur, staring into the crowd with an expression of anticipation and melancholy. At that moment, she looked as beautiful as anyone he'd ever seen. When she saw him crossing the lobby, she smiled and moved to meet him. But that whole evening, as Handle saw it, revolved around that one frozen image of his future wife leaning against a wall, looking sad, beautiful, eager.

Handle had spent the past two weeks with Marilyn's parents, trying to relax, with mixed results. He'd enjoyed the time but couldn't escape the nagging discontent that had driven him away from the city, his home, his wife. Louise, Marilyn's sister, had arrived from Los Angeles two days ago, giving him someone else to talk to. She'd just completed her second year of law school. Marilyn would finish her finals today, and by tomorrow she would be in Tennessee as well.

"You sleep later every day," his sister-in-law said, smiling at him as he walked down the stairs. Louise's eyes had always fascinated him, the same light brown as her skin but luminous.

He grinned at her. "I might have had a little too much to drink last night."

"That's safe to say." She waited for him to say something more, then moved her hands from her hips to her shoulders, crossing her arms. In one hand she held a book of Emily Dickinson. "You've missed breakfast, but if you talk really sweet, I *might* be persuaded to warm up the biscuits and make some gravy."

"Too early for me to think about food," Handle said, thinking how tired he was of milk gravy and flat biscuits. He thought he'd like a steak, a New York cut, but he smiled at his lovely sister-in-law. "Maybe later, Louise."

"Later will be too late." She laughed and walked out of the room. Handle watched the swish in her hips and knew he'd been away from his wife too long. But, then, the way Louise walked had always interested him. Her hips rolled like the shoulders of a swimmer.

He and Marilyn had been married six months when he'd first met Louise. The two sisters had walked in the front door of the apartment, each carrying suitcases and laughing. Louise's beauty had shocked him: her eyes, her walk, the trace of Tennessee in her voice that seemed to come and go as she wished. He thought of his wife again, her handsome face and long, angular body. He knew being away from her made Louise seem more appealing. Her presence always kept his interest in Louise in perspective.

He walked into the kitchen, took a bottle of orange juice from the refrigerator, and brought the bottle to his mouth. Orange juice and aspirin were key ingredients in his favorite hangover cure.

"Wayne Handle, we have glasses in this house, and I wish you'd use one."

Handle looked at his mother-in-law, standing with her hands on her hips just as Louise had stood earlier. That posture must run in the family, he thought. "Good morning, Annalee," he said and took another swig of orange juice. He noticed the flyswatter in her hand. "Kill anything yet?"

Her face lost its sternness. "I ought to kill you, drinking all night, telling foolish stories, sleeping the lifelong day away. What am I going to tell Marilyn when she gets here? That her husband's been acting like some teenage boy?" She giggled and the sound reminded Handle of his wife. "If you'd told that story about the alligator one more time, we'd have all shot you." She laughed out loud.

"They made me do it."

"Louise and Marvin are gluttons for punishment." Annalee laughed again and walked out the screen door into the sunlight. Another inherited trait, he thought: wandering off to end a conversation. He looked out the screen door just as Annalee brought her flyswatter down on the leg of her husband, who had been dozing in the porch swing. Marvin never lifted his head but raised his huge left arm and swatted Annalee on her behind. Who's the teenager? Handle wondered.

Before he'd met his in-laws, Handle had heard a story that had shaped his opinion of Annalee and Marvin. Their old dog, Hoot, had gone blind. Marvin speculated it stemmed from eating inky cap mushrooms, but Annalee insisted age had blinded the yellow dog. Too old to adjust, Hoot would become confused in the big yard, howling until someone came after him. He began shitting in the living room and lifting his leg on the furniture. Marvin couldn't bear the thought of putting Hoot to sleep. He'd found the dog as a pup, cradled in the boughs of the purple magnolia that marked the northeast corner of their property. Who put the dog there and why, they never discovered, but Marvin attached significance to finding a puppy in a tree. Annalee finally solved the problem. She made a trail with bacon grease from the front porch to the old barn where he liked to pee, to the thick grass near the purple magnolia where he liked to shit, and back to the porch. The old dog ran this circle the last two months of his life. When he finally died, Marvin insisted they bury him under the purple magnolia. Annalee dug the hole and buried the dog. The tree promptly died, leaving Marvin to speculate on the connectedness of all living things. Annalee argued that she may have severed the taproot while digging the grave, but Marvin ignored her.

Just as Handle turned away from the screen door, Marvin's thick voice boomed across the porch. "Handle, come quick. This woman's getting feisty. I need you to tell her that alligator story again." He paused as Annalee started laughing. "That ought to calm her down."

Handle yelled back through the screen. "I was on patrol, first year on the force . . ."

"Aggh." Annalee swatted Marvin one last time and ran into the yard with her hands over her ears. Handle's laughter hurt his head, and he decided to go to the bathroom to search for aspirin.

Four aspirin were left in the bottle. Cupping his hand under the running faucet, he swallowed all four. As he lifted his head from the sink, his face rose in the mirror on the medicine cabinet, a dun-brown face several shades drabber than when he'd left the city. His eyes appeared yellow. He cupped his hands again and slapped his face with cold water. Running his fingers through his hair, he parted it at just the spot where his teeth parted, in the middle. Twice during his stay, Annalee and Marvin had cut off arguments when they heard him approach. He realized they were acting especially cheerful for his benefit, going out of their way to make him feel comfortable, knowing he must be in some kind of trouble to have come to Tennessee alone. He wanted to give them something in return, the thing they needed—an explanation.

He wanted to tell them that his job had become too much, that the ugliness and violence of being a cop had become overwhelming. He believed that would be adequate. They could nod their heads knowingly or shake them sadly, then relax, even quarrel with him if they wanted. Better yet, if he could give them an incident—perhaps he'd killed a man in self-defense—they could forgive and console him. However, the incident he had to tell was neither violent nor vulgar, but he had been unable to deal with it and unable still to discuss it.

It had happened in a bar. Off duty, he'd waited for a friend who had tickets for the Mets. As he drank a beer and looked over the bar, he noticed a kid in the booth directly behind his barstool, a black kid, fairly young, whom he recognized as some kind of offender. He couldn't place the kid, but he'd seen the face connected with something serious. Across the booth from him, another boy, white and very young, squirmed in his seat. He could tell something was going on under the table, probably passing drugs.

Handle tried to watch them without being seen. He didn't know exactly what was happening or where he'd seen the black kid, but he had no doubt the kid was trouble. He could just tell. The bartender brought him another beer. As he looked up to pay for it, he noticed a mirror with a Budweiser ad and, in it, the kid, his lap, and a white hand groping his crotch. Even then, knowing they weren't dealing in anything but each other, Handle couldn't shake the feeling that the kid was no good.

His friend finally arrived, another cop, white, mumbling that there was enough time for another beer. "Turn around slow," Handle said. "The black kid in the booth, who is he?"

His friend looked, then turned back, shaking his head. "Don't know him, but he looks something like that Jenkins kid who was shot last week. You remember," he said, "that shit who stabbed women through the ribs as he raped them."

Handle became frightened, turning around so quickly that he knocked over his beer and startled the kid. The boy looked him straight in the face, and Handle could see he resembled the Jenkins boy some. He had the same high cheekbones, the same uplifted upper lip, the same empty stare, and he was black, most of all he was black.

Handle tried to ignore the incident, go on with his life, but he'd lost his edge, questioned too many decisions and motivations, discovering that he looked at black men a little harder than at whites. He knew the phrase for it: *he had an eye out for bad niggers.* Finally, he'd told Marilyn he needed to get away, even though she had two weeks of school left. She'd seen his uneasiness and seemed relieved that he could point to his job as the problem. Handle, however, couldn't tell her that he thought of himself as a racist.

He rinsed his face again with cold water and walked out of the bathroom. Across the hall, in the walk-in closet under the stairs, Louise tried to pull sheets from the top shelf. As she stretched for the sheets, her white muslin dress rose to her thighs, revealing her white underwear and the curves of her bottom. Handle thought of the summers she'd spent with them in New York. Once that first summer he had come home early, a little shaken from a scuffle with an afternoon drunk, and found her and Marilyn naked on the patio playing cards. "Expecting someone else?" he'd asked. Marilyn had been startled, but Louise laughed and reached behind her for her dress. Then she had been a year away from completing college. Now she was a year away from becoming a lawyer. Always something about her was unresolved.

Louise turned with the sheets in her hands and caught him staring. "You scoundrel," she said with a hint of accent. She threw the sheets at him. "You could have helped me out."

"It was more fun watching." He caught the sheets and threw them back. The top sheet inflated as it flew.

She laughed and stumbled as the sheets caught her full in the face. "Wayne Handle, you're the most worthless man I know."

He waited for her to pull the sheets from her face so he could see if that stern look was there, to see if that was an inherited trait as well as the habit of using his full name. But she lunged at him, pushing the sheets over his head, laughing as she knocked him off balance and they both fell to the hardwood floor.

He pulled the sheets off his head, looked at Louise sprawled face down at his feet, her dress up to her waist. Her body bounced with its own laughter. The throb of his headache quickened as he laughed. She sat up quickly and straightened her dress. "Worthless," she said, smiling. "Worthless."

A drizzle began in the afternoon and became a full-fledged rain before dark. At dusk, with stomachs full of mashed potatoes and mutton, the family sat in separate chairs on the porch and watched the rain fall. Handle thought the rain looked like pencil lines on cheap paper. For a moment he pictured himself in the first grade, his fat red pencil in his hand, copying the alphabet from the cards over the blackboard. He remembered Mrs. Hayes, his first-grade teacher, stalking the aisles with her ruler to swat anyone caught talking. Handle realized he was smiling. The image of that old woman, her white hair hovering around her black head like a cloud, seemed comical. But she had taught him how to read. In her class he had decided to become a teacher. He wondered when he'd lost track of that.

"There's nothing like rain, except maybe fire, that can hold a body for hours, just watching it," Marvin said. Marvin was so large that any chair he sat in was too small. Handle remembered his own father sitting in one of the first-grade desks, waiting to have a word with Mrs. Hayes, wanting to see if she could teach him to read the way she'd taught his son. The image of his father faded. Both Marvin and Annalee had taught in rural Tennessee schools. Handle had wanted to talk with them about teaching, but he'd never told anyone he'd wanted to be a teacher and couldn't bring himself to share his secret with them.

He looked back at the rain and picked up his bottle of beer. "The ocean," he said, feeling the cold bottle in his hands. "I could stare at the ocean all day." Handle pictured a wave coming toward him, looking like a cupped hand which would flatten just before reaching him.

"I've heard people say that," Marvin said.

"I can look at stars that way," Annalee said. "Nights without a moon."

Each of them turned to Louise, waiting for her to complete the circle of conversation. She said nothing, sitting with her legs tucked under her body, staring at the rain.

"Darling," Annalee said, looking at her daughter, "I've seen you staring at a man's bottom so long and hard I'd have sworn it was going to fall off."

Marvin smiled, Annalee and Handle laughed. Louise forced a smile, then let it fade. "Words," she said. "I can look at words on a page until they seem to glow." Handle could see the shine in her eyes.

"You always loved books," Marvin said. "I've never seen a child take to books so young."

Handle's eyes hadn't left Louise. Something about her sitting there, staring off into the darkening sky, her hair with drops of rain like jewels—he became afraid that he was falling in love, or that he had been in love since that first summer and had never admitted it, that he might scoop her up in his arms, here in front of her parents, and carry her to the room where he slept and make love with her. He tried to shrug off the feeling, staring out into the rain and reminding himself that Marilyn would be back by tomorrow night, and such thoughts would seem silly to him. But he couldn't resist looking back at her.

"Louise," Annalee said, rising from her chair, "you want to help with the dishes?"

Handle didn't want Louise to move. "I'll help you, Annalee," he said. As he stood, he heard Louise's voice, as if coming from a long distance, "Thank you."

Handle washed and Annalee dried. The window over the sink became covered with steam, and the sound of rain filled the room. Annalee hummed a tune Handle recognized but could not remember. He liked the feel of the hot water on his arms and hands, but Louise's eyes, her voice, hung in his mind.

"Will Marilyn need four years to get her degree?" Annalee ran a towel in circles over a dish.

"She could make it in three if her old classes transfer. Why?"

"Just wondering," she said and began humming again.

"What's that you're humming?"

She stopped, thought for a moment, then laughed. "Why, I don't know. I was just humming away, but as soon as you asked it left me. What did it sound like?"

Handle laughed. "Something like a cat in heat."

Annalee slapped his shoulder with the dish towel. "You shouldn't be mean to your mother-in-law. You don't talk that way to Marvin, and you're sure not mean to Louise."

Handle handed her another dish. He smiled but felt suddenly uneasy, wondering if his feelings toward Louise might be more obvious than he'd thought. He tried to discard the notion and concentrate on the dirty pot in his hands. They worked for a few moments to the sound of rain before Annalee started humming again.

She stopped abruptly. "Georgia on My Mind."

"Ray Charles," Handle said.

"Now that's out of the way, I'm going to ask you straight out, Wayne Handle."

Handle felt his stomach tense, afraid she might say something about Louise.

"Are you and my daughter going to have children?"

His stomach relaxed, but he didn't really know how to answer the question. "Marilyn's got to finish school."

Annalee stared at him for a second, then nodded. "School's a wonderful thing. Between Louise and Marilyn, I'm going to have the most educated daughters in Tennessee—if they were in Tennessee." She put the dish in the cupboard and took the pot from Handle. "The only thing I'd worry about is if Marilyn *did* get pregnant, Louise might run out and do the same, married or not." The screen door opened and Marvin walked through the kitchen to the living room, smiling at them as he passed. Annalee watched her husband, then turned back to the cupboard. "At least there'd be a few little ones around."

"While I'm in town tomorrow, I ought to buy you a puppy," Handle said. "Maybe two." He smiled at her, but she wasn't really amused. "Annalee, that's your dream, not ours."

She smiled weakly and patted his arm. "I know, sweetheart."

Handle put his arm around her in a half hug, but a new question formed for him: what was their dream? He finished the few remaining dishes, and Annalee shooed him out of the kitchen. The rain still fell steadily and Louise hadn't moved, feet tucked under her body, watching the darkness of evening fall with the rain. Talking with Annalee about his wife had diffused the charge that Louise carried. Handle took the chair next to her and looked off into the sky just as a flash of lightning painted a crooked path between dark clouds.

"Daddy's gone to bed," Louise said.

Handle nodded but looked past her to the rain. A thin stream of water dripping from the corner of the roof caught the light and looked like a long strand of twisting tinsel.

"We're all a little worried about you," Louise said.

Finally someone had just said it, Handle thought, but he didn't know what he could say in return. He might tell her that their worry showed in the kindness they extended him, but that sounded patronizing and avoided the question. Besides, he considered that the generosity of the family made it even more difficult to talk. When he'd first met Marvin and Annalee, he'd resented their marriage, believing it made Marilyn expect too much. Now, they'd been so careful to create an atmosphere of goodwill that to introduce his problems into the household seemed ugly and ungracious. Looking at Louise's patient face, he gave the most honest answer he could. "I don't think I can talk about it."

"Have you talked with Marilyn?"

"I wanted to." He folded his arms and looked back at the rain. "I thought once or twice this past week I might talk with Marvin or Annalee. I can't seem to do it."

"Is your marriage in trouble, Handle?"

He looked at her again, the soft curves of her cheek, the light brown of her eyes, then shook his head from side to side. "Sometimes I get this feeling. Riding in a patrol car with some white jackass, I get this queasy feeling, and I wonder who I'm trying to fool. I always convince myself it's better there's one cop who doesn't want to bust black heads, even when he has to. Now I believe that's just what they want me to think."

Louise still stared at him, waiting. He knew she wouldn't settle for an answer so general, but he couldn't tell her more. He stared back at her and found himself watching the minute changes in her face, how her eyebrows lifted and curved back to their normal shape as she moved from waiting for a response to a different attitude. Her eyes became slightly moist. Her lips moved almost imperceptibly as if mouthing a whisper. They sat quietly on the porch for several moments, just looking at one another while the rain fell.

"Oh, Handle," Louise said very softly. "What are you doing here without Marilyn?"

Handle felt something collapse inside him. He told her about the bar and the boy, the white groping hand, and that face, that blank brown face; he told her about the realization he'd come to about himself and how it had affected his work and his life. He spoke quickly, anxiously, watching her face, wondering what she would think of him. She listened patiently, but without giving away her thoughts. When Handle finished the story, he paused, but Louise said nothing and he didn't feel comfortable with the silence. "The department was all right. They know cops get crazy sometimes if they can't get away. And Marilyn understood or thought she did. She believed I needed to get away from dealing with rapists and pimps and junkies. I let her believe that. I didn't know how to tell her the truth."

"Why can't you tell her what you just told me?"

He tried to think of the real answer. Why had he been able to tell Louise what he couldn't tell his wife or her parents? What quality had he invested in her that he hadn't in the others? Perhaps it was just the moment, he thought. But looking at her again, he couldn't believe that was true. "I always wanted to be a teacher. Can you imagine that? I never told anyone. I wanted to teach kids to read."

Louise reached over and put her hand on his arm. "That first summer I met you, I don't know if you remember this, but Marilyn's friend was pregnant. She was your neighbor. I can't remember her name."

Handle nodded.

"When she miscarried, it was so awful. We thought she might die, the bleeding was so bad, and she was hysterical."

"I remember," Handle said.

"By the time you got home from work, she was hospitalized, but Marilyn and I were wrecks—we were scared. You were so good that night, Handle. You were so strong. I . . ." She stopped and stared at his face as if what she was about to say was written there. Then she closed her eyes. "You'll get over this," she said flatly.

Handle waited for her to open her eyes. He heard the screen door open, turned, and saw Annalee looking back at them. Only then did he realize Louise's hand was still on his arm.

"Still raining, I see," Annalee said in a voice barely above a whisper.

Handle nodded. The hand on his arm felt hot as an iron. Annalee walked by them to the porch swing. As she walked by, Louise lifted her hand and opened her eyes. The three of them sat without speaking for a long time. The rain fell and Annalee hummed another unrecognizable song.

Handle woke at two in the morning from another dream of the city, of running down an alley after a scared kid and realizing someone was running after him. The quietness of the country dark wakened him further. He pulled on his pants, then sat on the bed another moment, letting his eyes adjust to the dark and his ears to the quiet. He decided to have a beer, sit on the porch, and just listen to the still darkness.

The light from the refrigerator was so stark that the beer didn't look good to him. He took one anyway and started toward the porch. A light shone in the living room and he walked in to turn it off. In the corner of the room, under a lamp, Louise sat in a chair, reading a book. She was wrapped in a gray-blue comforter.

Handle stood in the doorway. "What are you reading?"

She didn't look up at first, finishing something, clearly aware of his presence before he spoke. "Emily Dickinson," she said, then reached out her hand for the beer.

Handle walked over and gave her the bottle, looking at the thin straps that held her white cotton nightshirt in place. "Why are you always reading that woman?"

"Because she wrote like I think, because she loved words for themselves."

Handle squatted to be at eye level with her and took back the beer. "You ought to read black writers," he said. "Richard Wright, Ellison, Baldwin."

"Those are all men. What makes you think I'm more black than I am woman?" She sat up straighter in the chair and turned the light toward the wall so she could see his face without the glare.

Handle looked into her eyes and started to smile, but he could see she was serious. "Because of your past. Because of your parents."

"One of my parents *is* a woman." She spoke without a trace of accent.

"But they're both black." He smiled, hoping the conversation would become less serious.

"Mostly," she said.

Handle lost his smile and moved closer to her. "What's got you talking this way?"

"We've got plenty of white in us, like it or not."

"All right, but who loves you? Who accepts you?"

"Women. The men, black men, white men, they want me, but they don't accept me. You'd be surprised how many men will make fools of themselves trying to get me to go out with them, sleep with them." She looked him in the eyes. "Even you, Handle. You're just like any other man. You look at me and picture me writhing under you, singing out your name."

Handle's first impulse was to deny it, but he stifled the urge, knowing she would just laugh. He felt curiously hurt yet moved, realizing he was seeing Louise clearly for the first time. He'd known her studious side and her playful side, but he'd never seen this part of her before, the part that tried to make the others converge into some meaningful whole.

Louise finally spoke again, looking away. "Besides, I've read all those men, and let me tell you they're more men than black."

Handle said nothing.

"And you, you're more man than you'll ever be black."

Handle straightened his back and furrowed his brow. "I'm a black man."

Louise giggled but stopped; her voice was without laughter. "You're a cop. They pay you to put niggers in jail."

He felt a heavy twist in his throat and an urge to slap her, but he held off. Her face still seemed hard, not phony sternness, but a real hard glare. "Where'd you get this anger, Louise? I've never seen it in you before."

"It's been here," she said, looking down at the book in her lap. "You think men have a corner on anger? All those angry black men you've read got you thinking a woman can't feel anger?"

"But whats made *you* angry?"

"Goddamn you, Handle. Don't you see what it is? You can be so damned stupid."

He waited for her to continue, not knowing what to say, recognizing in himself a familiar, uneasy feeling. An uncomfortable excitement began to build in his chest.

Louise stared down at her hands. "I want to sleep with my sister's husband," she whispered.

Handle put his hand on her cheek and turned her to face him.

"Christ, I hate this," she said. "I never wanted this to happen."

He moved his thumb across her cheek to catch a tear, then pulled her close. Her arms slowly moved around his body. He became aware suddenly of the quietness of the country. Both fear and desire filled him so that his chest shook to contain them. He clung to her and they sat in the dark for several minutes.

Louise lifted her head and kissed him lightly on the lips, and he found himself kissing her back. "If you weren't Marilyn's husband, I'd make love with you right here, right now. Or if I could just be sure."

Handle stared into her brown eyes and realized their luminous quality was a trace of green that floated in and out of the brown. He pressed his lips against hers and felt her tongue moving across his teeth. He pulled back and saw more tears running down her face.

"If I could be sure," Louise said. She shook her head from side to side. "Handle, I don't know whether I want you in spite of the fact you're Marilyn's husband or *because* you're her husband. If I could be sure, I don't think anything would matter." She put her hand behind his head and pulled him to her. They kissed, and she let her head fall against his chest.

The warmth of her face against his chest both saddened and excited him. He wondered if part of his desire was because she was Marilyn's sister. He didn't want to believe it was that ugly. They sat in the darkness for several minutes. Handle took a deep breath and held it, trying to calm himself. He didn't want to act without thinking, without trying to make sense of what he was feeling. It had been an emotional night, he told himself. Without his wife, he had turned to her sister. Tomorrow Marilyn would be back, and his feelings toward Louise would return to what they had been before.

He wanted to tell her this, tell her that what they were feeling was loneliness and a shared pain brought into focus by their friendship, that this and not love motivated them. Looking at her in his arms, he wavered, wondering what love was if not this. But he resolved to tell her that as much as they longed for each other, they shouldn't make love, that her sister would be here tomorrow and change what they believed they were feeling.

Before he could tell her, she lifted her head, brushed her lips across his cheek, stood slowly, and walked out of the room to her bed. Handle listened to her feet on the stairs and her bedroom door opening and closing. He waited a few moments, then walked into his room.

DAY 2

Handle slept late again. When he woke, he lay in bed listening. On the porch, Marvin sang to himself, a song Handle couldn't quite make out. He heard the noise of water running through the pipes and pictured Annalee washing the dishes after breakfast. He wondered about Louise. Was she still sleeping? Was she reading? He wondered if words sometimes appeared before her face, in bold print, independent even of paper.

He walked to the window and looked out at the trees, suddenly becoming aware of a memory he'd long forgotten. He believed it was his oldest memory, yet he visualized it clearly, as if it were happening. He stands on his mother's huge bed, his hands on the oak headboard, looking out the window, beyond the salt cedar's branches. A hen blown into the pond flaps its wings, claws the water, as thick misting rain shadows the yard and forms large clear drops on the boughs of the tree.

Handle wondered about the memory, its significance, because it seemed important, although he knew the event itself was unimportant. He couldn't even believe something of consequence about his life was tied up in the image. It was the clarity of the memory. He remembered it as if, for an instant, time had puddled and a moment passed before the flow resumed. He held on to the picture a few more seconds, then let it go.

He showered and dressed, paying special attention to his hair. He shaved and covered his neck with sweet-smelling aftershave lotion, unsure whether this care was for his wife whom he hadn't seen in two weeks or for her sister.

He loved his wife, but there had been times when he felt the need of another woman, when he found it inconceivable to think that he'd never make love to any woman but Marilyn. During such times women inevitably seemed available and desirable, but Handle had never had an affair. The conflict had nothing to do with his love for Marilyn. He needed the security of their marriage. But he also wanted to throw himself into relationships, to be consumed by the many and various women he desired. For years Louise had siphoned off those desires harmlessly. Their flirtatious friendship had stabilized his marriage.

Down the stairs, he heard Marvin still singing. "On the run all night, on the run all day . . ." Handle laughed.

Annalee's voice came through the open kitchen door. "Is that finally you, Handle?"

He stepped into the living room and looked into the corner where Louise sat with a book in her hands. "What is it today?" he asked softly.

She looked up at him solemnly, then smiled. "Gwendolyn Brooks, have you read her?"

He shook his head. "Never heard of her." Louise turned back to her book, and Handle tried for a moment to picture her as she had been last night, resting in his arms. Instead, he saw her once again on the porch with drops of water glistening in her hair. Their flirtatious friendship was over, he realized. The confessions of the past night had ended it. They would have to find a new way to deal with one another.

He walked out onto the porch. Clouds obscured much of the sky, but the sun still shone brightly. Perspiration formed along his forehead as soon as he stepped outside. Marvin stopped singing as Handle closed the screen door.

"Trains," Marvin said. His shirt had damp splotches at the armpits and the center of his chest.

"What about them?"

"My father could sit in the Chicago switching yard and watch trains come and go all night." Marvin smiled but his eyes were distant. "They meant something more to him than they ever did to me. I don't know exactly what. Freedom maybe. Adventure."

"Direction," Handle said, surprised at the sound of his voice. He pictured the tracks, the black ties and heavy rails. He liked the image, its solidity. And the train, he pictured the train moving down the tracks with its remarkable conviction. The image became so strong that he barely heard Marvin reply.

"Maybe. Direction's a hard thing to come by."

Handle intended to walk in the woods. The afternoon rains had kept him inside too much and the anticipation of Marilyn's arrival made him restless, so he decided to explore the woods before the sky darkened. A long field of new corn separated the woods from the house. The knee-high stalks had been recently thinned and weeded, hoed-out as Marvin called it, creating an appealing symmetry about the plants and rows.

Handle walked through the corn, inhaling the fragile odor of the green stalks and looking ahead at the woods. Perhaps the mud discouraged him, accumulating around the edges of his tennis shoes so that he had to stomp it off or lift his feet high and walk like a man in snowshoes. But the woods would be drier than the plowed rows and his shoes were already too muddy to wear into town to pick up Marilyn, so something else caused him to stop just before the perfect rows ended. He considered the question but couldn't say why.

He straddled a cornstalk, stared into the woods, and tried to think of the names of the trees. Maples he knew, the leaves like stars with winged pairs of seeds that pirouette to earth, but he didn't see any maples. The trees that marked the end of the field might have been sycamores or oaks, beeches or hickories. As long as he didn't know their names, they were just trees, blocking the sun and engendering darkness. Handle turned away from the woods.

As he began his walk back to the house, he spotted Louise leaning against the birdbath behind the barn. She waved as if washing a windowpane. The birdbath was the gray of concrete, the barn the gray of rotting lumber, but Louise's shirt was bloodred, conspicuous in the landscape, making her appear closer than she actually was. She straightened as he walked to her and put her hands in the pockets of her denim cutoffs.

"Why didn't you go in?" She twisted slightly from the waist as she spoke. The tail of her red shirt looped over her wrists.

Handle felt she'd read his thoughts. "Was it that obvious?"

"Marilyn and I used to play in the woods when we were kids." Her eyes left Handle for the woods. "If you go back far enough, there's a hollow. It was our secret place."

She smelled of cigarettes. On the ground next to the birdbath, white cigarette butts lay scattered like a mutilated alphabet. Handle realized he'd never seen her smoke in her parents' home, although she smoked often when she visited New York. The barn hid this spot from the house, and Handle realized that this too was a secret place for her. "I never had a secret place."

"All kids do," Louise said. "You've just forgotten."

A wasp flew by Handle's head. He followed its flight to the eave of the barn. "My father kept a pretty short leash." He looked back to Louise. She still stared out at the woods, and Handle suddenly became uneasy. Sweat gathered at his temples and the base of his jaw. The sheer greenness of the trees, the grass at his feet, became suffocating. Only the corn, the lone stalks separated by rich brown earth, soothed him. They had room to breathe.

Louise began giggling and turned toward Handle. She rested her hands against the birdbath and leaned against it again. "The day after Marilyn got caught in the barn with Bobby Dill—oh, they weren't doing anything. She was only in the eighth grade. But the day after, I took a boy out to our secret spot, the hollow. I couldn't let Marilyn get one up on me." She laughed. "Neither one of us knew what to do when we got there, so I acted mad and screamed terrible, mean things at him, hoping Marilyn or somebody would hear. But the hollow is too far out, no one could hear."

Louise laughed again and dipped her head. Handle laughed with her but still felt edgy. She shook her head. "I always had to outdo Marilyn. I thought I was over that."

Her head was still cast down, but Handle could see her face reflected in the rainwater in the birdbath, coppery and clear. Above them, wasps hummed at the openings of their finger-shaped nests. "When Marilyn gets here," he said, "I'm going to tell her . . ."

"I wouldn't." Louise looked up quickly from the bath.

"No, about my job, why I had to leave."

"I was afraid you meant . . ." She shook her head violently. "Last night on the porch, when you told me about that boy in the bar, I thought about the men I know, so sure of themselves they're blind or just the opposite, like puppies—I think of what I want in a man and I see it in you, but maybe that's not it. Maybe whatever I see in you I make myself want." She turned away from him, rested against the birdbath, and faced the dense trees. "What it really is—I see you and Marilyn happy and I want that. I guess I want to take it from her. It's awful, but it must be the truth."

Handle wanted to tell her she was being too hard on herself, but he didn't want to encourage her to believe she really loved him. At least he didn't think he wanted to. At the same time, he didn't want to believe her desire for him was just rivalry with her sister. In some dark corner of his heart, he wanted her to want *him*. But he also wanted it to be over. He said nothing. For several moments they stared at the fields. Above them, wasps fanned their mud nests, their whine as electric as the surge of blood.

Louise turned toward him, reached into the birdbath, and withdrew a penny. Waves rippled in circles from the point where her hand entered and left the water, and pennies sparkled beneath them like jewels. She placed one damp penny in his mouth, on his tongue, and put another in her mouth. Handle tasted the tart metal and watched Louise. He remembered the taste from childhood, and suddenly he remembered crawling on top of the bookcase in his parents' living room, pulling open the door to the linen closet that was above the clothes closet, and hoisting himself up. The closet was so high it was never used except by him, his secret place where, with the door just cracked open, he could watch the world from a safe distance. He remembered the narrow view afforded by the cracked door and the thrill of the jump down onto the couch. For a moment, he felt that thrill of the secret fall. He started to tell Louise but decided not to, even though she was the first person ever to find her way there. Instead, he tasted the penny and watched her watch him.

Louise finally took the penny from her mouth and dropped it back into the water. "Pennies," she said and smiled, then walked away from him, around the corner of the barn.

The temperature in Monroe, Tennessee, was close to ninety degrees. Handle sat on the bench outside the tiny bus depot. He had been unable to convince himself that the twenty-minute drive to the city would take only twenty minutes. In New York, he would have run into heavy traffic or an accident blocking the road and would have arrived just in time. But he wasn't in New York, so he sat on the bench to wait for the bus.

He looked up and down the city's main street. The air in Monroe didn't seem real to him. He was more comfortable with sky the color of primer paint. A weimaraner sniffed at his shoes, then walked a few yards away and shit on the concrete sidewalk. A man and a woman, holding hands, crossed the inter-section of Manhattan and Magnolia against the traffic light. The man had his shirt off. Tufts of black hair on his shoulders and back made Handle think of haircuts, of having clipped hair down the back of his shirt. The woman watched her feet as she walked, as if they began walking on their own and she just fol-lowed, curious and somehow saddened by the asphalt beneath them.

Ten minutes before the bus was due, an unshaven man wearing a check-ered coat a full size too large walked next to the bench where Handle sat. He held his arm stiffly behind his back, as if he was twisting his own arm to force himself to speak. He was talking to himself as he walked by Handle. "You never take into consideration the whole heart," he said as he passed the bench.

Handle thought of Amy Hansen, a past neighbor and former friend of Mar-ilyn's. He remembered Amy, pregnant and excited about becoming a mother, spending Saturdays with them while her husband worked driving a bus. Mari-lyn had wanted a child badly during that period. They discussed it almost every night. After the miscarriage, Amy lost her mind. She feared that one day her head would just fall off her shoulders. A redheaded woman with a beehive hairdo passed Handle's bench. She placed one spiked heel in the dog shit as she walked by. In a way Handle couldn't explain, the woman legitimized Amy's fear. Anything is possible, he thought.

The bus was on time. Marilyn stepped off looking softer and younger than he'd remembered. As he hugged her and kissed her, the constancy of his love for her returned instantly. Only after the feeling returned did he realize it had been gone at all. She was full of conversation about her final exams, her last-minute essay, her longing for him, but as they drove through the Tennessee countryside, Handle began thinking of the night before. He questioned whether he could talk with Marilyn but decided to try.

"I don't like being a cop," he said and looked at her. For an instant she had the same look he'd remembered in the lobby years ago: sad, eager, beautiful. "Most of all, I don't like thinking like a cop."

"I've never known you to think like anyone but Wayne Handle," she said.

"Well, Wayne Handle is a cop."

"So how do cops think?" She took hold of his arm with both hands.

"There are certain types we've got to keep on a short leash," Handle said.

"For instance?"

"For instance, blacks."

Marilyn nodded and looked off down the road. Her parents' farm became visible in the distance. "Sometimes you can feel things you don't really believe."

"But how do you tell?"

Handle watched as her gaze left the approaching farm and found him. He loved her gentle face, her unlined forehead and smooth cheeks, her dark and relentless eyes, the perfect ellipse of her mouth. "I love you, Wayne. Everything else I guess at." She laid her head against his shoulder as he guided the car off the main road toward the white farmhouse. He could see Marvin sitting on the porch, watching them approach.

"I thought for sure you'd be fat by now," Marvin said, stepping down the porch steps to greet his daughter. "But you get prettier every time I see you."

She had to jump to throw her arms around his neck. She laughed as she said, "Hi, Daddy." Handle could hear the drawl beginning to return with her first words.

Annalee came out of the screen door with Louise just behind her. "Oh, Marilyn, we were about to fall apart, waiting for you," her mother said, opening her arms.

Marilyn took a few quick steps to her mother and wrapped her arms around her. "Hi, Mama." Even as she hugged her mother, Handle could see his wife's eyes looking toward Louise. He watched as she burst into Louise's arms, saying, "Loosie, Loosie." Handle had forgotten how much taller Marilyn was, how Louise always looked childlike next to her.

The warmth cut loose in the yard was more than even the sky could bear, and large drops of rain began to fall. "Would you look at that," Marvin said. "These northern women always seem to bring the rain with them."

The rain continued through the afternoon and dinner. It was still raining when the table had been cleared, the dishes done, and Marilyn, Louise, Annalee, and Handle joined Marvin on the porch. Handle and Marilyn sat together, arms around each other.

"I can hardly believe we have the whole family together," Annalee said. "Of course, with daughters at either end of the country, I guess we shouldn't expect it too often, but it is nice we're all here."

"I had a dream about being here," Marilyn said. "I dreamed I was up in my room getting ready for bed. I was grown up, but the room was just like it was when I was little. The bed even had that frilly green bedspread Grandma made for me."

"I still have that bedspread," Annalee said.

"I heard a noise outside and I went to the window. All the stars were falling out of the sky into the yard. I ran down the stairs and out to the yard. When I got close, I could see that the stars were ceramic dolls with blue eyes and clothes of silver. They were beautiful."

Handle kissed Marilyn on the cheek.

"That's a lovely dream," Louise said.

Marvin and Annalee exchanged a long look. "Darling," Annalee began. "How well do you remember Grandmother Perkins?"

"I remember her more from pictures than anything else," Marilyn said.

"You were only four or five when she died. She was silly about you. I guess because you were the only grandchild she lived to see. Anyway, she was always making you things, like that bedspread."

"I never did like that thing," Marvin said.

"And giving you things, spoiling you every chance she got. One of the things she gave you was a doll, a white porcelain doll with blue eyes, and she may have been wearing silver clothes. I don't remember."

"I remember," Marvin said. "That doll had a frilly silver dress on."

"Daddy, I never knew you took an interest in dolls," Louise said.

"I remember because I broke the damn thing. It wasn't a doll made for children anyway, made to look at."

"She'd had it since she was a little girl," Annalee said. "But it had never been played with because her father hated the thing—it was so white and had blue eyes. She saved it for her kids, but Marvin was her only child, so she just hung on to it. I guess she knew she was dying and wanted you to have the doll even though you weren't old enough to take care of it."

"I wasn't old enough either. I dropped the damn thing and Mother was ready to take my head clean off." Marvin laughed. Annalee smiled and patted him on the shoulder. The sound of the rain returned as if it had been quiet while the story was being told.

"It's funny you'd remember that. You were so tiny," Annalee said.

"I didn't remember it," Marilyn said. "I dreamed it."

Marvin grunted. "I wonder why your mind stored that doll away all these years, just to bring it out now."

Handle looked out into the rain and thought of the recurring dreams he had of being chased down the streets of the city. He envied Marilyn for her dream. He thought of Marvin's grandfather telling his daughter to put the doll away. He respected the man for that gesture, however cruel it must have seemed to the little girl who would become Marvin's mother. He looked at his wife and wondered how many white dolls were locked within her, waiting to present themselves unexpectedly. He decided he didn't envy her the dream. It was, after all, just a beautiful nightmare.

The family talked and listened to the rain. They talked about Louise finishing school and Marilyn finally going back to school. They talked about the conversation of two nights ago, how they kept making Handle tell his alligator story over and over while Annalee complained. Marvin's thick voice shook the porch as he imitated Handle finishing the story. "There I was standing on a table in the corner of that rundown dive, with a damn alligator staring at me, looking hungry, and before my partner will call for help he wants to know if it's an alligator or a crocodile." Everybody laughed and drank wine or beer. "An alligator or a crocodile," Marvin repeated and laughed again. Handle wondered if they liked the story because the fool asking the question was white.

"Marvin Perkins, if I hear that story one more time, you'll be wondering whether what hit you was a pot or a pan," Annalee said. "Then you and Handle both'll be sleeping in the woods."

It was nearly eleven when the rain began to dissipate and the family moved inside and to bed.

Who can say why a man full of good food and just enough beer, tired from laughing with people he loves and making love with his wife, cannot sleep? And who can be sure that light is not sometimes detectable even through solid walls? At three in the morning, in the doorway of his in-laws' living room, Handle stared across into the far corner. Louise sat in the armchair, bare-shouldered, wrapped in the gray-blue comforter, hands in her lap with a book of poetry. The low reading lamp shone directly on the book, her brown hands, the folds in the comforter. "Louise," Handle said, his voice a hoarse whisper, almost inaudible. She didn't hear. In the indirect light, her face was like the reflection of a face in a dark window—rounded, softened by the night. Her eyes, cast down, gave her a sleepy look, but below their hoods they were lit like tiny candles.

She either hadn't seen him or chose to ignore him, waiting for him to step forward. He had been sure that Marilyn's arrival would stop his thoughts of Louise. When that didn't happen, he believed that after making love with his wife his desire for Louise would fade. But here he was, confident in his love for his wife, unable to sleep, thinking about her sister. He could still stop. He could walk back up the stairs, crawl across his sleeping wife, and return to the familiar, sleepless dark. Handle stepped backward, out of the room. He pivoted out of the doorway and leaned against the wall. His heart knocked around in his chest like a tennis shoe in a dryer. He closed his eyes, but the figure of her in the chair, wrapped in the comforter, took shape, as if imprinted on his retina.

Handle slid silently down the wall into a squat. Moonlight shone through the window onto the dining table, coating the polished mahogany with white light. On the floor, beyond the table, a half circle of light, scattered at the edges, approached him slowly. He pulled his feet back unconsciously, then he heard a page turn in the next room and dropped to his knees in the light. Crooking his head into the opening, he stared again at Louise, dark ovals shadowing the base of her neck, a black splinter separating her lips. He pulled back, settled flat on the floor, his back against the wall. Moonlight reached the middle of his thighs. He tried to sort out his thoughts, but they came too fast and he couldn't make sense of them. He felt suspended in mid jump, the instant before reaching one side or the other or beginning to fall.

Moonlight found his lap, lit half the doorway. The polished table glowed white, like the surface of a still lake. He tried to picture just such a lake to calm himself, but the pull of Louise in the next room permitted him no tranquility. He gripped the doorjamb backhanded to pull himself up, the throb of blood in his hand so strong he thought it might pulse red. He stood in the half-lit doorway, moonlight scattering at his feet.

Louise closed her book and looked up at him. His doubts fell away almost instantly, his thoughts slowed, and he became calm and sure. For a second, he thought of the conversation of the night before and wondered whether he came to her as a black man or just as a man. He couldn't answer the question or even consider it, not that the differences were indistinct, but they seemed unimportant. Something larger was present, something he'd hoped to contain in a secret place hopelessly small. This time he couldn't tell himself Marilyn's arrival would make it retreat. It wasn't the flickering of lust or the simple glow of desire that led him to her, but the total darkness of love.

He walked toward her but stopped before he reached her chair. She leaned forward when he stopped. "Does it surprise you I'm here?" she asked.

"No," Handle said. "It surprises me *I'm* here."

"This was always my favorite place to read, wrapped in a blanket after everyone had gone to sleep. It was always my part of the house." She ran her hand down the comforter, smoothing the wrinkles.

The room went silent. They stared at each other bravely. Louise lifted her hand to the reading lamp and turned out the light. Handle took another step forward, feeling a sudden urge to kneel before her. He squatted, at eye level with her, gripped the arm of the chair. Her hair smelled like cinnamon. A shuddering in his chest threatened to topple him. He went to one knee to balance himself.

"When Marilyn arrived," Louise said, "I knew immediately how I felt about her. And about you." She put her hand to his temple, the tips of her fingers resting there so lightly he couldn't be sure she touched him at all. He became afraid again, afraid she might reject him, afraid she might not. "I love my sister." Her fingers brushed across his cheek and jaw. "I would never do anything *just* to hurt her. When I realized that, I knew I loved you as well, Handle."

He took her hand from his face, cupped it in his hands as if it were a liquid he was about to drink.

"Mama and Daddy are old. They sleep like children," Louise said. "Marilyn was so tired. She won't wake." She opened the comforter and Handle looked at her body, the shapes and angles, the turns and shadows. He worried that Marilyn might wake and find him missing or that Marvin or Annalee might want a glass of milk or a breath of air and discover them. But the time for worry had passed and he was helpless to stop. "Just for tonight," Louise said, coming into his arms.

He kissed her lips, her breasts. He ran his mouth down her neck. As their bodies touched, the world stepped back and they entered a private realm. Handle spread the comforter on the floor and they lay together, holding each other, running their hands lightly over their bodies.

They made love slowly. And as they made love, Handle thought of the boy in the bar with another boy's white hand in his lap, he thought of Annalee and Marvin making love at just this pace, this slow pace. He thought of his wife, exhausted from the bus ride, wine, and lovemaking, sleeping in the dark quiet, and he thought of the dark itself, of his dark skin, of Louise's eyes with their flash of green, of rain falling straight to the earth, of pennies sparkling under rainwater, of Marvin as a little boy watching his father watch the trains in the Chicago switching yard, of a train charging ahead, full speed into the darkness, absolutely confident that the rails will take it home into the light, of Louise, here, with him, right now, making love with him, of this night, this instant.

They made love, and the evening seemed to condense into one moment. Handle held Louise close and kissed her lips, feeling as if the moment had a life of its own and that life beat within them both, independent of the dark world around them. And that, perhaps, was enough, he thought, an interval of clarity, one clear, resonant note that stops momentarily the daily march of events. He dressed slowly. He kissed Louise again and returned to sleep with his wife, confident he had witnessed the movement from now to then tremble, where love was as visible and tangible as the rain.

DAY 3

Although he'd lain awake much of the night, Handle woke feeling strong and refreshed, but when he looked at Marilyn dressing, a haze separated them. She caught him staring. "How did you sleep?" she asked.

He thought he should tell her fine, then thought that was silly, he should tell her the truth, that he'd been awake most of the night. But the real truth was that he'd made love with her sister. He felt awkward, so he shrugged his shoulders and rolled onto his side. His face burned with embarrassment.

"I slept like a child," Marilyn said. She sat on the edge of the bed and laid her hand on his back. "It's so peaceful here."

He didn't want to look at her, so he rooted his head into the pillow. Then he felt ridiculous, making the situation worse by acting guilty. He started to roll over to face her but decided that might be too bold, that if she got a good look at his face she would know. He worked his head into the pillow again, his eyes closed. "Uh-huh, peaceful," he said, but his voice didn't sound right to him.

Marilyn slapped him on the butt. "Wayne Handle, are you going back to sleep?"

What had come over him? He felt panicky with every question. He should turn to her, he thought. No, he should be still. He should be natural, as if nothing had happened. Handle tried to think of a natural thing to do. After a moment of deliberation, he scratched his jaw.

Marilyn resumed dressing. "You're going to sleep your life away."

He felt the slight tip of the bed for each leg as she pulled on her jeans. He heard her stand and zip her jeans, then she was back on the bed again, shifting her weight as she slipped on her socks and shoes. She seemed to be dressing very slowly.

"Should I save you any breakfast?"

He could feel her right above him, but he kept his eyes closed. "No," he said. Then she was breathing down his neck. Her lips pressed against his cheek, liquid and hot. He waited for the sound of the door opening and closing, then opened his eyes a crack to be sure she was gone.

Handle sat up in the bed. He had never been unfaithful to Marilyn and up to now hadn't thought of the past night in those terms. It had seemed different, separate from his life with Marilyn. He believed he'd tried to do what was right in order to be true to Louise, to himself, to love. He closed his eyes and thought of Louise. He remembered the softness of her cheek against his chest, the smell of her body, the rhythm of her breathing, the cinnamon smell of her hair. No, he thought, making love with Louise was as genuine as taking a breath.

When he opened his eyes, he saw Marilyn's negligee draped across the dresser and he lost his surety. He stood and walked to the window. The sky had cleared, and the unobscured sun shone so brightly that it seemed to be answering a question he could not formulate. The low limbs of the trees were calm, but wind whipped through the high branches.

Handle took a long shower and shaved slowly. He thought of Marilyn and their marriage. For an instant, he thought he should take her aside and suggest they have children, but he knew the idea grew out of fear and guilt. He wondered whether he was afraid of losing her or just afraid of her knowing he'd betrayed her. He had believed that his lovemaking with Louise had a certain purity, a clarity that transcended convention. But he knew he couldn't explain that to Marilyn and knew that although he'd been honest with himself and Louise, he'd betrayed Marilyn nonetheless. He cupped his hands under the faucet and took a drink. The swallow of water felt like a stone in his throat.

He dressed slowly, then sat on the bed trying to think. He heard steps on the stairs. Sure it was Marilyn, he jumped from the bed and walked to the door, hoping to be moving, to appear to have direction when he met her. He stepped into the hall with his head down. The figure near the top of the stairs froze. Louise held a book in one hand, the other clutched her skirt. She looked like a schoolgirl caught in the hall without a pass.

Handle looked past her. The stairs and room below were empty. She crossed her arms in front of her chest and smiled weakly. He wanted to grab her by the shoulders and shake her but knew immediately that was dishonest. He nodded at her and hurried down the stairs.

Handle sat in the porch swing with his head tilted back and his eyes closed. The sun on his face felt good and gave him an excuse to be still. For the whole of the morning he'd tried to control the gnawing at his stomach that made him feel like a criminal. Then, lying in the sun, pretending to relax, it occurred to him that he *was* a criminal. He thought of all the punks he'd arrested who had said it seemed right at the time.

"Handle."

He recognized Marvin's deep voice but didn't want to open his eyes. "Yes," he said.

"Taking the women shopping. Might have a couple of beers if you're interested."

"Think I'll stay here."

Marvin laughed. "I dreamed about alligators last night." He laughed again. "I was raising them like cows."

Handle offered a smile and opened his eyes, shading them from the sun with his hand. Marvin and Annalee stood just in front of him, their backs to the sun, two dark shapes connected like an amoeba in the last stages of splitting. Handle realized they were holding hands. They looked somehow comic and he laughed.

They smiled back at him, then turned and walked to their car. Handle watched them walk. The screen door opened and his wife stepped onto the porch. "You want some magazines or anything, Wayne?"

Handle looked at her for a long time before he answered by shaking his head. She smiled at him, then hurried to catch up with her parents. He watched her go, feeling she might be gone a long time. He closed his eyes and listened to the car as it drove away. He took a deep breath and tried to relax.

He decided not to think about Marilyn or Louise or anything. Wind pushed through the leaves and birds played out a tune he could almost imagine as a saxophone solo. He tried to picture himself as a teacher in a crowded class-room. But the screen door opened and the swing swayed with the weight of another. He kept his eyes closed.

Louise's voice came out of his darkness. "We should talk, Handle."

He nodded but kept his eyes closed. "I feel terrible."

"I know."

"Every time I see Marilyn, I think I'm going to cry," he said. It wasn't exactly true, but the truth was worse.

"Maybe you just need to cry."

Her voice sounded thick and low, then he heard vibration in her breathing and knew she'd begun to cry. Until his eyes became accustomed to the light, she was a blur of color. But her shape settled, and he saw her clearly: a woman, eyes red from crying, arms folded across her chest to stop herself from shaking. He saw her separate from his vision of her, as a person absolutely apart from him. A new part of her was naked, and Handle might have recognized the same in himself, but he was unable to resist touching her.

Louise shrugged his arms off her. "Someone could see," she said.

Handle looked out over the empty fields and still trees, then followed Louise inside. "It seemed right," he said when they reached the living room.

She turned and pressed her hands against his chest. They sat on the couch and held one another. Handle tried to make sense of what he felt. He closed his eyes and thought of his wife and how afraid he was of losing her. Already, he knew, he had created a distance between them. Then he thought of arriving with Marilyn at the farm, how she had burst into Louise's arms. He began to cry, knowing how much Louise had lost as well. He held her tighter, feeling closer to her than ever because of the loss they shared.

When they quit crying, Handle found he could not let her go. His arms felt solid, like cement. He knew he had to let go, but he couldn't move. His heart pounded so vigorously that he recognized it as a muscle working inside him. He kissed her. She began crying again but kissed him back. Every time he lifted a hand, it returned to her. He could pull back, but he could not pull away.

He followed Louise up the stairs to her room, where they made love again, without the clarity of emotion or the genuine belief in its honesty they'd had the night before but with the sincerest of necessity. While they made love, they listened for sounds of the car returning. They hurried, wondering how they had kept from worrying about being caught the night before. They dressed quickly afterward.

"We can never let this happen again," Louise said.

Handle had his hand on the door. "I know," he said.

They left the room separately without kissing or saying good-bye.

Handle could not stay in the house with Louise. He walked through the long, straight rows of corn quickly, directly to the woods and into the thick brush that bordered the fields. High weeds licked the insides of his legs. The woods were dense and quiet, the trees still. Sunlight through the trees speckled the ground with moving patterns, like an active disease magnified to become visible. He walked quickly, head down, leading with his arms like a swimmer, through the woods. Louise and Marilyn played here as children, he thought as he ducked under a low limb and pushed himself through a narrow space between two trees. He was flooded with smells, the sharp green smell of the trees with new leaves, the dusty odor of bark, the mildly bitter smell of certain weeds when they broke under his step. The boy in the bar, his blank brown face, flashed in his vision, as if the boy were behind a tree watching him. Handle ignored the image and kept walking. A fallen trunk blocked his way, lying at a diagonal between trees, its white guts open, soft and spongy from rain and decay. Handle carefully placed his foot in a white pocket and lifted himself over. He pushed on, breathing heavily, his heart thudding against his chest. He lifted a thin limb and stepped under it into a narrow path. Turning immediately, he followed the path, increasing his speed. The path widened and he began to run, hands flailing at limbs and leaves. It struck him how much this was like his dream, how the path seemed like an alley, but he didn't slow down to think. His heart labored again like a muscle. The splotches of sunlight became larger. Then the forest opened up. The trees fell away. He'd reached the hollow.

His lungs aching, the muscles in his legs twitching, Handle stood erect and looked over the hollow. Milkweed and morning glories rimmed the clearing, muddled with tall grass and jimsonweed. In the middle, about fifteen yards from him, a clump of cattails grew out of the high grass. Handle leaned against a tree to catch his breath. This had been their secret place, he thought. He tried to picture them as little girls in short ruffled dresses and corn rows. His mind wouldn't cooperate, giving instead himself as a little boy with his father, not in the country but in the city, a sidewalk. A policeman tells his father that colored men do not look directly at white women and that anyone his age shouldn't have to be told. His father's face, blank and brown, his head nodding, as he assures the policeman that he wasn't doing anything and he certainly won't do it again. Handle walked into the weeds and high grass to the center. Water sloshed against his shoes and he smelled the acrid, stagnant pool of shallow water at the heart of the hollow.

As he stood among the cattails, he heard his father's voice calling someone a coal black son of a bitch. The sound of his father's voice stopped Handle, fixed him among the cattails, stationary as a tree stump. Was it that simple? Handle felt he'd just remembered a secret, as pictures of his father flashed relentlessly in his mind—his father proud his skin was lighter than his brother-in-law's, his father nodding politely to the policeman, then cursing about some niggers making it hard on the rest. Handle grabbed a handful of cattails and broke off their heads. He dropped all but one, threw it, and watched it spin like a propeller. He closed his eyes and there in his personal darkness were Louise and Marilyn.

He walked back to the edge of the hollow, but he couldn't find the path.

He circled the clearing, but he'd become disoriented and had no idea which way to turn. He circled the hollow again in the opposite direction, but it did no good. Already, clouds thickened the sky. Finally, he just set out into the woods.

The randomness of the trees, the irregular angles of the branches, oppressed him. He hesitated under a thorn tree, wanting to make some kind of sense of his direction, wishing he could create a reasonable order. But the woods relinquished none of their confusion. Handle decided to simplify the world. He would think of Marilyn. He would concentrate solely on his wife and wander the woods with her image, casting out the others. He decided his love for her would prevail.

With this resolution, he began walking again. He pushed through the dense woods for over an hour before he found the trail, and with each step he pledged his love for Marilyn, Marilyn, Marilyn. By the time he emerged from the woods, he felt renewed, confident his love for his wife would defeat the darkness that threatened them.

Handle insisted that he and Marilyn prepare supper. Marvin had bought a country ham while he'd been in town. They began by slicing the ham into thick steaks. Then Marilyn tore off leaves of lettuce while Handle cut tomatoes into crescents. He found himself full of enthusiasm for the work and for his wife, kissing her on the cheek or the back of the neck after each detail of the meal was completed.

Marilyn had set out several potatoes. Handle rummaged through the silverware drawer for a potato peeler, then began peeling them, working very quickly.

Marilyn laughed. "Those were going to be baked potatoes."

Handle smiled and shrugged. "How about mashed potatoes?" She just laughed again, so he began peeling them once more. The peeling went quickly. He chopped them into smaller pieces to boil. Handle liked the appearance of the pieces of potatoes with cut edges and straight sides. He chopped them rapidly and tossed them into a pan, working with so much concentration and enthusiasm that Marilyn began to laugh. He smiled at her, then laughed himself, pressing the pan of chopped potatoes into his side. That they were together, doing something and laughing over it, delighted him and he laughed harder. He laughed until he had tears in his eyes and still laughed. He dropped the pan of potatoes and doubled over laughing. He sank to the floor and sat flat, back against a cupboard, legs straight out in front of him, and laughed. He laughed until Marilyn began to cry. He could see she was crying, but he couldn't stop laughing until she held him so tightly against her chest that she suffocated the laughter.

"You're scaring me, Wayne," she whispered. They helped each other up the stairs to bed, where they lay holding one another until Handle fell asleep.

By suppertime, rain fell like strands of hair perfectly combed. Annalee and Louise finished preparing the meal Handle and Marilyn had abandoned. They set the table, then Annalee took the dishes away and set the table again with her best china, a blue willow design passed down to her from Marvin's mother. Since Handle and Marilyn still had not come down to eat, Annalee decided to bathe and change clothes. She chose a yellow summer dress with a large ruffled collar. The dress was a gift from Marvin. She'd worn it only once, the day he'd given it to her, more than a year ago. Designed for a younger woman, the dress made Annalee look old and lean. Marvin always bought her clothes meant for younger women, due not so much to his incomprehension of fashion, although he knew nothing about it, but to his blindness to his wife's aging. Annalee knew the dress was unattractive on her and incongruent with the rainy weather, but she wanted to wear something cheerful.

Marvin sat at the head of the table. Annalee and Louise sat to his right, Handle and Marilyn to his left. He lay ham steaks on each of the plates passed to him, smelling each one and licking his lips. He still wore the overalls and work shirt he'd worn into town. Having carefully cultivated the image of a country farmer, Marvin always wore overalls when he went into town. Everyone knew he leased out his farmland, and his spotless, pressed overalls would fool no one who didn't know, but he enjoyed the masquerade and his friends played along willingly.

Louise hadn't bathed or changed clothes. The heat of the kitchen combined with the general humidity caused her white blouse to stick and wrinkle against her skin. A gravy stain ran from her first button across her heart and disappeared under her arm. Her hair, greasy with sweat, formed wet arrows across her forehead. It matted flat on one side of her head and puffed out on the other, giving her head a lopsidedness associated with anger, with defiant carelessness. Her face had the flat, dissatisfied look of a child being punished.

As Marvin passed out the ham steaks, he told Handle about his dream of raising alligators. "Milking them was the worst," he said. "They're set so close to the ground."

Afraid to laugh after his laughing fit, Handle smiled and nodded. He kept his eyes on Marvin serving the ham or on Annalee, garish as a sunflower in her yellow dress. He didn't want to see Louise or Marilyn. Sitting at the table with both of them overtaxed his circuits. But as he accepted his plate from Marvin, he couldn't help looking at Louise. She appeared haggard and angry. Marvin still looked at him, and Handle felt obligated to say something. He didn't want the supper to be one of those long, silent meals where people eat slowly and chew quietly. He had hoped they would talk around him. Now he had to offer something. His collar felt tight around his throat, although his shirt was unbuttoned almost halfway down his chest. "I was thinking about Amy Hansen," he offered, unsure where the words had come from.

Marilyn placed her hand over his and gently squeezed. She smiled at him. Her hand was unusually warm.

"She was your neighbor, wasn't she?" Annalee asked, a question she and everyone at the table knew the answer to.

Handle didn't know what to say. Words were too treacherous. He shook his head. "What ever happened to her?" he said faintly. It was understood that the question was not to be answered.

He suddenly remembered a little boy who'd killed his brother during an argument. He remembered the boy sitting in the back of the patrol car while they waited for the juvenile officers. The boy kept asking about his brother, "What's going to happen to him now?" Handle shook his head as if to shake the memory out. As quickly as it left, his father entered, on the sidewalk, hearing the white cop tell him colored men did not look directly at white women. Self-hatred washed over him for a moment, a sensation he recognized but had never before named, a legacy from his father.

Annalee had begun telling a story about a student she'd had the last year she taught, a little boy, half the size of his classmates, who gave her a poem the last day of classes. She had committed the poem to memory:

> Boys have bubbles when they talk too fast
> Girls scrape their knees worse for dresses
> Dogs eat shoes in the closet
> Teachers give everything names.

Handle filled with sadness. It became obvious to him that his life had taken a wrong turn, that he should have been a teacher. It struck him that Louise looked like a troubled child. Then he realized why she looked so bad. She'd made herself unattractive so he would have less trouble ignoring her. The realization came so suddenly he gasped for air and stared at her, knowing her matted hair and dirty shirt were emblems of love. She looked back at him and he could believe the space between them was illuminated by a field of intense yellow light. By the time she looked down, Handle felt panicky, sure they'd given themselves away. But Marilyn ate undisturbed and Marvin drank milk. Annalee's face, however, was vacant with fear and recognition.

"The rain seems so odd to me," Marilyn said, looking up from her plate. "I guess because it had been so clear in New York." She picked up her napkin and wiped the sweat from Handle's forehead. "It's so humid," she said.

No one picked up the conversation. Annalee just stared straight ahead. Handle could no longer look at her. He couldn't look at Louise, her love for him disfiguring her. He couldn't look at his wife, caring for him while she sat directly across from his lover, her sister. He looked at Marvin but had to turn away from him, so oblivious to the destruction going on around him. He looked down at his plate and realized he hadn't eaten a bite.

"I was just thinking about old Hoot," Marvin said. "Blind as a stump from eating those inky cap mushrooms. Used to chew a whole mouthful up at once." He looked at Annalee. She wasn't listening. "Annalee still claims he was just too old to see, but I know better."

"Remember when he sniffed Reverend Lee's leg, then peed on him right in the living room?" Marilyn laughed as she spoke.

Handle knew how this story was told. Annalee was ignoring her parts.

"He shit in my bed," Louise said flatly, without looking up.

Annalee turned and stared at Louise as if she'd spoken in a foreign language.

"Would have died as a pup but I ran out in the freezing cold after he'd been attacked by whatever bird it was had hatched him in the first place," Marvin chewed ham as he spoke.

Annalee was supposed to say there wasn't any such bird, so Marilyn could talk about the perfect white ground and the little dog, head up in the snow, steam rising from his exposed intestines, the snow next to him soiled by blood and shit. But Annalee wasn't speaking. She stared at Louise and Louise stared back now. Finally Louise spoke, still looking at her mother. "Mama saved the dog. She took him to the vet."

"You women always stick together," Marvin looked at Handle. "We never get credit for a thing in this household. Fact is, I practically gave the dog mouth to mouth."

"But Mama got his sight back," Marilyn said.

They looked at Annalee again. She finally turned away from Louise and back to her plate. "The dog's been dead for years," she said.

Handle wanted her to finish the story. She was supposed to tell about the bacon grease, making the path for the dog, so Marilyn could say "to the old barn where he liked to pee," and Louise could say "to the purple magnolia where the grass was thick and soft where he liked to shit," then Marvin would jump in saying how he'd found the dog in the branches, *in the branches,* and Annalee would say that was no reason to bury him there and kill the tree. Handle could hear it all in his mind, the way it was supposed to go. "Just goes to show," Marvin would say, "that all living things are joined one way or another, everything touches everything else." Annalee would scoff, say she'd probably cut the taproot while digging the grave. But the story had been killed and hovered over them.

Louise had begun to cry silently, catching the tears with her fingers before they even left her eyes. Handle could not bear to be at the table any longer. "Excuse me," he said, but he wasn't sure he said it loud enough for anyone to hear.

He stepped into the hall, thinking he would wash his face in the bathroom sink and compose himself. He opened the door and stepped into the room quickly, closing the door behind him. The room was pitch dark. He felt for the wall switch but couldn't find it. He slapped the wall high and low, but the light switch was gone. He felt the other side. The wall was gone, the room had changed. He stepped forward. Something landed on his face. He ducked, swatted at it, but when he stood again it was back on his face. He grabbed it, a string. Pulling it, the room lit—the walk-in closet. He had turned the wrong way. He pulled the light cord again, stepped out of the closet, and crossed the hall into the bathroom.

Handle and Marilyn went to bed shortly after supper, but Handle couldn't sleep. He lay next to his wife in the dark and began to shiver as if with a fever. He sat up in bed with his back to his wife.

"Wayne."

He looked over his shoulder at her.

"Talk with me, Wayne." She switched on the light next to the bed.

"I love you," Handle said, still with his back to her. "You've got to believe that."

She placed her hand on his back. "You're just confused."

He could only stare at her.

"When we get back to New York, if you can't go back to work, then we'll find something else. Sometimes people get trapped into doing things they don't believe, and they don't even realize they're trapped. You realize it, Wayne, that's why it's so hard for you." She put an arm around him and pressed her face against his back. "Now that you've realized what's happened, it may be easier to deal with."

Handle lay back beside her in the bed. He needed to be in their bedroom. This room was too clean, too large. He needed the dark wood dresser they'd found together and began refinishing and never finished, the closet so stuffed with clothes the door was always open. He needed the clutter of married life to remind him who he was.

"It's just the police," Marilyn said. "You meet so many desperate people." She took his chin, turned him to face her. "You're not racist, Wayne. You know you love me. How could you love me if you were racist? How could you love yourself?" She kissed his forehead. "You love me, you just told me so. And you love Mama and Daddy. You love . . ."

Handle cupped his palm over her mouth to stop her. He pulled her close and kissed her. She turned out the light and they kissed once more.

It was still dark. Handle had slept twice during the night, once for almost an hour. He let his eyes adjust to the darkness and looked at the shape his wife made in the bed as he slipped on his pants.

He walked down the stairs quietly, carefully, and stepped into the living room. Louise was in the corner. She had no book. There was no light. The comforter was wrapped tightly around her. When she saw him, she began shaking her head. She covered her face with her hands.

"I've been here all night," she whispered. "I was hoping you wouldn't come."

She stood. They held each other, afraid to talk. She led him out of the living room into the hall. She opened the door to the walk-in closet and spread the comforter. With the door closed, the closet was absolutely dark. They positioned themselves carefully away from the walls, which might creak if pressed against. They made love, controlling their breathing as much as they could, pausing if they heard a noise. When they finished, they kissed once, but neither could say that what they'd done was right or that it was over or that there was any escape.

ANDRE DUBUS

A Father's Story

My name is Luke Ripley, and here is what I call my life: I own a stable of thirty horses, and I have young people who teach riding, and we board some horses too. This is in northeastern Massachusetts. I have a barn with an indoor ring, and outside I've got two fenced-in rings and a pasture that ends at a woods with trails. I call it my life because it looks like it is, and people I know call it that, but it's a life I can get away from when I hunt and fish, and some nights after dinner when I sit in the dark in the front room and listen to opera. The room faces the lawn and the road, a two-lane country road. When cars come around the curve northwest of the house, they light up the lawn for an instant, the leaves of the maple out by the road and the hemlock closer to the window. Then I'm alone again, or I'd appear to be if someone crept up to the house and looked through a window: a big-gutted grey-haired guy, drinking tea and smoking cigarettes, staring out at the dark woods across the road, listening to a grieving soprano.

My real life is the one nobody talks about anymore, except Father Paul LeBoeuf, another old buck. He has a decade on me: he's sixty-four, a big man, bald on top with grey at the sides; when he had hair, it was black. His face is ruddy, and he jokes about being a whiskey priest, though he's not. He gets outdoors as much as he can, goes for a long walk every morning, and hunts and fishes with me. But I can't get him on a horse anymore. Ten years ago I could badger him into a trail ride; I had to give him a western saddle, and he'd hold the pommel and bounce through the woods with me, and be sore for days. He's looking at seventy with eyes that are younger than many I've seen in people in their twenties. I do not remember ever feeling the way they seem to; but I was lucky, because even as a child I knew that life would try me, and I must be strong to endure, though in those early days I expected to be tortured and killed for my faith, like the saints I learned about in school.

Father Paul's family came down from Canada, and he grew up speaking more French than English, so he is different from the Irish priests who abound up here. I do not like to make general statements, or even to hold general beliefs, about people's blood, but the Irish do seem happiest when they're dealing with misfortune or guilt, either their own or somebody else's, and if you think you're not a victim of either one, you can count on certain Irish priests to

288

try to change your mind. On Wednesday nights Father Paul comes to dinner. Often he comes on other nights too, and once, in the old days when we couldn't eat meat on Fridays, we bagged our first ducks of the season on a Friday, and as we drove home from the marsh, he said: For the purposes of Holy Mother Church, I believe a duck is more a creature of water than land, and is not rightly meat. Sometimes he teases me about never putting anything in his Sunday collection, which he would not know about if I hadn't told him years ago. I would like to believe I told him so we could have philosophical talk at dinner, but probably the truth is I suspected he knew, and I did not want him to think I so loved money that I would not even give his church a coin on Sunday. Certainly the ushers who pass the baskets know me as a miser.

I don't feel right about giving money for buildings, places. This starts with the Pope, and I cannot respect one of them till he sells his house and everything in it, and that church too, and uses the money to feed the poor. I have rarely, and maybe never, come across saintliness, but I feel certain it cannot exist in such a place. But I admit, also, that I know very little, and maybe the popes live on a different plane and are tried in ways I don't know about. Father Paul says his own church, St. John's, is hardly the Vatican. I like his church: it is made of wood, and has a simple altar and crucifix, and no padding on the kneelers. He does not have to lock its doors at night. Still it is a place. He could say Mass in my barn. I know this is stubborn, but I can find no mention by Christ of maintaining buildings, much less erecting them of stone or brick, and decorating them with pieces of metal and mineral and elements that people still fight over like barbarians. We had a Maltese woman taking riding lessons, she came over on the boat when she was ten, and once she told me how the nuns in Malta used to tell the little girls that if they wore jewelry, rings and bracelets and necklaces, in purgatory snakes would coil around their fingers and wrists and throats. I do not believe in frightening children or telling them lies, but if those nuns saved a few girls from devotion to things, maybe they were right. That Maltese woman laughed about it, but I noticed she wore only a watch, and that with a leather strap.

The money I give to the church goes in people's stomachs, and on their backs, down in New York City. I have no delusions about the worth of what I do, but I feel it's better to feed somebody than not. There's a priest in Times Square giving shelter to runaway kids, and some Franciscans who run a bread line; actually it's a morning line for coffee and a roll, and Father Paul calls it the continental breakfast for winos and bag ladies. He is curious about how much I am sending, and I know why: he guesses I send a lot, he has said probably more than tithing, and he is right; he wants to know how much because he believes I'm generous and good, and he is wrong about that; he has never had much money and does not know how easy it is to write a check when you have every thing you will ever need, and the figures are mere numbers, and represent no sacrifice at all. Being a real Catholic is too hard; if I were one, I would do with my house and barn what I want the Pope to do with his. So I do not want to impress Father Paul, and when he asks me how much, I say I can't let my left hand know what my right is doing.

He came on Wednesday nights when Gloria and I were married, and the kids were young; Gloria was a very good cook (I assume she still is, but it is difficult to think of her in the present), and I liked sitting at the table with a friend who was also a priest. I was proud of my handsome and healthy children. This was long ago, and they were all very young and cheerful and often funny, and the three boys took care of their baby sister, and did not bully or tease her. Of course they did sometimes, with that excited cruelty children are prone to, but not enough so that it was part of her days. On the Wednesday after Gloria left with the kids and a U-Haul trailer, I was sitting on the front steps, it was summer, and I was watching cars go by on the road, when Father Paul drove around the curve and into the driveway. I was ashamed to see him because he is a priest and my family was gone, but I was relieved too. I went to the car to greet him. He got out smiling, with a bottle of wine, and shook my hand, then pulled me to him, gave me a quick hug, and said: 'It's Wednesday, isn't it? Let's open some cans.'

With arms about each other we walked to the house, and it was good to know he was doing his work but coming as a friend too, and I thought what good work he had. I have no calling. It is for me to keep horses.

In that other life, anyway. In my real one I go to bed early and sleep well and wake at four forty-five, for an hour of silence. I never want to get out of bed then, and every morning I know I can sleep for another four hours, and still not fail at any of my duties. But I get up, so have come to believe my life can be seen in miniature in that struggle in the dark of morning. While making the bed and boiling water for coffee, I talk to God: I offer Him my day, every act of my body and spirit, my thoughts and moods, as a prayer of thanksgiving, and for Gloria and my children and my friends and two women I made love with after Gloria left. This morning offertory is a habit from my boyhood in a Catholic school; or then it was a habit, but as I kept it and grew older it became a ritual. Then I say the Lord's Prayer, trying not to recite it, and one morning it occurred to me that a prayer, whether recited or said with concentration, is always an act of faith.

I sit in the kitchen at the rear of the house and drink coffee and smoke and watch the sky growing light before sunrise, the trees of the woods near the barn taking shape, becoming single pines and elms and oaks and maples. Sometimes a rabbit comes out of the treeline, or is already sitting there, invisible till the light finds him. The birds are awake in the trees and feeding on the ground, and the little ones, the purple finches and titmice and chickadees, are at the feeder I rigged outside the kitchen window; it is too small for pigeons to get a purchase. I sit and give myself to coffee and tobacco, that get me brisk again, and I watch and listen. In the first year or so after I lost my family, I played the radio in the mornings. But I overcame that, and now I rarely play it at all. Once in the mail I received a questionnaire asking me to write down everything I watched on television during the week they had chosen. At the end of those seven days I wrote in *The Wizard of Oz* and returned it. That was in winter and was actually a busy week for my television, which normally sits out the cold months without once warming up. Had they sent the questionnaire during baseball season, they would have found me at my set. People at the stables talk about shows and performers I have never heard of, but I cannot get interested; when I am in the mood to watch television, I go to a movie or read a detective novel. There are always good detective novels to be found, and I like remembering them next morning with my coffee.

I also think of baseball and hunting and fishing, and of my children. It is not painful to think about them anymore, because even if we had lived together, they would be gone now, grown into their own lives, except Jennifer. I think of death too, not sadly, or with fear, though something like excitement does run through me, something more quickening than the coffee and tobacco. I suppose it is an intense interest, and an outright distrust: I never feel certain that I'll be here watching birds eating at tomorrow's daylight. Sometimes I try to think of other things, like the rabbit that is warm and breathing but not there till twilight. I feel on the brink of something about the life of the senses, but either am not equipped to go further or am not interested enough to concentrate. I have called all of this thinking, but it is not, because it is unintentional; what I'm really doing is feeling the day, in silence, and that is what Father Paul is doing too on his five-to-ten-mile walks.

When the hour ends I take an apple or carrot and I go to the stable and tack up a horse. We take good care of these horses, and no one rides them but students, instructors, and me, and nobody rides the horses we board unless an owner asks me to. The barn is dark and I turn on lights and take some deep breaths, smelling the hay and horses and their manure, both fresh and dried, a combined odor that you either like or you don't. I walk down the wide space of dirt between stalls, greeting the horses, joking with them about their quirks, and choose one for no reason at all other than the way it looks at me that morning. I get my old English saddle that has smoothed and darkened through the years, and go into the stall, talking to this beautiful creature who'll swerve out of a canter if a piece of paper blows in front of him, and if the barn catches fire and you manage to get him out he will, if he can get away from you, run back into the fire, to his stall. Like the smells that surround them, you either like them or you don't. I love them, so am spared having to try to explain why. I feed one the carrot or apple and tack up and lead him outside, where I mount, and we go down the driveway to the road and cross it and turn northwest and walk then trot then canter to St. John's.

A few cars are on the road, their drivers looking serious about going to work. It is always strange for me to see a woman dressed for work so early in the morning. You know how long it takes them, with the makeup and hair and clothes, and I think of them waking in the dark of winter or early light of other seasons, and dressing as they might for an evening's entertainment. Probably this strikes me because I grew up seeing my father put on those suits he never wore on weekends or his two weeks off, and so am accustomed to the men, but when I see these women I think something went wrong, to send all those dressed-up people out on the road when the dew hasn't dried yet. Maybe it's because I so dislike getting up early, but am also doing what I choose to do, while they have no choice. At heart I am lazy, yet I find such peace and delight in it that I believe it is a natural state, and in what looks like my laziest periods I am closest to my center. The ride to St. John's is fifteen minutes. The horses and I do it in all weather; the road is well plowed in winter, and there are only a few days a year when ice makes me drive the pickup. People always look at someone on horseback, and for a moment their faces change and many drivers and I wave to each other. Then at St. John's, Father Paul and five or six regulars and I celebrate the Mass.

Do not think of me as a spiritual man whose every thought during those twenty-five minutes is at one with the words of the Mass. Each morning I try, each morning I fail, and know that always I will be a creature who, looking at Father Paul and the altar, and uttering prayers, will be distracted by scrambled eggs, horses, the weather, and memories and daydreams that have nothing to do with the sacrament I am about to receive. I can receive, though: the Eucharist, and also, at Mass and at other times, moments and even minutes of contemplation. But I cannot achieve contemplation, as some can; and so, having to face and forgive my own failures, I have learned from them both the necessity and wonder of ritual. For ritual allows those who cannot will themselves out of the secular to perform the spiritual, as dancing allows the tongue-tied man a ceremony of love. And, while my mind dwells on breakfast, or Major or Duchess tethered under the church eave, there is, as I take the Host from Father Paul and place it on my tongue and return to the pew, a feeling that I am thankful I have not lost in the forty-eight years since my first Communion. At its center is excitement; spreading out from it is the peace of certainty. Or the certainty of peace. One night Father Paul and I talked about faith. It was long ago, and all I remember is him saying: Belief is believing in God; faith is believing that God believes in you. That is the excitement, and the peace; then the Mass is over, and I go into the sacristy and we have a cigarette and chat, the mystery ends, we are two men talking like any two men on a morning in America, about baseball, plane crashes, presidents, governors, murders, the sun, the clouds. Then I go to the horse and ride back to the life people see, the one in which I move and talk, and most days I enjoy it.

It is late summer now, the time between fishing and hunting, but a good time for baseball. It has been two weeks since Jennifer left, to drive home to Gloria's after her summer visit. She is the only one who still visits; the boys are married and have children, and sometimes fly up for a holiday, or I fly down or west to visit one of them. Jennifer is twenty, and I worry about her the way fathers worry about daughters but not sons. I want to know what she's up to, and at the same time I don't. She looks athletic, and she is: she swims and runs and of course rides. All my children do. When she comes for six weeks in summer, the house is loud with girls, friends of hers since childhood, and new ones. I am glad she kept the girl friends. They have been young company for me and, being with them, I have been able to gauge her growth between summers. On their riding days, I'd take them back to the house when their lessons were over and they had walked the horses and put them back in the stalls, and we'd have lemonade or Coke, and cookies if I had some, and talk until their parents came to drive them home. One year their breasts grew, so I wasn't startled when I saw Jennifer in July. Then they were driving cars to the stable, and beginning to look like young women, and I was passing out beer and ashtrays and they were talking about college.

When Jennifer was here in summer, they were at the house most days. I would say generally that as they got older they became quieter, and though I enjoyed both, I sometimes missed the giggles and shouts. The quiet voices, just low enough for me not to hear from wherever I was, rising and falling in proportion to my distance from them, frightened me. Not that I believed they were planning or recounting anything really wicked, but there was a female seriousness about them, and it was secretive, and of course I thought: love, sex. But it was more than that: it was womanhood they were entering, the deep forest of it, and no matter how many women and men too are saying these days that there is little difference between us, the truth is that men find their way into that forest only on clearly marked trails, while women move about in it like birds. So hearing Jennifer and her friends talking so quietly, yet intensely, I wanted very much to have a wife.

But not as much as in the old days, when Gloria had left but her presence was still in the house as strongly as if she had only gone to visit her folks for a week. There were no clothes or cosmetics, but potted plants endured my neglectful care as long as they could, and slowly died; I did not kill them on purpose, to exorcise the house of her, but I could not remember to water them. For weeks, because I did not use it much, the house was as neat as she had kept it, though dust layered the order she had made. The kitchen went first: I got the dishes in and out of the dishwasher and wiped the top of the stove, but did not return cooking spoons and pot holders to their hooks on the wall, and soon the burners and oven were caked with spillings, the refrigerator had more space and was spotted with juices. The living room and my bedroom went next; I did not go into the children's rooms except on bad nights when I went from room to room and looked and touched and smelled, so they did not lose their order until a year later when the kids came for six weeks. It was three months before I ate the last of the food Gloria had cooked and frozen: I remember it was a beef stew, and very good. By then I had four cookbooks, and was boasting a bit, and talking about recipes with the women at the stables, and looking forward to cooking for Father Paul. But I never looked forward to cooking at night only for myself, though I made myself do it; on some nights I gave in to my daily temptation, and took a newspaper or detective novel to a restaurant. By the end of the second year, though, I had stopped turning on the radio as soon as I woke in the morning, and was able to be silent and alone in the evening too, and then I enjoyed my dinners.

It is not hard to live through a day, if you can live through a moment. What creates despair is the imagination, which pretends there is a future, and insists on predicting millions of moments, thousands of days, and so drains you that you cannot live the moment at hand. That is what Father Paul told me in those first two years, on some of the bad nights when I believed I could not bear what I had to: the most painful loss was my children, then the loss of Gloria, whom

I still loved despite or maybe because of our long periods of sadness that rendered us helpless, so neither of us could break out of it to give a hand to the other. Twelve years later I believe ritual would have healed us more quickly than the repetitious talks we had, perhaps even kept us healed. Marriages have lost that, and I wish I had known then what I know now, and we had performed certain acts together every day, no matter how we felt, and perhaps then we could have subordinated feeling to action, for surely that is the essence of love. I know this from my distractions during Mass, and during everything else I do, so that my actions and feelings are seldom one. It does happen every day, but in proportion to everything else in a day, it is rare, like joy. The third most painful loss, which became second and sometimes first as months passed, was the knowledge that I could never marry again, and so dared not even keep company with a woman.

On some of the bad nights I was bitter about this with Father Paul, and I so pitied myself that I cried, or nearly did, speaking with damp eyes and breaking voice. I believe that celibacy is for him the same trial it is for me, not of the flesh, but the spirit: the heart longing to love. But the difference is he chose it, and did not wake one day to a life with thirty horses. In my anger I said I had done my service to love and chastity, and I told him of the actual physical and spiritual pain of practicing rhythm: nights of striking the mattress with a fist, two young animals lying side by side in heat, leaving the bed to pace, to smoke, to curse, and too passionate to question, for we were so angered and oppressed by our passion that we could see no further than our loins. So now I understand how people can be enslaved for generations before they throw down their tools or use them as weapons, the form of their slavery—the cotton fields, the shacks and puny cupboards and untended illnesses—absorbing their emotions and thoughts until finally they have little or none at all to direct with clarity and energy at the owners and legislators. And I told him of the trick of passion and its slaking: how during what we had to believe were safe periods, though all four children were conceived at those times, we were able with some coherence to question the tradition and reason and justice of the law against birth control, but not with enough conviction to soberly act against it, as though regular satisfaction in bed tempered our revolutionary as well as our erotic desires. Only when abstinence drove us hotly away from each other did we receive an urge so strong it lasted all the way to the drugstore and back; but always, after release, we threw away the remaining condoms; and after going through this a few times, we knew what would happen, and from then on we submitted to the calendar she so precisely marked on the bedroom wall. I told him that living two lives each month, one as celibates, one as lovers, made us tense and short-tempered, so we snapped at each other like dogs.

To have endured that, to have reached a time when we burned slowly and could gain from bed the comfort of lying down at night with one who loves you and whom you love, could for weeks on end go to bed tired and peacefully sleep after a kiss, a touch of the hands, and then to be thrown out of the marriage like a bundle from a moving freight car, was unjust, was intolerable, and I could not or would not muster the strength to endure it. But I did, a moment at a time, a day, a night, except twice, each time with a different woman and more than a year apart, and this was so long ago that I clearly see their faces in my memory, can hear the pitch of their voices, and the way they pronounced words, one with a Massachusetts accent, one midwestern, but I feel as though I only heard about them from someone else. Each rode at the stables and was with me for part of an evening; one was badly married, one divorced, so none of us was free. They did not understand this Catholic view, but they were understanding about my having it, and I remained friends with both of them until the married one left her husband and went to Boston, and the divorced one moved to Maine. After both those evenings, those good women, I went to Mass early while Father Paul was still in the confessional, and received his absolution. I did not tell him who I was, but of course he knew, though I never saw it in his eyes. Now my longing for a wife comes only once in a while, like a cold: on some late afternoons when I am alone in the barn, then I lock up and walk to the house, daydreaming, then suddenly look at it and see it empty, as though for the first time, and all at once I'm weary and feel I do not have the energy to broil meat, and I think of driving to a restaurant, then shake my head and go on to the house, the refrigerator, the oven; and some mornings when I wake in the dark and listen to the silence and run my hand over the cold sheet beside me; and some days in summer when Jennifer is here.

Gloria left first me, then the Church, and that was the end of religion for the children, though on visits they went to Sunday Mass with me, and still do, out of a respect for my life that they manage to keep free of patronage. Jennifer is an agnostic, though I doubt she would call herself that, any more than she would call herself any other name that implied she had made a decision, a choice, about existence, death, and God. In truth she tends to pantheism, a good sign, I think; but not wanting to be a father who tells his children what they ought to believe, I do not say to her that Catholicism includes pantheism, like onions in a stew. Besides, I have no missionary instincts and do not believe everyone should or even could live with the Catholic faith. It is Jennifer's womanhood that renders me awkward. And womanhood now is frank, not like when Gloria was twenty and there were symbols: high heels and cosmetics and dresses, a cigarette, a cocktail. I am glad that women are free now of false modesty and all its attention paid the flesh; but, still, it is difficult to see so much of your daughter, to hear her talk as only men and bawdy women used to, and most of all to see in her face the deep and unabashed sensuality of women, with no tricks of the eyes and mouth to hide the pleasure she feels at having a strong young body. I am certain, with the way things are now, that she has very happily not been a virgin for years. That does not bother me. What bothers me is my certainty about it, just from watching her walk across a room or light a cigarette or pour milk on cereal.

She told me all of it, waking me that night when I had gone to sleep listening to the wind in the trees and against the house, a wind so strong that I had to shut all but the lee windows, and still the house cooled; told it to me in such detail and so clearly that now, when she has driven the car to Florida, I remember it all as though I had been a passenger in the front seat, or even at the wheel. It started with a movie, then beer and driving to the sea to look at the waves in the night and the wind, Jennifer and Betsy and Liz. They drank a beer on the beach and wanted to go in naked but were afraid they would drown in the high surf. They bought another six-pack at a grocery store in New Hampshire, and drove home. I can see it now, feel it: the three girls and the beer and the ride on country roads where pines curved in the wind and the big deciduous trees swayed and shook as if they might leap from the earth. They would have some windows partly open so they could feel the wind; Jennifer would be playing a cassette, the music stirring them, as it does the young, to memories of another time, other people and places in what is for them the past.

She took Betsy home, then Liz, and sang with her cassette as she left the town west of us and started home, a twenty-minute drive on the road that passes my house. They had each had four beers, but now there were twelve empty bottles in the bag on the floor at the passenger seat, and I keep focusing on their sound against each other when the car shifted speeds or changed directions. For I want to understand that one moment out of all her heart's time on earth, and whether her history had any bearing on it, or whether her heart was then isolated from all it had known, and the sound of those bottles urged it. She was just leaving the town, accelerating past a night club on the right, gaining speed to climb a long, gradual hill, then she went up it, singing, patting the beat on the steering wheel, the wind loud through her few inches of open window, blowing her hair as it did the high branches alongside the road, and she looked up at them and watched the top of the hill for someone drunk or heedless coming over it in part of her lane. She crested to an open black road, and there he was: a bulk, a blur, a thing running across her headlights, and she swerved left and her foot went for the brake and was stomping air above its pedal when she hit him, saw his legs and body in the air, flying out of her light, into the dark. Her brakes were screaming into the wind, bottles clinking in the fallen bag, and with the music and wind inside the car was his sound, already a memory but as real as an echo, that car-shuddering thump as though she had struck a tree. Her foot was back on the accelerator. Then she shifted gears and pushed it. She ejected the cassette and closed the window. She did not start to cry until she knocked on my bedroom door, then called: 'Dad?'

Her voice, her tears, broke through my dream and the wind I heard in my sleep, and I stepped into jeans and hurried to the door, thinking harm, rape, death. All were in her face, and I hugged her and pressed her cheek to my chest and smoothed her blown hair, then led her, weeping, to the kitchen and sat her at the table where still she could not speak, nor look at me; when she raised her face it fell forward again, as of its own weight, into her palms. I offered tea and she shook her head, so I offered beer twice, then she shook her head, so I offered whiskey and she nodded. I had some rye that Father Paul and I had not finished last hunting season, and I poured some over ice and set it in front of her and was putting away the ice but stopped and got another glass and poured one for myself too, and brought the ice and bottle to the table where she was trying to get one of her long menthols out of the pack, but her fingers jerked like severed snakes, and I took the pack and lit one for her and took one for myself. I watched her shudder with her first swallow of rye, and push hair back from her face, it is auburn and gleamed in the overhead light, and I remembered how beautiful she looked riding a sorrel; she was smoking fast, then the sobs in her throat stopped, and she looked at me and said it, the words coming out with smoke: 'I hit somebody. With the *car.*'

Then she was crying and I was on my feet, moving back and forth, looking down at her, asking *Who? Where? Where?* She was pointing at the wall over the stove, jabbing her fingers and cigarette at it, her other hand at her eyes, and twice in horror I actually looked at the wall. She finished the whiskey in a swallow and I stopped pacing and asking and poured another, and either the drink or the exhaustion of tears quieted her, even the dry sobs, and she told me; not as I tell it now, for that was later as again and again we relieved it in the kitchen or living room, and, if in daylight, fled it on horseback out on the trails through the woods and, if at night, walked quietly around in the moonlit pasture, walked around and around it, sweating through our clothes. She told it in bursts, like she was a child again, running to me, injured from play. I put on boots and a shirt and left her with the bottle and her streaked face and a cigarette twitching between her fingers, pushed the door open against the wind, and eased it shut. The wind squinted and watered my eyes as I leaned into it and went to the pickup.

When I passed St. John's I looked at it, and Father Paul's little white rectory in the rear, and wanted to stop, wished I could as I could if he were simply a friend who sold hardware or something. I had forgotten my watch but I always know the time within minutes, even when a sound or dream or my bladder wakes me in the night. It was nearly two; we had been in the kitchen about twenty minutes; she had hit him around one-fifteen. Or her. The road was empty and I drove between blowing trees; caught for an instant in my lights, they seemed to be in panic. I smoked and let hope play its tricks on me: it was neither man nor woman but an animal, a goat or calf or deer on the road; it was a man who had jumped away in time, the collision of metal and body glancing not direct, and he had limped home to nurse bruises and cuts. Then I threw the cigarette and hope both out the window and prayed that he was alive, while beneath that prayer, a reserve deeper in my heart, another one stirred: that if he were dead, they would not get Jennifer.

From our direction, east and a bit south, the road to that hill and the night club beyond it and finally the town is, for its last four or five miles, straight through farming country. When I reached that stretch I slowed the truck and opened my window for the fierce air; on both sides were scattered farmhouses and barns and sometimes a silo, looking not like shelters but like unsheltered things the wind would flatten. Corn bent toward the road from a field on my right, and always something blew in front of me: paper, leaves, dried weeds, branches. I slowed approaching the hill, and went up it in second, staring through my open window at the ditch on the left side of the road, its weeds

alive, whipping, a mad dance with the trees above them. I went over the hill
and down and, opposite the club, turned right onto a side street of houses, and
parked there, in the leaping shadows of trees. I walked back across the road to
the club's parking lot, the wind behind me, lifting me as I strode, and I could
not hear my boots on pavement. I walked up the hill, on the shoulder, watching the branches above me, hearing their leaves and the creaking trunks and
the wind. Then I was at the top, looking down the road and at the farms and
fields; the night was clear, and I could see a long way; clouds scudded past the
half-moon and stars, blown out to sea.

I started down, watching the tall grass under the trees to my right, glancing into the dark of the ditch, listening for cars behind me; but as soon as I
cleared one tree, its sound was gone, its flapping leaves and rattling branches
far behind me, as though the greatest distance I had at my back was a matter
of feet, while ahead of me I could see a barn two miles off. Then I saw her skid
marks: short, and going left and downhill, into the other lane. I stood at the
ditch, its weeds blowing; across it were trees and their moving shadows, like
the clouds. I stepped onto its slope, and it took me sliding on my feet, then
rump, to the bottom, where I sat still, my body gathered to itself, lest a part of
me should touch him. But there was only tall grass, and I stood, my shoulders
reaching the sides of the ditch, and I walked uphill, wishing for the flashlight
in the pickup, walking slowly, and down in the ditch I could hear my feet in
the grass and on the earth, and kicking cans and bottles. At the top of the hill
I turned and went down, watching the ground above the ditch on my right,
praying my prayer from the truck again, the first one, the one I would admit,
that he was not dead, was in fact home, and began to hope again, memory
telling me of lost pheasants and grouse I had shot, but they were small and the
colors of their home, while a man was either there or not; and from that memory I left where I was and while walking in the ditch under the wind was in the
deceit of imagination with Jennifer in the kitchen, telling her she had hit no one,
or at least had not badly hurt anyone, when I realized he could be in the hospital now and I would have to think of a way to check there, something to say
on the phone. I see now that, once hope returned, I should have been certain
what it prepared me for: ahead of me, in high grass and the shadows of trees,
I saw his shirt. Or that is all my mind would allow itself: a shirt, and I stood
looking at it for the moments it took my mind to admit the arm and head and
the dark length covered by pants. He lay face down, the arm I could see near
his side, his head turned from me, on its cheek.

'Fella?' I said. I had meant to call, but it came out quiet and high, lost inches
from my face in the wind. Then I said, 'Oh God,' and felt Him in the wind and
the sky moving past the stars and moon and the fields around me, but only
watching me as He might have watched Cain or Job, I did not know which, and
I said it again, and wanted to sink to the earth and weep till I slept there in the
weeds. I climbed, scrambling up the side of the ditch, pulling at clutched grass,
gained the top on hands and knees, and went to him like that, panting, moving through the grass as high and higher than my face, crawling under that sky,
making sounds too, like some animal, there being no words to let him know I

was here with him now. He was long; that is the word that came to me, not tall. I kneeled beside him, my hands on my legs. His right arm was by his side, his left arm straight out from the shoulder, but turned, so his palm was open to the tree above us. His left cheek was cleanshaven, his eye closed, and there was no blood. I leaned forward to look at his open mouth and saw the blood on it, going down into the grass. I straightened and looked ahead at the wind blowing past me through grass and trees to a distant light, and I started at the light, imagining someone awake out there, wanting someone to be, a gathering of old friends, or someone alone listening to music or painting a picture, then I figured it was a night light at a farmyard whose house I couldn't see. *Going,* I thought. *Still going.* I leaned over again and looked at dripping blood.

So I had to touch his wrist, a thick one with a watch and expansion band that I pushed up his arm, thinking *he's left-handed,* my three fingers pressing his wrist, and all I felt was my tough finger-tips on that smooth underside flesh and small bones, then relief, then certainty. But against my will, or only because of it, I still don't know, I touched his neck, ran my fingers down it as if petting, then pressed, and my hand sprang back as from fire. I lowered it again, held it there until it felt that faint beating that I could not believe. There was too much wind. Nothing could make a sound in it. A pulse could not be felt in it, nor could mere fingers in that wind feel the absolute silence of a dead man's artery. I was making sounds again; I grabbed his left arm and his waist, and pulled him toward me, and that side of him rose, turned, and I lowered him to his back, his face tilted up toward the tree that was groaning, the tree and I the only sounds in the wind. Turning my face from his, looking down the length of him at his sneakers, I placed my ear on his heart, and heard not that but something else, and I clamped a hand over my exposed ear, heard something liquid and alive, like when you pump a well and after a few strokes you hear air and water moving in the pipe, and I knew I must raise his legs and cover him and run to a phone, while still I listened to his chest, thinking *raise with what? cover with what?* and amid the liquid sound I heard the heart, then lost it, and pressed my ear against bone, but his chest was quiet, and I did not know when the liquid had stopped, and do not know now when I heard air, a faint rush of it, and whether under my ear or at his mouth or whether I heard it at all. I straightened and looked at the light, dim and yellow. Then I touched his throat, looking him full in the face. He was blond and young. He could have been sleeping in the shade of a tree, but for the smear of blood from his mouth to his hair, and the night sky, and the weeds blowing against his head, and the leaves shaking in the dark above us.

I stood. Then I kneeled again and prayed for his soul to join in peace and joy all the dead and living; and, doing so, confronted my first sin against him, not stopping for Father Paul, who could have given him the last rites, and immediately then my second one, or, I saw then, my first, not calling an ambulance to meet me there, and I stood and turned into the wind, slid down the ditch and crawled out of it, and went up the hill and down it, across the road to the street of houses whose people I had left behind forever, so that I moved with stealth in the shadows to my truck.

When I came around the bend near my house, I saw the kitchen light at the rear. She sat as I had left her, the ashtray filled, and I looked at the bottle, felt her eyes on me, felt what she was seeing too: the dirt from my crawling. She had not drunk much of the rye. I poured some in my glass, with the water from melted ice, and sat down and swallowed some and looked at her and swallowed some more, and said: 'He's dead.'

She rubbed her eyes with the heels of her hands, rubbed the cheeks under them, but she was dry now.

'He was probably dead when he hit the ground. I mean, that's probably what killed—'

'Where was he?'

'Across the ditch, under a tree.'

'Was he—did you see his face?'

'No. Not really. I just felt. For life, pulse. I'm going out to the car.'

'What for? Oh.'

I finished the rye, and pushed back the chair, then she was standing too.

'I'll go with you.'

'There's no need.'

'I'll go.'

I took a flashlight from a drawer and pushed open the door and held it while she went out. We turned our faces from the wind. It was like on the hill, when I was walking, and the wind closed the distance behind me: after three or four steps I felt there was no house back there. She took my hand, as I was reaching for hers. In the garage we let go, and squeezed between the pickup and her little car, to the front of it, where we had more room, and we stepped back from the grill and I shone the light on the fender, the smashed headlight turned into it, the concave chrome staring to the right, at the garage wall.

'We ought to get the bottles,' I said.

She moved between the garage and the car, on the passenger side, and had room to open the door and lift the bag. I reached out, and she gave me the bag and backed up and shut the door and came around the car. We sidled to the doorway, and she put her arm around my waist and I hugged her shoulders.

'I thought you'd call the police,' she said.

We crossed the yard, faces bowed from the wind, her hair blowing away from her neck, and in the kitchen I put the bag of bottles in the garbage basket. She was working at the table: capping the rye and putting it away, filling the ice tray, washing the glasses, emptying the ashtray, sponging the table.

'Try to sleep now,' I said.

She nodded at the sponge circling under her hand, gathering ashes. Then she dropped it in the sink and, looking me full in the face, as I had never seen her look, as perhaps she never had, being for so long a daughter on visits (or so it seemed to me and still does: that until then our eyes had never seriously met), she crossed to me from the sink and kissed my lips, then held me so tightly I lost balance, and would have stumbled forward had she not held me so hard.

I sat in the living room, the house darkened, and watched the maple and the hemlock. When I believed she was asleep I put on *La Boheme,* and kept it at the same volume as the wind so it would not wake her. Then I listened to *Madame Butterfly,* and in the third act had to rise quickly to lower the sound: the wind was gone. I looked at the still maple near the window, and thought of the wind leaving farms and towns and the coast, going out over the sea to die on the waves. I smoked and gazed out the window. The sky was darker, and at daybreak the rain came. I listened to *Tosca,* and at six-fifteen went to the kitchen where Jennifer's purse lay on the table, a leather shoulder purse crammed with the things of an adult woman, things she had begun accumulating only a few years back, and I nearly wept, thinking of what sandy foundations they were: driver's license, credit card, disposable lighter, cigarettes, checkbook, ballpoint pen, cash, cosmetics, comb, brush, Kleenex, these the rite of passage from childhood, and I took one of them—her keys—and went out, remembering a jacket and hat when the rain struck me, but I kept going to the car, and squeezed and lowered myself into it, pulled the seat belt over my shoulder and fastened it and backed out, turning in the drive, going forward into the road, toward St. John's and Father Paul.

Cars were on the road, the workers, and I did not worry about any of them noticing the fender and light. Only a horse distracted them from what they drove to. In front of St. John's is a parking lot; at its far side, past the church and at the edge of the lawn, is an old pine, taller than the steeple now. I shifted to third, left the road, and, aiming the right headlight at the tree, accelerated past the white blur of church, into the black trunk growing bigger till it was all I could see, then I rocked in that resonant thump she had heard, had felt, and when I turned off the ignition it was still in my ears, my blood, and I saw the boy flying in the wind. I lowered my forehead to the wheel. Father Paul opened the door, his face white in the rain.

'I'm all right.'

'What happened?'

'I don't know. I fainted.'

I got out and went around to the front of the car, looked at the smashed light, the crumpled and torn fender.

'Come to the house and lie down.'

'I'm all right.'

'When was your last physical?'

'I'm due for one. Let's get out of this rain.'

'You'd better lie down.'

'No. I want to receive.'

That was the time to say I want to confess, but I have not and will not. Though I could now, for Jennifer is in Florida, and weeks have passed, and perhaps now Father Paul would not feel that he must tell me to go to the police. And, for that very reason, to confess now would be unfair. It is a world of secrets, and now I have one from my best, in truth my only, friend. I have one from Jennifer too, but that is the nature of fatherhood.

Most of that day it rained, so it was only in early evening, when the sky cleared, with a setting sun, that two little boys, leaving their confinement for some play before dinner, found him. Jennifer and I got that on the local news, which we listened to every hour, meeting at the radio, standing with cigarettes, until the one at eight o'clock; when she stopped crying, we went out and walked on the wet grass, around the pasture, the last of sunlight still in the air and trees. His name was Patrick Mitchell, he was nineteen years old, was employed by CETA, lived at home with his parents and brother and sister. The paper next day said he had been at a friend's house and was walking home, and I thought of that light I had seen, then knew it was not for him; he lived on one of the streets behind the club. The paper did not say then, or in the next few days, anything to make Jennifer think he was alive while she was with me in the kitchen. Nor do I know if we—I—could have saved him.

In keeping her secret from her friends, Jennifer had to perform so often, as I did with Father Paul and at the stables, that I believe the acting, which took more of her than our daylight trail rides and our night walks in the pasture, was her healing. Her friends teased me about wrecking her car. When I carried her luggage out to the car on that last morning, we spoke only of the weather for her trip—the day was clear, with a dry cool breeze—and hugged and kissed, and I stood watching as she started the car and turned it around. But then she shifted to neutral and put on the parking brake and unclasped the belt, looking at me all the while, then she was coming to me, as she had that night in the kitchen, and I opened my arms.

I have said I talk with God in the mornings, as I start my day, and sometimes as I sit with coffee, looking at the birds, and the woods. Of course He has never spoken to me, but that is not something I require. Nor does He need to. I know Him, as I know the part of myself that knows Him, that felt Him watching from the wind and the night as I kneeled over the dying boy. Lately I have taken to arguing with Him, as I can't with Father Paul, who, when he hears my monthly confession, has not heard and will not hear anything of failure to do all that one can to save an anonymous life, of injustice to a family in their grief, of deepening their pain at the chance and mystery of death by giving them nothing—no one—to hate. With Father Paul I feel lonely about this, but not with God. When I received the Eucharist while Jennifer's car sat twice-damaged, so redeemed, in the rain, I felt neither loneliness nor shame, but as though He were watching me, even from my tongue, intestines, blood, as I have watched my sons at times in their young lives when I was able to judge but without anger, and so keep silent while they, in the agony of their youth, decided how they must act; or found reasons, after their actions, for what they had done. Their reasons were never as good or as bad as their actions, but they needed to find them, to believe they were living by them, instead of the awful solitude of the heart.

I do not feel the peace I once did: not with God, nor the earth, or anyone on it. I have begun to prefer this state, to remember with fondness the other one as a period of peace I neither earned nor deserved. Now in the mornings while I watch purple finches driving larger titmice from the feeder, I say to Him: I would do it again. For when she knocked on my door, then called me, she woke what had flowed dormant in my blood since her birth, so that what rose from the bed was not a stable owner or a Catholic or any other Luke Ripley I had lived with for a long time, but the father of a girl.

And He says: I am a Father too.

Yes, I say, as You are a Son Whom this morning I will receive; unless You kill me on the way to church, then I trust You will receive me. And as a Son You made Your plea.

Yes, He says, but I would not lift the cup.

True, and I don't want You to lift it from me either. And if one of my sons had come to me that night, I would have phoned the police and told them to meet us with an ambulance at the top of the hill.

Why? Do you love them less?

I tell Him no, it is not that I love them less, but that I could bear the pain of watching and knowing my sons' pain, could bear it with pride as they took the whip and nails. But You never had a daughter and, if You had, You could not have borne her passion.

So, He says, you love her more than you love Me.

I love her more than I love truth.

Then you love in weakness, He says.

As You love me, I say, and I go with an apple or carrot out to the barn.

Lust

*L*eo was from a long time ago, the first one I ever saw nude. In the spring before the Hellmans filled their pool, we'd go down there in the deep end, with baby oil, and like that. I met him the first month away at boarding school. He had a halo from the campus light behind him. I flipped.

Roger was fast. In his illegal car, we drove to the reservoir, the radio blaring, talking fast, fast, fast. He was always going for my zipper. He got kicked out sophomore year.

By the time the band got around to playing "Wild Horses," I had tasted Bruce's tongue. We were clicking in the shadows on the other side of the amplifier, out of Mrs. Donovan's line of vision. It tasted like salt, with my neck bent back, because we had been dancing so hard before.

Tim's line: "I'd like to see you in a bathing suit." I knew it was his line when he said the exact same thing to Annie Hines.

You'd go on walks to get off campus. It was raining like hell, my sweater as sopped as a wet sheep. Tim pinned me to a tree, the woods light brown and dark brown, a white house half hidden with the lights already on. The water was as loud as a crowd hissing. He made certain comments about my forehead, about my cheeks.

We started off sitting at one end of the couch and then our feet were squished against the armrest and then he went over to turn off the TV and came back after he had taken off his shirt and then we slid onto the floor and he got up again to close the door, then came back to me, a body waiting on the rug.

You'd try to wipe off the table or to do the dishes and Willie would untuck your shirt and get his hands up under in front, standing behind you, making puffy noises in your ear.

*

He likes it when I wash my hair. He covers his face with it and if I start to say something, he goes, "Shush."

304

For a long time, I had Philip on the brain. The less they noticed you, the more you got them on the brain.

My parents had no idea. Parents never really know what's going on, especially when you're away at school most of the time. If she met them, my mother might say, "Oliver seems nice" or "I like that one" without much of an opinion. If she didn't like them, "He's a funny fellow, isn't he?" or "Johnny's perfectly nice but a drink of water." My father was too shy to talk to them at all unless they played sports and he'd ask them about that.

The sand was almost cold underneath because the sun was long gone. Eben piled a mound over my feet, patting around my ankles, the ghostly surf rumbling behind him in the dark. He was the first person I ever knew who died, later that summer, in a car crash. I thought about it for a long time.

"Come here," he says on the porch.
    I go over to the hammock and he takes my wrist with two fingers.
    "What?"
    He kisses my palm then directs my hand to his fly.

Songs went with whichever boy it was. "Sugar Magnolia" was Tim, with the line "Rolling in the rushes/down by the riverside." With "Darkness Darkness," I'd picture Philip with his long hair. Hearing "Under My Thumb" there'd be the smell of Jamie's suede jacket.

We hid in the listening rooms during study hall. With a record cover over the door's window, the teacher on duty couldn't look in. I came out flushed and heady and back at the dorm was surprised how red my lips were in the mirror.

One weekend at Simon's brother's, we stayed inside all day with the shades down, in bed, then went out to Store 24 to get some ice cream. He stood at the magazine rack and read through *MAD* while I got butterscotch sauce, craving something sweet.

I could do some things well. Some things I was good at, like math or painting or even sports, but the second a boy put his arm around me, I forgot about wanting to do anything else, which felt like a relief at first until it became like sinking into a muck.

*

It was different for a girl.

When we were little, the brothers next door tied up our ankles. They held the door of the goat house and wouldn't let us out till we showed them our underpants. Then they'd forget about being after us and when we played whiffle ball, I'd be just as good as they were.

Then it got to be different. Just because you have on a short skirt, they yell from the cars, slowing down for a while, and if you don't look, they screech off and call you a bitch.

"What's the matter with me?" they say, point-blank.

Or else, "Why won't you go out with me? I'm not asking you to get married," about to get mad.

Or it'd be, trying to be reasonable, in a regular voice, "Listen, I just want to have a good time."

So I'd go because I couldn't think of something to say back that wouldn't be obvious, and if you go out with them, you sort of have to do something.

I sat between Mack and Eddie in the front seat of the pickup. They were having a fight about something. I've a feeling about me.

Certain nights you'd feel a certain surrender, maybe if you'd had wine. The surrender would be forgetting yourself and you'd put your nose to his neck and feel like a squirrel, safe, at rest, in a restful dream. But then you'd start to slip from that and the dark would come in and there'd be a cave. You make out the dim shape of the windows and feel yourself become a cave, filled absolutely with air, or with a sadness that wouldn't stop.

Teenage years. You know just what you're doing and don't see the things that start to get in the way.

Lots of boys, but never two at the same time. One was plenty to keep you in a state. You'd start to see a boy and something would rush over you like a fast storm cloud and you couldn't possibly think of anyone else. Boys took it differently. Their eyes perked up at any little number that walked by. You'd act like you weren't noticing.

The joke was that the school doctor gave out the pill like aspirin. He didn't ask you anything. I was fifteen. We had a picture of him in assembly, holding up an IUD shaped like a T. Most girls were on the pill, if anything, because they couldn't handle a diaphragm. I kept the dial in my top drawer like my mother and thought of her each time I tipped out the yellow tablets in the morning before chapel.

If they were too shy, I'd be more so. Andrew was nervous. We stayed up with his family album, sharing a pack of Old Golds. Before it got light, we turned on the TV. A man was explaining how to plant seedlings. His mouth jerked to the side in a tic. Andrew thought it was a riot and kept imitating him. I laughed to be polite. When we finally dozed off, he dared to put his arm around me, but that was it.

You wait till they come to you. With half fright, half swagger, they stand one step down. They dare to touch the button on your coat then lose their nerve and quickly drop their hand so you—you'd do anything for them. You touch their cheek.

The girls sit around in the common room and talk about boys, smoking their heads off.

"What are you complaining about?" says Jill to me when we talk about problems.

"Yeah," says Giddy. "You always have a boyfriend."

I look at them and think, As if.

I thought the worst thing anyone could call you was a cock-teaser. So, if you flirted, you had to be prepared to go through with it. Sleeping with someone was perfectly normal once you had done it. You didn't really worry about it. But there were other problems. The problems had to do with something else entirely.

*

Mack was during the hottest summer ever recorded. We were renting a house on an island with all sorts of other people. No one slept during the heat wave, walking around the house with nothing on which we were used to because of the nude beach. In the living room, Eddie lay on top of a coffee table to cool off. Mack and I, with the bedroom door open for air, sweated and sweated all night.

"I can't take this," he said at three A.M. "I'm going for a swim." He and some guys down the hall went to the beach. The heat put me on edge. I sat on a cracked chest by the open window and smoked and smoked till I felt even worse, waiting for something—I guess for him to get back.

One was on a camping trip in Colorado. We zipped our sleeping bags together, the coyotes' hysterical chatter far away. Other couples murmured in other tents. Paul was up before sunrise, starting a fire for breakfast. He wasn't much of a talker in the daytime. At night, his hand leafed about in the hair at my neck.

There'd be times when you overdid it. You'd get carried away. All the next day, you'd be in a total fog, delirious, absent-minded, crossing the street and nearly getting run over.

The more girls a boy has, the better. He has a bright look, having reaped fruits, blooming. He stalks around, sure-shouldered, and you have the feeling he's got more in him, a fatter heart, more stories to tell. For a girl, with each boy it's as though a petal gets plucked each time.

Then you start to get tired. You begin to feel diluted, like watered-down stew.

Oliver came skiing with us. We lolled by the fire after everyone had gone to bed. Each creak you'd think was someone coming downstairs. The silver loop bracelet he gave me had been a present from his girlfriend before.

On vacations, we went skiing, or you'd go south if someone invited you. Some people had apartments in New York that their families hardly ever used. Or summer houses, or older sisters. We always managed to find someplace to go.

We made the plan at coffee hour. Simon snuck out and met me at Main Gate after lights-out. We crept to the chapel and spent the night in the balcony. He tasted like onions from a submarine sandwich.

The boys are one of two ways: either they can't sit still or they don't move. In front of the TV, they won't budge. On weekends they play touch football while we sit on the sidelines, picking blades of grass to chew on, and watch. We're always watching them run around. We shiver in the stands, knocking our boots together to keep our toes warm, and they whizz across the ice, chopping their sticks around the puck. When they're in the rink, they refuse to look at you, only eyeing each other beneath low helmets. You cheer for them but they don't look up, even if it's a face-off when nothing's happening, even if they're doing drills before any game has started at all.

Dancing under the pink tent, he bent down and whispered in my ear. We slipped away to the lawn on the other side of the hedge. Much later, as he was leaving the buffet with two plates of eggs and sausage, I saw the grass stains on the knees of his white pants.

Tim's was shaped like a banana, with a graceful curve to it. They're all different. Willie's like a bunch of walnuts when nothing was happening, another's as thin as a thin hot dog. But it's like faces; you're never really surprised.

Still, you're not sure what to expect.

I look into his face and he looks back. I look into his eyes and they look back at mine. Then they look down at my mouth so I look at his mouth, then back to his eyes then, backing up, at his whole face. I think, Who? Who are you? His head tilts to one side.
    I say, "Who are you?"
    "What do you mean?"
    "Nothing."
    I look at his eyes again, deeper. Can't tell who he is, what he thinks.
    "What?" he says. I look at his mouth.
    "I'm just wondering," I say and go wandering across his face. Study the chin line. It's shaped like a persimmon.
    "Who are you? What are you thinking?"
    He says, "What the hell are you talking about?"

Then they get mad after, when you say enough is enough. After, when it's easier to explain that you don't want to. You wouldn't dream of saying that maybe you weren't really ready to in the first place.

Gentle Eddie. We waded into the sea, the waves round and plowing in, buffalo-headed, slapping our thighs. I put my arms around his freckled shoulders and he held me up, buoyed by the water, and rocked me like a sea shell.

I had no idea whose party it was, the apartment jam-packed, stepping over people in the hallway. The room with the music was practically empty, the bare floor, me in red shoes. This fellow slides onto one knee and takes me around the waist and we rock to jazzy tunes, with my toes pointing heaven-ward, and waltz and spin and dip to "Smoke Gets in Your Eyes" or "I'll Love You Just for Now." He puts his head to my chest, runs a sweeping hand down my inside thigh and we go loose-limbed and sultry and as smooth as silk and I stamp my red heels and he takes me into a swoon. I never saw him again after that but I thought, I could have loved that one.

You wonder how long you can keep it up. You begin to feel as if you're showing through, like a bathroom window that only lets in grey light, the kind you can't see out of.

They keep coming around. Johnny drives up at Easter vacation from Baltimore and I let him in the kitchen with everyone sound asleep. He has friends waiting in the car.

"What are you, crazy? It's pouring out there," I say.

"It's okay," he says. "They understand."

So he gets some long kisses from me, against the refrigerator, before he goes because I hate those girls who push away a boy's face as if she were made out of Ivory soap, as if she's that much greater than he is.

The note on my cubby told me to see the headmaster. I had no idea for what. He had received complaints about my amorous displays on the town green. It was Willie that spring. The headmaster told me he didn't care what I did but that Casey Academy had a reputation to uphold in the town. He lowered his glasses on his nose. "We've got twenty acres of woods on this campus," he said. "If you want to smooch with your boyfriend, there are twenty acres for you to do it out of the public eye. You read me?"

Everybody'd get weekend permissions for different places, then we'd all go to someone's house whose parents were away. Usually there'd be more boys than girls. We raided the liquor closet and smoked pot at the kitchen table and you'd never know who would end up where, or with whom. There were always disasters. Ceci got bombed and cracked her head open on the banister and needed stitches. Then there was the time Wendel Blair walked through the picture window at the Lowes' and got slashed to ribbons.

He scared me. In bed, I didn't dare look at him. I lay back with my eyes closed, luxuriating because he knew all sorts of expert angles, his hands never fumbling, going over my whole body, pressing the hair up and off the back of my head, giving an extra hip shove, as if to say *There*. I parted my eyes slightly, keeping the screen of my lashes low because it was too much to look at him, his mouth loose and pink and parted, his eyes looking through my forehead, or kneeling up, looking through my throat. I was ashamed but couldn't look him in the eye.

You wonder about things feeling a little off-kilter. You begin to feel like a piece of pounded veal.

At boarding school, everyone gets depressed. We go in and see the house-mother, Mrs. Gunther. She got married when she was eighteen. Mr. Gunther was her high school sweetheart, the only boyfriend she ever had.
    "And you knew you wanted to marry him right off?" we ask her.
    She smiles and says, "Yes."
    "They always want something from you," says Jill, complaining about her boyfriend.
    "Yeah," says Giddy. "You always feel like you have to deliver something."
    "You do," says Mrs. Gunther. "Babies."

After sex, you curl up like a shrimp, something deep inside you ruined, slammed in a place that sickens at slamming, and slowly you fill up with an overwhelming sadness, an elusive gaping worry. You don't try to explain it, filled with the knowledge that it's nothing after all, everything filling up finally and absolutely with death. After the briskness of loving, loving stops. And you roll over with death stretched out alongside you like a feather boa, or a snake, light as air, and you . . . you don't even ask for anything or try to say something to him because it's obviously your own damn fault. You haven't been able to—to what? To open your heart. You open your legs but can't, or don't dare any-more, to open your heart.

It starts this way:
    You stare into their eyes. They flash like all the stars are out. They look at you seriously, their eyes at a low burn and their hands no matter what starting off shy and with such a gentle touch that the only thing you can do is take that tenderness and let yourself be swept away. When, with one attentive finger they tuck the hair behind your ear, you—
    You do everything they want.
    Then comes after. After when they don't look at you. They scratch their balls, stare at the ceiling. Or if they do turn, their gaze is altogether changed. They are surprised. They turn casually to look at you, distracted, and get a mild distracted surprise. You're gone. Their blank look tells you that the girl they were fucking is not there anymore. You seem to have disappeared.

Bullet in the Brain

*A*nders couldn't get to the bank until just before it closed, so of course the line was endless and he got stuck behind two women whose loud, stupid conversation put him in a murderous temper. He was never in the best of tempers anyway, Anders—a book critic known for the weary, elegant savagery with which he dispatched almost everything he reviewed.

With the line still doubled around the rope, one of the tellers stuck a "POSITION CLOSED" sign in her window and walked to the back of the bank, where she leaned against a desk and began to pass the time with a man shuffling papers. The women in front of Anders broke off their conversation and watched the teller with hatred. "Oh, that's nice," one of them said. She turned to Anders and added, confident of his accord, "One of those little human touches that keep us coming back for more."

Anders had conceived his own towering hatred of the teller, but he immediately turned it on the presumptuous crybaby in front of him. "Damned unfair," he said. "Tragic, really. If they're not chopping off the wrong leg, or bombing your ancestral village, they're closing their positions."

She stood her ground. "I didn't say it was tragic," she said. "I just think it's a pretty lousy way to treat your customers."

"Unforgivable," Anders said. "Heaven will take note."

She sucked in her cheeks but stared past him and said nothing. Anders saw that the other woman, her friend, was looking in the same direction. And then the tellers stopped what they were doing, and the customers slowly turned, and silence came over the bank. Two men wearing black ski masks and blue business suits were standing to the side of the door. One of them had a pistol pressed against the guard's neck. The guard's eyes were closed, and his lips were moving. The other man had a sawed-off shotgun. "Keep your big mouth shut!" the man with the pistol said, though no one had spoken a word. "One of you tellers hits the alarm, you're all dead meat. Got it?"

The tellers nodded.

"Oh, bravo," Anders said. "*Dead meat.*" He turned to the woman in front of him. "Great script, eh? The stern, brass-knuckled poetry of the dangerous classes."

She looked at him with drowning eyes.

The man with the shotgun pushed the guard to his knees. He handed the shotgun to his partner and yanked the guard's wrists up behind his back and locked them together with a pair of handcuffs. He toppled him onto the floor with a kick between the shoulder blades. Then he took his shotgun back and went over to the security gate at the end of the counter. He was short and heavy and moved with peculiar slowness, even torpor. "Buzz him in," his partner said. The man with the shotgun opened the gate and sauntered along the line of tellers, handing each of them a Hefty bag. When he came to the empty position he looked over at the man with the pistol, who said, "Whose slot is that?"

Anders watched the teller. She put her hand to her throat and turned to the man she'd been talking to. He nodded. "Mine," she said.

"Then get your ugly ass in gear and fill that bag."

"There you go," Anders said to the woman in front of him. "Justice is done."

"Hey! Bright boy! Did I tell you to talk?"

"No," Anders said.

"Then shut your trap."

"Did you hear that?" Anders said. "'Bright boy.' Right out of 'The Killers.'"

"Please be quiet," the woman said.

"Hey, you deaf or what?" The man with the pistol walked over to Anders. He poked the weapon into Anders' gut. "You think I'm playing games?"

"No," Anders said, but the barrel tickled like a stiff finger and he had to fight back the titters. He did this by making himself stare into the man's eyes, which were clearly visible behind the holes in the mask: pale blue and rawly red-rimmed. The man's left eyelid kept twitching. He breathed out a piercing, ammoniac smell that shocked Anders more than anything that had happened, and he was beginning to develop a sense of unease when the man prodded him again with the pistol.

"You like me, bright boy?" he said. "You want to suck my dick?"

"No," Anders said.

"Then stop looking at me."

Anders fixed his gaze on the man's shiny wing-tip shoes.

"Not down there. Up there." He stuck the pistol under Anders' chin and pushed it upward until Anders was looking at the ceiling.

Anders had never paid much attention to that part of the bank, a pompous old building with marble floors and counters and pillars, and gilt scrollwork over the tellers' cages. The domed ceiling had been decorated with mythological figures whose fleshy, toga-draped ugliness Anders had taken in at a glance many years earlier and afterward declined to notice. Now he had no choice but to scrutinize the painter's work. It was even worse than he remembered, and all of it executed with the utmost gravity. The artist had a few tricks up his sleeve and used them again and again—a certain rosy blush on the underside of the clouds, a coy backward glance on the faces of the cupids and fauns. The ceiling was crowded with various dramas, but the one that caught Anders' eye was Zeus and Europa—portrayed, in this rendition, as a bull ogling a cow from behind a haystack. To make the cow sexy, the painter had canted her hips suggestively and given her long, droopy eyelashes through which she gazed back at the bull with sultry welcome. The bull wore a smirk and his eyebrows were arched. If there'd been a bubble coming out of his mouth, it would have said, "Hubba hubba."

"What's so funny, bright boy?"

"Nothing."

"You think I'm comical? You think I'm some kind of clown?"

"No."

"You think you can fuck with me?"

"No."

"Fuck with me again, you're history. *Capiche?*"

Anders burst out laughing. He covered his mouth with both hands and said, "I'm sorry, I'm sorry," then snorted helplessly through his fingers and said, "*Capiche*—oh, God, *capiche,*" and at that the man with the pistol raised the pistol and shot Anders right in the head.

The bullet smashed Anders' skull and ploughed through his brain and exited behind his right ear, scattering shards of bone into the cerebral cortex, the corpus callosum, back toward the basal ganglia, and down into the thalamus. But before all this occurred, the first appearance of the bullet in the cerebrum set off a crackling chain of ion transports and neuro-transmissions. Because of their peculiar origin these traced a peculiar pattern, flukishly calling to life a summer afternoon some forty years past, and long since lost to memory. After striking the cranium the bullet was moving at 900 feet per second, a pathetically sluggish, glacial pace compared to the synaptic lightning that flashed around it. Once in the brain, that is, the bullet came under the mediation of brain time, which gave Anders plenty of leisure to contemplate the scene that, in a phrase he would have abhorred, "passed before his eyes."

It is worth noting what Anders did not remember, given what he did remember. He did not remember his first lover, Sherry, or what he had most madly loved about her, before it came to irritate him—her unembarrassed carnality, and especially the cordial way she had with his unit, which she called Mr. Mole, as in, "Uh-oh, looks like Mr. Mole wants to play," and, "Let's hide Mr. Mole!" Anders did not remember his wife, whom he had also loved before she exhausted him with her predictability, or his daughter, now a sullen professor of economics at Dartmouth. He did not remember standing just outside his daughter's door as she lectured her bear about his naughtiness and described the truly appalling punishments Paws would receive unless he changed his ways. He did not remember a single line of the hundreds of poems he had committed to memory in his youth so that he could give himself the shivers at will— not "Silent, upon a peak in Darien," or "My God, I heard this day," or "All my pretty ones? Did you say all? O hell-kite! All?" None of these did he remember; not one. Anders did not remember his dying mother saying of his father, "I should have stabbed him in his sleep."

He did not remember Professor Josephs telling his class how Athenian prisoners in Sicily had been released if they could recite Aeschylus, and then reciting Aeschylus himself, right there, in the Greek. Anders did not remember how his eyes had burned at those sounds. He did not remember the surprise of seeing a college classmate's name on the jacket of a novel not long after they graduated, or the respect he had felt after reading the book. He did not remember the pleasure of giving respect.

Nor did Anders remember seeing a woman leap to her death from the building opposite his own just days after his daughter was born. He did not remember shouting, "Lord have mercy!" He did not remember deliberately crashing his father's car into a tree, or having his ribs kicked in by three policemen at an anti-war rally, or waking himself up with laughter. He did not remember when he began to regard the heap of books on his desk with boredom and dread, or when he grew angry at writers for writing them. He did not remember when everything began to remind him of something else.

This is what he remembered. Heat. A baseball field. Yellow grass, the whirr of insects, himself leaning against a tree as the boys of the neighborhood gather for a pickup game. He looks on as the others argue the relative genius of Mantle and Mays. They have been worrying this subject all summer, and it has become tedious to Anders: an oppression, like the heat.

Then the last two boys arrive, Coyle and a cousin of his from Mississippi. Anders has never met Coyle's cousin before and will never see him again. He says hi with the rest but takes no further notice of him until they've chosen sides and someone asks the cousin what position he wants to play. "Shortstop," the boy says. "Short's the best position they is." Anders turns and looks at him. He wants to hear Coyle's cousin repeat what he's just said, but he knows better than to ask. The others will think he's being a jerk, ragging the kid for his grammar. But that isn't it, not at all—it's that Anders is strangely roused, elated, by those final two words, their pure unexpectedness and their music. He takes the field in a trance, repeating them to himself.

The bullet is already in the brain; it won't be outrun forever, or charmed to a halt. In the end it will do its work and leave the troubled skull behind, dragging its comet's tail of memory and hope and talent and love into the marble hall of commerce. That can't be helped. But for now Anders can still make time. Time for the shadows to lengthen on the grass, time for the tethered dog to bark at the flying ball, time for the boy in right field to smack his sweat-blackened mitt and softly chant, *They is, they is, they is.*

PART 3

Magazines, Journals, and Quarterlies Publishing Short Stories

Editorial Addresses of American and Canadian Magazines Publishing Short Stories

When available, the annual subscription rate and the name of the editor follow the address.

African American Review
Stalker Hall 212
Indiana State University
Terre Haute, IN 47809
$24, Joe Weixlmann

Agni Review
Creative Writing Department
Boston University
236 Bay State Road
Boston, MA 02115
$12, Askold Melnyczuk

Alaska Quarterly Review
Department of English
University of Alaska
3211 Providence Drive
Anchorage, AK 99508
$8, Ronald Spatz

Alfred Hitchcock's Mystery
   Magazine
1540 Broadway
New York, NY 10036
$34.97, Cathleen Jordan

American Letters and Commentary
Suite 56
850 Park Avenue
New York, NY 10021
*$5, Jeanne Beaumont, Anna
   Rabinowitz*

American Literary Review
University of North Texas
P.O. Box 13615

Denton, TX 76203
$15, Lee Martin

American Short Fiction
Parlin 108
Department of English
University of Texas at Austin
Austin, TX 78712-1164
$24, Joseph Krupa

American Voice
332 West Broadway
Louisville, KY 40202
*$15, Sallie Bingham, Frederick
   Smock*

Analog Science Fiction/Science Fact
1540 Broadway
New York, NY 10036
$34.95, Stanley Schmidt

Another Chicago Magazine
Left Field Press
3709 North Kenmore
Chicago, IL 60613
$8, Sharon Solwitz

Antietam Review
82 West Washington Street
Hagerstown, MD 21740
$5, Suzanne Kass

Antioch Review
P.O. Box 148
Yellow Springs, OH 45387
$35, Robert S. Fogarty

Apalachee Quarterly
P.O. Box 20106
Tallahassee, FL 32316
$15, Barbara Hamby

Appalachian Heritage
Berea College
Berea, KY 40404
$18, Sidney Saylor Farr

Arkansas Review
Dept. of English and Philosophy
P.O. Box 1890
Arkansas State University
State University, AR 72467
$20, Norman Lavers

Ascent
English Dept.
901 8th St.
Moorehead, MN 56562
$9, W. Scott Olsen

Atlantic Monthly
77 N. Washington Street
Boston, MA 02114
$15.94, C. Michael Curtis

Baltimore Review
P.O. Box 410
Riderwood, MD 21139
Barbara Westwood Diehl

Bananafish
P.O. Box 381332
Cambridge, MA 02238-1332
Robin Lippincott

Bellingham Review
MS 9053
Western Washington University
Bellingham, WA 98225
$10, Robin Hemly

Baffler
P.O. Box 378293

Chicago, IL 60637
$20, Thomas Frank, Keith White

Bellowing Ark
P.O. Box 45637
Seattle, WA 98145
$15, Robert R. Ward

Beloit Fiction Journal
Beloit College
P.O. Box 11
Beloit, WI 53511
$9, Fred Burwell

Big Sky Journal
P.O. Box 1069
Bozeman, MT 59771-1069
$22, Allen Jones, Brian Baise

Black Warrior Review
P.O. Box 2936
Tuscaloosa, AL 35487-2936
$14, Christopher Chambers

Blood & Aphorisms
P.O. Box 702
Toronto, Ontario
M5S ZY4 Canada
$18, Michelle Alfano, Dennis Black

BOMB
New Art Publications
10th floor
594 Broadway
New York, NY 10012
$18, Betsy Sussler

Border Crossings
Y300-393 Portage Avenue
Winnipeg, Manitoba
R3B 3H6 Canada
$23, Meeka Walsh

Boston Book Review
30 Brattle Street
Cambridge, MA 02138
$24, Theoharis Constantine

Boston Review
Building E53
Room 407
Cambridge, MA 02139
$15, editorial board

Bottomfish
DeAnza College
21250 Stevens Creek Blvd.
Cupertino, CA 95014
$5, David Denny

Boulevard
4579 Laclede Avenue #332
St. Louis, MO 63108
$12, Richard Burgin

Briar Cliff Review
3303 Rebecca Street
P.O. Box 2100
Sioux City, IA 51104-2100
$4, Phil Hey

Bridges
P.O. Box 24839
Eugene, OR 97402
$15, Clare Kinberg

The Bridge
14050 Vernon Street
Oak Park, MI 48237
$8, Helen Zucker

BUZZ
11835 West Olympic Blvd.
Suite 450
Los Angeles, CA 90064
$14.95, Renee Vogel

Callaloo
Dept. of English
Wilson Hall
University of Virginia
Charlottesville, VA 22903
$35, Charles H. Rowell

Calyx
P.O. Box B
Corvallis, OR 97339
$18, Margarita Donnelly

Canadian Fiction
Box 946, Station F
Toronto, Ontario
M4Y 2N9 Canada
$34.24, Geoffrey Hancock

Capilano Review
Capilano College
2055 Purcell Way
North Vancouver,
British Columbia
V7J 3H5 Canada
$25, Robert Sherrin

Carolina Quarterly
Greenlaw Hall 066A
University of North Carolina
Chapel Hill, NC 27514
$10, Shannon Wooden

Century
P.O. Box 150510
Brooklyn, NY 11215-0510
$33, Robert J. Killheffer

Chariton Review
Division of Language & Literature
Northeast Missouri State University
Kirksville, MO 63501
$9, Jim Barnes

Chattahoochee Review
DeKalb Community College
2101 Womack Road
Dunwoody, GA 30338-4497
$15, Lamar York

Chelsea
P.O. Box 773
Cooper Station
New York, NY 10276
$13, Richard Foerster

Chicago Review
5801 South Kenwood
University of Chicago
Chicago, IL 60637
$18, Andrew Rathman

Cimarron Review
205 Morrill Hall
Oklahoma State University
Stillwater, OK 74078-0135
$12, Gordon Weaver

Cities and Roads
P.O. Box 10886
Greensboro, NC 27404
$15.75, Tom Kealey

Clackamas Literary Review
196 South Molalla Ave.
Oregon City, OR 97045
$6, Jeff Knorr and Tim Schell

Colorado Review
Department of English
Colorado State University
Fort Collins, CO 80523
$18, David Milofsky

Columbia
415 Dodge
Columbia University
New York, NY 10027
$13, Gregory Cowles

Commentary
165 East 56th Street
New York, NY 10022
$39, Neal Kozodoy

Confrontation
English Department
C. W. Post College of Long
   Island University
Greenvale, NY 11548
$8, Martin Tucker

Conjunctions
21 East 10th St.
#3E
New York, NY 10003
$18, Bradford Morrow

Cream City Review
University of Wisconsin,
   Milwaukee
P.O. Box 413
Milwaukee, WI 53201
$12, Andrew Rivera

Crescent Review
P.O. Box 15069
Chevy Chase, MD 20825-5069
$21, J. Timothy Holland

Crucible
Barton College
College Station
Wilson, NC 27893
Terence Grimes

Cut Bank
Department of English
University of Montana
Missoula, MT 59812
*$12, Marcus Hersh and
   Amanda E. Ward*

Denver Quarterly
University of Denver
Denver, CO 80208
$25, Bin Ramke

Descant
P.O. Box 314, Station P
Toronto, Ontario
M5S 2S8 Canada
$25, Karen Mulhallen

Descant
Department of English
Texas Christian University
Box 32872

Fort Worth, TX 76129
$12, Neal Easterbrook

Double Take
Center for Documentary Studies
1317 West Pettigrew Street
Durham, NC 27705
$32, Robert Coles

Eagle's Flight
P.O. Box 832
Granite, OK 73547
$5, Rekha Kulkarni

Elle
1633 Broadway
New York, NY 10019
$24, Patricia Towers

Epoch
251 Goldwin Smith Hall
Cornell University
Ithaca, NY 14853-3201
$11, Michael Koch

Esquire
250 West 55th Street
New York, NY 10019
*$17.94, Rust Hills,
   Erika Mansourian*

Eureka Literary Magazine
Eureka College
P.O. Box 280
Eureka, IL 61530
$10, Loren Logsdon

event
c/o Douglas College
P.O. Box 2503
New Westminster, British Columbia
V3L 5B2 Canada
$15, Christine Dewar

Farmer's Market
Elgin Community College

1700 Spartan Drive
Elgin, IL 60123
$10, Rachael Tecza

Fiction
Fiction, Inc.
Department of English
The City College of New York
New York, NY
$7, Mark Mirsky

Fiction International
Department of English and
   Comparative Literature
San Diego State University
San Diego, CA 92182
$14, Harold Jaffe, Larry McCaffery

Fiddlehead
UNB Box 4400
University of New Brunswick
Fredericton, New Brunswick
E3B 5A3 Canada
$16, Don McKay, Bill Gaston

Fish Stories
5412 N. Clark, South Suite
Chicago, IL 60640
$10.95, Amy G. Davis

Five Points
Department of English
Georgia State University
University Plaza
Atlanta, GA 30303-3083
$15, Pam Durban

Florida Review
Department of English
University of Central Florida
P.O. Box 25000
Orlando, FL 32816
$7, Russell Kesler

Folio
Department of Literature

The American University
Washington, DC 20016
$10, Cynthia Lollar

Fourteen Hills
Department of Creative Writing
San Francisco State University
1600 Holloway Avenue
San Francisco, CA 94132
$12, Amanda Kim

Gargoyle
Paycock Press
c/o Atticus Books and Music
1508 U Street, NW
Washington, DC 20009
*$20, Richard Peabody and
    Lucinda Ebersole*

Geist
1062 Homer Street #100
Vancouver, Canada
V6B 2W9
$20, Stephen Osborne

Genre
7080 Hollywood Blvd.
Suite 1104
Hollywood, CA 90028
$19.95, Ronald Mark Kraft

Georgetown Review
400 East College Street,
    Box 227
Georgetown, KY 40324
$10, John Fulmer

Georgia Review
University of Georgia
Athens, GA 30602
$18, Stanley W. Lindberg

Gettysburg Review
Gettysburg College
Gettysburg, PA 17325
$24, Peter Stitt

Glimmer Train Stories
812 SW Washington Street
Suite 1205
Portland, OR 97205
$29, Susan Burmeister, Linda Davies

Good Housekeeping
959 Eighth Avenue
New York, NY 10019
$17.97, Arleen L. Quarfoot

GQ
350 Madison Avenue
New York, NY 10017
$19.97, Ilena Silverman

Grain
Box 1154
Regina, Saskatchewan
S4P 3B4 Canada
$23.95, Connie Gault

Grand Street
131 Varick Street
New York, NY 10013
$40, Jean Stein

Granta
2-3 Hanover Yard
Noel Road Islington
London, England N1 8BE
$32, Ian Jack

Great River Review
211 West 7th Street
Winona, MN 55987
$12, Pamela Davies

Green Hills Literary Lantern
North Central Missouri College
Box 375
Trenton, MO 64683
$5.95, Jack Smith

Green Mountain Review
Box A 58

Johnson State College
Johnson, VT 05656
$12, Tony Whedon

Greensboro Review
Department of English
University of North Carolina
Greensboro, NC 27412
$8, Jim Clark

Gulf Coast
Department of English
University of Houston
4800 Calhoun Road
Houston, TX 77204-3012
$22, Derrick Burleson

Gulf Stream
English Department
Florida International University
North Miami Campus
North Miami, FL 33181
$4, Lynne Barrett,
   John Dufresne

G.W. Review
Box 20B, The Marvin Center
800 21st Street
Washington, DC 20052
$9, Jane A. Roh

Habersham Review
Piedmont College
Demorest, GA 30535-0010
$12, Frank Gannon

Harper's Magazine
666 Broadway
New York, NY 10012
$18, Lewis H. Lapham

Harvard Review
Poetry Room
Harvard College Library
Cambridge, MA 02138
$12, Stratis Haviaris

Hawaii Review
University of Hawaii
Department of English
1733 Donagho Road
Honolulu, HI 96822
$25, Lisa Chang

Hayden's Ferry Review
Box 871502
Arizona State University
Tempe, AZ 85287-1502
$10, Melissa Olson, Verania White

High Plains Literary Review
180 Adams Street, Suite 250
Denver, CO 80206
$20, Robert O. Greer, Jr.

HR
University of Hawaii, Manoa
1733 Donagho Road
Honolulu, HI 96822
$25, Robert Sean Macbeth,
   S. Gonzalez

Hudson Review
684 Park Avenue
New York, NY 10021
$24, Paula Deitz, Frederick Morgan

Image
323 S. Broad Street
P.O. Box 674
Kendall Square, PA 19348
$30, Gregory Wolfe

Ink
P.O. Box 52558
St. George Postal Outlet
264 Bloor Street
Toronto, Ontario
M5S 1V0 Canada
$8, John Degan

International Quarterly
P.O. Box 10521

Tallahassee, FL 32302
$22, Catherine Reid, Virgil Suarez

Iowa Review
Department of English
University of Iowa
308 EPB
Iowa City, IA 52242
$18, David Hamilton

Iris
Box 323 HSC
University of Virginia
Charlottesville, VA 22908
$17, Kristen Staby Rembold

Italian Americana
University of Rhode Island
College of Continuing Education
199 Promenade Street
Providence, RI 02908
$15, Carol Bonomo Albright

Jewish Currents
22 East 17th Street, Suite 601
New York, NY 10003-3272
$20, editorial board

Journal
Department of English
Ohio State University
164 West 17th Avenue
Columbus, OH 43210
$8, Kathy Fagan, Michelle Herman

Kairos
Dundurn P.O. Box 33553
Hamilton, Ontario
L8P 4X4 Canada
$12.95, R.W. Megens

Kalliope
Florida Community College
3939 Roosevelt Blvd.
Jacksonville, FL 32205
$12.50, Mary Sue Koeppel

Karamu
English Department
Eastern Illinois University
Charleston, IL 61920
$6.50, Peggy L. Brayfield

Kenyon Review
Kenyon College
Gambier, OH 43022
$22, Marilyn Hacker

Kiosk
English Department
306 Clemens Hall
SUNY
Buffalo, NY 14260
$6, Lia Vella

Laurel Review
Department of English
Northwest Missouri State University
Maryville, MO 64468
$8, Craig Goad, David Slater,
    William Trowbridge

Lilith
250 West 57th Street
New York, NY 10107
$16, Susan Weidman

Literal Latté
Suite 240
61 East 8th Street
New York, NY 10003
$25, Jenine Gordon

Literary Review
Fairleigh Dickinson University
285 Madison Avenue
Madison, NJ 07940
$18, Walter Cummins

Louisiana Literature
Box 792
Southeastern Louisiana University
Hammond, LA 70402
$10, David Hanson

Lynx Eye
1880 Hill Drive
Los Angeles, CA 90041
$20, Pam McCully, Kathryn
*   Morrison*

Madison Review
University of Wisconsin
Department of English
H. C. White Hall
600 North Park Street
Madison, WI 53706
$15, Joley Wood

Malahat Review
University of Victoria
P.O. Box 1700
Victoria, British Columbia
V8W 2Y2 Canada
$15, Derk Wynand

Manoa
English Department
University of Hawaii
Honolulu, HI 96822
$18, Ian MacMillan

Many Mountains Moving
2525 Arapahoe Road
Suite E4-309
Boulder, CO 80302
$18, Naomi Horii, Marilyn
*   Krysl*

Massachusetts Review
Memorial Hall
University of Massachusetts
Amherst, MA 01003
$15, Jules Chametsky, Mary Heath,
*   Paul Jenkins*

Matrix
1455 de Paisonneuve Blvd. West
Suite LB-514-8
Montreal, Quebec
H3G IM8 Canada
$15, Terence Byrnes

Michigan Quarterly Review
3032 Rackham Building
University of Michigan
Ann Arbor, MI 48109
$18, Laurence Goldstein

Mid-American Review
Department of English
Bowling Green State University
Bowling Green, OH 43403
$12, Rebecca Meacham

Midstream
110 East 59th Street
New York, NY 10022
$21, Joel Carmichael

Midwesterner
Big Shoulders Publishing
343 S. Dearborn Street
Suite 610
Chicago, IL 60604
(has ceased publication)

Minnesota Review
Department of English
State University of New York
Stony Brook, NY 11794-5350
$12, Jeffrey Williams

Mississippi Review
University of Southern
   Mississippi
Southern Station, P.O. Box 5144
Hattiesburg, MS 39406-5144
$15, Frederick Barthelme

Missouri Review
1507 Hillcrest Hall
University of Missouri
Columbia, MO 65211
$19, Speer Morgan

Modern Words
350 Bay Street #100
San Francisco, CA 94133
$20, Garland Richard Kyle

Ms.
230 Park Avenue
New York, NY 10169
$45, Marcia Ann Gillespie

Nassau Review
English Department
Nassau Community College
One Education Drive
Garden City, NY 11530-6793
Paul A. Doyle

Nebraska Review
Writer's Workshop, ASH 212
University of Nebraska
Omaha, NE 68182-0324
*$10, Art Homer, Richard
    Duggin*

New Delta Review
Creative Writing Program
English Department
Louisiana State University
Baton Rouge, LA 70803
$7, Mindy Meek

New England Review
Middlebury College
Middlebury, VT 05753
$23, Stephen Donadio

New Letters
University of Missouri
4216 Rockhill Road
Kansas City, MO 64110
$17, James McKinley

New Orleans Review
P.O. Box 195
Loyola University
New Orleans, LA 70118
$18, Ralph Adamo

New Quarterly
English Language Proficiency
    Programme

University of Waterloo
Waterloo, Ontario
N2L 3G1 Canada
*$11.50, Peter Hinchcliffe,
    Kim Jernigan, Mary Merikle,
    Linda Kenyon*

New Renaissance
9 Heath Road
Arlington, MA 02174
$11.50, Louise T. Reynolds

New Yorker
25 West 43rd Street
New York, NY 10036
$32, David Remnick

Nightsun
School of Arts and Humanities
Dept. of English
Frostburg State University
Frostburg, MD 21532-1099
$5, Brad Barkley

Nimrod
Arts and Humanities Council
    of Tulsa
2210 South Main Street
Tulsa, OK 74114
$15, Francine Ringold

North American Review
University of Northern Iowa
1222 West 27th Street
Cedar Falls, IA 50614
$18, Robley Wilson, Jr.

North Dakota Quarterly
University of North Dakota
P.O. Box 8237
Grand Forks, ND 58202
$25, William Borden

Northeast Corridor
Department of English
Beaver College

450 S. Easton Road
Glenside, PA 19038-3295
$10, Susan Balee

Northwest Review
369 PLC
University of Oregon
Eugene, OR 97403
$20, John Witte

Notre Dame Review
Department of English
University of Notre Dame
Notre Dame, IN 46556
$15, Valerie Sayers

Oasis
P.O. Box 626
Largo, FL 34649-0626
$22, Neal Storrs

Ohio Review
Ellis Hall
Ohio University
Athens, OH 45701-2979
$16, Wayne Dodd

Ontario Review
9 Honey Brook Drive
Princeton, NJ 08540
$12, Raymond J. Smith

Onthebus
Bombshelter Press
6684 Colgate Avenue
Los Angeles, CA 90048
$28, Jack Grapes

Open City
225 Lafayette Street
Suite 1114
New York, NY 10012
$24, Thomas Beller, Daniel Pinchbeck

Other Voices
University of Illinois at Chicago

Department of English
(M/C 162) 601 South Morgan Street
Chicago, IL 60680
$20, Lois Hauselman

Oxford American
115 ¹/₂ South Lamar
Oxford, MS 38655
$16, Marc Smirnoff

Oyster Boy Review
103B Hanna Street
Carrboro, NC 27510
$12, Chad Driscoll, Damon Suave

Paris Review
541 East 72nd Street
New York, NY 10021
$34, George Plimpton

Parting Gifts
3413 Wilshire Dr.
Greensboro, NC 27408-2923
Robert Bixby

Partisan Review
236 Bay State Road
Boston, MA 02215
$22, William Phillips

Playboy
Playboy Building
919 North Michigan Avenue
Chicago, IL 60611
$24, Alice K. Turner

Pleiades
Department of English
Central Missouri State University
P.O. Box 800
Warrensburg, MO 64093
$10, R. M. Kinder

Ploughshares
Emerson College
100 Beacon Street

Boston, MA 02116
$21, Don Lee

Porcupine
P.O. Box 259
Cedarburg, WI 53012
$13.95, group editorship

Potpourri
P.O. Box 8278
Prairie Village, KS 66208
$12, Polly W. Swafford

Pottersfield Portfolio
The Gatsby Press
5280 Green Street, P.O. Box 27094
Halifax, Nova Scotia
B3H 4M8 Canada
$18, Ian Colford

Prairie Fire
423-100 Arthur Street
Winnipeg, Manitoba
R3B 1H3 Canada
$24, Andris Taskans

Prairie Schooner
201 Andrews Hall
University of Nebraska
Lincoln, NE 68588-0334
$22, Hilda Raz

Press
125 West 72nd Street
Suite 3-M
New York, NY 10023
$24, Daniel Roberts

Prism International
Department of Creative Writing
University of British Columbia
Vancouver, British Columbia
V6T 1W5 Canada
$16, Ian Cockfield

Provincetown Arts
650 Commercial Street

Provincetown MA 02657
$10,Christopher Busa

Puerto del Sol
P.O. Box 3E
Department of English
New Mexico State University
Las Cruces, NM 88003
$10, Kevin McIlvoy

Quarry Magazine
P.O. Box 1061
Kingston, Ontario
K7L 4Y5 Canada
$22, Mary Cameron

Quarterly West
312 Olpin Union
University of Utah
Salt Lake City, UT 84112
$12, Margot Schilpp

RE:AL
School of Liberal Arts
Stephen F. Austin State University
P.O. Box 13007
SFA Station
Nacogdoches, TX 75962
$15, Dale Hearell

Redbook
959 Eighth Avenue
New York, NY 10017
$11.97, Dawn Raffel

Riversedge
Dept. of English
University of Texas, Pan-American
1201 West University Drive, CAS 266
Edinburg, TX 78539-2999
$12, Dorey Schmidt

River Styx
Big River Association
14 South Euclid
St. Louis, MO 63108
$20, Richard Newman

Room of One's Own
P.O. Box 46160
Station D
Vancouver, British Columbia
V6J 5G5 Canada
$22, collective

Salamander
48 Ackers Avenue
Brookline, MA 02146
$12, Jennifer Barber

Salmagundi
Skidmore College
Saratoga Springs, NY 12866
$18, Robert Boyers

San Jose Studies
c/o English Department
San Jose State University
One Washington Square
San Jose, CA 95192
$12, John Engell, D. Mesher

Santa Monica Review
Center for the Humanities
Santa Monica College
1900 Pico Boulevard
Santa Monica, CA 90405
$12, Lee Montgomery

Saturday Night
Suite 400
184 Front Street E
Toronto, Ontario
M5V 2Z4 Canada
$26.45, Robert Weaver

Seattle Review
Padelford Hall, GN-30
University of Washington
Seattle, WA 98195
$9, Charles Johnson

Seventeen
850 Third Avenue

New York, NY 10022
$14.95, Susan Brenna

Sewanee Review
University of the South
Sewanee, TN 37375-4009
$18, George Core

Shenandoah
Washington and Lee University
P.O. Box 722
Lexington, VA 24450
$15, R. T. Smith

The Slate
Box 58119
Minneapolis, MN 55458
*$15, Chris Dall, Rachel Fulkerson,
    Jessica Morris*

Sonora Review
Department of English
University of Arizona
Tucson, AZ 85721
$12, Hannah Hass

So to Speak
4400 University Drive
George Mason University
Fairfax, VA 22030-444
$7, Nolde Alexius

South Carolina Review
Department of English
Clemson University
Clemson, SC 29634-1503
$10, Frank Day, Carol Johnston

South Dakota Review
University of South Dakota
P.O. Box 111 University
    Exchange
Vermillion, SD 57069
$15, Brian Bedard

Southern Exposure
P.O. Box 531

Durham, NC 27702
$24, Jordan Green

Southern Humanities Review
9088 Haley Center
Auburn University
Auburn, AL 36849
$15, Dan R. Latimer,
   Virginia M. Kouidis

Southern Review
43 Allen Hall
Louisiana State University
Baton Rouge, LA 70803
$20, James Olney, Dave Smith

Southwest Review
Southern Methodist University
P.O. Box 4374
Dallas, TX 75275
$20, Willard Spiegelman

Spec-lit
Columbia College Chicago
600 South Michigan Ave.
Chicago, IL 60605
$6.95, Phyllis Eisenstein

Story
1507 Dana Avenue
Cincinnati, OH 45207
$22, Lois Rosenthal

Story Head
1340 W. Granville
Chicago, IL 60660
$16, Mike Brehn, Joe Peterson

Story Quarterly
P.O. Box 1416
Northbrook, IL 60065
$12, Margaret Barrett,
   Anne Brashler, Diane Williams

Sun
107 North Roberson Street

Chapel Hill, NC 27516
$30, Sy Safransky

Sun Dog
The Southeast Review
406 Williams Building
Florida State University
Tallahassee, FL 32306-1036
$8, Russ Franklin

Sycamore Review
Department of English
Heavilon Hall
Purdue University
West Lafayette, IN 47907
$10, Jon Briner

Talking River Review
Division of Literature
Lewis-Clark State College
500 8th Avenue
Lewiston, ID 83501
$10, group editorship

Teacup
P.O. Box 8665
Hellgate Station
Missoula, MT 59807
$9, group editorship

Thema
Box 74109
Metairie, LA 70053-4109
$16, Virginia Howard

Thin Air
P.O. Box 23549
Flagstaff, AZ 86002
$9, Jeff Huebner, Rob Morrill

Third Coast
Dept. of English
Western Michigan University
Kalamazoo, MI 49008-5092
$11, Heidi Bell, Kellie Wells

13th Moon
Department of English
SUNY at Albany
Albany, NY 12222
$18, Judith Emlyn Johnson

32 Pages
Rain Crow Publishing
101-308 Andrew Place
West Lafayette, IN 47906-3932
$10, Michael S. Manley

Threepenny Review
P.O. Box 9131
Berkeley, CA 94709
$16, Wendy Lesser

Tikkun
5100 Leona Street
Oakland, CA 94619
$36, Michael Lerner

Trafika
P.O. Box 250822
New York, NY 10025-1536
$35, Scott Lewis, Krister Swartz,
Jeffrey Young

Treasure House
Suite 3A
1106 Oak Hill Avenue
Hagerstown, MD 21742
$9, J. G. Wolfensberger

TriQuarterly
2020 Ridge Avenue
Northwestern University
Evanston, IL 60208
$24, Susan Firestone Hahn

University of Windsor Review
Department of English
University of Windsor
Windsor, Ontario

N9B 3P4 Canada
$19.95, Alistair MacLeod

Unmuzzled Ox
105 Hudson Street
New York, NY 10013
$8.95, Michael Andre

Urbanus
P.O. Box 192561
San Francisco, CA 94119
$8, Peter Drizhal

Vignette
4150-G Riverside Drive
Toluca Lake, CA 91505
$29, Dawn Baille, Deborah Clark

Virginia Quarterly Review
One West Range
Charlottesville, VA 22903
$18, Staige D. Blackford

Wascana Review
English Department
University of Regina
Regina, Saskatchewan
S4S 0A2 Canada
$10, J. Shami

Washington Square
Creative Writing Program
New York University
19 University Place, 2nd floor
New York, NY 10003-4556
$6, Helen Ellis

Weber Studies
Weber State College
Ogden, UT 84408
$10, Neila Seshachari

Wellspring
770 Tonkawa Road
Long Lake, MN 55356
$8, Meg Miller

West Branch
Department of English
Bucknell University
Lewisburg, PA 17837
$7, Robert Love Taylor, Karl Patten

Western Humanities Review
University of Utah
Salt Lake City, UT 84112
$20, Barry Weller

What?
P.O. Box 1669
Hollywood, CA 90078
$12, collective

Whetstone
Barrington Area Arts Council
P.O. Box 1266
Barrington, IL 60011
$7.25, Sandra Berris, Marsha
  Portnoy, Jean Tolle

Wind
RFD Route 1
P.O. Box 809K
Pikeville, KY 41501
$7, Quentin R. Howard

Windsor Review
Department of English
University of Windsor
Windsor, Ontario
N9B 3P4 Canada
$19.95, Alistair MacLeod

Witness
Oakland Community College
Orchard Ridge Campus
27055 Orchard Lake Road
Farmington Hills, MI 48334
$12, Peter Stine

Worcester Review
6 Chatham Street
Worcester, MA 01690
$10, Rodger Martin

Wordwrights
Argonne Hotel
1620 Argonne Place NW
Washington, DC 20009
$10, collective

Xavier Review
Xavier University
Box 110C
New Orleans, LA 70125
$10, Thomas Bonner, Jr.

Yale Review
1902A Yale Station
New Haven, CT 06520
$27, J. D. McClatchy

Yalobusha Review
P.O. Box 186
University, MS 38677-0186
$6, Jill E. Grogg

Yankee
Yankee Publishing, Inc.
Dublin, NH 03444
$22, Judson D. Hale, Sr.

Yemassee
Department of English
University of South Carolina
Columbia, SC 29208
$15, Stephen Owen

Zoetrope
AZX Publications
126 Fifth Avenue, Suite 300
New York, NY 10011
Adrienne Brodeur

ZYZZYVA
41 Sutter Street, Suite 1400
San Francisco, CA 94104
$28, Howard Junker